The author has grown up in Europe and is specialised in the preservation, restoration and reconstruction of historic sites. His fields of expertise are the Antiquity and Middle Ages. He currently lives in Australia.

Dedication

The proceeds of this book will be used for animal rescue.

Martin Zierholz

The Perennial Plants

A reference to perennial plants and their use in Landscape Architecture,
Garden Design and Horticulture

AUSTIN MACAULEY PUBLISHERS™

LONDON * CAMBRIDGE * NEW YORK * SHARJAH

Copyright © Martin Zierholz (2018)

The right of Martin Zierholz to be identified as author of this work has been asserted by him in accordance with section 77 and 78 of the Copyright, Designs and Patents Act 1988.

All rights reserved. No part of this publication may be reproduced, stored in a retrieval system, or transmitted in any form or by any means, electronic, mechanical, photocopying, recording, or otherwise, without the prior permission of the publishers.

Any person who commits any unauthorised act in relation to this publication may be liable to criminal prosecution and civil claims for damages.

A CIP catalogue record for this title is available from the British Library.

ISBN 9781786934895 (Paperback)
ISBN 9781786934901 (Hardback)
ISBN 9781786934918 (E-Book)
www.austinmacauley.com

First Published (2018)
Austin Macauley Publishers Ltd.
25 Canada Square
Canary Wharf
London
E14 5LQ

Acknowledgements

There are many people, organisations and places that I wish to acknowledge and that are essentially part of this book or contributing to it with shared time, experience, knowledge or pictures. As this book summarises experiences of many decades and many places, I will try to do this in reasonably chronological order.

My old Masters from whom I learned the trade of Horticulture and the science, craft and art of Landscape Architecture: Master Matthias, Master Otfried Preussler, Professor Dürschmied, Doctor Weiler and Professor Zimmermann.

With the warmest memories, my time with the residence and nursery of the Countess of Zeppelin, Aglaja von Rumohr geborene von Stein-Zeppelin; the nursery is now with her daughter Karin. Many pictures in and on this book are either from my time in the nursery or other early work and study (they are scanned paper photographs as digital technology was not available at the time) or have been sent recently for this book by Anne Rostek from and on behalf of the nursery. There are also pictures from Anne herself, thank you very much Anne.

Other contributions, pictures and courtesies are from UNESCO World Heritage, Montacute House, The National Trust, Kew Gardens, Sissinghurst Gardens and the Spanish Heritage Council, the Alhambra, Château Vaux-le Vicomte, Villa Adriana with the University of Rome, the Staudengärtnerei Häussermann, Baumschule Horstmann, the Museum of Solnhofen, the Deutsches Archäologisches Institut, the Deutsche Stiftung Denkmalschutz, the Wilhelma zoologic & botanic gardens in Stuttgart, Schloss Ludwigsburg and das Blühende Barock.

From Europe, then on my time in Australia with the Royal Botanic Gardens Sydney, Bruce Rann and Frank Howarth and all my friends, colleagues and staff who introduced me to a new culture (and taught me Australian-English), a new climate and plants. It was a fantastic time.

Time, pictures and plant experiences are shared with Eleanor Hall, Barbara Arnott, Beth Chatto, Gabriel Miriero, Stephan Willenberger, Frances Pryor, Angelika Kaufmann, Madlyn Howe, the brothers Wilfried and Anton Büchli, Frank Schmid, Brett Samon, John Seymour, Frieder Ungenberger, Tracey Willmott, Ingrid Meier, Krzew Mojzesza, Miriam Goldstein, Karin Feldmann, Herbert Porstmeier, Klaus Mödinger and Claudia Zierholz.
Thank you very much to all.

As these acknowledgements cover several decades, many journeys around the world, many happy and sad events and my memory is human, there may be unintended oversights or errors. Should you be aware of any oversights or errors, I ask kindly to contact me please on: E-mail: kittyandmarti@gmail.com

Iris fields in Sulzburg/Baden, southern Germany
Staudengärtnerei Gräfin von Zeppelin

The picture shows the Iris fields looking downslope toward the village, church and glasshouses. At the time I worked there, a pair of falcons was nesting in the church tower.

1 - Blandfordia nobilis in Queanbeyan, Australia summer 2014
Author's home garden

A book of seasons and the cycles of life

Table of Contents

Landscape Architecture Principles of Design — 14

Perennial Plants, Their Habitats and Behaviour — 16

Perennial Plantings and Borders Structure, Composition and Cycles — 29

The Perennial Plants: Characteristics, Propagation and Use in the Landscape — 39

Already as a child I was fascinated by natural beauty, animals, plants and landscapes. With this picture of an ancient fossil, I imagined it to be a miniature landscape one could just walk into and keep walking and disappear from the troubles of the world.

2 - Early plant life; fossil of Solnhofen in Germany around 155 million years old
Courtesy Museum of Solnhofen, Germany

Landscape Architecture
Principles of Design

When designing new landscapes or restoring historic gardens, the greatest joy for me lies in the smallest detail. It is in the flowers, foliage, textures and life cycles of perennial plants. Like the beautiful ornaments on a carpet or textiles, it is the colouring of the landscapes that brings them to life, gives joy and reminds us of the limitation of our lives.

With this following chapter and this entire book, I wish to share inspiration, knowledge and experience, tools and choices for anyone enjoying the passions of working in and with our living, designed environment. There are of course innumerous ways of approaching landscape architecture and garden design. They are forms of art and philosophy and passions based on the crafts of landscape architecture and horticulture. These crafts must be technically mastered before they can become art. Ultimately everyone may then find their own individual artistic way of creation and expression. Therefore, I intend this book as a professional discussion and inspiration, continuing the millennia of traditional crafts by which I have been inspired from when starting out as an apprentice. I have learned from old masters in very conservative environments and as hard as it sometimes was, this gave me a solid foundation for my life that I am most grateful for to this day. Graduating from this foundation I learned to authentically restore, reconstruct and preserve historic landscape designs, build contemporary landscapes and grow any desired plant species with joy. Building and growing on from there, I then developed my own ways of creating new unique landscapes. Learning never ends.

Therefore, with this book I try to share an extract of what I have learned from my old masters, combined with my own experiences accumulated over the years of work in historic and contemporary gardens in the northern and southern hemispheres. This is to give choice and inspiration for life and joy, not rigid structures. Indeed, many of the most inspiring achievements in landscape and garden design have found new ways of creating and designing. But all convincing designs and successful ways of creating landscapes have been based on the traditional foundation of solid knowledge about nature, soils and plants.

After shaping or restoring the topography and grades, the landscape architect structures the design with the hard fabric elements. Then she or he populates it firstly with the evergreen trees and shrubs, the vegetal skeleton and framework and secondly, moulds the main deciduous elements into this design structure. I would not want to imagine a world without trees. Their unique habit, expressing their soul, their kindness and dignity, the majesty or humility of a species combined with its age, telling about the time they had. And after these main elements of the designed landscape are in place, perennials and annuals then 'dress' our gardens, to use a metaphor.

The purpose of this introductory chapter in relation to landscape architecture is to frame the greater structure for the book subject of perennial plants. Topography, hard fabric structures and soft fabric structural elements are forming the frame for the colours and textures of our scenes.

In landscape architecture, the design intent determines the main principles of construction of the topography, the hard fabric and the planting of the evergreen and deciduous structures of the soft fabric. There are three main design principles that encompass landscape architectural and garden designs; the natural, the semi-formal and the formal principles. These applied principles guide the designed landscape to the *Unity of Design*.

Once the designed landscape is formed, different habitats and microclimates develop within its features according to the surface gradients, hard fabric construction and the structural elements of the soft fabric.

The architectural composition of a landscape and garden is constituted in:

1. The design intent, formulated in its plan
2. The topography, natural or created
3. Its structural and decorative features of the hard fabric
4. Its vegetation, species and plant communities, proportions, spacing, respective heights and colour schemes
5. Its water, running or still, reflecting the sky
6. The surrounding landscape, vistas, exposure or shelter and backgrounds

These constituents are subject to the laws of nature; they are perishable and renewable. Therefore, the appearance and physical reality of a landscape and garden reflects the perpetual balance between the cycle of the seasons, the growth and decay of nature and the work of the artist and craftsman in its dynamic preservation.

3 - Water feature in front of the Moorish Garden, Wilhelma in Stuttgart, southern Germany
Courtesy of the Wilhelma; Work in Stuttgart 1992

Perennial Plants, Their Habitats and Behaviour

The plants and their use in the landscape described in this book are mainly from dry (semi-arid and arid), moderate (Mediterranean, humid subtropical, coastal) and continental (humid-continental and sub-arctic) temperate zones of the world. I discuss some peripheral species from tropical and polar regions (tundra and highlands).

With this selection, almost any landscape and garden design in the temperate northern and southern hemispheres can be created.

One of the most fundamental pieces of knowledge is where a plant species originates and under what environmental conditions it has evolved and thrives. This knowledge gives us the basis for successful cultivation in our designed setting, the built environment. A key to successful landscape architecture is to assess the existing environmental conditions and model, alter and adjust what we can toward our planned design objectives, and to assess what we cannot change and under these limitations create the appropriate conditions and habitats for the plant species we want to grow for our desired design intent.

The first and foremost differentiation of planting designs determines if the design intent is to be natural, semi-formal or formal. In larger landscape settings, all these design principles may be present but are usually divided into clearly distinct sectors of the landscape. For example, in the Royal Palace in Ludwigsburg in southern Germany, the garden sectors immediately surrounding the palace buildings are strictly formal (Baroque). Outside this area an ordered semi-formal perimeter walk leads into a natural woodland, the Fairy-tale garden. Within this woodland garden are displays of the well-known fairy tales of the brothers Grimm, like *Hansel and Gretel*, *Rapunzel* and *Snow White and the Seven Dwarfs* and no family with children should miss this.

4 - Formal garden design, Baroque, Royal Palace of Germany in Ludwigsburg
Courtesy of Das Blühende Barock; Restoration Work in Ludwigsburg 1994

5 - Detail of the formal garden design, seasonal planting in summer 1994, picture taken from the corner of the upper balcony
Courtesy of Das Blühende Barock; Restoration Work in Ludwigsbug 1994

When we decide on the formality or natural intent of our design, we need to assess the resources available to maintain this intent and advice our clients on this. In those old historic gardens of Europe that I was part of, the knowledge of maintenance requirements was almost always already given as these landscapes had usually been maintained for several centuries. In some cases, gardens were millennia old, like gardens of the Roman Empire but had been fallen into disrepair due to passing of adverse times like war, or the decline and fall of the Roman Empire in this case. These landscapes had to be restored or reconstructed according to their state and according to the Venice (Florence) Charter of the International Council of Monuments or Sites (ICOMOS). Personally, I found the work in historic landscapes and gardens most fascinating and inspiring. However, the restoration and preservation of historic gardens is the subject of a separate book dealing specifically with this vast topic.

Generally, the more formal a design is, the more natural the design is, the less resources are needed to maintain the status quo and design intent. Whilst this is usually known by experience in the management of old and well-maintained gardens it is sometimes inadequately understood in younger landscapes or new gardens and we need to advise our clients on these dynamics.

6 - Courtyard of the Generalife, Alhambra, Spain with Hemerocallis in summer
Courtesy of the Spanish Heritage Council; Work and study in Spain 1988

In the following, I would like to go over the different natural habitats of perennial plants to understand their requirements in the designed landscape. Once these principles are understood, the landscape architect or garden designer will be able to create sustainable plant communities that draw on the strengths of the species and create an aesthetic sense in any landscape context across the world.

The Main Habitats of Perennial Plants

Habitat forest and woodlands including their margins

8 – Habitat Forest - the Black Forest in southern Germany
Work at the Staudengärtnerei Gräfin von Zeppelin, Badenweiler 1992

Imagine walking in the deep forest. Cool shade, gentle light and the trunks of trees rising like the columns of a cathedral and forming a sheltering canopy. Shade, coolness and moisture but also root pressure and competition are important factors to consider. Depending if it is an evergreen or deciduous forest the understorey of perennial plants can create pictures that vary greatly between these habitats and their seasons. A light and happy carpet of Anemone sylvestris between the smooth grey columns of Fagus sylvatica before the airy light green of the first leaves pushes out is one example. An entirely different mood of a forest habitat may be the strong darkness of conifer forests like Abies, Taxus and Picea where the trunks of trees

7 - Natural perennial planting along a garden path in early autumn with Limonium latifolium, Chrysanthemum x hortorum and Aster divaricatus 2015
Courtesy Staudengärtnerei Gräfin von Zeppelin, Germany

sometimes appear to be stern guardians of the underworld and only some softening ferns occupy moist areas. Gnomes or other forest spirits could be just around the corner. To a point these sceneries are where many of our well-known fairy tales originate.

On the other side of the world, we can experience the humid lushness and abundance of life within a subtropical rainforest or marvel at the size of tree ferns and their delicate, yet tough fronds.

9 – The same habitat on the other side of the world, Subtropical rainforest on Fraser Island, Australia
Courtesy Gabriel Mirtero

Woodlands are more open with widely varying levels of shade and light conditions, soil properties and moisture. Differing levels of root pressure or shelter from the structuring trees determines what species thrive. Accordingly, the scenes and moods that can be created by the tree types, their canopies and associated perennials are very varied also. From intimate, sheltered little garden rooms with a chair to majestic scenes of grandeur, we can find and create a huge palette of moods. A carpet of Helleborus, Epimedium and Symphytum with Astilbe in the background along a path leading away from the troubles of the world.

10 - Woodland margin design with Meconopsis betonicifolia, Geranium x magnificum, Digitalis purpurea, Aruncus dioicus, Astilbe and Cimicifuga in southern Germany
Work and study in Weihenstephan 1988

Habitat Scrublands, Heathlands and Mallee

When environmental conditions do not support the larger trees any more, the structure of some habitats is formed and dominated by smaller and larger shrubs or multi-stemmed small trees. Grasses, herbaceous and perennial plants and geophytes in various compositions accompany them.

11 - Mediterranean Garigue with Thymus and Cistus
Courtesy Stephan Willenberger

These habitats may be in cold, hot or coastal environments but all share a high level of exposure to adverse growing conditions and this is important to note for our design intentions and choice of plant species. It means in terms of design that plants from these environments are tough and can withstand harshness and exposure; indeed, to develop their natural characteristics they *need* exposure. If these plant species are set into a mild, sheltered microclimate and fertile, well-watered soils, they grow atypically and very often fail. But we may use them in conditions where many other species would struggle to survive, like road embankments in civil engineering projects, places with extreme winds, rock gardens, shallow soils and baking hot sun, freezing cold or both.

12 - Mallee habitat near Mildura, Australia
Travel study

Examples of hot scrublands would be the Mediterranean Garrigue and Macchia or the Australian Mallee habitat. Characteristics are hot and dry summers with rainfall predominantly in spring and autumn and this is when the plants are most active. Soils are usually shallow, poor and often sandy or gravelly.

Examples of the cold counterparts would be northern heathlands, high altitudes above the tree line or tundra. Tree growth in these places is limited by cold temperatures and short growing seasons. Coastal zones are often exposed to high winds and salt spray and its typical vegetation has evolved to cope with that.

Habitat Prairies and Steppes

We often connect the term 'prairie' with the vast grasslands of North America and grazing buffalos. This is correct but prairies are also part of other temperate grasslands, savannas, and shrublands with similar temperate climates, moderate rainfall, and a composition of grasses, herbs, and shrubs rather than trees dominating the structure of the landscape. Temperate grassland regions include the Pampas of Argentina, Brazil and Uruguay as well as the seemingly never-ending steppes of Eurasia.

Steppes are grasslands with herbaceous perennials and characterised by an absence of trees. However, a surprising multitude of beautiful plants grows in these vast open spaces among the waves of grasses swaying in the wind. One of the poets and pioneers of perennial plant knowledge, Karl Förster, has called the grasses "the hair of the earth". Many annuals, bulbous, tuberous and other perennial plants have evolved to live among the grasses of the vast steppes.

13 - Habitat Prairie, Fynbos, South Africa
Courtesy Gabriel Miriero

In our landscape designs, we may think of prairies and steppes also as spaces for free thinking and for meditation. Spaces to clear the mind. These spaces may separate as well as connect different landscape habitats and sectors of the designed environment. One could step out from the abundance of a cottage garden with its variety of textures, flowers and colours into the wide-open space of the steppe and walk or stand among the grassland to let the senses settle and calm down. Mindful of this openness and clarity, one becomes open and receptive for the different impressions of the adjoining part of the landscape, maybe the inviting structure of the shrubs of a scrubland.

All these habitats of course can naturally merge into one another with innumerous forms and variations in between them.

14 - Habitat Steppe, Painted Desert, Australia with Ptilotus nobilis (Mulla-Mulla)
Courtesy Gabriel Miriero

Habitat Rockeries and Alpine

The alpine habitat and occurs at high elevation and above the tree line. Alpine plants grow together as a plant community in alpine tundra, also see above habitat 'scrublands'. These plants include perennial grasses, sedges, forbs, cushion plants, mosses, and wonderful lichens. Alpine plants are adapted to the harsh conditions of the alpine environment, which include low temperatures, strong winds, dryness, ultraviolet radiation, and a short growing season.

An alpine garden (or alpinarium, alpinum) is a domestic or botanical garden specialising in the collection and cultivation of alpine plants that would naturally be growing naturally at high altitudes around the world, such as in the Caucasus, Pyrenees, Rocky Mountains, Alps, Himalayas and Andes.

15 - Alpine habitat, Mont Blanc, France
Travel studies 1986

The alpine garden or rockery tries to recreate the conditions of the plants' place of origin, for example, large stones and gravel beds. A very important factor are the properties of the underlying rock and the PH of the soils. Though the plants can often cope with low temperatures they require good drainage as one can imagine from the slopes where water drains away by gradient and the rocky nature of the subsoils. The soil used is typically poor sandy, gracelly or rocky and extremely well-drained. One of the main obstacles in developing an alpine garden is the conditions which exist in some lowland areas, in example particularly mild or severe winters, heavy rainfall and/or lack of high UV. As an example, the famous 'Edelweiss' (Leontopodium alpinum) requires dry conditions and high UV exposure to develop its natural thick, white felty appearance. This is hard to imitate in the lowlands and I remember from my apprentice days that the cultivated plants in lower altitudes always looked greenish and elongated compared to plants from high altitudes. For other species, unfavourable lowland conditions may be mitigated by growing the plants in an alpine house or unheated greenhouse, which tries to reproduce the ideal conditions. In one of my old workplaces, the Royal Botanic Gardens in Sydney (coastal mild habitat) we installed a misting system for plants among them many orchids that came from higher altitudes to simulate the mountain environment of their original habitat. The first historically true alpine garden was created by Anton Kerner von Marilaun in 1875 in Tirol (Tyrol) in Austria on the Blaser Mountain at an altitude of just above 2,000 metres.

16 - Alpine dry-stone wall planting with Dianthus, Phlox, Saxifraga and Aster alpinus
Work in Badenweiler, Germany 1991

Habitat Moorland, Swamp and the Water's Edge

Habitats found in upland areas in temperate grasslands, savannas, and shrublands as well as montane grasslands and shrublands biomes that are characterised by low-growing vegetation on acidic soils are moorlands. They are closely related to heathlands and like in heathlands the most important factor is the water table. Generally, moor refers to highland, high rainfall zones with a high water table, with water being at least occasionally visible and the ground feels somewhat unstable, whereas heathland refers to zones with a lower water table that may have moist soils but can also be reasonably dry.

Moorland habitats are most extensive in the subtropics and tropical Africa but also occur in northern and western Europe, Northern Australia, North America, Central Asia, and the Indian subcontinent. Most of the world's moorlands are very diverse and complex ecosystems. In the extensive moorlands of the tropics, biodiversity can be extremely high. Moorland also resembles the tundra (where the subsoil is permafrost or permanently frozen soil) and is appearing as the tundra retreats and moorland then inhabits the area between the permafrost and the natural tree zone.

Habitat Water

Water depth or duration of flooding and temperatures are the main defining factors of this habitat. Other factors are availability of nutrients and salinity.

When we design water features for our landscapes and gardens, it is prudent to remember the high level of maintenance that usually comes with it when these features are part of formal designs for presentation. This is different and less so with natural designs or designs that include naturally existing water features, creeks or rivers into their structure.

Aquatic plants are plants that have adapted to living in aquatic environments (saltwater or freshwater). They are also referred to as hydrophytes or macrophytes.

The water plants we use in the landscape have originated in different plant families and they can be ferns or angiosperms (including both monocots and dicots).

The well-known Amazon Water Lily is one of the largest aquatic plants in the world. It is at home in warm water and I remember when we were growing it in the Royal Wilhelma in Stuttgart in southern Germany, we had to move it in and out of the shelter of the glasshouse with the seasons.

Some aquatic plants are used as important food sources like wild rice (Zizania), water caltrop (Trapa natans), Chinese water chestnut (Eleocharis dulcis), Indian Lotus (Nelumbo nucifera), water spinach (Ipomoea aquatica) and watercress (Rorippa nasturtium-aquaticum).

17 - Design with water plants, Nymphaea, Nelumbo and Victoria amazonica
Courtesy of the Wilhelma, Work in Stuttgart, Germany 1992

The Cultivated Garden Beds

This 'habitat' really is entirely artificial and consists of the by us created variety of garden beds. This is usually done to provide the best possible growing conditions to present showy plants with spectacular flowers that have often been in cultivation for centuries, which subsequently have become somewhat 'soft' and would not survive in the wild. Another well-known purpose of course are garden beds for food production and medicinal herb gardens. All have in common that the soil is carefully prepared and cultivated for the specific purpose and plant species that will populate the design. It is a very rewarding but also maintenance-intense undertaking.

18 - Perennial border design in sunny orientation with Dictamnus albus, Nepeta
Germany 2015, Courtesy Anne Rostek

It goes without saying that the description of the natural habitats is intended to assist with the design of landscapes and gardens, not to categorise the living, organic environment into a rigid structure. These habitats of course merge into one another, sometimes abruptly but more often gradually and imperceptibly, forming innumerous variations and little worlds in themselves.

One of the purposes of this book is to give the reader an understanding of the huge variety of perennial plant habitats and a broad palette of concepts and species to have the choices of creating landscapes with knowledge and pleasure.

Like the musician, the painter, the poet, and the rest, the true lover of flowers is born, not made. And he is born to happiness in this vale of tears, to a certain amount of the purest joy that earth can give her children, joy that is tranquil, innocent, uplifting, unfailing. Given a little patch of ground, with time to take care of it, with tools to work it and seeds to plant in it, he has all he needs. -- Celia Thaxter (1835-1894)

Perennial Plantings and Borders
Structure, Composition and Cycles

Structure

The structure of a design is formed by the hard fabric and its evergreen soft fabric elements. This skeleton and framework defines the composition. The evergreen elements form visual points, paths and rooms, they guide the eye along flows and into garden spaces, form rooms or invite one to go into open spaces.

All our plantings are based on the foundation of the design intent. The first decision of planting designs is if the plantings intent is to be natural, semi-formal or formal.

Natural; informal and nature-like plantings create scenes and moods which we would eventually find in a landscape untouched by humans. The imagination of a never-ending journey to yet undiscovered worlds leading us into the natural landscapes. We collectively find panoramic views and landscapes attractive that invite the mind and body to exploration.

In the picture example below, we are drawn into the landscape and toward the mountain range in the background. This is achieved by the structure of the plantings and the way they are framing the grassed area leading to the path.

19 - Kirstenbosch Botanic Garden, South Africa 1992
Courtesy of the Kistenbosch Botanic Gardens, South Africa

Leaving the open landscape, we may enter forests or bushlands that create a feeling of protection and cover, their paths inviting to be followed on to secluded places, shelter and the treasure of peace.

In the below pictured example the hand of the landscape gardener is hardly visible and it could be an untouched natural landscape. The path is grassed and leads along Viola, Cyclamen and Polygonatum into the deeper forest.

20 - Natural landscape, grassed forest path with Polygonatum 'Weihenstephan',
Work and study in Weihenstephan, Germany 1986

Composition

The artistic composition of perennial plantings and borders I compare to the composition of classic music like Vivaldi's *Four Seasons*. It is my favourite piece of music and reflects the cycle of seasons that we essentially work with in our designs. The cycles of seasons are an integral part of the design in the living environment. View the entire design holistically including the changes of the seasons.

Great designs are much more than just a collection of pretty plants just like great food is not just a random mixture of good ingredients.

21 - Natural mixed planting with stepping stones along a woodland border
Work in Germany 1985

The vegetal components of perennial plant designs reflect in principle the composition of the greater landscape design; it is just on a smaller scale but it is utilising the same principles of design. The largest evergreen plants form the skeleton or framework of the design and they are composed upon the foundation of the hard fabric structure. In the historic tradition of European perennial borders, evergreen conifers are often used to form the dark background to set off the colourful perennials in front of them. Sometimes a stone wall or brick wall is used for the same purpose. Start the visual imagining of your design in the deep dormancy of winter and firstly compose your skeletal structure of evergreen plants.

22 - Garden structure in winter, semi-formal garden design
Courtesy Frances Pryor

The structure of this garden is defined by the evergreen elements of conifers and in this case, I would consider the hedge of Carpinus betulus (Hainbuche) also as an evergreen element as it retains the foliage for the protection of the young buds through winter. Another important aspect of design here is that the structural grasses are kept through winter and are cut back in early spring just before growth starts again. This way the body of the dry leaves and seed keep forming the mood of the design, with hoar frost or snow painting the romantic scene.

The Framework or Skeleton of Evergreen Components

This skeleton of soft fabric with evergreen plants will hold the design together and make it work, just like in anatomy the bones hold the muscles together, give them direction and purpose and enable them to function. Compose this framework of evergreen plants building upon the structural parameters of the hard fabric. Especially give attention to the height structure and all visual aspects; for example it is important if a planting is viewed only from one visual approach from a path or if it is meant to be viewed from all sides and people may walk all around it. The traditional teachings start with a low border, medium centre and tall background. This is a timeless principle that always works and is convincing. However different ideas can also be very attractive but always keep in mind *why* you do things in a certain way, remember the reasons for decisions and the intent of the design.

One of the most important things to remember when composing this foundation of a design is to imagine this planting's structure in the deep dormancy of winter. It is easy to fall for the temptation of so many pretty flowers. Almost all flowers are short-lived. They are the icing on the cake, not the cake itself, to use a metaphor. But all flowers are presented at their best on a well-laid foundation and structure of foliage and texture. When the design is convincing in the dormant season, chances are it will look convincing when plants are actively growing, flowers are in bloom and it will be beautiful throughout all seasons.

23 - Classic perennial border set against a stone wall background, Pitmeddon, England
Courtesy Beth Chatto

The Main Body of Structural Herbaceous and Feature Plants

The next 'building block' are the structural herbaceous plants including the ornamental grasses. These are herbaceous plants that define the appearance of the planting throughout the growing seasons but have a dormant period, usually but not always in winter. They can either be medium to large bodied plants or small to medium plants, used in large numbers and groups with the purpose of forming the main body of the planting or border.

The history of the perennial border design as specifically designed ornamental borders dates to around 1890. At the time George Nicholson, curator for the Royal Botanic Gardens at Kew, England, promoted perennial-only gardens, steering the gardeners of the time away from the regimented old garden styles. This movement was significant because the representative ornamental gardening to that time relied primarily on bedding plants. Since then the history of perennial use has introduced the border garden, the island garden and the mixed garden. Originally these border perennial gardens were set against a backdrop of a hedge. Perennials were grouped together and tiered with the tallest at the back and the shorter in the front. The purpose was to separate the lawn area from the border. Island beds were introduced in the 1950s. These beds were set in the lawn area and could be viewed from all sides. Taller specimens were placed in the centre of the bed.

Perennial plantings for this book are much more varied and include large natural landscapes where perennials form an integral part of the design with the woody ornamentals in a holistic philosophy. The only boundaries are really set by the imagination of the artist and craftsman or craftswoman.

24 - Perennial border design on the formal eastern terrace of Government House Grounds in Sydney, Australia, restoration of a High-Victorian or Gardenesque design (1870s)
Restoration Work in Sydney, Australia 1998

Feature Plants

These are plants that are very conspicuous in their prime when in flower and then either significantly contribute to or even dominate the main body of the design. I would use Eremurus groups as an example of a feature plant. When in flower the Eremurus dominate the planting and draw the eye of the plant connoisseur toward them. Compared with structural herbaceous species they are either for most of the year inconspicuous or entirely absent due to their long dormancy. As an example of such a structural herbaceous plant, I may give the late flowering Chrysanthemum: for most of the growing seasons the body of Chrysanthemum forms an important part of the perennial border with its foliage, the lovely late flowers being of course a more than welcome added benefit in autumn and going into winter. The criterion to keep in mind for the artist is the contribution to the overall design intent throughout the year.

25 - Examples of feature plants from the Sichtungsgarten Weihenstephan, Germany
Work and study in Weihenstephan 1987

Complementing Herbaceous Plants and Supplementing Bulbs

Upon this main body of structural herbaceous and feature plants we partner plants that with their life cycle, texture and flower complement the structural plants. All these plants have periods where they are less visible or less effective in the display; for example dormancy, late active or having had to be pruned back after flowering for maintenance reasons. Therefore, it is wise to place plants with them that during these times 'take over' with foliage or flower. As an example, the bearded Iris are structural plants and very showy when in flower. But they have both a winter and summer dormancy as in their original habitat they get just about no rain in summer and during these times they are almost invisible. Therefore, I usually place plants with them and in the foreground of them that are active and pretty during these times, for example in front of bearded Iris I would plant evergreen and low silvery Artemisia like the simple Artemisia absinthium. They are fantastic as they have similar requirements on soil properties and exposure, they are sociable with these types of Iris and give throughout the year a humble but effective beautiful presence. Around the Iris the Aster amellus are a great choice as their foliage combines extremely well with them throughout the year and their flowers appear when the Iris are dormant. Many smaller or medium bulbous plants can fulfil the same important role; as always, know your species and what it needs and does throughout the year. Of course, bulbous plants may be chosen as the main theme of a design and the same principles of combining species to their advantage can be applied.

With these structures and principles, I would like to inspire and give assistance, choices and joy as perennials may be confusing in their vast diversity and constantly changing appearances and life cycles. Nothing stays the same and perennial plantings and borders are never finished.

26 - Natural parkland design in the Palace Garden, Stuttgart, Germany
Work and study in Stuttgart 1989

Design Hierarchy, Principles and Structure

Design Hierarchy
The parameter decisions of hard fabric structure

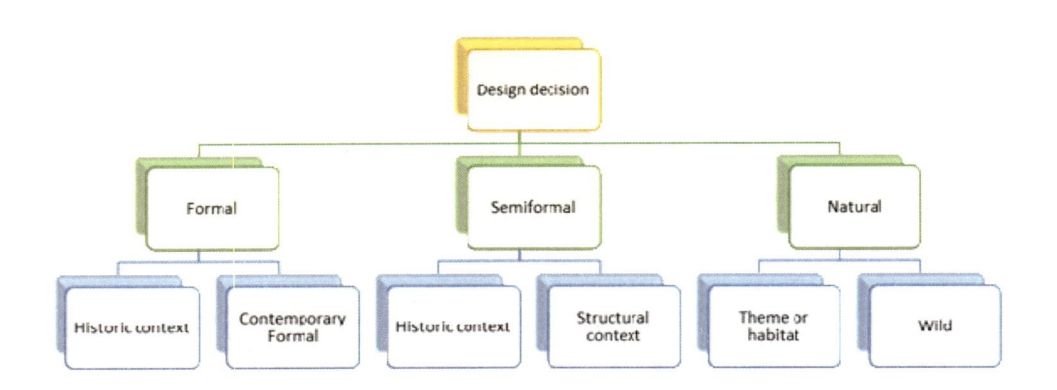

```
                        Design decision
            ┌───────────────┼───────────────┐
          Formal        Semiformal         Natural
         ┌──┴──┐         ┌──┴──┐          ┌──┴──┐
    Historic  Contemporary  Historic  Structural  Theme or  Wild
    context    Formal       context    context    habitat
```

Design Principles and Structure
The subsequent decisions of soft fabric structure and detail

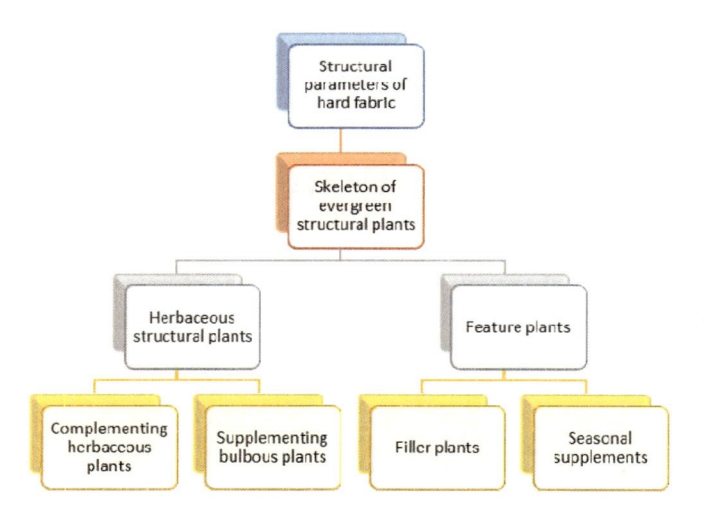

```
        Structural parameters of hard fabric
                      │
        Skeleton of evergreen structural plants
                      │
            ┌─────────┴─────────┐
        Herbaceous           Feature plants
     structural plants
         ┌──┴──┐              ┌──┴──┐
  Complementing  Supplementing  Filler   Seasonal
   herbaceous    bulbous plants  plants  supplements
     plants
```

The Master Plan

Please note that for historic reconstructions or restorations obviously the Master Plan is already given and the design parameters are set unless they are unknown and require archaeological investigation and architectural definition.

The Perennial Plants: Characteristics, Propagation and Use in the Landscape

The following alphabetical listing of perennial plants introduces the genus as such and then details some of the most important species, varieties and cultivars and their use in the landscape.

In selecting plant species, I aimed to assist the professional landscape architect and horticulturist as well as the plant enthusiast. The species described are for use in large scale professional landscapes and parks, as well as species for intensely maintained smaller garden situations and almost all design situations in the temperate northern and southern hemispheres are covered.

Acaena; Rosaceae

The genus Acaena inhabits mountainous regions in the southern hemisphere. There are around a hundred species; some are sub shrubs, others herbaceous plants with slightly woody base sprouts that form roots at their nodes. The leaves are alternating, pinnate with small side leaves, flowers are hermaphroditic, spherical or in clusters and prickly.

Acaena are good weed-suppressing ground cover but live long only on poor soils that they are adapted to, somewhat comparable to some *Thymus*. They grow fast and prefer sunny or dappled shade situations.

Propagation is by horizontal cuttings with two or more nodes or division of already rooted shoots and taken best in late summer.

Acaena adscendens / Vahl 1805 (syn. Acaena affinis)
Originating in South America, Macquarie Islands in the Tasmanian Sea, South New Zealand, this is amore shrubby type around twenty-five centimetres high with blue-green leaves. This species tolerates root pressure from trees or shrubs which is useful in many situations in the landscape.

Acaena anserinifolia / (Forster et Forster) Druce 1917 (syn. Acaena sanguisorba)
This species comes from New Zealand and South-East Australia where it inhabits tussock grasslands as well as open ground. Flowers in summer, strongly growing, I would recommend it for use in natural compositions as ground cover, for example in heathland plantings.

Acaena buchananii / Hook f. 1864
The blue-green foliage is very attractive close or from a distance, the species should be used in moist situations that may include creek beds or moist grasslands. Flowering time is summer; nutrients should be kept low in cultivation.

27 – Acaena buchananii

The picture is taken in the early morning after a night of high humidity and one can observe the dew drops formed on the serrated leaves – this Acaena can, like Alchemilla mollis, push out excess moisture through its leaves to preven fluid overload and fungal infection.

Acaena caesiiglauca / (Bitter) Bergmanns 1939 (A. caerulea hort. A. Glauca hort.)
Coming from New Zealand, this subtle Acaena with normally distinctly blue foliage flowers in early summer occupies open grasslands in its natural habitat. And this is the way it should be used in the designed landscape, in natural plantings, maybe dotted in sways and drifts among grasses and small shrubs.

Acaena magellanica / (Lam.) Vahl 1805
This interesting species occurs naturally in Patagonia, southern Chile and around the southern parts of Argentina. Its shoots may be up to a metre long and appear glowing red when young; the colour changes to a green-blue when maturing. It flowers in early summer and requires cool conditions; in my experience, it does perform well in sub-alpine conditions.

Acaena microphylla / Hook. f.
This cute Acaena has lovely brown to coppery-red foliage and is common in cultivation; there are several horticultural selections and cultivars available. Useful in smaller spaces for its foliage, the following cultivars are recommended: 'Kupferteppich' (Copper Carpet) and 'Pulchella'. 'Pulchella' is best in garden situations where it can be seen up close.

Acaena novae-zealandiae / Kirk 1871

As the name gives away, this strong-growing Acaena originates in New Zealand, its shoots may be up to a metre long with nice dark-green foliage and flowers in early summer. This is a species that does also well in larger applications in the landscape, however it requires considerable maintenance until fully established.

Acantholimon; Plumbaginaceae

The German common name 'Igelkissen' for this genus translates into something like 'hedgehog pillow' which is an apt description for the growth of most of its species. It is less well known in cultivation. However, many species are highly attractive when cultivated and used correctly.

Main habitats are the southern dry regions of the Balkans, Creta and extend to the mountains of western and central Asia into Pakistan and Tibet.

Knowledge of these habitats is the key to successful cultivation. They are best treated as alpines and grown on withered, aged and mineral soils in association with rocks on either alkaline, volcanic or acidic subsoil depending on the species origin.

They are slightly prickly cushions on a woody base; some grow to more than a metre across. Full sun or open heathlands are required for best development. Good companion plants are Astralagus, Genista, Ericaceae, grasses and small bulbs.

Propagation requires some experience. Seed is a good method but often it is hard to get viable seed. I recommend mature tip cuttings from late summer to late autumn in a light, sandy mix, some Perlite may be helpful as are hormones.

Acantholimon albanicum / O. Schwarz et E.K. Meyer

Growing naturally in southern Albania, strong-growing to around a metre across, of medium height, this species is easy to cultivate and flowers dark pink in late spring. Highly recommended, it is attractive through its body and intensely coloured flowers.

Acantholimon androsaceum / (Jaub. et. Spach)

This species originates in the southern Balkans and features a very dense, blue-green and smaller cushion. Bright pink flowers are delightful in early summer.

Acantholimon armenum / Boiss et A Huet

The pink flowers occur on quite long, fifteen to sixteen centimetres stalks above a dense grey-blue greenish cushion in summer. The calyx after flowering is papery, like parchment and remains decorative until late autumn. Originates in Armenia and Kurdistan.

28 – Acantholimon armenum planted on porous rock
Work and study in Weihenstephan, Germany 1988

Acantholimon bracteatum / (Girard) Boiss

Flowering very brightly from pink to light red, this species is very attractive and extends naturally from Armenia and Anatolia through to north-western Iran. The natural habitat emphasises the use in the landscape for dry rockeries.

Acantholimon diapensioides / Boiss

Originating in north-eastern Afghanistan and Pamir, this small species may be more for the collector. It flowers white to pink and has grey to blue-green dense foliage forming its cushion; it requires full sun for best development.

Acantholimon glumaceum / (Jaub. et Spach)

Growing into a green cushion of around fifty centimetres this species from Armenia is easy in cultivation and flowers pink in late spring/early summer.

Acantholimon lycopodioides / (Girard)

This species comes from eastern Afghanistan, northern Pakistan, Pamir and western Tibet. The cushion is compact and flat, with white to light-pink flowers in late spring and early summer.

Acantholimon venustum / Boiss

Extending from northern Syria to southern and eastern Anatolia and northern Iraq, this is one of the most beautiful species with very long, curved glowing dark-pink abundant flowers that are held above the foliage cushion. Performs great in rockeries or larger dry-stone walls.

Acanthus; Acanthaceae

This genus is represented by around twenty species in Asia, Africa and southern Europe. Most species are strong herbaceous perennials or small shrubs with ornamental foliage. Good drainage in normal garden soils is required. It is important to use the species according to its size. Natural or semi-formal landscape designs suit the nature of this genus best. Most species can easily be propagated by root cuttings in winter. It may be of interest that the Acanthus leaf has been extensively used as an ornament in ancient architecture, secular and ecclesiastical.

Acanthus dioscosidis / Willd

Occurs naturally from Turkey to the Lebanon and Iraq to western Iran on dry mountain slopes, up to two thousand two hundred metres above sea level. It flowers in early summer with pink or purple showy inflorescences. I would use this species in dry and well-drained alkaline soil in full sun.

Acanthus hungaricus / (Borb.) Baen

This species comes from the Balkans, south-west Romania and Croatia. Its habitat are forests, shrub lands and rocky slopes, it is one of the most ornamental species and very valuable in the landscape. According to its original habitat I would use it in large rockeries or in correlation with shrubs or the edges of woodlands. It also is a useful cut flower.

Acanthus mollis / I

The possibly most common species in garden situations comes from Portugal and the western Mediterranean regions. It is a large species with ornamental foliage and showy flowers in early summer. Its cultivation requirements are deep soils with good drainage. Use in the landscape in natural planting designs or informal perennial borders, its dark leaves create a great background for colourful flower drifts planted in front of it.

Acanthus spinosus I (A. spinosissimus Pers; A. caro-alexandri)

South-eastern Italy, the Balkans, Algeria and around the eastern Mediterranean regions are the natural home of the species featuring strong pink flowers in early summer. Its natural habitats are along and around smaller shrubs in the Macchia; accordingly, I would use it in groups and accents around low natural designs or informal perennial borders.

29 – Acanthus spinosus
Courtesy Stephan Willenberger

Acanthus syriacus / Boiss

Coming from south-eastern turkey, western Syria, the Lebanon and Palestine, this species prefers dry places in full sun. It features white and chocolate-coloured flowers and may be propagated by root cuttings, seed or division.

Achillea; Asteraceae

This important genus comprises around a hundred-different species in temperate zones of Europe and western Asia. They come as small ground-covers, medium and tall (up to a hundred and fifty centimetres) perennials and most love the full sun. The foliage is graceful and fine, ranging from dark-green to grey and silvery.

Use in the landscape varies; the small species are ideal for the rockery, alpine settings or in containers, good to use with Campanula, Dianthus and Acantholimon, maybe some small bulbs. The taller and stronger species are best used in the sunny and drier perennial border, more in the natural and informal planting but with the right care they can complement a semi-formal perennial border. They are good cut flowers and produce very good dried flower arrangements.

Cultivation is in most cases easy; sun and good drainage – it should be mentioned that Achillea thrive on poor soils, therefore hold back with the fertiliser and use low N but higher P & K. Some alpine species are a little tricky, this is mentioned in the species description below. For areas with more moisture, Achillea ptarmica is a good choice and combines very well with the purples of Salvia nemorosa.

Propagation is best by division, however A. millefolium and similar species are doing well by seed also, when used in natural plant communities where genetic diversity is welcome and desired.

Acillea ageratifolia / (Sibth. Et Sm) Boiss

This species with large white flowers comes from alkaline soils, gravel and rocks of the Balkans. In cultivation, add medium to large graded limestone gravels to the soil for best results.

Achillea atrata / I

This is one of the trickier species from an alpine background; it has green leaves and resembles a moss. White flowers. It prefers a cool and moist gravelly soil and is probably more for the collector.

Achillea canescens

This around thirty centimetres high species features silvery-white ornamental foliage and flowers white in summer. It originates in western Greece and extends into northern Albania and Montenegro. It requires light and sandy soils with good drainage and should not be fertilised, another collector's species.

Achillea chrysocoma / Friv (A. aurea Lam)

From Albania and Macedonia, this small species does well in small rockeries or dry-stone walls. The foliage is small and green, the flowers are yellow. I would combine it with Thymus, Helianthemum and Anaphalis or other small partners.

Achillea filipendulina / Lam (A. eupatorium; M. Bieb)

An excellent cut flower, growing to a hundred and fifty centimetres with grey-green fine foliage. Golden-yellow firm flowers in early summer, the selection 'Parker' is recommended. If the central flower is taken out early, the side flowers gain strength and are very showy. In the perennial border, it combines well with Echinops, Helenium, Anaphalis and Artemisia or ornamental grasses like Panicum with Salvia nemorosa and Solidago.

30 – Achilea filipendulina
Courtesy Angelika Kaufmann

Achillea millefolium / L

Yarrow, from Europe to western Asia, the Caucasus mountain range and northern Iran, it is widespread. It grows up to fifty centimetres tall and flowers from white to pink and red in summer and late summer. Good companion plants are Artemisia ludoviciana 'Silver Queen', Calamagrostis x acutiflora, Centranthus ruber 'Coccineus', Helictotrichon sempervirens, Malva moschata 'Alba', Panicum virgatum, Salvia nemorosa and Stachys byzantine. There are some selections; recommended are 'Cerise Queen', 'Fire King' and 'Sammetriese' ('Red Giant'). Cultivation is easy, use is best in more natural or informal planting designs.

Achillea ptarmica / L

Also called the swamp Yarrow, this more moisture preferring Achillea is widespread from Europe to western Asia. It flowers white and can easily be combined with other moisture-loving perennials in the open border or meadow.

Achillea umbellata var. argentea (Achillea argentea) / Sibth. Et Sm

This silvery beauty comes from Greece where it lives amongst rocks and gravel. It should be used accordingly in the small rock garden or alpinum in full sun, this species is more for the collector.

Aciphylla; Apiaceae

This genus is represented by around fifty species, most of them in Australia. They inhabit higher altitudes, from the sub-alpine to alpine regions. Cultivation is best in acidic and well-drained but at the same time moisture-holding soils. Use in the landscape is best either as collector's species or as accent in alpine rockeries.

Aciphylla horrida / W.R.B. Oliver
The rosettes are a metre or more in diameter, this aptly named species comes from New Zealand. The flower stalks may be up to one and a half metres or more.

Aciphylla squarrosa / J.R. et G. Forst
Also from New Zealand this species follows creeks or water courses and features blue-green foliage. It is easy to cultivate, requiring more water in summer and drier conditions in winter.

Aconitum; Ranunculaceae

Wolfsbane, Monkshood or Aconite are common names associated with Aconitum (usually with A. napellus), a genus that contains around four hundred perennial plants, except the annual Aconitum gymnandrum. The genus extends from the boreal to temperate zones of the northern hemisphere. It mostly occupies grasslands and other open areas of mountains and higher altitudes, but sometimes descends into the valleys.

It is one of the most toxic plants, used in medicine as well as (in the Middle Ages...) to poison wolves and other predators, hence the common name wolfsbane. It has also been used as an arrow or spear poison due to the high toxicity of the plant containing the alkaloids aconitine, mesaconitine, hypaconitine and jesaconitine. These lead to cardiac and respiratory difficulties or death. The concentration is highest in the seed after ripening and the rootstock in the dormant season, winter. When propagating this plant, it is recommended to wear gloves.

The genus prefers by and large cool and moist soil conditions; in drier areas it is recommended to use it in semi-shaded situations, maybe together with Aruncus dioicus, Campanula latifolia var. macrantha, Astilbe species and varieties, Cimicifuga and Anemone japonica in natural or informal designs. However, it does also very well in formal bed situations and is great as a cut flower, this is best achieved in full sun with ample soil moisture and sufficient fertiliser, especially A. napellus is a gross feeder. In cultivation, I would not remove the leaves in autumn too early when they start to discolour, so don't be too tidy there as the plant still gathers nutrients into the roots. This will result in a stronger plant and more flowers next growing season.

Propagation is by seed (cold-moist stratification is required) or division of the root tubers. Remember to wear gloves!

Aconitum alboviolaceum / Kom
As the species name suggests, this interesting Aconitum flowers purple and white. It comes from Korea and Manchuria. It is strong growing and flowers well even in shade, I would recommend it for natural designs in association with shrubs and trees.

Aconitum anglicum Stapf
The English 'Iron Hat' grows up to a hundred and fifty centimetres tall and flowers profusely in early summer; it is an exquisite species for smaller garden situations and may also be used in rockeries.

Aconitum anthora / L
Quite different to most Aconitum species, this gracefully fine-leafed plant prefers drier situations and full sun. It originates in the Pyrenees and margins of the Alps up to two thousand metres above sea level. Yellow flowers appear in late summer, it combines well with Cistus in natural heathland communities.

Aconitum carmichaelii / Debaux (A. fisheri F.B. Forb. et Hemsl non Rchb.)

A very strong Monkshood coming from central China, it can grow up to three hundred centimetres tall and flowers blue-purple in late summer. Whilst the straight species may be best in natural and informal designs, there is a beautiful cultivar 'Arendsii' that is a valuable cut flower and does combine very well in the more formal perennial borders.

Aconitum moldavicum ssp moldavicum / Hacq

The name gives away its origins; this remarkable Aconitum may be up to two hundred centimetres tall in good cultivation and flower colours range from bright purple to crimson red in late summer. It requires sun, moisture and a lot of food. It would be desirable to select outstanding colour variations as cultivars, highly recommended.

Aconitum napellus / L emend. Skalicky (A. pyramidale Mill. A. vulgare DC)

The true Wolfsbane inhabits terrain from low lying river flats up to alpine zones from Spain to Scandinavia and the Balkans. The root tuber is somewhat like a carrot and it can grow up to two hundred centimetres tall. The blue to purple flowers appear in summer and they are great cut flowers. The name 'Wolfsbane' comes from the old use of the plant to poison wolves to protect livestock of settlements. A sheep or cattle carcass was saturated with the Aconitum roots and then placed where wolves would likely find them. After ingestion of the toxins, the wolves would die.

It is one of my favourite European perennials for the interesting flowers that resemble armoured helmets of the pikemen of the late Middle Ages and Renaissance, hence giving them the German common name of 'Sturmhut' (freely translated into Combat Helmet). The highly toxic plant had been used to poison arrows for many centuries. During the Middle Ages, a special permission from the king was required to grow this plant, somewhat like a modern gun licence.

Cultivation is in rich and moist soils; the species is a gross-feeder. Propagation is by seed or division of the rootstock in winter: Extreme care must be taken when handling the carrot-like rootstock as the concentration of the toxins is highest during the winter dormancy. I always instructed my staff to wear gloves when working with them.

31 – Aconitum napellus; Pyrenees 1982
Travel study

Aconitum toxicum / Rchb

The German common name is 'Siebenbürger Eisenhut', which I would loosely translate into 'Seven castles iron hat'. The name refers to an area in Germany combined with the medieval protective armour for the head. With large purple flowers in late summer and up to two hundred centimetres tall, this is an excellent feature along margins of woods or shrubs. The subspecies A. toxicum ssp. toxicum is also highly recommended.

Aconogonon; Polygonaceae

Formerly named Polygonum, this genus extends from Europe to eastern Asia including the Himalayas and south-western China. Almost all are used in herbal medicine for their tannin content; some are used as vegetables in cooking. Propagation is by seed, best when fresh.

Acogonogonon campanulatum / (Hook f)

This valuable perennial originates in the Himalayas and grows to around sixty centimetres. It flowers for a long time, from summer into late autumn with pink, almost bell-like inflorescences and is best used in a sheltered position in semi-shade.

Aconogonum sericeum / (Pall) H. Hara (Persicaria sericea, Polygonum sericeum)

Growing up to a metre tall with an abundance of white flowers in mid-summer, it is a reliable and long-living perennial. I would use it mainly in natural designs and informal plant communities in the middle or background. Propagation is best by seed, cuttings are possible from soft side-shoots before flowering.

Actacea; Ranunculaceae

The genus is commonly named after the Saint Christopherus (Christophskraut) and inhabits the northern temperate zones of the world. Found in forests in shady places the Actaea have graceful foliage and decorative berries as fruit.

Actacea alba / (L) Miller (A. spicata var. alba, A. pachypoda)

This is probably the largest and most beautiful species featuring white berries on thick red stems in summer and autumn. Good partners are Smilacina racemosa and Gillenia trifoliata. It comes from America.

32 -Actaea alba
Staudengärtnerei Häussermann, Stuttgart in Germany

Actacea spicata / L (A. nigra)

An enduring tough perennial that survives even under Picea and Abies canopies where many ferns fail. The plant grows to around eighty centimetres, often found under Fagus and mixed forests. It has white flowers and black berries.

Actinotus; Apiaceae

Actinotus helianthii

The 'Flannel Flower' is a special perennial with soft, silvery-grey beautifully divided foliage that is a most attractive feature. The plant grows to fifty centimetres high and has daisy-like white flowers up to eight centimetres across. Even that the species' name suggests and the flower superficially resembles it, the plant is not related to the Sunflowers that are Asteraceae. The plant requires sandy, extremely well-drained and poor soils, in its original habitat the soil profile is often no more than five centimetres deep but the plants grow around sandstones which provide protection of the roots from the fierce summer sun. If you translate this knowledge into providing the right environment in cultivation, it is a very graceful, long-living and gently self-sowing species great in rockeries or natural designs. A great cut flower, it is propagated by seed (erratic germination) or cuttings – do not keep those too wet, just on the verge of dry like silvery Artemisia cuttings.

Adenophora; Campanulaceae

Around forty species are known of this genus, closely related to Campanula. Use in the landscape for the higher species is in perennial borders as well as natural informal planting designs including combinations with loosely planted shrubs. The smaller ones are doing well in rockeries or even in pots. Most accept normal garden soil, preferably slightly alcaline and sun or light shade. Propagation is best by seed, the plants like being undisturbed and do not transplant well.

Adenophora confusa / Nannfeldt
The plant grows up to ninety centimetres tall and originates in western China. The nodding flower bells are deep blue and around two centimetres.

33 – Adenophora confusa
Courtesy Stephan Willenberger

Adenophora divaricata / Franch et Sav

Manchuria, Japan and Korea are the natural habitats of this bell-flower. Its valuable properties are a very long flowering period from summer until late autumn with blue bells.

Adenophora tashiroi / Makino et Nakai

This dwarf species originates in Japan and is found in some places in Korea. It flowers in summer with lovely purple bells and should be grown in loose gravels, great also in pots. A species that is best for the plant enthusiast and collector.

Adiantum; Pteridaceae

This genus of ferns contains around a hundred and fifty different species. It has representatives almost everywhere in the world, most of them in tropical America. Most grow along creeks and rivers, in the rainforest or wet rockeries, so plenty of moisture is required for cultivation.

Adiantum pedatum L

Peacock's fern or horseshoe fern are some of the common names referring to the easily identified leaf structure. It extends from northern America to eastern Asia and the Himalayas and is a graceful foliage and background plant. It is reasonably tough for a fern and prefers some shade. I have used it within Rhododendron and other Ericaceae plantings as ground cover and complementing species and it did very well.

34 – Adiantum pedatum
Courtesy Angelika Kaufmann

Adiantum venustum / D. Don

From the Himalayas and Nepal, the 'women's hair fern' as it is often commonly called does this name justice. It is a fine beauty requiring moisture and shade where it develops into a delicate ground cover or softens harsh edges in a design.

Adonis; Ranunculaceae

There are between twenty and forty perennial and annual species in this genus. Use in the landscape varies greatly and is according to the original habitat of the species concerned. Some grow in association with sheltered woods and shrubs (A. amurensis, A. brevistyla), whilst others (A. vernalis) are exposed heathland plants, often in association with Gentiana cruciata, Globularia punctata, Inula ensifolia, Pulsatilla and other species of this community. Propagation is by seed – early harvest is important.

Adonis sibiria / Patrin ex Ledeb (Adonanthe sibirica)
Originating in north-west and eastern Russia and extending into northern Asia, these valuable small perennial lives in open forests and meadows. In cultivation, it prefers sun and good drainage and has lovely orange-yellow and long-lasting flowers. Propagation is by seed with fresh seed being best; however germination is often erratic and patience is in order.

Adonis vernalis / L (Adonanthe veralis)
This may be the best-known Adonis with its main habitat extending from eastern, central and southern Europe into Russia and Scandinavia. This species lives on dry, alkaline soils and flowers yellow in spring, there are sometimes very interesting seedling variations that are worth cultivating. Use in the landscape in flowery meadows and partners like Carlina acaulis, Euphorbia cyparissias, Potentilla arenaria, Pulsatilla grandis and perhaps grasses from similar plant communities.

35 – Adonis vernalis, Romania, Transylvania
Travel study 1988

Aethionema; Brassicaceae

These are small perennials with mostly blue-green foliage, comparable to Iberis and useful in small rockery situations or alpine tubs. Use in association with Acantholimon, small Achillea and Alyssum, Helianthemum, Arenaria and alpine Dianthus, Euphorbia capitata and Festuca.

Aethionema armenum / Boiss
The pink flowering attractive little sub-shrub has blue-grey foliage and lives in Anatolia. Keep the soil well drained, light and poor in cultivation, otherwise it has a short lifespan. Propagation is by cuttings in late summer.

Agapanthus; Alliaceae

This south African genus has around ten identified species and numerous garden hybrids and cultivars. They are in principle quite tough but for best flower production they require moisture and food in the development in spring. Propagation is easy by division.

Agapanthus campanulatus ssp campanulatus / Bell

Natal and northern provinces are the original habitat of this Agapanthus with a clear blue flower in summer, there is a white cultivar available.

Agapanthus praecox / Willd

This is the most common Agapanthus that has many variations, including a white variety. Discovered in 1809, it is now very widely used in gardens around the world and is even known to 'escape' into the Australian bush.

Agastache; Lamiaceae

Most species of this genus come from North-America or Mexico, an aromatic perennial related to the mints.

Agastache cana / Wooton et Standley

This very attractive grey-leaved plant requires hot and dry conditions for in cultivation. It grows to around sixty centimetres with pink to orange flowers in summer and late summer. Pruning back in early autumn assists the plants with lateral growth and strengthens the rootstock, resulting in more flowers in the next growing season.

Agastache rugosa / Kuntze

Originating in Korea and extending into northern China, this representative of the genus grows to around eighty centimetres tall. A graceful garden plant combining well with many other perennials, it contains many varieties ranging in colour from white to pink, blue and purple, possibly the best purple may be 'Serpentine'.

Agave; Agavaceae

A well-known genus that contains many striking structural species coming mainly from the Americas. Most have fleshy, succulent leaves and are often armed with spikes. The flower stalk develops only after several years and inflorescence is usually followed by the death of the plant, however many offshoots would have developed, like in *Sempervivum*. These plants come from hot and dry mountains and deserts and are best combined with plants from such communities. Placement in the landscape or urns needs to be carefully considered as most pose a danger through their spikes.

Agave attenuata / Galeotti

This soft-leaved and 'unarmed' species comes from central Mexico and is very attractive in urns or dry succulent garden beds. Due to its softness, it can be planted in accessible areas as is does not possess the stinging capacity of most of its relatives.

Agave megalacanta / Hemsl

This Mexican Agave forms attractive small groups of plants through its offshoots and features almost triangular young leaves that broaden into an oval shape as they mature.

Agave parryi / Engelm

Texas to southern Arizona and northern Mexico are home to this silvery-green leaved Agave. The inflorescence may be up to six metres high with large, up to eight centimetres across yellow flowers.

Agave hutahensis / Engelm

This species grows naturally on gravelly soils from northern Arizona and southern Utah into northern Mexico. It also has a very tall flower spike and is best used in the larger landscapes for structural and architectural purposes.

Agave victoriae-reginae

Named after Queen Victoria (reginae derives from rex, regis, the ruling king or queen) this is a small species from the Chihuahuan Desert. It is very interesting as the maturing leaves peeling off leave a white stripe across the old leaves and this develops into a very ornamental pattern. It is slow growing and does also very well in urns but needs to be kept out of reach due to its sharp spikes. In Government House grounds in Sydney (1995 – 2002), we kept them in sandstone urns around the formal eastern terrace but we cut off the spikes to protect the people.

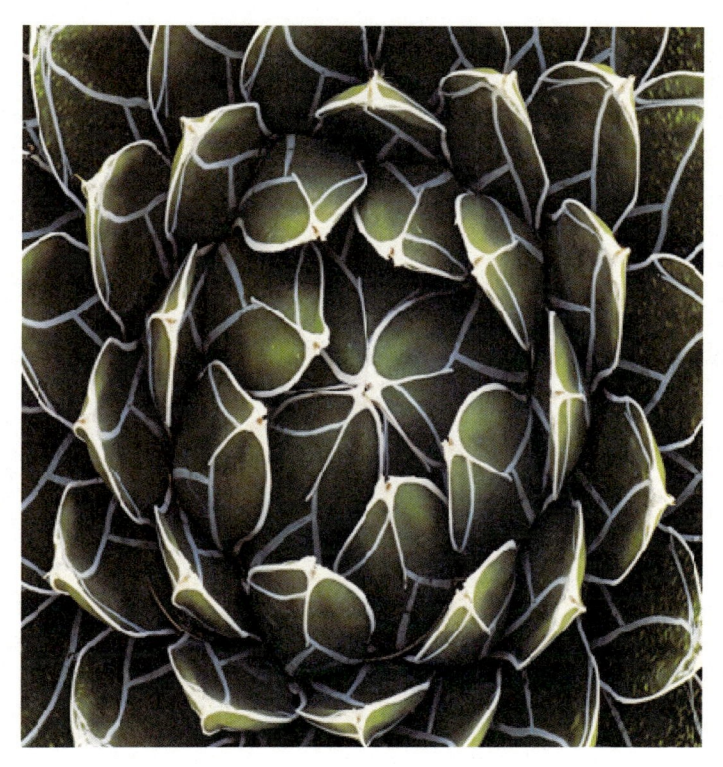

36 – Agave victoriae-reginae
Government House grounds in Sydney, Australia, work in Sydney 1998

Ajuga; Lamiaceae

This genus contains annual as well as perennial species, together there are around forty of them. Most are very useful ground cover for semi-shade and shade and require moisture.

Ajuga genevensis / L

Ajuga genevensis is a widespread species that ranges from southern Sweden to France and Turkey to the Caucasus mountains. It naturally occurs along the margins of woodlands or on open heath associated with shrubs, mostly on alkaline soils. It brings a glowing blue colour into plantings. I would use it together with Pulsatilla, Festuca and Helianthemum species.

Ajuga reptans / L

This fast-growing species is at home in Europe but extends well into Tunisia, Algeria and Iran and east into the Caucasus mountain range. It develops into dense carpets that may be very useful under and around shrubs and trees, as fill among taller perennials or as foreground and border plant to name a few examples. Thalictrum, Trollius, Astilbe, Cimicifuga, Lysimachia and Tradescantia are good partners, however the competitive nature of this species requires regular maintenance so it does not overwhelm its neighbours. Propagation is easy by division, cuttings and seed are also easy should larger numbers be required.

37 – Ajuga reptans
Work in Canberra, Australia 2012

Alcea; Malvaceae

This genus originates mainly in south-west and middle Asia and the eastern Mediterranean regions where dry summers and mild winters characterise the climate. Most representatives of this genus develop very fast into handsome plants and feature impressive flower displays from summer through to autumn. They are prone to fungal leaf diseases (*Puccinia malvacearum*) and insect attack however. Propagation is easy by seed and from experience I would recommend keeping re-propagating fresh young plants for displays.

Alcea ficifolia / L

As the name suggests, this species is often called the fig-leaved Hollyhock and originates in the warmer areas of Siberia and Asia and there are several nice garden hybrids available that flower in tones of yellow, copper, pink, red and white from summer through to autumn.

Alcea rosea / L

Coming from Anatolia and south-east Asia this species' hybrids are popular and common in horticulture. From pink to dark red, salmon, yellow and white, the flowers are also good for the vase. They are best used as groups in the background of natural or cottage garden scenarios, maybe in combination with Salvia officinalis, tall bearded Iris, Lilium candidum and Campanula pyramidalis. They stand out even from a distance and therefore may also be used together with Delphinium, Helenium and similar perennials.

38 – Alcea rosea
Courtesy Madlyn Howe

Alcea rugosa / Alef
This more than two-metre-tall species hails from southern Russia and the Ukraine where it inhabits dry valleys and rocky hill slopes. It is a robust species that is less prone to the Rust problems of the other species and features pale or deep yellow, sometimes orange yellow flowers up to five centimetres across.

Alchemilla; Rosaceae

The 'Lady's Mantle' genus contains around a thousand different species. However, many are quite similar and difficult to differentiate and for the purpose for this book this is not necessary. Those that have significance for our landscapes and gardens come from subalpine zones of Europe, Africa and Asia where they accompany shrub and woodland communities. They are herbaceous, winter-dormant low perennials that prefer sun to dappled shade with the soils being not too dry. Propagation is by cuttings and seed (cold-moist stratification).

Alchemilla caucasica / Buser

This small Alchemilla originates in the Caucasus as the name suggests and I would use it mainly in the sunny alpine rockery in small groups. It connects other plants very well and gives the design a sense of cohesion and unity. It flowers in summer, extending into early autumn.

Alchemilla mollis / Buser, Rothm

The species that probably gave the genus its name is at home in Anatolia, Iran, the Caucasus, the Balkans and Romania, where it inhabits meadows and the margins of woodlands. It forms large stands and is reasonably robust, a very useful plant also along borders when its winter dormancy does not matter to the design intent. From my time at the nursery of Her Highness the Countess of Zeppelin in Germany I remember we used it on both sides along the small pathway leading up from the private residence into the nursery quarters. It was a wonderful picture with its clouds of flowers and in cold mornings with high humidity the leaves pushed out small droplets of water along its serrated edges that looked like pearls or tears.

39 – Alchemilla mollis
An early morning picture taken in autumn when the Alchemilla pushed out excess moisture from its leaf tips forming these lovely pearls of dew
Courtesy Staudengärtnerei Gräfin von Zeppelin, Germany, border of Rose Walk

Alchemilla splendens / Christ ex Gremli
The western Alps are the home of this smaller pretty Alchemilla that prefers alkaline soils and limestone subsoils. It is best used in alpine rockeries in small groups in among the feature species as it brings a planting well together.

Alisma; Alismataceae

There are around ten species of this plant of swamps, shallow water or wet areas near the water's edge. The German common name translates freely into 'the Frog's Spoon' which refers to its spoon-like leaf shape. Frogs have not yet been observed eating with it. It is almost a cosmopolitan genus and inhabits temperate, subtropical and tropical zones of Europe, America, Asia and Australia. Use in the landscape mostly in natural designs or in clearly defined and *confined* spaces in semi-formal or even formal settings.

Alisma gramineum / Lej (Alisma loeselii; Gorski)
The fine-leafed 'Frog's Spoon' has decorative inflorescences and fruiting bodies that stand around half a metre above the water. It is best used along ponds or in the running water of creeks and like water features.

Alisma plantago-aquatica / L

This species features up to a metre above the water a decorative inflorescence that holds well as cut flower in the vase. It is quite a structural plant with its upright habit accentuating the water. It is strong, best used on its own and in wild, natural designs as it tends to overwhelm plants near it.

Allium; Allicaceae

This is a reasonably large genus with around six hundred and ninety species, widespread and extending from Europe, Asia, America, Sri Lanka and into Africa. Many are used in the kitchen as herbs or vegetables and there are many ornamental species for use in natural settings or formal perennial borders.

Allium aflatuense B. Fedtsch

This species originates in central Asia and grows to around a hundred and fifty centimetres. It is an excellent cut flower, also in dried arrangements. Good drainage and full sun with not too much competition from other plants is required. During and after the flowering phase the leaves tend to die back, therefore I found it works best not in the immediate foreground but set back in a planting behind species that provide structure in front of it.

Allium christophii Trautv

Also 'listening' to the glamorous name of 'The Star of Persia', this very showy species originates as this common name suggests in the ancient empire of Persia, today Iran, Iraq and into Turkey. It inhabits rocky and gravelly mountain slopes from around nine hundred up to two thousand three hundred metres altitude. This gives us a good indication on how to cultivate the plants; obviously good drainage and full sun and it does not mind the cold. It has beautiful bright purple round inflorescences that catch the eye when in flower. It invites planting in steppe-like settings with partners that complement it when dormant, like Sedum or Acaena; I would use it also in rockeries among low evergreen perennials and sub-shrubs. The dried fruiting bodies keep for years in dry flower arrangements.

40 – Allium christophii
Courtesy Frank Schmid

Allium karataviense Regel

This special Leek features broad, curved and metallic blue leaves and is for that reason in Germany called 'Blue Tongue Leek'. It comes from central Asia and requires alkaline gravels to thrive. This now is a species more for the collector in the rockery, steppe or alpine garden rather than a perennial border and the inflorescences are around thirty centimetres high. The dried fruit and seeds are good for dry flower arrangements.

Allium neapolitanum Cyr

Named after the beautiful Italian city, this species is also known as the Daffodil Garlic. It inhabits meadows and fields that are well-drained. The flowers are up to twelve centimetres across, white and come up in late spring. It likes full sun or semi-shade and grows well in association with smaller shrubs; it is a very valuable species in the garden and as cut flower. There is a selection called 'Grandiflorum' available that features larger flowers.

Alstroemeria; Alstroemeriaceae

The 'Inca-Lily' comes as the name suggests from South America, Mexico to Argentina, Peru and Chile. It grows naturally under and around open shrublands that provide some shelter. It prefers warm, sunny or semi-shaded places with good drainage. Good partners are perennials with the same preferences as Artemisia arborescens, Perovskia abrotanum, Eryngium species and Iris germanica. Alstroemeria may spread in irregular clusters and therefore I would use in mainly in natural, wild planting designs.

Alstroemeria aurea Graham

The possibly toughest and strongest species from Chile and Argentina grows to around a metre and bears orange-yellow flowers through summer. There are different selections and hybrids that I can recommend like

'Lutea' (yellow with red stripes), 'Dover Orange' (deep orange with markings) and 'Orange King' (large orange flowers).

41 – Alstroemeria aurantiaca
Travel study, Liguria, Italy 1982

Alstroemeria ligtu (A. pulchella)
This is the parent of the most hybrids today in garden cultivation with the common name of 'St. Martin's flower'. The species grows between fifty and sixty centimetres with white, pale mauve and pink flowers. Its hybrids (usually cross A. ligtu var. angustifolia x A. haemantha) are larger and more intensely coloured than the species.

Alstoemeria patagonica Phil (A. pygmaea)
Quite an exceptional small rockery or alpine species, it grows to around ten centimetres high depending on exposure. In my opinion, it does well in full exposure to sun and wind, clinging to white rocks where it forms dense clusters. This species is probably more for the alpine collector and botanic enthusiast. Propagation is by seed and fresh seed is best, it usually takes around three years before the first flowers appear from seedlings.

Althea, Malvaceae

Mostly known as Hollyhock, this genus is widespread from Western Europe to Middle Asia where it grows in moist and even swampy valleys. Handsome perennials that are best combined with Hemerocallis and ornamental grasses with similar moisture requirements.

Althea cannabina L
This species grows up to three metres tall with several shoots; the flowers are shades of pink with dark eyes and prominent stamens. An elegant and light plant best used in large natural spaces and meadows.

Althea officinalis L

The old medicinal plant (leaves and roots help against coughs) is a traditional species for herb and cottage gardens. It inhabits Europe, Siberia, Asia and northern Africa, grows up to two metres and prefers moist meadows. The flowers are up to five centimetres across and usually pale pink, however there may be strong local variations in colour. Lythrum salicaria, Asclepias incarnata and Carmassia species are good partners. Propagation is by seed or root cuttings during dormancy.

42 – Althaea officinalis
Herb garden in the Royal Botanic Gardens Sydney Australia 2001

Alyssum, Brassicaceae

The genus comprises around a hundred and fifty different species. Some are annual, some are perennial and some are sub-shrubs, becoming woody at the base. It occurs from central and southern Europe through to Asia and northern Africa; most species are at home in the Mediterranean though. A great representative of the genus is Alyssum montanum, one of the sub-shrubs. It is best used in a rockery or dry-stone wall or container, I have also successfully used on vegetated roofs. Aubrieta, low Phloxes, Arabis caucasica and Iberis sempervirens are fantastic as complementing partners. Good drainage and light soils are essential, use fertilisers only very sparingly as they are adapted to poor soils and die quickly if overfed. Propagation is easy by seed. Powdery or downy mildew may be encountered in years with high humidity.

Alyssum alpestre L

A lovely rockery plant forming fifteen-centimetre-high pillows and preferring gravelly soils, Alyssum alpestre bears masses of pale yellow flowers that cover the entire plant in early summer.

Alyssum argenteum All

A true alpine for dry places and around forty centimetres high with a woody base, this perennial is at home in southern Europe. Golden-yellow flowers are loosely held.

43 – Alyssum argenteum
Courtesy Angelika Kaufmann

Alyssum caespitosum Baumg

This from Turkey coming perennial is very attractive through its silvery and dense carpets of leaves in the rockery. It grows only to around five centimetres high and I find it is best used in conjunction with rocks in very exposed locations. The flowers are golden-yellow in late spring.

Alyssum moellendorffianum Aschers

A very pretty species ideally suited for the top of dry stone walls or large stone tubs, it comes from Croatia and western Bosnia. It grows to fifteen centimetres and forms a dense carpet in full sun and requires excellent drainage.

Alyssum montanum L

The German common name translates loosely into something like Mountain Rock Herb and it naturally extends from Europe to northern Africa, Asia and into Syria. It grows in a large variety of soils and gets up to twenty centimetres high with yellow flowers in late spring and early summer. It is very easy and can be used in a wide range of applications.

44 – Alyssum montanum 'Berggold'
Dry stone wall in Badenweiler, Germany

Amsonia; Apogynaceae

A small genus with twenty species from North America related to Oleander and Vinca. Propagation of desirable selections is by cuttings in early summer.

Amsonia ciliata Walt
This up to a hundred and fifty-centimetre-high perennial inhabits open forests and should be used accordingly and as a fill in the background. The flowers are pale blue.

Amsonia tabernaemontana Walt
This species grows to around a metre and holds the metallic-blue flowers in clusters. Like the Nerium, it may be best used on its own as understorey in low-maintenance open forest parks.

Anacamptis; Orchidaceae

There is only one species in this genus, the German common name is 'Dog's Herb'.

Anacamptis pyramidalis Rich
This Orchid inhabits the European Alps, the Mediterranean, south-west Asia and northern Africa. The deep red flowers are held pyramidal, hence the Latin name description. The deep red brightens as the flower matures in summer; it grows up to eighty centimetres tall. This is an interesting species to use, maybe for the collector, in natural meadows or other informal plantings; it requires dry, sunny and alkaline conditions. It is difficult to establish as this species depends on a symbiosis with mycorrhizal fungi. It is a protected species.

45 – Anacamptis pyramidalis
Courtesy Stephan Willenberger

Anacyclus; Asteraceae

There are twelve species representing this genus. They are common around the Mediterranean, southern Europe, northern Africa and the Middle East. Propagation is by seed or basal cuttings.

Anacyclus depressus Ball
This pretty but short-lived perennial is at home in the mountains of Morocco. As the species name suggests it is a ground-hugging little plant that is covered in flowers in early summer. Good drainage is essential and on good sites it self-sows. Good combinations are Crassula, Sedum, Helichrysum milfordiae, Origanum rotundifolium and dry grasses like Stipa.

46 – Anacyclus depressus
Rockery garden in Korntal, Stuttgart, Germany 1985

Anaphalis; Asteraceae

In Europe, Asia and North America we can find thirty-five species of this genus. They are mostly grey or silvery and furry-leaved small perennials for the rockery or alpinum in full sun. Other sun and dry-loving perennials like Eryngium, Lavandula, Salvia, Dictamnus or Verbascum combine well with them. Propagation is by division, soft tip cuttings in spring (do not over-water, no mist!) or seed.

Anaphalis margaritacea Benth
The 'Silver Immortelle' or 'Pearly Everlasting' originates in northern America, Japan and north-eastern Asia, it has been introduced to Europe. Its habitats are dry steppes, slopes and open shrublands and it may be used as a pioneer plant where soil has been disturbed and needs replanting.

Anaphalis triplinervis Sims et Clarke
This up to fifty-centimetre-high growing perennial hails from the Himalayas and flowers white in summer and the foliage is very decorative. There are two selections that can be recommended, 'Sommerschnee' (Summer Snow) and 'Silberregen' (Silver Rain).

Anchusa; Boraginaceae

At home in the temperate zones of Europe, Africa and western Asia, these perennials prefer warm and dry places. The German common name translates loosely into 'Oxen Tongue' and refers to the rough, hairy surface of the leaves. I find it best in natural, wild designs and plant communities, for more formal designs these plants are not 'dressy' enough but in the right place they perform beautifully. Propagation is by seed or root cuttings – these should be taken early in autumn and winter and potted rather shallow and not over-watered.

Anchusa azurea Miller
A characteristic plant of the Mediterranean, this species extends into northern Africa. It grows up to one and a half metres tall and has a carrot-like root. The flowers are outstanding with a deep blue, close to Gentiana, sometimes playing into purple. It combines well with Achillea, Papaver orientale and the tall bearded Iris. However, this combination should be planted in the middle or background due to the prolonged dormancies of these species, I usually utilise some evergreen partners that give the planting structure throughout the year. There are some very good selections like 'Loddon Royalist', 'Royal Blue' and 'Dropmore'.

Anchusa cespitosa Lam
This very beautiful perennial from Crete requires some attention, especially excellent drainage as it grows naturally in gravel but it is worth the effort.

Anchusa leptophylla ssp incana Roem et Schult
Coming from Armenia this around forty-centimetre-high beauty also requires excellent drainage and has a most beautiful glowing blue inflorescence in summer and into early autumn. Good partners are Festuca glauca, Hypericum, Linum and similar species with those requirements.

Andropogon; Poaceae

This genus of ornamental grasses extends from the tropics to the cool-temperate zones of the world. The cultivated species are used in formal or informal gardens, they are growing clumpy and most flower in late summer through to late autumn. Personally, I recommend in cold climates to leave old flowers and leaves right through the winter as they look very attractive covered with snow or coated with ice crystals in hoar frosts. Cut back down to ground level in early spring. Propagation is by seed or division in early spring, can also be done in winter in case work runs out in a nursery but the divided plants should not be over-watered during dormancy.

Andropogon gerardii Vitman
This grass comes from America (from the North down to Mexico) and is a great feature for large perennial borders or steppe plantings. It grows up to two metres tall with blue-green leaves and reddish stems and looks wonderful in early or late light. The selection 'Präriesommer' (summer in the prairies) is more compact and flowers even more profusely, a great structural plant.

Andropogon ternaries Michx
This lovely beard grass comes originally from Delaware, Florida, and Texas. The leaves are bluish and colour in autumn to a rich copper red with silvery inflorescences. Good to use as cut flower.

Androsace; Primulaeae

This genus of very interesting members of the Primula family has been repeatedly classified and re-classified by botanists and is still under discussion. There are annuals, biennials and perennial species. Most of the perennials form dense pillows or rosettes with some real treasures amongst them. For this book, I would like to focus mainly on the cultivation requirements, the species listing is according to the sections of the genus.

Cultivation requirements for group A; dense pillow-forming and hairy species from the Himalayas, section Chamaejasme: Excellent drainage in full sun, protection from wet soils in winter and hoar frosts as well as intense heat in summer, therefore often best cultivated in an alpine house. They do very well in ceramic unglazed pots with gravels, sand, Perlite, Vermiculite or Seramis and only around twenty-five per cent of aged organic soil. The so-prepared pots are sunk in moist sand, so that capillary action creates low moisture in the pots. Alternatively, open beds with conditions as described above can be created; excellent drainage, perfect aeration and protection from extremes of temperatures are paramount. Nutrition needs to be poor in nitrogen and low in concentration; I made good experiences with cactus fertiliser (NPK 5-8-25) at a third of the recommended strength. These species are recommended only for the experienced grower/collector/botanist.

Cultivation requirements for group B; some of the hardier Chamaejasme, the species of subsection Aretia, the species of subsection Dicranothrix except for Androsace pyrenaica and some of the section Douglasia. These are treated in principle as described above but are tougher and easier; for example they tolerate more moisture and humidity in winter or more heat in summer. They are sensitive to hoar frosts and require protection, though.

Cultivation requirements for group C; these are the carpet-forming species, i.e. Androsace sarmentosa and its relatives. They are by and large more robust but still need good drainage and larger particle size soils like gravel mixed with sand; do not plant in loam or clay or mixes with high percentages of organic matter. Propagation is easy by separation of the runners once they start forming roots, a little bit like strawberries.

Cultivation requirements for group D; these are the most robust representatives of this genus. Good drainage and full sun with light, open soils are the key to success. They can be real little gems in the small rock garden, in tubs or an alpinum and do not require species protection. Propagation is by division of the (often short) runners once roots start to form if only small numbers are required for production. Seed propagation is another method and used if larger numbers are required. Please note that some require different clones of its own species for fertile seed to form, these are self-sterile forms. Sowing is best in autumn and early winter; best practice is to let the seed absorb some moisture for ten days without frost and then expose them to winter temperatures to overcome the dormancy and germination inhibitors. They still may be erratic germinators and it is well worth keeping seed trays for a year with these treasures.

Section Andraspis

Androsace albana Stev

This pretty species is at home in the Caucasus, north-eastern Turkey and north-western Iran. The flowers are white to pink with a bright yellow eye and seven to ten millimetres across. Cultivation requirements for group D.

Androsace armena Duby

Also coming from the Caucasus, Turkey and north-western Iran, this species usually behaves like a biennial but under good cultivation can endure for several years. In any case, it is recommended to harvest and save the seed. The rosettes are up to twelve centimetres across and the flowers are creamy white to pale pink with a red eye that darkens as the flower matures. Highly recommended decorative species, it requires cultivation under group D.

Androsace chaixii Gem et Godt

Originating in the mountains of south-eastern France this short-lived attractive species is often found clustered around rocks and is best used in a similar manner as filler in the small rockery or alpinum. Flowers are up to seven millimetres across and pink; cultivation requirements group D.

Androsace multiscapa Duby

Inhabiting higher altitudes from a thousand to three thousand five hundred metres in the Taurus Mountains of Turkey and the Lebanon, this species is ideal for informal borders of an alpinum or tubs of any size grown in gravel and rocks. Flowers are white to pink with a yellow eye; cultivation requirements for group D.

Section Aizoidium

Androsace bulleyana Fort

This species grows naturally in the higher altitudes of western Yunnan, from eighteen hundred metres to over three thousand two hundred metres elevation. The hairy rosettes can become more than ten centimetres wide, the flowers are deep carmine red and are carried in dense umbels. This is usually a biennial plant and is very easy to grow from seed. The strong colour makes this species very valuable in the rockery; cultivation requirements as for group D.

Section Aretia

Subsection Aretia

Androsace alpina Lam

This rather well-known species is at home in the Alps and inhabits gravelly slopes above two thousand metres. The loose pillows branch out and look for good places among the rocks. The flowers are white to pink with a golden-yellow eye and come up in spring, sometimes there is a second flush of flowers in late summer. Whilst this species prefers slightly more moist soils it requires excellent drainage and free airflow; cultivation requirements for group A.

47 – Androsace alpina
Travel study, mountains in Switzerland 1985

Androsace ciliata DC

From the beautiful Pyrenees comes this very lovely and relatively easy to grow species. It inhabits gravelly slopes and often occupies disturbed areas after rock falls or landslides at altitudes between two thousand five hundred and three thousand two hundred metres. Prolific flowering in shades of pink with the highlight in early spring but some flowers appear pretty much throughout the year. It requires some protection from too much water in winter; cultivation requirements are for group B.

Androsace delavayi Franch

The Himalayas to western China are home to this little delicacy. It grows in very high altitudes from four thousand to five thousand three hundred metres in acidic rocky and gravelly soils. Accordingly, I would consider it difficult to grow unless the collector has a proper alpine house with professional climate controls in lower altitudes. The plant forms dense pillows or extends into little carpets; the leaves feature silky hairs at the margins. The flowers are bright to dark pink. Propagation is by cuttings or seed; cultivation requirements are for group A.

Androsace hausmannii Leyb

This species now prefers alkaline gravels and rocks; it naturally grows in the eastern Alps in altitudes above one thousand nine hundred metres. It flowers white, pale pink or hues of pink on white with a yellow eye, usually short-lived but easy to propagate by seed. Cultivation requirements are under group A.

Androsace helvetica All

Guess where this species comes from? While it is named after Switzerland, it naturally extends far beyond the country's borders in altitudes of fifteen hundred to three thousand two hundred metres. The flowers are white with yellow eye in spring, there is a large variation within this species and it would be well worth selecting attractive forms; cultivation requirements as for group A.

48 – Androsace helvetica
Travel study, Switzerland

Androsace vandellii (Turra) Chiov

This species is one of my favourites; it only occurs in rock crevices of acidic mountains in altitudes of 900 to 3,500 metres in the Alps, the Pyrenees and the Sierra Nevada. The plant forms very dense, silvery-grey pillows that look like they would have been glued onto pure rock. It flowers profusely in pure white with a yellow eye; cultivation requirements of group A.

Subsection Dicranothrix

Androsace carnea L

Growing right across the western mountains of Europe, this species is somewhat variable but all types prefer lime-free rocky and gravelly conditions, flowers are pink or white; cultivation requirements of group B.

Androsace pyrenaica Lam

The species inhabits altitudes over two thousand five hundred metres on granite and forms dense pillows of grey hairy rosettes. Flowers are pure white with yellow eye and have a very sweet scent; cultivation requirements for group A.

Section Chamaejasme

Subsection Villosae

Androsace globifera Duby

Coming from the southern slopes of the Himalayas and unusually for Androsace, grow into monsoonal zones at altitudes between three thousand five hundred to four thousand five hundred metres. It grows reasonably large, into pillows up to a metre in diameter and features mauve to pale purple flowers with yellow eyes and is very attractive. In cultivation, I found it does well in moist sand and does not like to dry out in summer. Propagation is easy by cuttings, cultivation requirements other than I described above as for group A and B.

Androsace jacqemontii Duby

This species originates in the Indian part of the Himalayas where it lives in altitudes of three thousand five hundred to four thousand five hundred metres and forms dense carpets. The flowers are bright pink, it is a very pretty Androsace and easy to cultivate; cultivation requirements as for group C.

Androsace sarmentosa Wall

The Himalayas and western China are the home of this species that usually grows in altitudes between two thousand seven hundred and three thousand five hundred metres. This species is the parent of most of the common Androsace in cultivation and easy to grow given basic horticultural knowledge. There are many selections available in the trade, 'Brilliant' being probably the most outstanding red one.

Subsection Hookeriana

Androsace hookeriana Klatt

At home in eastern Nepal to western China, this Androsace inhabits moister zones and grows in altitudes between three thousand seven hundred to four thousand five hundred metres. It forms open carpets and has white to bright pink flowers in spring, this is one of the few Androsace that does well in dappled shade, it also inhabits open mountain forests; cultivation requirements of group B.

Subsection Mucronifoliae

Androsace himalaica Hand-Mazz

North-eastern Afghanistan, northern Pakistan and the western Kashmir are home to this graceful species that lives in altitudes of up to three thousand metres. It forms large carpets and its flowers are white to pink in spring and it forms viable seed easily; cultivation requirements of group B.

Androsace sempervivioides Jacquem ex Duby

This species lives on grassy slopes and disturbed mountainsides between three thousand and four thousand metre altitude. The plant forms open carpets with pale to dark pink flowers and it has a strong sweet scent; cultivation requirements of group C.

Subsection Strigillosae

Androsace strigillosa Franch
This is a very early summer flowering plant that comes from the Himalayas where it inhabits open woodlands and grasslands of altitudes between two thousand five hundred and four thousand five hundred metres. The flowers are white on the upper side of the petal and pink to red below. Propagation is easy by seed or cutting; cultivation requirements for group B.

Subsection Sublanatae

Androsace nortonii Ludlow
Nepal, southern Tibet and Bhutan are the homes of these small pillow-forming plants. Pink flowers with dark centres and yellow eye. Propagation is best by cuttings; cultivation requirements for group B.

Subsection Douglasia

Androsace Montana Gray Wendelbo
Coming from North America, this species prefers drier conditions on stony slopes. Its leaves are grey-green with a red hue on older plants that form pillows or small carpets, the flowers are of a glowing pink or mauve. This species crosses easily with A. nivalis and A. laevigata and its hybrids are propagated by cuttings; cultivation requirements for group B.

Androsace nivalis Lindl Wendelbo
This is another American species that grows in altitudes of up to three thousand six hundred metres on acidic gravels. It forms loose carpets and its older parts have a reddish tinge, the flowers are pink-purple to a brownish red and are very beautiful. Unfortunately, it usually is somewhat short-lived; cultivation requirements of group B.

Section Pseudoprimula

Androsace croftii Watt
This Androsace lives in eastern Nepal and the Sikkim province on altitudes of around four thousand metres. The flowers are a warm, dark brown-red and it prefers sandy gravels and rocks, in cultivation use loam or humus only very sparingly, this species tolerates to be grown on the shady side of a rockery or alpinum; cultivation requirements of group B.

Anemone; Ranunculaceae
There are some one hundred species in this genus of which most are from the cool-temperate or cold zones of the northern hemisphere. These perennials often feature a strong, sometimes bulbous root system and many can be propagated by root cuttings during dormancy.

Due to the variations in their requirements I have divided the species listing according to their use in the landscape, so that the landscape architect can choose according to the intended design.

Species of the habitat forest
The species that are at home in the forests and woodlands are mostly from the section Anemonanthea. All these are active very early in the season, often flower before the leaves appear in a deciduous forest and withdraw into dormancy after flowering. They may be useful to 'mark' other forest/woodland dwelling perennials that come up later as they complement each other well. Important in cultivation is that the leaf litter of trees is not cleared away from the forest floor/parkland as these plants need this medium to live.

Subsection Sylvia

Anemone altaica Fisch ex C.A. Mey
From the northern European Russia comes this delicate beauty with light blue or purple markings on its white petals. The flowers appear before the leave in early spring and seeing a carpet of those perennials when walking through the forests is unforgettable.

Anemone nemorosa L
The small white Bush Wind-Rose (common name translated from German) often is the first sign of spring in the forests and like the above A. altaica is a beautiful sight when walking the forests. There are numerous varieties and selections, but all are best used in natural designs of large parks or English landscape gardens. Propagation is by seed or division.

Subsection Tuberosa

Anemone apennina L
This species is at home in southern Europe, from the Pyrenees over Italy and into Bulgaria. It is a very valuable wild species for natural designs.

Subsection Stolonifera

Anemone baicalensis Turcz
Eastern Siberia, China and Korea are the home to this strong grower; it flowers a bit later than the above described species and requires more moisture. The use in the landscape is like the above with the addition . that does well in more open situation like around open shrubs.

Species of the forest and woodland margins

All species of this group belong botanically into the subsection Brevistylae of the section Anemonanthea, derived from the Latin description of eriocephalus, which means 'Woolly-headed'. If you have a look at their fruit and seed heads, it becomes clear why. For this book, I wanted to reduce botany to a very minimum, but because this is a funny one I thought I'd mention it.

Some require a moist and well-structured soil with good buffering capacity. Important to mention that transplanting and division should only be done in spring when they become active, that is different to many Anemone from other sections. There are exceptions to the rule, of course; examples are Anemone rupicola and Anemone sylvestris, which prefer alkaline soils that can be sandy or gravelly and are drier in summer. Both are strong growers and consequently need strong partners, they would overgrow small delicate species. One of my childhood memories are extensive Anemone sylvestris carpets in the Beech (Fagus sylvatica) forests on the limestone expanses of the Swabian Alb (Schwäbische Alb) where I would walk by myself for hours and get lost in dreams.

Anemone hupehensis Lem
There is often confusion in the correct terminology. In the common trade, this wild species from western China is very often incorrectly called *Anemone japonica*, but like the famous *Geranium – Pelargonium* the incorrect name is more widespread and better known. I guess if the plants are used in the right place and bring joy in the private or professional landscape it does not matter all that much. Now, the right places and cultivation are in grasslands associated with shrubs or the warmer, sunnier side of trees. They are strong growers and tend to overwhelm smaller, slower perennials. I would use them in wild and natural settings rather than the formal perennial border; they do offer themselves to the cottage garden too. There are several

hybrids available like 'Bowles Pink', 'Splendens', September Charm' (bred by Georg Arends in 1935 and the September refers obviously to the season of the northern hemisphere) and others.

Anemone hupehensis var japonica Thunb

This is an old cultivar from southern China that was introduced to Japan later, so the name is somewhat misleading. 'Japanese Windflower' may be the most commonly used name; it is a graceful, long-lived and strong perennial, flowering from early into late autumn. Propagation is commercially done by root cuttings in winter when the plants are dormant; this also suits the labour availability in colder climate nurseries. There are numerous cultivars ranging in colour from white to pink and red and with single and double flowers.

49 – Anemone hupehensis var japonica
Work in Canberra, Australia 2014

Anemone x hybrid Paxt

This term describes many hybrids that were created by George Gordon between 1845 and 1848 in Chiswick, England and promoted in Kew gardens. These are mostly crosses between Anemone hupehensis var japonica and Anemone vitifolia and vary greatly in their appearance, but are all very garden-worthy.

Anemone sylvestris L

This important species extends from Europe into Siberia, the Alps and the Balkans, the Caucasus, where it lives in the habitats of shrublands, in conifer forests. It grows along roads and paths, on slopes or in meadows, mostly on alkaline soils. It is a very variable and adaptable species that I would 'sprinkle' around in a wild, natural design and then just let it live its own life. It will characterise the planting when in flower and just blend in when not in season. There are also several horticultural selections and cultivars available.

Anemone tomentosa Maxim

Coming from China, this species has velvety leaves and stems as the Latin name describes. One of the most beautiful cultivars is Anemone tomentosa 'Superba' bred by Karl Foerster in Germany; it flowers profusely and is a wonderful sight in early or late light in autumn.

Species of the Rockery

This is a group of more specialised Anemone, more for the rockery, the alpinum and the collector, as most are delicate and need to be protected from strong neighbours.

Section Anemone; Subsection Longistylae

Anemone baldensis L
The Alps, Croatia, the Iberian Peninsula and Tirol are home to the 'Tyrolean wind flower', a small species that inhabits rocky and gravelly poor soils and meadows in the alpine zones. It prefers alkaline ground and flowers in summer.

Section Anemone; Subsection Brevistylae

Anemone caroliniana Walter
This species originates in Wisconsin to Illinois, southern Dakota and down to Florida and Texas (not in Carolina). It grows to twenty-five centimetres and has an interesting colour variation from white to pink and red and sometimes sapphire blue!

Anemonopsis; Ranunculaceae

There is only one genus from the Japanese mountain forests.

Anemonopsis macrophylla Sieb et Zucc
This delicate and beautiful elf-like perennial grows up to eighty centimetres high. It is best used in moist, semi-shaded forests where the visitor can admire it in a corner or along the forest path. The leaf litter should be left for the plant to grow into.

Angelica; Apiaceae

There are around fifty species. Some are biennial, most are perennial, the common name translated from German means, 'Angel's Herb'. Some are used in herbal medicine. Propagation is by seed.

Angelica archangelica L
This species is the actual 'Angel's Herb' (Engelswurz, also referring to the German term of Erz-Engel). It grows in moist meadows, along rivers and creeks. This species is biennial and grows to a handsome two hundred and fifty centimetres. The leaves are fragrant and it features greenish flowers at the height of summer. The variety A. archangelica var. sativa is used to make herbal liquor from its roots.

50 – Angelica archangelica
Courtesy Angelika Kaufmann

Angelica sylvestris L

As the Latin name tells us, this herb lives in the forests and woodlands where enough water is available. It extends from Europe into the Caucasus and Siberia and is an old medicinal herb, known at least since the Middle Ages.

Anigozanthos; Haemodoraceae

The 'Kangaroo Paws' are a small genus of Western Australian perennials. All of them are fantastic and interesting perennials for their unique woolly flowers over a huge range of colours and their strap-like or terete foliage. Their use in the landscape is in the natural design, prairies, meadows, in association with shrubs and they make great rockery plants. Propagation is best by division or tissue culture.

Anigozanthos flavidus

This is a large species growing to two hundred centimetres tall with strap-like foliage to a metre long and variable flowers. Unlike most Anigozanthos, this one tolerates wet conditions and average soils. They are bird-pollinated and attract honey-eaters like the Eastern Spinebill. Their foliage is an attractive structural feature in natural and informal perennial borders and near water features but sometimes suffers from fungus.

51 – Anigozanthos flavidus x 'Sunset'
Author's home garden in Queanbeyan, Australia - I often had trouble with snails who appear to just love them

Anigozanthos humilis
A small special Kangaroo Paw with its foliage short and sickle-shaped to twenty centimetres and the orange to red and brown flowers stand to thirty centimetres. This species prefers alkaline and well-drained, poor, sandy or gravelly soils.

Anigozanthos manglesii
The 'Red and Green Kangaroo Paw' is the floral emblem of Western Australia and grows to forty centimetres high with grey-green strap-like leaves. The red-stemmed flower spikes stand up to a metre above the foliage with a brilliant display of forest green with a red base. The plant is often short-lived; more

longevity can be achieved by drier, sandier soils and a higher K-ratio in the fertiliser. Fungal infections with ink disease (Dreschleria irisid) and snails can be a problem.

Anigozanthos preissii
This small species with around twenty-five-centimetre-long semi-terete leaves and often poor root system has some of the largest beautiful orange flowers in the genus standing more than half a metre above the leaves. Cultivation can be challenging, I would use it in sandy or gravelly poor soils in rockeries in full sun or dappled shade, again a higher K-ratio in the fertiliser assists and the species is well worth the effort!

Anthotium; Goodeniaceae

Anthotium rubriflorum
This small but outstanding perennial grows to around ten centimetres high with its rosette of lanceolate to spathulate leaves. The head of brilliant red flowers is held fifteen to twenty centimetres above and appears in spring. It requires full sun, poor soils and excellent drainage. Propagation is by seed or leaf cuttings.

Antennaria; Asteraceae

Around fifty species of Antennaria occupy the temperate and cool-temperate zones of the northern hemisphere; some exceptions are in South America. Most species form beautiful flowering carpets and require full sun and have adapted to poor soils. They are well suited to rockeries, container plantings or green roofs. Good partners are small Achillea, Helianthemum, Marrubium, Paronychia, Onosma and small Artemisia. They are also good with Erica and Calluna as well as Thymus, small Dianthus and dry grasses like Festuca in heath-like designs. Propagation is by division or seed. The German common name means 'Little Kitten Paws'.

Antennaria carpatica (Wahlenb) Bluff et Fingerh
This species originates in the Pyrenees, Alps and is at home in the Carpathian ranges. It grows to around twenty centimetres with hairy leaves and flowers brown to red from late spring to early autumn. It is important to provide free-draining, gravelly mineral soils.

Antennaria dioica (L) Gaertn
This species extends from the cool-temperate northern zones into sub-arctic areas on poor soils in meadows, pastures, heathlands and sand dunes and on loamy, drier soils. Around twenty centimetres high with woolly white, yellow to red flower heads in early summer it also features woolly grey foliage that is tough and can structure smaller planting designs in rockeries as an example. There are some garden cultivars available like the red 'Grillfeuer' (fire on the BBQ) or the white 'Perlkissen' (pearl pillow) or the pink 'Nyewood's Variety'.

Anthemis; Asteraceae syn Cota

This genus of Asteraceae comprises around a hundred species in Europe, western Asia, northern Africa and around the Mediterranean. Most representatives have a distinct aromatic fragrance. The smaller species are valuable for the rockery, the alpinum or tubs in full sun and gravelly soils. The taller ones are useful in perennial borders, the cottage garden and may be used as cut flowers. Propagation is by seed and division; the taller species are best done by soft tip cuttings early in the growing season.

Anthemis carpatica Walst et Kit ex Willd

The Pyrenees, eastern Alps and Carpathian to Balkan ranges are home to this around twenty-five centimetres high Anthemis that grows in altitudes between one thousand eight hundred to two thousand three hundred metres. It flowers yellow with a white centre in early summer and requires poor, gravelly or sandy soils. There is a recommended selection in the trade called 'Karpatenschnee' (Carpathian Snow).

Anthemis tinctoria L

The German common name 'Färberkamille' (Dyers Chamomile) refers to the old use of the flowers to dye wool yellow. It occurs throughout Europe and western Asia and has been introduced into North America. The species prefers dry meadows, slopes and the presence of rocks or gravel with soils poor and well-drained. The plant grows to around sixty centimetres and flowers from summer to autumn. There are several horticultural selections, hybrids and cultivars available ranging from white to many different shades of yellow.

52 – Anthemis tinctoria syn Cota tinctoria
Courtesy of Wikimedia

Anthericum; Anthericaceae

There are around sixty-five species in this genus, often called 'Grass Lilies'. Many of them come from warmer regions of Africa, Mexico and South America; there are three species in Europe. They are best used in natural, wild steppe or dry meadow designs. Propagation is by division in spring or seed which requires cold-moist stratification.

Anthericum lilago L

This species originates in southern Europe but extends into North Africa and Asia Minor. It inhabits dry meadows and open Oak and Pine forests with slightly acidic poor soils, where it can form lovely scenes in late spring and early summer.

53 – Anthericum lilago
Travel study in Switzerland 1986

Anthericum ramosum L

Southern and middle Europe and the Caucasus are home to this Grass Lily. The deep-rooted plant has quite similar preferences to Anthericum lilago, but also descends into valleys and dos not mind loamy soils. It flowers somewhat later in summer. On good locations, it often self-sows, creating lovely scenes.

Anthirrhinum; Scrophulariaceae

The 'Lion's Mouth' is represented with around forty species, mostly around the Mediterranean. Some occur in North America on the Pacific side. There are annual, perennial and shrubby species; many people usually know it from the popular annual displays. Whilst most hybrids used in the annual displays often suffer from rust, especially if the plants are kept for more than one season, the wild species if planted correctly do not experience this problem. Most Anthirrhinum prefer dry locations Propagation is by seed or soft-tip cuttings, some shrubby species propagate well from semi-hardwood cuttings in late summer once growth matures.

Anthirrhinum hispanicum ssp hispanicum Chav

As the common name gives away, this species is at home in the Iberian Peninsula on sunny, rocky hillsides. Knowing this one would use this subtle beauty in dry stone walls or in the alpinum; it grows to fifteen centimetres and flowers creamy-white to yellow.

Anthirrhinum molle L

The central and eastern Pyrenees with their limestone soils are habitat for this around twenty-five centimetres high sub-shrub with hairy leaves. It flowers white to mild pink from summer to autumn and is also a great to use in the rockery or dry-stone walls.

Apocynum; Apogynaceae

A relative of the well-known Nerium oleander, this genus comprises around a hundred species in temperate Asia and northern America. It is a poisonous genus with some species are today used in herbal medicine, usually in homoeopathy. The plants have also been used for their fibre. Most plants are strong growers and may become too invasive; this needs to be kept in mind.

Apocynum androsaemifolium L
North America; this is a strongly spreading 'Dog's Bane' (German; Hundsgiftgewächs). Use best in natural, wild designs. Due to its hardiness, it works out well along pathways.

Aponogeton; Aponogetonaceae

This genus contains around twenty-five species from Africa, Madagascar, southern Asia and northern Australia. One of the common names is 'Water-Wheat' and logically refers to its habitat of living and swimming in the water. The flower colours vary from white, yellow or purple.

Aponogeton distachyos L
This mainly African species also occurs in the North of Australia and in South America where it has been introduced. Like so many water species, once introduced it propagates itself wildly due to a very competitive nature and consequently needs to be used very carefully. It is a beautiful water plant for sunny, shallow ponds up to fifty centimetres depth and flowers white.

Aquilegia; Ranunculaceae

A genus that is very popular and well-known in the Anglo-Saxon and German garden history, where it is known with the common names of Columbine or Akelei. There are a hundred and twenty species with small to large representatives; an interesting aspect is that some of the red flowering species in America are pollinated by the Colibri birds. The use in the landscape is varied; the taller species usually prefer moist places in the dappled shade of shrubs or trees, whereas the yellow American species prefer it drier and more exposed to the sun. The smaller, more delicate Aquilegias are best used in the cooler rockeries in shadier locations. The tall species are moderately suited as cut flowers.

54 – Aquilegia vulgaris x hybrids
Work in Canberra, Australia 2014

Aquilegia alpina L

As the name suggests, this species is at home in the Alps where it populates meadows or lives among shrubs and trees at altitudes of one thousand six hundred to two thousand metres. This Aquilegia prefers cool locations with not too much sun and requires acidic soils. The flowers appear in spring and have a subdued blue to purple colour; it grows to eighty centimetres tall.

Aquilegia aurea Janka

This medium, up to forty-centimetre-tall yellow species is slow-growing and naturally occurs in Bulgaria and Macedonia. I would use it in natural, wild sceneries where it is just left to its own devices and over time creates its own niche.

Aquilegia canadensis l

The red Columbine from Canada and eastern and middle America grows to around forty centimetres and lives naturally in forests or the shade of big rocks. The species varies greatly and it can provide pleasant surprises if it is just let go and self-sows or hybridises with others.

Aquilegia coerulea James

As the knowledgeable reader suspects, this is also known as Aquilegia caerulea and in my opinion the discussion is too academic to warrant further comment here. The 'Blue Columbine' originates in the USA where it inhabits moist to fresh soils in dappled shade, almost always in close association with forests or woodlands. It is a very beautiful Ranunculaceae propagated by seed. Again, I would use it in natural or wild designs or the cottage garden where, once planted, the plants are just let go.

Aquilegia flabellata Sieb et Zucc

An important cultivated from, also known as Aquilegia akitensis. There are variable forms in the trade which includes distinctly two-coloured variations and white and white double forms (Aquilegia flabellata 'Nana Alba Plena').

Aquilegia longissima Gray ex Watson

The 'Longspur Columbine' of the USA and Arizona grows to over one metre high and flowers bright to golden yellow, a very interesting addition to meadows.

Aquilegia scopulorum Tidestr

Also called the 'Utah Columbine', this up to thirty-centimetre-high species has nice blue-green foliage that is quite dense compared to most other Aquilegias. The flowers are large, lavender to purple and the petals are white to yellow; they are very variable. The species is very attractive and desired for gravel beds and the alpinum with a close relative, A. scopulorum var. perplexans from Nevada that features red, blue, white or two-coloured plants that give a very happy display in larger numbers.

Aquilegia viridiflora Pall

A very interesting species from western China, this Aquilegia grows to around half a metre and has lovely, nodding yellow-brown or reddish-brown flowers. It prefers semi-shade and moisture in the soils, but not too heavy soils like clay, there should be good drainage and permeability.

Aquilegia vulgaris L

That is the 'common' Columbine or Akelei from Europe extending into the Ukraine. Its natural habitats are open, light-filled forests or woodlands, meadows or in association with shrubs. It does not mind a bit of calcium in the soil, which should never completely dry out. In garden cultivation with a loving hand, it can grow to a hundred and fifty centimetres high and flowers mostly purple or blue, but also pink or white is not uncommon. In our front yard in Queanbeyan, a pink form has established itself without any guiding hand after the original planting and keeps popping up within the grasses. There are numerous cultivars and selections in the trade.

Arabis; Brassicaceae

This humble genus features around a hundred and twenty species, with most of them coming from the mountains of northern and middle Europe, the Mediterranean, Africa, Asia and America, quite a widespread genus really. Use in the landscape is accordingly rockeries, dry stone walls or in combination with pathways and paving.

Arabis caucasica Schldl

This around twenty-centimetre small Arabis comes from the Canary Islands and Madeira, the Mediterranean and extends into the Caucasus. The plant forms nice carpets with grey felt-like leaves and flowers white in early spring. It is very popular in garden cultivation due to its pretty, solid carpets of foliage that combines with almost anything, but does best in rockeries, or in association with rocks, but also along paths, paving and borders. A nice touch is early wild tulips or similar bulbous plants growing through the foliage and it combines also very well with Alyssum and Aubrieta.

Aralia; Araliaceae

This genus comprises around forty perennials, shrubs or small trees with mostly large, almost maple-like ornamental serrated foliage. Most require large spaces to fully develop and are recommended as foliage feature plants for larger gardens or landscapes, where they work well in association with woody ornamentals. They do require shade and are sensitive to strong winds.

Aralia californica Watson

This species grows to around three metres and naturally comes from the western USA where it grows along creeks, rivers or in moist forests. The leaves are up to thirty centimetres long and the plant features numerous showy white flowers in summer.

Aralia cordata Thunb

Japan, the Sakhalin, Manchuria, Korea and China are the home of this around a metre and a half high perennial. It prefers moist zones in woodlands along creeks or rivers. The young shoots (Udo) are used as vegetable or salad in Japan.

Arctostaphylos; Ericaceae

In North and Middle America, we can find around seventy species of Arctostaphylos. They are ground-hugging plants with dark-green foliage with short flowers and prominent decorative berries that are useful as ground cover. The German common name translates into something like 'Bear's Grapes'.

Arctostaphylos alpina Spreng

All around the northern hemisphere we can find the alpine 'Bear's Grapes' in higher altitudes of fifteen hundred metres and above. The species requires acidic good soils, offering themselves as good partners to Rhododendron and Erica. I have used them in low heath land plantings together with small conifers in alpine rockeries. This plant features a wonderful red autumn foliage.

Arctostaphylos uva-ursi Spreng

A former medicinal plant that was exported from Germany in the last centuries. Europe and America are the home to this plant which grows as a flat ground cover with its shoots becoming woody. They are great for poor gravelly soils and tolerate almost any PH. They disappear when being shaded over. The use in the landscape is like the above A. alpina in heathland designs with dwarf conifers, Erica and Genista. Propagation is by cuttings taken in autumn. I use longer, already branched shoots of the current growing season for best results.

Arenaria; Caryophyllaceae

Spread all around the world except for Australia are approximately one hundred and sixty species of Arenaria; one of the common names is 'Sand-Herb'. They are perennials or small sub-shrubs that require full sun and good drainage and are easy, except for species from very high altitudes of the Himalayas, Alaska and Japan. They are best used in container plantings, dry stone walls or small rockeries and the alpinum. Propagation is by seed or division, best in late summer.

Arenaria armerina Bory

Coming from southern Spain, this mat-forming up to ten centimetres high species holds its white flowers in terminal heads in early summer. It prefers alkaline, well-drained soils and full sun; it is easy to combine it with other rockery species.

Arenaria grandiflora L

This species naturally occurs from central Europe through to the higher African mountain ranges. It features very large white flowers in summer and forms dense ornamental mats, like mini-turf areas.

Arenaria montana L

South-western Europe is the home of this small pillowy species that prefers limestone soils and has, for its size, large, white flowers.

55 – Arenaria montana
Courtesy Klaus Mödinger

Arenaria procera Spreng

A grassy-leafed, up to twenty-five-centimetre-high plant that originates around the Mediterranean and Eastern Europe. It flowers in summer and prefers dry and sunny locations with sandy soils.

Arenaria tetraquetra L

A very small (rarely over five centimetres high) species, that hails from the Pyrenees. It is a lovely plant used in the right places; for example one can create gorgeous miniature landscapes (Penjing) with it.

Argemone; Papaveraceae

This interesting genus is represented with twenty-eight species in America, the West Indies and Hawaii. The main habitat is semi-arid zones of the annual or perennial plants. There is one shrub, *Argemone fruticosa*, that is rarely cultivated. As the habitat suggests to the knowledgeable horticulturist, these plants are best used in dry, sunny natural or wild designs, steppes or rocky slopes. Annual species may last several years if the spent flower is cut off down to ground level and is not allowed to go to seed. The plant usually produces a new basal set of leaves. Alternatively, of course they can self-sow in good locations. It goes almost without saying that this type of scene should not be fertilised with high N. Propagation is by seed; early pricking off into long tubes is recommended because of the development of a taproot. Some of the perennial species can be propagated by root cuttings during their dormancy, observe polarity.

Argemone mexicana L

The species is at home in Central America and extends into Guatemala, Nicaragua and Texas. It is a pioneer plant, often occupying disturbed land and ascends to around one thousand six hundred metres altitude. It is an annual with bright yellow flowers and prickly, very ornamental leaves. In keeping with its nature, I have used this plant often in large natural semi-desert like steppes where its tendency to self-sow is welcome. It does disappear by itself once other, longer lived species establish themselves in the design, good to use in xerophytic plant communities.

56 – Argemone mexicana
Courtesy Wilfried Büchli

Argemone munita E. M. Durand et Hilagard

California, Nevada, Arizona and Utah are the natural habitat for this grey-leaved species with large, showy flowers. It requires sandy or gravelly poor soils and grows into altitudes of up to two thousand six hundred metres. Good partners are other grey-leaved plants, silvery or hairy foliage textures and plants of similar habitats.

Arisaema; Araceae

This genus contains around a hundred and fifty species, mainly from Asia and North America. Cultivation requires organic, loamy soils in semi-shade or shade, most of these plants are forest-dwellers.

They should be planted near the paths to be able to adore their subtle and unusual beauty. Propagation is by seed, best when fresh.

Arisaema amurense Maxim
From Russia to Japan this species lives in forests and grows to around fifty centimetres high. It flowers are mostly brown with white stripes in early summer, it is easy to cultivate and should be left just to roam freely around the trees; it then creates all by itself wonderful little magic scenes.

Arisaema sikokianum Franch et Sav
This striking species originates in China and Japan and when in flower in early summer, looks almost like it comes from a different planet. Propagation is slow and usually difficult; artificial pollination is recommended.

Aristolochia; Aristolochiaceae

This genus 'listens' to the common name of 'Dutchman's Pipe'. It does not however grow naturally in Holland but is at home in the temperate and tropical zones and comprises around three hundred species. There are climbing plants, shrubs or perennials with mostly large, heart-shaped leaves. Propagation is by seed or division.

Aristolochia clematitis Osterluzei
This Mediterranean species is an old medicinal plant and was as such cultivated in Italy, France and Spain. It naturally grows on sunny slopes with gravelly or sandy, well-drained soils – its large leaves appear to contradict somewhat the natural habitat. It grows to around a metre and establishes itself in vineyards and dry-stone walls, along hedges, or fences. As use in the landscape I would recommend natural, wild designs where it may be used as foliage contrast. Good partners are Dictamnus, Asphodeline, Scrophularia sambucifolia and Campanula trachelium. It is a slow starter, but after two or three years it becomes very strong and can hold its own.

Aristolochia rotunda L
Italy, Spain, Portugal and Greece as well as Turkey are home to this a bit smaller species. It lives in drier meadows, along hedges and scattered on grassy slopes. The leaves are smaller and look a little like oysters growing along the stems. The flowers are up to four centimetres long, axillary and are yellowish to red.

Armeria; Plumbaginaceae

There are around thirty species of 'Grass Carnations' in Europe, Asia, northern Africa and America. Most are coastal plants that form dense, pretty pillows that sometimes become woody at the base. The flowers are held in little balls above the foliage and vary from white, pink to red. Use in the landscape in the alpinum, rockeries, the heath gardens, drystone walls and as ornamental border along paths. They are easy to grow but should not be over-fertilised as this shortens the lifespan and makes the dense pillows fall apart. Propagation is best by small divisions requiring a little practice, but the pure species are also possible by seed.

Armeria alliacea Cav Hoffmgg et Link
This tall, up to fifty centimetres high species originates extends from Portugal to south-western Germany, northern Italy and north-west Africa. It prefers dry and sandy soils and flowers in summer with white or pink flower heads. There are some garden selections available; 'Formosa' hybrids with pink to white; 'Grandiflora' with pink and 'Leucantha' with white showy flowers.

Armeria caespitosa Boiss
Coming from central Spain and growing on poor soils, this small (five centimetres) plant is very attractive with shades of pink or white. It is best used in rockeries, dry stone arrangements or stone tubs.

Armeria maritima Willd
This may be, in horticulture, the most important and widely used species, with numerous hybrids and selections available. It naturally occurs all around the northern hemisphere, Europe, Asia America and into northern Africa. It is mainly a coastal species and occupies salt marshes and roadsides. The plant is up to twenty-five centimetres tall with solid, grass-like, slightly fleshy leaves and flowers pink in early summer. If the spent flowers are removed promptly, a second flush of flowers usually results. It can be widely used, but should not be overshaded by tall neighbours; rockeries, dry stone walls, along pathways or in mixed perennial plantings with partners such as Antennaria dioica, Campanula portenschlagiana, Campanula poscharskyana, Carex Montana, Dianthus gratianopolitanus, Thymus serpyllus, Veronica incana and species from a similar background.

Armeria maritima
Work in Canberra, Australia 2011

Arnica; Asteraceae

There are thirty-two species of Arnica in the northern and temperate zones.

Arnica montana L
Europe, Scandinavia, Poland and Russia are home to this well-known species that prefers altitudes from a thousand to around two thousand eight hundred metres in height. It lives in poor meadows and heathlands and is quite adaptable but does not like alkaline soils. It is also sensitive to fertiliser, so use it in plant communities adapted to these poor soil conditions. The flowers are of a deep buttery yellow in spring and early summer and the entire plant is quite aromatic. It is an important medicinal plant and still in use. Propagation is by seed and fresh is best.

58 – Arnica montana
Courtesy Anton Büchli

Artemisia; Asteraceae

The drier areas of the northern temperate zones are the natural habitat of Artemisia or 'Wormwoods'. There are perennials and sub-shrubs of this important genus that is used for medicinal as well as ornamental purposes. Most have finely divided silvery, grey or white foliage and are grown for this reason; the flowers are mostly insignificant. Most species are also highly aromatic; not always pleasant, some are distinctly bitter. Depending on classification botanists count between two to four hundred species in this genus. Most are at home in dry to very dry places, meadows, steppes and semi-deserts. According to the use in the landscape I have divided the genus into three main groups: the larger shrubby types; the medium-sized sub-shrubs and the herbaceous perennial species types. Many are important as medicinal plants.

The Shrubby and Larger Artemisia:

Artemisia abrotanum L

Coming originally from Spain, this species is widely used around Europe with silvery, dense foliage on numerous stems; it forms a dense structural plant. It grows to a hundred and twenty centimetres high. It is recommended to prune it back in spring and stay in the soft parts of the plant for best looks. The entire plant is highly aromatic.

59 – Artemisia abrotanum used in a silver themed perennial border together with Santolina chamaecyparissus, Asphodeline lutea, Lychnis calcedonica

The silvery foliage as the theme accentuates the colour of the flowers and is effective throughout all seasons
Work in Canberra, Australia 2014

Artemisia absinthium L

The famous (or notorious) 'Absinth' extends from Europe to Siberia. It prefers alkaline soils in areas with low rainfall, indeed it resents high humidity. The plants grow either as a low, around thirty-centimetre-high ground cover or as shrubs up to a hundred and twenty centimetres high. It was and still is used for medicinal purposes or to produce the liquor of Absinth, hence the species' name. One of the historic uses (or abuses) was during the times of the Parisienne art scene in the early twentieth century with Pablo Picasso, Toulouse-Lautrec and other artists of the expressionist/modern era, when the artists supposedly used the liquor for inspirational purposes.

Artemisia arborescens L

The 'Silver-Wormwood' is a, at the base, woody species and grows to around a metre. This species has the silveriest foliage of all Artemisia and is for that reason popular in ornamental horticulture; however, in colder areas it suffers from frost. Like most Artemisia it resents high humidity and it should not be watered overhead or fertilised with high N.

Artemisia procera Willd

This shrub from Europe, the Caucasus and Siberia starts off stiff upright, but at maturity becomes wide and broad. It is large, up to two hundred and fifty centimetres tall. The foliage is more grey-green and strongly aromatic. Its size suggests using it in the background of perennial borders to provide structure.

The Sub-Shrubs and Medium-Sized Artemisia:

Artemisia armeniaca Lam
At home in Armenia this blue-silvery plant has a unique appearance and is an interesting foliage contrast in the perennial border. It grows to around a hundred centimetres.

Artemisia genipi Weber
The Alps are the original habitat of this Artemisia that features grey-silvery, sometimes almost purplish foliage. For this reason, it is also called the 'Black Artemisia' (Schwarze Edelraute' in German). It resents alkaline soils and occupies altitudes between two thousand four hundred and three thousand one hundred metres. The recommended use in the landscape is in the rockery or alpinum.

Artemisia schmidtiana Maxim
Also called 'Angel's Hair' (Engelhaar, translated from German), this very beautiful species has silvery-white, attractive foliage and forms dense, but strong-growing pillows. One of my favourite uses is as a border and to let it hang over a stone wall where it defines the border but at the same time softens up harsh architectural edges. Recommended partners are Campanula portenschlagiana, Geranium sanguineum, Geranium subcaulescens and Helianthemum. The Clone 'Nana' is very widespread in cultivation and sometimes mixed up with the actual species. Both require poor, sandy soil in dry and very sunny environments, I know one specimen that is more than a hundred years old in southern Germany.

Artemisia splendens Willd
Armenia, Iran and the Caucasus are home to this species. Its variety brachyphylla is usually the one in cultivation and more widely known in horticulture. It is very beautiful, but sensitive to too much water, in winter. As the above, use in rockeries with poor gravelly or sandy soils and it will be a feature plant with its silvery-white foliage.

Artemisia stelleriana Besser
This species comes from Korea, Japan and Kamchatka, it has 'escaped' into northern Europe and North America. It naturally grows in sand dunes along the coast and other dry sandy environments. It should be used accordingly and rewards the grower with strikingly white, felt-like foliage on woody stems up to sixty centimetres tall. Propagation is by cuttings (not in the mist propagator!) and divisions of rooted side-shoots.

Artemisia vallesiaca All
At home in Switzerland, France and northern Italy, this species requires alkaline soils and dry, well-drained conditions in full sun. It has a rich aroma and grows to around forty centimetres high. It is one of the most beautiful silvery-grey Artemisias.

The Perennial Artemisias:

Artemisa dracunculus L
The up to a hundred and twenty-centimetre-high aromatic perennial is used as a spice and occurs naturally in Eastern Europe, Russia and northern America. The most used and possibly best 'Estragon' in the kitchen is the 'German Estragon' also called 'Thüringischer Estragon' which has the finest flavour, mildly peppery and bitter-sweet. This species is also the toughest and easy to cultivate for the kitchen or to use in ornamental borders.

Artemisia glacialis L

Not so much in glaciers as the species name suggests but in rocky environments between two and three thousand metre altitude grows this special Artemisia. It features grey-white silky and hairy leaves and forms small pillows in gravels. Cultivation is recommended for the experienced grower, as it is not easy, the water requirements are like an alpine cactus and this knowledge is a key to success.

Artemisia lactiflora Wall ex DC

The upright, up to a hundred and fifty-centimetre-tall perennial has large leaves and is probably the only one which flowers in autumn. It is a significant feature in the perennial border. It comes from China. This is also a species that requires more moisture or resents hot sun if there is not enough water available in the soil. It is especially beautiful together with blue autumn Asters. There are several selections to be recommended; 'Elfenbeinturm' (Ivory Tower), 'Guizhou' and 'Rosaschleier'.

Artemisia ludoviciana Nutt

This species comes from North America where it lives in the prairies on sandy and dry soils. It is considered a holy, sacred plant by the Cheyenne. The plant grows to a hundred and twenty centimetres high, is aromatic and the foliage is very decorative.

Artemisia pontica L

The 'Roman' Artemisia naturally grows in dry meadows, on slopes, vineyards and rocky places that are warm and dry. Mildly aromatic, it can get to eighty centimetres and may be used to cover larger areas in natural perennial designs.

Artemisia vulgaris L

This is the common 'Beifuss' or 'Wermut' that often grows along pathways or roadsides. It is a medicinal plant and used to assist with digestion of heavy meals or to cure general digestive difficulties.

Arum; Araceae

This genus is represented by twenty-five species, all of which form tubers that spread like rhizomes. They grow in areas with sufficient moisture in winter and spring and they endure dry summers well. Use in the landscape in the semi-shade of shrubs and trees. Propagation is easy by division. In the right place, Arums can become very competitive and consequently should be used with strong partners in more natural and wild designs.

Arum alpinum Schott et Kotschy

Throughout the elevated, between four hundred and fifty and seventeen hundred metres high altitudes of Europe grow this medium green Arum that flowers profusely with a yellow to orange inflorescence. The orange to red fruits are showy and numerous.

Arum italicum Miller

This species features narrow or broad, arrow-like dark-green leaves. The inflorescence produces orange to red berries that stand out in the shade of shrubs and trees.

Aruncus; Rosaceae

This is a small genus with four species that inhabit the northern temperate zones. They are forest-dwellers and prefer shade and semi-shade with ample soil moisture and higher air humidity. They are however more tolerant of dry conditions than the Astilbe which resemble them in appearance.

Aruncus dioicus Walter Fernald

This species naturally grows in forested valleys in shady places, often along creeks. The perennial grows to two metres tall and lives very long. It is an excellent tall background plant for natural areas, or in association with water features. The German common name translates into 'Goat's Beard'.

60 – Aruncus dioicus
Courtesy Anton Büchli

Arundo; Poaceae

There are three species of Arundo in the Mediterranean and extending into Asia. They are tall, up to six metres, ornamental grasses that need considerable placement as they can become very strong and overgrow other areas, especially where a lot of moisture is prevalent.

Arundo donax

Often used for erosion control, this strong plant is widely spread around the warmer areas of Europe. Good to plant also as background in natural areas and along strong-flowing watercourses.

Asclepias; Asclepiadaceae

The common name for this genus is 'Silk-Plant' and it refers to the beautiful soft hairs on the fruit, once you touch those the name will be remembered. There are around a hundred species, mostly in America; some are in southern Africa. There are shrubs, sub-shrubs, herbaceous perennials and annuals in this genus. The stems contain a mildly poisonous milky sap (a little like Euphorbia). Propagation is by seed or division. Most species come from dry backgrounds, steppes, semi-deserts and prairies and should be used accordingly for best results. The silky white hairs attached to the seed remain on the plant for a long time and are of subtle beauty. For this reason, I have used them in rockeries near the pathways, to be admired.

Asclepias cordifolia Jeps

This species is at home in western North America and grows naturally on dry slopes, between open shrubs or woodlands. It is up to eighty centimetres tall and the pink flowers possess a mild perfume, it flowers in summer. The plant requires dry, well-drained soils in cultivation and is very beautiful used together with grasses, perennials or sub-shrubs from similar environments like Stipa, Helianthemum, Acantholimon and Romneya.

Asclepias exaltata Mühlenb

This large, up to a hundred and eighty-centimetre-tall perennial occurs naturally in the USA where it grows in shrublands and open woodlands. The flowers are a special mauve with creamy heads and it is a very showy species that needs to be used only in larger designs.

Asclepias speciosa Torr

The 'Showy Milkweed' comes from western North America, California, and extends into Texas. This species now requires moisture and grows in its natural habitat along creeks and rivers. It grows to around a metre and the entire plant is covered by felt-like hairs and the flowers are reddish in summer.

Asclepias tuberosa L

This American species grows in dry meadows, grassy places and slopes where it flowers orange in summer. Important for cultivation is drainage and slightly acidic soil conditions, it resents alkaline soils. Good cut flower.

61 – Asclepias tuberosa
Courtesy Angelika Kaufmann

Asparagus; Asparagaceae (Liliaceae)

There are around three hundred species of the well-known Asparagus genus, mainly covering Europe, Africa and Asia. Most are perennials, with the base becoming slightly woody with age. For this book, we look here at those perennial plants that originate in dry regions of the Mediterranean and Asia. Asparagus have a unique beauty with their fine foliage and the lovely yellow autumn colour and the berries on female plants. My cats are very fond of them for meditation and we called the planting 'the Asparagus Forest' in their honour.

Asparagus officinalis L

This is now the well-known and healthy vegetable. Its origins are around Europe and Asia; it has a long history of cultivation. Naturally it grows on dry and sandy places and its habitat extends into altitudes of up to thirteen hundred metres. The plant grows to around a hundred and fifty centimetres high and may also be used in larger perennial borders.

Asparagus pseudoscaber Aschers et Graebn

This very decorative species comes from Yugoslavia and the Ukraine and has similar requirements to the above vegetable. It is large, up to two metres high and may be used in groups or singly in larger perennial borders where it stands out in late autumn with its rich display of berries.

Asperula; Rubiaceae

Around a hundred species of annual, perennial or small shrubs represent this genus. The main occurrences are in the Mediterranean, greater Europe but there are sixteen species in eastern Australia and Tasmania. The higher ones are suited to sunny or semi-shaded margins of woodlands, slopes or rockeries with alkaline soils. Propagation is by seed and division. The alpine species are best used among rocks in the alpinum, in dry stone walls or tubs. They combine well with Aethionema, Alyssum, Armeria, Draba, Iberis or small Dianthus.

Asperula capitata Kit et Schult

Carpathia and Bulgaria are home to this small, to around twenty-centimetre-high perennial that requires alkaline soil conditions. The flowers are purple in summer.

Asperula cynanchia L

Almost all over Europe we can find this around fifty-centimetre-high perennial in dry grasslands, Pine forests and meadows. It flowers purply-pink in summer and into early autumn. Good partners would be Aster amellus Bupleurum falcatum, Euphorbia cyparissias, Scabiosa columbaris and similar perennials.

Asphodeline; Asphodelaceae (Liliaceae)

This genus extends from the Mediterranean into Asia and has biennial and perennial species with fleshy roots. The plants grow in well-drained soil and full sun is best for healthy development. Plant is small groups in rockeries or drier borders; they also do well along and on top of dry stone walls. Propagation is by seed, (germination is somewhat erratic, so don't lose patience) or by division.

Asphodeline liburnica Rchb

The plant grows eighty centimetres to a bit over a metre high and offers itself to natural designs through its graceful habit and irregular appearances.

Asphodeline lutea Rchb

This species originates in the Mediterranean and extends into Syria. It grows on rocky and gravelly, alkaline soils where it becomes up to a metre high. Its features are striking yellow flowers in summer, contrasting with the fleshy grey-blue leaves.

62 – Asphodeline lutea
Travel study, Italy 1987

Asphodeline taurica Kunth

Greece, western Asia and the Caucasus are home to this showy species that thrives on rocky slopes, dry grasslands and in open woodlands, also preferring alkaline soils. The plant reaches up to eighty centimetres in height with dense white flowers. I would use it in larger groups where it is very conspicuous in rockeries or on slopes.

Asphodelus; Asphodelaceae

The Mediterranean, greater Europe and northern Africa have around twelve species of this showy genus. Most have bluish or grey-green fleshy leaves that almost look like a succulent grass when not in flower. They are impressive feature plants with their white or pink inflorescence and are best used in hot, dry locations where they stand out and above lower plantings like steppes or rockeries. Propagation is by seed in spring after harvesting the previous autumn or division.

Asphodelus aestivus Brot

All around the Mediterranean can we find this species that further extends into Portugal, Asia and North Africa. It naturally occurs in dry grasslands, steppes or heathlands with dry, sandy or gravelly soils, sometimes it is scattered in open pine forests where enough sunlight can penetrate to the forest floor. The impressive flower stalk can grow up to two metres high and are held above a rosette of fifty-centimetre-long leaves.

Asphodelus albus Miller

This species main habitat is in dry meadows, grasslands, slopes and steppes of the Mediterranean and extends into Eastern Europe. The white, sometimes mild pink flowers are up to a hundred and fifty centimetres high and very showy. The plant is slow to establish and requires three or more years before it shows its full potential.

63 – Asphodelus albus
Work in Kew, England; Courtesy Kew Gardens

Asphodelus ramosus L

In south-western Europe and down to Greece, we can find this Asphodelus with lightly branched flower stalks that feature white flowers. Cultivation and use in the landscape is as for the above.

Asplenium; Aspleniaceae

This large genus of ferns contains around seven hundred species, some botanists also include the Ceterach and Phyllitis but we will look at those separately in this book. It is a cosmopolitan genus; its representatives can be found all over the world. For successful cultivation, it is imperative to learn how the respective species lives and subsequently provide the right environment for it.

Asplenium adiantum-nigrum L

The black-stemmed Fern comes originally from moist forests of Middle and South Europe, Asia and Africa. It grows in damp soils but also can establish itself on rock walls. It starts early in spring and as in most ferns the development of its leaves is of subtle beauty. Use in the landscape in naturally shady and moist environments, preferably with a mild microclimate. It may be used in shady courtyards as a gentle background plant.

Asplenium septentrionale Hoffmann

This, a little unusual fern, inhabits mountains of the European Alps, Asia and north America where it grows in sunny, warm and dry rocks of up to two thousand eight hundred metres altitude. It is important to keep in mind that it prefers acidic soils conditions and use it in the landscape to soften up rocky areas or dry-stone walls.

Asplenium trichomanes L

One of my favourite common names is 'Steinfeder' which translates into 'Rock Feather' and this gives a good indication of the fine appearance of this small, up to thirty-centimetre-high fern. The lovely feathery leaves give a friendly appearance to garden scenes in dappled shade, nice to use also in combination with creeks or other water features in sheltered secluded places. One could imagine little elves sitting there and meditating!

Astelia; Asteliaceae

In Australia, New Zealand, Chile and the Falkland Islands are twenty-five species of Astelia. They are conspicuous structural plant with dense rosettes of sword-like silvery-grey leaves; the inflorescence is usually somewhat hidden in amongst the leaves. They prefer a cooler, semi-shaded location and suffer from harsher frosts (below -10ºC). The leaves are great in the vase. Propagation is by seed (slow and erratic) and by division.

Astelia banksii Cunn

This New Zealand species naturally grows along the coast up to two and a half metres high and has five centimetres wide leaves. A very good structural plant in the right place, the inflorescences are an upright stalk and have bright green to creamy white flowers with white berries that darken to purple-black when maturing.

Astelia nivicola Cockayne ex Cheeseman

Also from New Zealand, this species inhabits mountain meadows in altitudes from seven hundred to seventeen hundred metres. It is a low plant with up to fifty-centimetre-long silvery leaves that brightens up semi-shaded places where sufficient moisture is.

Aster; Asteraceae

Around six hundred species, most of them perennials, represent the genus Aster, which is part of one of the larger families in the Kingdom Plantae. Most know the flower structure well; indeed, when children paint flowers they usually paint Asteraceae. For this book, we shall only look at the perennial species; there are some shrubby and annual ones as well. They occur from Europe to Asia, America and South Africa. They generally do well in any good garden soil, preferring full sun to light shade. Some can stand for decades without rejuvenation whilst some need to be taken up and divided/rejuvenated every two or three years. Propagation is best by cuttings and division. Cuttings are best from the first growth in spring, whilst division offers itself as a winter activity, I remember we dug up the plants and divided them in the workroom in southern Germany (cold fingers). Wild species and certain breeds also come well from seed, of course. In the following listing, I divided them by flowering time to assist with the use in the landscape.

Spring-Flowering Asters:

Aster alpinus L

This hairy, up to thirty-centimetre-high species occurs all around the European Alps, the mountain ranges of West and Middle Asia and the western North America. It has large flowers with mostly purple or mauve, sometimes pink or white colours. I recommend using it mainly in the alpinum, rockeries and tubs with very good drainage. It does not like too much fertiliser and lives longer if the soil is kept poor (remember the original habitat).

Aster diplostephioides C.B. Clarke

Coming from the Himalayas, Tibet and China and down to India and Pakistan, this up to fifty-centimetre-high perennial is famous for its numerous and long lilac-coloured petals. The flowers are up to nine centimetres wide; it is certainly one of the outstanding Aster species.

Aster himalaicus C.B. Clarke

Growing on rocks and open slopes, up to twenty-five centimetres high, this Aster flowers violet-blue and features up to seventy petals around its flower head, it is very pretty but is best used in more natural and wild designs rather than the formal perennial border.

Aster tongolensis Franch

This species comes from western China where it grows in forests, on meadows and along creeks. It is up to forty centimetres high and flowers profusely, with shiny purple-blue petals around an orange-yellow flower head. Despite its natural habitat often being semi-shaded, this wonderful plant can be used in full sun provided enough moisture is in the soil; it is a great complementation for the semi-formal and formal perennial borders. I would use it in combination with, but behind, autumn-flowering Asters, so that the layout and colour of the autumn species dominate the structure of the bed throughout most of the year.

Aster yunnanensis Franch

As the name suggests, this plant is at home in Yunnan, western China and Tibet where it grows in meadows and the margins of woodlands and forests. It becomes up to fifty centimetres high and the flowers are a lovely dark-blue with golden-brown heads.

Summer and autumn-flowering Asters:

Who does not know Asters in the garden? They are almost a symbol of late summer and autumn and maybe a symbol for flowers themselves. For best horticultural practice, I would like to point out here that the species from a European and Asian background are by and large weaker and less competitive than their North American relatives and consequently should be used accordingly. Most European-Asiatic species are medium plants from the steppes that prefer warm and well-drained soil conditions.

European and Asian Asters

Aster amellus L

Also called 'Mountain Aster', this species extends from France to northern Italy, from Macedonia to Siberia, Armenia, Anatolia and into western Asia. It inhabits alkaline, well-drained and rocky or gravelly soil and grows also in association with shrubs. The plant is hairy, becomes sixty centimetres tall and features large flowers, usually blue or purplish, but sometimes white or pink. It prefers full sun and does well in beds with Papaver orientale and the tall bearded Iris as they inhabit the same environments and complement each other with flowering time and dormancy. In nature, they are long-lived and tough species – in the garden they require light, dry and well-drained soil to have the same longevity and not too much N in fertiliser, just like the Iris and the Poppies. Spring plantings are preferable to autumn.

Aster x frikartii Frikart

This is a Swiss hybrid with lovely large flowers and long stems that are good cut flowers. Flowering time is late summer to autumn and like the above, this plant is sensitive to wet soils and is best planted in spring. There are some outstanding selections; 'Jungfrau' (Virgin) with dark purple, 'Mönch' (Monk; both are named after the Swiss mountains) with large purple flowers and 'Wunder von Stäfa' (Miracle of Stäfa) growing to eighty centimetres with pure blue flowers.

Aster linosyris Bernh syn Galatella linosyris

The lovely common name of 'Goldhaar-Aster' (Golden-hair Aster) indicates a quite different species with no petals on their flower heads. Nonetheless this is a very showy, bright and beautiful perennial for the steppe and heath plantings and combines extremely well with light grasses, Aster amellus and other plants from similar environments. Naturally it inhabits southern Europe, England and south-eastern Sweden but extends into Russia and northern Africa. A very special Aster and one of my personal favourites for unusual garden scenes.

64 – Aster linosyris syn Galatella linosyris
Courtesy Klaus Mödinger

Aster pyrenaeus Dsf ex DC

Southern France and the Pyrenees are home to this up to ninety-centimetre-high perennial with light blue to mauve flowers in late summer and autumn. It is by and large tougher than the similar Aster amellus but its colour is less intense. The best hybrid I would recommend is the in 1912 bred 'Lutetia', named after the Roman name for the ancient French city.

Aster sedifolius L

A widely spread species, from Europe to Asia, this simple Aster with mauve or mild purple flowers is best used in natural or semi-formal heathlands. It is long-lived and robust; also, the selection 'Nana' (around thirty centimetres) is great in the landscape.

North-American Asters

Most of these Asters require more moisture and richer soils and are stronger growing than their European and Asian relatives.

Aster amethystinus Nutt (A. ericioides x A. novae-angliae)

This attractive and tall Aster combines well with Helianthus and tall grasses which colour up in autumn. It flowers profusely with mild blue flower heads on multi-branched stems.

Aster azureus Lindl

The 'Sky-blue Aster' (translated from German) comes from Ontario, Georgia, Minnesota, Kansas, Alabama and Texas. It grows on the margins of woodlands and becomes up to a hundred and twenty centimetres tall. It flowers in pure blue in autumn and is a great addition in the middle or background of larger perennial borders.

Aster cordifolius L

This very tall, up to a hundred and eighty-centimetre-high multi-branched Aster inhabits woodlands or shrublands from Nova Scotia to Ontario, Minnesota, Georgia, Missouri, Oregon, Montana and Alabama. Colours on small flower heads vary from blue or purple to sometimes white or mild pink. It flowers into late autumn and is therefore very valuable in the herbaceous perennial border waving farewell to the growing season.

Aster dumosus L

This may be one of the most important Aster types in common horticultural use; the German common name is 'Kissen-Aster' which loosely translates into 'Pillow-Aster'. This refers to the dense, soft, rounded appearance of the perennial in leaf or flower. Originally it comes from Maine, Ontaria, Michigan, Illinois and down to Florida, Louisiana and Texas. There is some academic discussion as to the demarcation between Aster dumosus and Aster novi-belgii, but for this book, this is not relevant. Relevant is the successful cultivation and appropriate placement in the landscape of the numerous lovely hybrids that are available. As is clear from their origin, they prefer rich and well-cultivated garden soils with sufficient moisture, especially in summer. Personally, I prefer to use them in the foreground or the edges of herbaceous perennial borders, because they provide structure and colour at a time when most other perennials are already in the process of withdrawing for winter dormancy. Good partners are ornamental grasses.

Aster ericioides L

A multi-branched and profusely flowering perennial coming from British Columbia, Georgia and Texas. It grows to around a metre and flowers white, sometimes mild pink. This species is more drought tolerant than its other American relatives and consequently can be used to great advantage in prairies or steppes along with Liatris, Sidalcea or Solidago and steppe grasses. It also is a good cut flower; there are several recommendable cultivars in the trade.

Aster novae-angliae L

The 'rough-leaved Aster', referring to its hairy leaves, originates in Quebec to Alberta, Maryland, North Carolina, Colorado and New Mexico. It grows on open, moist places, along the margins of woodlands and along rivers and creeks. It is a tall perennial of up to a hundred and eighty centimetres and is normally stiff upright. On cloudy days, the flowers close, this may be a reason why it is not as popular as the closely related and similar Aster novi-belgii. However, it is less susceptible to powdery mildew, which is often a problem for the latter, especially when autumn days are warm and the nights are cold, producing condensation moisture on the leaves. There are many good cultivars and hybrids in the trade ranging from white, pink, red to blue and deep purple.

65 – Aster novae belgii 'Purple Dome'
Courtesy Staudengärtnerei Häussermann, Stuttgart, Germany

Aster novi-belgii L

Quite like the above, this Aster has smooth leaves and comes originally from Quebec, Maine and Georgia. It inhabits moist to swampy places and consequently requires sufficient water in cultivation. The 'smooth-leaved Aster' get to around a hundred and fifty centimetres high and is probably one of the most important Asters for the autumn in herbaceous perennial borders. Propagation is by cuttings in spring or division in winter, they require sufficient food and water especially during the summer months for good development and rich flowers. Again, as in the above, there are very many good cultivars, selections and hybrids in the trade.

Astilbe; Saxifragacae

There are around thirty-five species in this genus. One of the common names is 'Meadowsweet'. The come mainly from eastern Asia and are low to medium plants with attractive, fine foliage and feathery flowers, usually in summer. Most of them prefer moist, but not water-logged soils and semi-shade. Propagation is by division in winter or rooted runners.

Astilbe x arendsii Arends

This is a group of horticultural hybrids by Georg Arends with varying colours and flowering times. They combine very well with Aconitum, Anemone, Astrantia, Bergenia, Brunnera, Campanula, Cimicifuga racemosa, Epimedium, but also Hosta, Primula, Rodgersia, Tiarella and many ferns. The choice of hybrids depends on flowering time and colour preferences. In the right setting, they can create magical scenes where one could imagine elves hiding in amongst the plants.

66 – Astilbe x arendsii 'Else Schluck'
Courtesy Angelika Kaufmann

Astilbe chinesis var. pumila hort

This exceptional Astilbe tolerates drought and full sun; it is a fantastic ground cover and flowers profusely from late summer to autumn. There are several cultivars available that vary from shades of pink to purple.

Astilbe grandis Stapf ex Wils

A large, up to two-metre-tall species of Astilbe with an open habit and up to a metre-long flowers in creamy-yellow white. A very good background plant for shaded and semi-shaded areas but more for the natural designs as the plant is too strong for more formal perennial borders and tends to overgrow others.

Astilbe japonica Gray

The Japanese Astilbe has many valuable hybrids, most of which flower in summer, earlier than other Astilbes. Sufficient moisture is essential for good growth and long life as well as a rich soil with a lot of organic matter; leaf litter is great.

Astilboides; Saxifragaceae

Only one species in this genus:

Astilboides tabularis Engl

Formerly named Rodgersia tabularis, this showy perennial grows to a metre high and its rhizomes grow shallowly, just under the surface of the soil. The flowers are white and like its relatives, the Astilbes, in early summer. It is however mostly grown for its foliage; the large round and serrated leaves are held on long stems and stand out in a design. The plant essentially requires cool and moist places in the shade or semi-shade of deep-rooted trees (shallow rooted trees compete too strongly with the perennial). It enjoys places near water, creeks, rivers or water features but does not want to stand *in* the water. The plant needs a lot of space over time and is best partnered with strong species of the same habitat, Aconitum, Astilbe, Ligularia,

Cimicifuga or large ferns would be examples. Propagation is by division in autumn or spring, or by seed in winter.

67 – Astilboides tabularis, courtesy of Wikimedia, picture by Nestmaker

Astralagus; Fabaceae

This is a large genus of around fifteen hundred species everywhere in the world except Australia. There are annuals, biennials, perennials, sub-shrubs and shrubs represented. Almost all prefer dry, well-drained soils in full sun and are great to use in rockeries, tubs or the alpinum. Their tendency to develop a strong taproot makes propagation by seed into deep tubes one of the best options.

Astralagus angustifolius L

Crete, the southern Balkans and Asia are home to this sub-shrub that grows to thirty centimetres in height and up to a metre wide. It flowers white in early summer. The use in the landscape is in sunny, rocky places, dry stone walls included. This species can be propagated by cuttings in autumn that are embedded in a sandy mix.

Astralagus centralpinus Braun-Blanq

This alpine species has woolly-hairy leaves and shoots and grows to a metre tall. The yellow flowers are showy and appear in summer. It is a very attractive plant for dry perennial borders, natural or semi-formal.

Astralagus massiliensis Lam

Coming from the coastal areas of south-western Europe where it grows in open heathlands. It is a nice sub-shrub forming fifty-centimetre-high pillows and flowers white in late spring and early summer. Good to use in larger rockeries or as structural plant in bigger, dry perennial borders in informal groups.

Astralagus monspessulanus L

An alpine plant spread from the Pyrenees, the southern Alps to the Balkans, Ukraine and northern Africa. It inhabits altitudes of up to two thousand six hundred metres and grows to around twenty centimetres high, often hugging rocks and sending a deep taproot into the gravelly or sandy soil. The flowers are large and red, very conspicuous and beautiful.

Astralagus purshii Dougl

This American species grows low, to around twenty centimetres high, has dense grey hairy leaves and occupies dry grasslands and mountain ridges of up to two thousand three hundred metres. The flowers appear in summer and are creamy-white, it is a lovely plant for rockeries.

Astralagus sempervirens Lam

The Pyrenees, southern Alps and the Balkans are home to this special sub-shrub that grows to fifteen centimetres high and fifty centimetres across. It ascends to two thousand eight hundred metres altitude and flowers pink or in shades of white. It is a long-lived species for sunny rockeries and should be planted in gravelly soils. Propagation is easy by seed, hard by cutting.

Astrantia; Apiaceae

These humble perennials are distributed from Europe to Asia where they live in the dappled shade of deciduous forests and woodlands. Consequently, they prefer shadier places with moisture in the rich soil and air humidity not too low.

Astrantia major L

A predominantly European species which inhabits forests and woodlands, mountain meadows and protected shrublands. It is a variable and adaptable plant, flowering mild pink in summer. There are some horticultural selections available in the trade; in general, I would use the plant in natural designs and let it go wild along forest paths that invite exploration and adventure.

Athyrium; Dryopteridaceae

The genus of 'Women's Fern' (translated from German) contains around two hundred species spread all over the world, but mostly in the mountains of Asia.

Athyrium filix-femina Roth

The 'Forest-Women's Fern' ascends from moist valleys up to two thousand metres altitude. As with many ferns it requires ample moisture and should not dry out. It prefers acidic soils and is not found on alkaline soils. The lovely leaves reach up to a hundred and twenty centimetres in length and the unfolding of the young leaf in spring is of aesthetic beauty. Once given a sheltered moist and protected place, the fern will develop its very own character and is very long-lived. Nice partners are mossy rocks, maybe Actaea, and other shade loving plants. Please do not remove the leaf litter from deciduous trees sheltering them, as this forms a great protection for the heart of the plant and will develop into the best soil for this beautiful fern. There are around three varieties of the species.

Athyrium niponicum Hance

The 'Japanese Women's Fern' is also at home in Korea and China. The leaves are up to seventy centimetres long and the green is somewhat lighter than in other Athyriums. As the above it requires a sheltered and shaded place with rich and most soil, I have seen it used wonderfully in combination with mossy rocks in monasteries as gardens for meditation.

Atropa; Solanaceae

This genus is a well-known medicinal and poisonous plant; the German name 'Tollkirsche' translates loosely into something like 'Mad Cherry'.

Atropa bella-donna L

Also called the 'Deadly Nightshade', this Mediterranean and Eurasian species grows to a hundred and fifty centimetres high and produces as fruit a black, shiny berry. The plant prefers moist and shady places in warm regions. The foliage and berries are highly toxic, containing tropane alkaloids. These toxins include scopolamine and hyoscyamine, which cause a bizarre delirium and hallucinations. These constituents are also used as pharmaceutical anticholinergics. The drug atropine is derived from the plant. It has a long history of use as a medicine, cosmetic, and poison and has even been used as anaesthetic for surgery in the Roman Empire. The genus name Atropa comes from Atropos, one of the three Fates in Greek mythology. The name "bella donna" is derived from the Italian language and means "beautiful woman" because the herb was used in eye-drops by women, to dilate the pupils of the eyes to make them appear beautiful and seductive.

Atropa belladonna
By Tom Oates at the English language Wikipedia, CC BY-SA 3.0

Aubrieta; Brassicaceae

This ornamental perennial comes from the mountains of Europe, Asia Minor and the Mediterranean. There are twelve species and they are very showy, covered with flowers in spring. They prefer full sun in well-drained soils, preferably with gravel or sand and of alkaline conditions. Propagation is by cuttings put into a sandy mix; I recommend cutting the plants back after flowering and using this material.

Aubrieta columnae Guss

From Italy, Sicily, Albania and Romania comes this up to ten-centimetre-high pillow-forming species with purple flowers.

Aubrieta deltoidea L

This beautiful species is at home in Sicily, the Balkans and Asia Minor. Around 10cm high, the dense pillow is a strong growing. The flowers are blue and white and stand well above the foliage.

Aubrieta x cultorum Bergm

The Aubrieta hybrids are the most important and well-known forms that we find in the gardens. Some of those, like the blue 'Tauricola' can become more than a hundred years old and can still be found on dry stone walls. Their pillows of flowers trailing over the rocks are one of my first childhood memories of flowers and I stood there often, mesmerised for a long time by their little abundant flowers. The colours range from white to red and pink, blue and purple. Some personal recommendations are the blue 'Blaumeise' (Blue Finch, named after a lovely little bird), 'Hamburger Stadtpark' in purple, 'Gloriosa' in pink, 'Red Dyke' in red and 'Winterberg' in white. I recommend visiting your local nursery and ask what is available.

69 – Aubrieta x cultorum 'Hartswood Purple'
Staudengärtnerei Häussermann in Stuttgart, Germany

Aurinia; Brassicaceae

Aurinia saxatilis Desv (Alyssum saxatilis)
From the warmer parts of Europe and Asia minor comes this small perennial that almost always grows in association with rocks and gravel. It gets to forty centimetres high and becomes a little woody at the base as the plant matures. It flowers rich yellow in spring. Use is the same as for Alyssum, dry stone walls, rockeries or on green roofs as they are very drought tolerant and want to bake in the sun. Propagation is by cuttings in late autumn and early winter, best put in straight sand and not kept too wet or humid.

70 – Aurinia saxatilis
Courtesy Klaus Mödinger

Azorella; Apiaceae

This perennial comes from South America, the Andes but also occurs in New Zealand. It colonises open, moist places between rocks and prefers light soils and cool locations. It is a special texture plant, maybe more for the collector than the landscape architect or horticulturist. One can create intimate small garden scenes with it combined with Hebe, small conifers and grasses like Carex. Propagation is by division of the rosettes and best done in autumn and early winter.

Azorella trifurcate Pers
This species originates in Chile and the southern Andes, it is long-lived given the right environment; it should not dry out but at the same time requires good drainage.

Baccharis; Asteraceae

A large genus that comprises around three hundred and fifty species including perennials, shrubs and even small trees. They are very decorative and desired plants for collectors but in my opinion, should be used more widely in designs.

Baccharis halimifolia L

This tall, up to two-metre-high perennial comes from North America where it grows in sandy coastal environments. In autumn, it features ice bronze-brown foliage with the female plants additionally being decorated with white fruits. This species is best suited to large displays or as a structural feature plant on poor soils.

Baccharis odorata var. spathulata Pers

This small, thirty-centimetre-high shrub grows along the margins of swamps in the Andes from Columbia to Bolivia. The small leaflets are beautifully fragrant and it features yellow flowers. It is a special beauty requiring careful preparation of the environment.

Baccharis pilularis

These plants are found in a variety of habitats, from coastal bluffs, oak woodlands, and grasslands, including on hillsides and in canyons, but usually below eight hundred metres.

Also called Coyote brush, this species is known as a secondary pioneer plant in communities such as coastal sage scrub and chaparral. It does not regenerate under a closed shrub canopy because seedling growth is poor in the shade. The shrub is generally smaller than three metres in height. This and other *Baccharis* species are nectar sources for most of the predatory wasps, native skippers (small butterflies), and native flies in their ranges.

Use in the landscape in open, informal and natural heathland and prairie designs.

71 – Baccharis pilularis
Courtesy Watershed Nurseries, United States

Ballota; Lamiaceae

A small genus with around thirty-five species in Europe and western Asia. They feature attractive flower stalks that are used in floristry. Many Mediterranean species are well suited to xerophytic environments, dry steppes or on dry stone constructions, all prefer full sun. Propagation is by soft cuttings from the first growth in spring, like Chrysanthemum; the woody species are best propagated by semi-hardwood cuttings in autumn.

Ballota acetabulosa Benth
From the limestone rocks of Greece hails this fifty-centimetre-high sub-shrub with lovely grey-felt-like and heart-shaped leaves. Mauve flowers appear in summer, it requires a warm, protected location with excellent drainage.

Ballota nigra L
This up to eighty-centimetre-high herbaceous perennial originates in the Balkans but has migrated to a larger area in Europe, mainly along railroad lines or on disturbed areas on farmland. The pure species is less important for horticulture, but there are some attractive cultivars available: 'Archer's Variety', forty centimetres with white variegated foliage and purple flowers – this variety prefers light shade though. Another cultivar is 'Zanzibar' which is strong growing and has yellow dotted foliage.

Ballota pseudodictamnus L
Western Turkey and Cyrenaica (Libya) are home to the fifty-centimetre-high sub-shrub. The small leaves are very hairy and the inflorescence reminds on Moluccella, the 'Bells of Ireland' that are very popular in the floral trade. The plant requires a well-drained and sunny, hot location to perform well and should be cut back in spring – but only stay in the 'soft bits' with the pruning, do not cut back into woody, older parts.

Balsamorhiza; Asteraceae

This is a small genus with twelve species in the North America and Canada. It is more of a collector's plant for the larger rockery or natural, wild garden in full sun. Propagation is best by seed.

Balsamorhiza rosea Nels et Macbr
This perennial prefers dry, rocky slopes or lives along cliff faces. It has large yellow flowers that change into a glowing bronze when maturing. It is a rare species and very sought after by collectors.

Balsamorhiza sagittata Nutt
The up to fifty-centimetre-high plant occupies dry slopes, grasslands and valleys. The glowing yellow flowers are up to ten centimetres across and make a great display planted in large groups among ornamental grasses and other perennials of the same community.

Baptisia; Fabaceae

There are thirty species representing this genus from eastern and southern America. The plants have thick, strong rhizomes and conspicuous flowers in white, yellow or purple. Their cultivation requires full sun and they are quite drought tolerant, they resemble Lupins and should be used accordingly in the landscape, the large and perennial border in natural gardens and parks or in informal groups.

Baptisia alba Vent
This attractive, white perennial has interesting foliage that is reddish-bronze or blackish when young and a feature. It flowers in summer and originally comes from prairies, open woodlands or grasslands and reaches up to 1.2 metres height. I recommend cutting back after flowering, unless the seed is wanted for harvesting, of course.

Baptisia australis R. Br
Inhabiting more moist soils than its relatives, this Baptisia grows to a metre and a half and has long, Lupin-like flower stalks up to forty centimetres long in blue-purple.

Baptisia tinctoria Vent
This up to a metre-tall species grows on dry, poor and sandy soils. It flowers quite prolifically in yellow with smaller flowers in summer.

Begonia; Begoniaceae

This is a well-known genus with over nine hundred herbaceous perennials, mostly from tropical and subtropical zones. They are very widespread also in the horticultural trade with numerous cultivars and hybrids; I would not dare to guess a number here. Begonias prefer moist, rich soils in semi-shade, few are suited to full sunny conditions. They combine very well with foliage texture plants, ferns or bamboos. Propagation is easy by either the small plantlets formed by many species or by leaf cutting, I remember that when I used to teach at school I often used Begonias as examples for leaf cuttings.

Begonia grandis ssp. evansia Dryand
Coming from China and Japan, this strong, up to sixty-centimetre-high Begonia forms asymmetrical, showy leaves that are green with red veins. Pink terminal flowers are produced from summer through to late autumn.

Begonia ravenii Peng et Chen
This mountain-dwelling Begonia ascends to altitudes of up to two thousand metres and grows with subterranean rhizomes. It features large, up to thirty-centimetre-tall leaves and has loosely held pink flowers.

Belamcanda; Iridaceae

Belamcanda chinensis Redoute
There is only this one species in this genus. The 'Leopard Flower' (translated from German) grows naturally in Bhutan, China, India, Japan, Korea, Nepal, Russia and Vietnam in altitudes of up to two thousand two hundred metres. It is often rather short-lived and gets to one and a half metres in good soils. There are many variations that are not (yet) botanically exactly classified, with colours ranging from yellow to red-orange and dwarf forms are known. The standard form we usually find available in the trade has a pretty, light orange with reddish dots, a little like a leopard's coat. I would use it in informal perennial borders in association with structural plants, also from an eastern Asian background as it sometimes just

disappears. In that case, the designer then has the structural plant as feature still there and is not left with an unintended hole. Propagation is best by seed. It should be mentioned that the fruits are highly valued in dried flower arrangements.

Bellis; Asteraceae

Fifteen species are in this genus from Europe and the Mediterranean. They are low, spreading perennials.

Bellis perennis L
The well-known 'Gänseblümchen' (little goose flower) extends from Europe down into Syria where it lives in meadows. They are popular in displays, as border along paths flowering in spring, easy, reliable and tough. There are many cultivars available in the trade.

Bergenia; Saxifragaceae

This is a small genus with seven species coming from East Asia. They are strong growing perennials with flat, thick roots and large, leathery leaves; most of them are evergreen. Often used in the landscape for their toughness, tolerating almost any soil in semi-shade or shade. The appearance with the upright ear-like leaves is somewhat different to most planting designs and they may look a bit odd. However they can be combined with rocks or walls or used along creeks and under trees in larger groups. I find that good partners are Epimedium, Astilbe, Geranium. Lysimachia and Campanula, but also ferns and semi-shade-loving grasses like Carex. Propagation is easy by division in spring, if the nursery man requires larger numbers cuttings of the rhizomes yield usually plenty. Seed is also possible but slow.

Bergenia cordifolia Sternb
This Asian plant has up to forty centimetres long leathery and strongly veined leaves. The flowers appear in spring and have colours from pink to mauve. It is an evergreen species and therefore useful in many herbaceous design situations.

Bergenia purpurascens Engl
From stony mountain sides in western China comes this smaller species with slightly reddish leaves and dark red flowers in spring.

Bergenia hybrids
There are numerous garden hybrids of Bergenia available as they breed easily. Most flower in spring, some so early that the flowers push up above the snow (in areas where there is snow, of course). Flower colours arrange from white to pink and red and purple. I would recommend checking with your local suppliers what is available.

Berlandiera; Asteraceae

Berlandiera lyrata Benth
The 'Chocolate Flowers' comes from North America where their original habitat is dry meadows and prairies between twelve hundred and eighteen hundred metres altitude. They are around forty centimetres tall, have white hairs along the stems and leaves and glowing yellow flowers. From spring to summer is the main flowering time and (who would have guessed it?) they smell like lovely warm chocolate!

Biarum; Araceae

These unusual tuberous plants are at home in the Mediterranean on stony, dry soils and should be used accordingly in rockeries, on dry, gravelly slopes as collector's species. They flower from summer to autumn.

Biarum davisii Turrill
Crete and south-western Turkey are home to this species with small leaves and its unusual flower that looks like it would come from an enchanted forest.

Biarum tenuifolium Schott
From Portugal, Spain, Italy and east to Greece and Turkey extends the habitat of this species with twenty-centimetre-long leaves that flowers irregularly in spring and in autumn and winter. It is a robust plant which is quite a show when it flowers as they appear in large numbers. I would plant it close to a path, maybe on top of a low dry-stone wall or a rockery where people can have a close look.

Bistorta; Polygonaceae

This genus was formerly known as *Polygonum* and describes species that grow in clumps, pillows and carpets, often with underground rhizomes. Propagation is by seed, rooted rhizome cuttings or division.

Bistorta affinis Greene
The plant comes originally from the Himalayas and grows in flat carpets, around twenty centimetres high. The flowers are pink and white and become more reddish as they fade. It is essentially a mountain plant and the use in the landscape is accordingly in cool and moist areas. It is a reliable and strong ground cover with partners like Anemone hupehensis, Ceratostigma, Bergenia and Campanula. Many bulbs like Narcissus also combine well with it and push easily through the carpet. There are several cultivars available; some that I can recommend are 'Hartswood' and 'Superbum'.

Bistorta amplexicaulis Ronse
Also from the Himalayas this taller, up to a metre-high species grows in strong clumps and flowers red, pink and white in summer. It is a reliable and fast-growing species for larger, more natural herbaceous borders for partners such as Cimicifuga, Geraniums, Miscanthus and Tanacetum.

Blandfordia; Blandfordiaceae

This small and remarkable genus of the 'Christmas Bells' has four described species. It is essentially Australian and has grass-like tufts of foliage and very showy flowers. Propagation is best by seed (flowers in the third year) or by division in spring or after flowering in later summer.

Blandfordia grandiflora
This, probably best-known species grows to fifty centimetres high with thick, tufted grass-like leaves. The flower spikes can carry up to ten large bell-shaped flowers from pure yellow to deep red with yellow tips in colour. As the name suggests these usually occur in summer (Christmas-time in the southern hemisphere) but they do spot-flower at other times too. They require lot of moisture for best cultivation. In their original habitat, they grow in sandy soils, but in my experience a good garden soil will do just fine and they can be grown in wet spots in a rockery. Always grow in full sun or only slightly shaded, like in the dappled shade of an open Eucalypt.

Blandfordia nobilis

This species is somewhat smaller but otherwise like B. grandiflora; its flowers are more funnel than bell-shaped and always red with yellow tips. This species requires good drainage and does not like it wet like the above.

Blandfordia nobilis is pictured in the introduction to this book.

Blandfordia punicea

A larger Christmas Bell from Tasmania that grows to a metre tall, with rush-like strong foliage that creates a lovely structural feature in the perennial border. The flower spike has a head of red flowers with yellow tips in summer. This plant prefers some shade and cooler conditions than the 'mainland Australians'.

72 - Blandfordia punicea
Courtesy Brett Samon

Blechnum; Blechnaceae

A distinct and as far as ferns go easily identified genus of ferns with around two hundred species. They occur in the temperate zones of the northern hemisphere but larger numbers are in the subtropical and oceanic areas of Chile and New Zealand.

Blechnum penna-marina Kuhn

The evergreen 'Sea-Feather' is at home in New Zealand, Tasmania, South America and some Pacific islands. It is a small fern, covering the ground and forming little carpets. Cool, acidic soils, rich in organic matter, provide ideal conditions for this humble beauty that is best used in shady rockeries or as companion for Cyclamen, Hepatica, Narcissus and the like.

Blechnum spicant Roth

This may the best known and most commonly used fern of this genus from Europe that also occurs in northern America. It is a strong, simple and evergreen fern, growing to eighty centimetres high, which may be used in many applications. The species is a forest-dweller and should be used accordingly in the landscape; it is a lovely feature plant that provides structure in low light situations, even in conifer forests like Picea. Unlike many ferns it prefers alkaline soils. Good partners are Corydalis, Myosotis, Trollius and moisture-loving Iris, these of course in the sunnier spots of the landscape. Propagation is easy by division.

Bletilla; Orchidaceae

The around ten known species of this genus come from East Asia. They are ground orchids preferring well-drained, gravelly but also organic soils in full sun or semi-shade. Their use in the landscape is best close to a path of a rockery or on top of small walls where their intricate flower structure can be admired. However, they can also be used in association with shrubs and together with bulbous plants that are not too competitive. Propagation is best by division in spring or seed.

Bletilla striata Richb

Coming from Japan and China, this around forty to fifty-centimetre-high species has beautiful pink flowers that are striped on the lower petal, the lip – hence the species' name striata, which means 'striped'. It flowers in early summer and prefers a warm location that is reasonably moist during the growing season.

73 – Bletilla striata
Courtesy Stephan Willenberger

Boltonia; Asteraceae

This genus looks very like the actual Aster and the German common name translates into something like 'Pseudo-Aster'. The differences between these two genera are merely academic and refer to the number of pappus hairs. It comes from North America.

Boltonia asteroids Herit
A very tall, up to a hundred and eighty-centimetre perennial that has willow-like foliage and numerous, loosely-held flowers that can vary from white to pink and mauve. Use in the landscape in the background of semi-formal or natural perennial borders. It is a strong grower that requires space.

Boltonia asteroides var latisquama Cronquist
This variety of the species is better suited to the more formal perennial border. It has larger flowers, usually varying from light blue to purple. It flowers in summer and into early autumn, prefers full sun but is easy to grow and good as a cut flower.

Borago; Boraginaceae

The six species of this genus containing the well-known herb Borago officinalis are at home in the Mediterranean in sunny, rocky or other well-drained locations. The flowers feature a lovely blue. However, the plant may become too strong or invasive through the numerous seedlings that are produced.

Borago pygmaea Chater et Greuter
This smaller species occupies moist and often more shady places. The flowers are pure blue from summer into late autumn.

Brachyscome; Asteraceae

Brachyscome multifida
This species forms a neat little pillow of fine feathery leaves up to half a metre across and ten centimetres high. Lilac-blue daisy flowers appear in spring and summer. The plant prefers well-drained soils in full sun but does well in dappled shade. Propagation is by cuttings.

74 – Brachyscome 'Mauve Bliss'
Queanbeyan, Australia 2013

Brachyscome procumbens
An up to thirty-centimetre-high stoloniferous perennial that bears blue-mauve flowers from spring to autumn. This is an unassuming, graceful plant that is hardy and long-flowering, also suited as bedding plant. Propagation is by seed or cutting.

Brimeura; Hyacinthaceae

This genus has only two species; for garden cultivation only one, Brimeura amethystina, is of importance.

Brimeura amethystina Chouard
This species comes from the Pyrenees and extends into north-eastern Spain and north-western Yugoslavia. It is at home in meadows and prefers alkaline soils. It flowers blue in spring, together with Tulipa sprengeri. Good partners are Acaena, Anthemis, Geranium subcaulescens and Geranium cinereum, small Achilleas and similar small, pillow-forming sub-alpine perennials.

75 – Brimeura amethystina
Courtesy Angelika Kaufmann

Briza; Poaceae

The 'Trembling Grass' genus is a cosmopolite with very decorative fruit often used in dry flower arrangements.

Briza media L
This beautiful grass forms mats with its infertile shoots, grows to fifty centimetres high and flowers in summer. It prefers dry and poor soils. I use it in the landscape, often in drifts and sways to visually link dry, natural planting designs together.

76 – Briza media
Courtesy University of Trieste, Italy

Brodiaceae; Alliaceae

This genus comes from North America and produces great cut flowers. By and large these species are more for the collector. Propagation is usually by bulblets that require two to three years to flower. Seed is slow and erratic.

Brodiaea californica Lindl

As the name suggests, this species comes from California but is more widespread in the USA. It naturally grows in rocky or gravelly meadows where it can reach up to seventy centimetres in height with its bright or dark purple, sometimes pink, flowers in summer. For the use in the landscape, I would recommend natural, wild meadows or steppes where it can develop its own special places.

77 – Brodiaea californica
Courtesy John Seymour

Brodiaea coronaria Engl

Also from the USA and California, this small, up to twenty-five-centimetre-high species grows in the same dry, rocky or gravelly habitat. The flowers are pale or dark purple and appear in summer.

Bruckenthalia; Ericaceae

There is only one species in this genus that is closely related with the more widely known Erica. It has similar properties in that it is essentially a sub-shrub, becoming woody at the base and forming dense carpets.

Bruckenthalia spiculifolia Richb

Romania, Turkey and the Balkans are the original habitat of this small sub-shrub that is very valuable in the group of heath plants because it flowers in summer, a time when most of its relatives, Erica and Calluna, are without colour. Like most heathland plants it requires full exposure to sun and wind for healthy, dense development. Cultivation is best in soils rich in organic matter. Propagation is by semi-hardwood cuttings.

78 - Bruckenthalia spiculifolia
Courtesy Brett Samon

Brunnera; Boraginaceae

There are three species in this genus related to the Forget-Me-Not.

Brunnera macrophylla Johnst

This large, heart-shaped leaved Brunnera comes from the Caucasus mountains; the reason why its German common name is the 'Caucasus Vergiss-mein-nicht', the 'Caucasus Forget-Me-Not'. It is essentially a forest-dwelling plant, tolerating many different soil types provided it is in shade or semi-shade and given enough moisture. The leaves appear after the flowers in spring and the plant forms solid clumps, making it a reliable ground cover and weed suppressor. If the plant likes its surroundings, it self-sows and sometimes migrates to other spots on its own. Good companions are Epimedium, Doronicum orientale, Geum coccineum, Waldsteinia geoides, Lamiastrum galeobdolon, Primula and quite a few bulbs may complement it well also. Propagation is by root cuttings in winter, observing polarity. There are by now numerous hybrids and cultivars available in the trade.

79 – Brunnera macrophylla
Work in Canberra, Australia 2013

Bulbine; Asphodelaceae

Bulbine bulbosa
A bulbous plant growing to forty centimetres high with succulent linear leaves. Yellow, star-like flowers form on an upright stem to sixty centimetres high in spring and summer. The plant requires ample water; gently self-sows in the right places, for example a rockery. Propagation is by seed.

Bulbocodium; Colchicaceae

Only two species are in this genus that come from south-eastern Europe.

Bulbocodium vernum L
Cup or star-shaped pale pink-purple flowers appear very early in spring. The plant lives naturally in alpine meadows, in the landscape I would use it dotted around in the rockery or near paths or buildings, as it is one of the first bulbous perennials to flower and combines well with pillow-forming perennials or early flowering open shrubs like Hamamelis.

80 – Bulbocodium vernum
Courtesy Wikimedia

Butomus; Butomaceae

Only one species in this genus, it comes from Europe and temperate Asia.

Butomus umbellatus L

The up to a hundred and thirty-centimetre-high plant grows naturally along and in slow-flowing or still water features, into a depth of around fifty centimetres. The flowers are white with red veins and make this species a valuable addition to the water's edge. I would plant it along with Iris pseudacorus, Alisma and Sagittarius. It also combines well with various smaller Nymphaeae that extend into deeper water. Propagation is by division or seed.

81 – Butomus umbellatus
Courtesy Wikimedia

Calamagrostis; Poaceae

This is a large genus of grasses with around two hundred and thirty species that occurs almost everywhere in the world. I have listed here the, for ornamental horticulture and landscape architecture, most important ones.

Calamagrostis x acutiflora Rehb

A sterile cross from the wild with several decorative selections. 'Karl Foerster' is an upright cultivar, cut back very early in spring before it becomes active. 'Waldenbuch' is a smaller selection that is suited for the smaller garden. I recommend leaving the fruit right into winter until it falls naturally as it looks very beautiful in hoar frosts. Propagation is by division in spring.

Calamagrostis brachytricha Steud

This species comes from Japan and Korea where it has the common name of 'Diamond Grass'. It grows up to a hundred and fifty centimetres high, flowering in autumn. It is a very ornamental plant that can be used in a large variety of applications, even in formal designs due to its upright and strict appearance.

Calamintha; Lamiaceae

The 'Mountain Mint' is a small genus of seven species with a distribution around the warmer zones of Europe and into Asia. Propagation is usually best by soft-tip cuttings, pure species also by seed.

Calamintha grandiflora L

The natural habitat of this pink flowering aromatic plant is a Beech forest (Fagus sylvatica) with not too dry soils where it grows in semi-shade. The perennial is a very good 'filler' plant in between taller partners, indifferent to the PH of the soil.

Calamintha nepeta ssp nepeta

A very attractive and long-flowering species that comes from southern Europe and northern Africa. From summer into autumn light purple or white flowers appear. The plant is also aromatic and can be used in the landscape almost everywhere in drier places, including along borders or as companion to taller plants in rockeries.

82 - Calamintha nepeta
Courtesy Staudengärtnerei Gräfin von Zeppelin, Germany

Calanthe; Orchidaceae

This genus of terrestrial orchids has around a hundred and fifty species in tropical and temperate zones of Asia, Polynesia and Madagascar. Its habitats are evergreen or deciduous forests from sea level to around three thousand metre altitudes. Cultivation should be in shaded and protected locations with generally poor soils Propagation is by division of the pseudo bulbs. Use in the landscape may be in special small garden rooms or openings under trees and larger shrubs where their special beauty can be 'discovered' and appreciated close up.

Calanthe discolour Lindl
This species lives in mixed forests of Korea, Japan and Taiwan. It should be planted in cool, shaded spots and the soil should be rich in organic matter like aged leaf litter. The flowers stand around fifty centimetres tall and the colours of its cultivars vary from brown, orange, white, red or yellow.

Calceolaria; Scrophulariaceae

There are around two hundred species in this genus; most come from South America. They are exotic, bizarre-looking perennials that require high humidity and well-drained, light soils in cultivation. Use in the landscape in smaller rockeries near paths or seating opportunities where they can be seen close up. Probably more suited to the collector than larger-scale landscapes.

Calceolaria biflora Lam
This special beauty comes from Chile and Argentina where it forms clumps or colonies in consistently damp locations, extending from sea level to altitudes of around two thousand eight hundred metres. The plant grows to around fifty centimetres high with short rhizomes and flowers in a strong yellow, sometimes with red dots in early summer.

Calceolaria fothergillii
Courtesy Frieder Ungenberger

Calochortus; Liliaceae

In western America and Mexico are around seventy species of this sun-loving genus. Most of them are plants for the passionate collector and require some expertise in growing. One of the common names for them is 'Tulip of the Mormons'; the reasons for this are not known to me. The flowers vaguely resemble tulips. Propagation is by seed (erratic germination) or separation of the small bulbils that are formed in the axis of the stems. Some even form bulbils at the soil surface that can be removed and replanted, it usually takes two years for them to flower.

Calochortus barbatus Painter
The natural habitats of this species are meadows and stony slopes of Mexico. It grows up to forty centimetres high and has pendulous branches that bear bell-shaped yellow flowers with brown hairs in late summer.

Calochortus luteus M
This wonderful plant comes from grasslands and steppes in California where it extends into open woodlands with enough sun penetration. It has one of the loveliest yellows. Use in the landscape either in smaller natural rockeries or meadows, together with non-competitive species where it can develop.

84 – Calochortus luteus
Courtesy Ensigntherapy

Caltha; Ranunculaceae

There are around forty species in the northern and southern temperate zones of the world. They are essentially swamp plants and need to be used at the water's edge or in constantly wet places. Like many swamp plants they are strong growers and competitive, therefore need similarly strong partner plants as companions. I would use it in the natural landscape with low maintenance requirements (or resources) as the species pretty much looks after itself after planting.

Caltha palustris L
From the northern hemisphere comes this buttery yellow species that grows along creeks or ponds from the lowlands to the mountains, up to around two thousand five hundred metres altitude. Flowering time is early spring and the plant reaches up to fifty centimetres height. Propagation is easy by division in late winter. They can be planted in clumps and will usually flower already in the next season – or for the nursery; the divisions can be potted up and sold as flowering plants in spring, so have a very short turn-around time.

Caltha polysepala Hochst
This species comes from the Caucasus, the Balkans and extends into northern Iran. It is not only a swamp species but also extends into shallow water into around thirty centimetres depth. Around sixty centimetres tall, its flowers are much larger than those of Caltha palustris. Good partners are other strong plants of the water's edge like Iris pseudacorus, Lysichitum americanum or other water Iris like I. versicolour or I. chrysographes.

Camassia; Hyacinthaceae

This is a small genus with only around five species. They are bulbous plants of moist meadows in full sun or part shade. They thrive in moist, loamy but still well-drained soils with partners like Trollius,

Dodecatheon, Achillea ptarmica, Echinaca purpurea and Doronicum plantagineum. Propagation is more efficient by seed than bulbils.

Camassia leichtlinii Watson

The USA and Rocky Mountains are home to this around a hundred and thirty-centimetre-high Camassia whose colours range from white or blue to purple. It prefers sun and moist, acidic soils, there are several good cultivars available in the trade. Use in natural meadows in the informal landscape.

Camassia quamash Greene

Also from America, this species is smaller, up to eighty centimetres high with light blue to deep purple flowers in spring. This plant is better suited to smaller gardens, cottage gardens and rockeries. The cooked bulb has been used for food by Native Americans.

Campanula; Campanulaceae

The genus Campanula comprises around three hundred species and most of these inhabit the temperate zones of the northern hemisphere. Meadows, alpine slopes and forests are their main habitats. In size, Campanula range from alpine ground-hugging dwarfs to human-size perennials; in colour from whites and light blues to deep purples. Their use in the landscape is accordingly very variable and includes alpine rockeries, natural plantings and formal perennial borders. In perennial borders, they combine well with Achillea, Oenothera, Coreopsis, Chrysanthemum, Lilium and Papaver; in the shadier borders Astilbe, Aruncus, Digitalis Polygonatum or Cimicifuga are good companions. The smaller alpine species I would partner with the small Achillea, Arenaria, Thymus, Gypsophila and Linum flavum, but these are of course only a few selected examples. Most Campanula propagate easily by seed. In the following listing, the species are grouped according to their use in the landscape.

1. Group: Species thirty centimetres high or taller for borders and natural designs

Campanula glomerata L

Extending from Europe into northern Africa and Iran is the 'Bellflower', an up to sixty-centimetre-high species with deep purple terminal flower heads in summer. It is best used in natural designs on alkaline soils. Good partners are Achillea, Cerastium tomentosum, Coreopsis lanceolata, Coreopsis verticillata (including 'Moonbeam'), Helianthemum, Hypericum polyphyllum, Linum flavum, Oenothera tetragona, Pulsatilla x tonguei, Thymus serpyllum and other species from the same habitat.

85 - Campanula glomerata
Courtesy Baumschule Horstmann, Germany

Campanula lactiflora Bieb

The up to two-metre-tall, profusely flowering Campanula lactiflora is at home in the Caucasus and western China. It flowers milky-light blue to mauve-blue in summer. I would recommend it for sunny and semi-shaded larger perennial borders and in the informal landscape in association with shrubs and trees. They combine well with Artemisia lactiflora, Aster divaricatus, Aster cordifolius, Astilbe, Deschampsia, Digitalis, Iris sibirica, Luzula, Lythrum and ferns. As can be seen from the above partners, the species requires somewhat more moisture. There are several very nice selections and cultivars in the trade, ranging in colour from pure white ('Alba') to dark blue ('Superbum').

Campanula latifolia L

Coming from all over Europe, Siberia, Iran and Asia, the broadleaved 'Forest Bell-Flower' may be one of the most important species for landscape architecture and horticulture. The plant reaches one and a half metres and flowers purple-blue in summer. It can be used in a wide range of applications in the landscape, from formal perennial borders to natural plantings, forests and parks. When planted in the full sun, the species requires consistent moisture. It partners well with Aruncus, Astilbe, Hosta, larger Carex, Luzula and many ferns. Campanula latifolia var. macrantha has similar properties but larger and darker flowers – highly recommended!

Campanula persicifolia L

The peach-leaved Bell Flower, also called Willow Bell or Peach's Bell, hails from Siberia and the Balkans. The species grows to around a metre tall and flowers in summer. It is a beautiful wild perennial naturally growing in meadows and open woodlands that can be used in natural as well as formal designs. It combines well with Achillea, Coreopsis, Hemerocallis, Leucanthemum, Lysimachia, Papaver orientale and tall Phlox. There are many good cultivars in the trade.

1. Group: Small species for rockeries, walls and container plantings

Campanula aucheri DC

This valuable rockery species comes from the eastern Caucasus, Armenia and Iran. It has a carrot-like root and around two and a half centimetre wide purple flowers in spring. It grows strongly and is excellent for filling rock crevices and in dry stone walls; the only drawback is its popularity with snails.

Campanula carpatica Jacq

As the name suggest, this species is at home in the Carpathian Mountains; an English common name is 'Tussock Bellflower'. In its original habitat, it inhabits semi-shaded or sunny places in limestone soils and rocky places. It can be highly recommended for its gentle nature as it self-sows without becoming weedy and characterises locations with the right conditions.

In landscapes and gardens, we usually use horticultural cultivars, hybrids or selections. Some fall true from seed, some must be propagated vegetatively; true from seed are:

'Blaue Clips' with round form and sky-blue flowers; 'Pearl Deep Blue' with dark blue and earlier flowering time; 'Silberschale' with pure white flowers.

Vegetative propagation is required for:

'Kobaltglocke' with dark purple; 'Spechtmeise' with purple-blue flowers and 'Zwergmöve' with silvery-white flowers (Karl Foerster 1956).

Campanula cochleariifolia Lam

The 'Dwarf Bellflower' or 'Fairies' Thimbles' is widespread in the European mountains. It is a small ground-hugging plant growing to only around fifteen centimetres, flowering with a light purple-blue in summer. It is one of the loveliest delicate bellflowers for the rockery or dry-stone walls. It spreads with runners through crevices and creates beautiful little flowering carpets even on poor soils. Good companions are Alchemilla hoppeana, Cerastium villosum, Dianthus gratianopolitanus, Gentiana acaulis, Linum flavum 'Compactum', Saxifraga colyledon, Thymus and Petrorhagia.

Campanula garganica Ten

This species hails from Monte Gargano in Italy and western Greece. It is a very valuable spreading plant for sunny and semi-shaded rockeries and along paths. Its star-like purple flowers appear in early summer. It self-sows without becoming invasive.

Campanula portenschlagiana Schult

One of the best rockery plants, this species comes from Dalmatia and is very reliable, be it on dry, sunny or shady and moist places in rockeries or dry-stone walls. It creeps into and fills cracks and holes in walls or fills spaces between rocks with its purple, four to six-millimetre-wide flowers in summer. Propagation may be done all year round by cuttings.

86 – Campanula portenschlagiana
Courtesy Staudengärtnerei Gräfin von Zeppelin, Germany

Campanula poscharskyana Degen

This species is somewhat like C. garganica but differs in that the plant is larger, stronger growing and more open in habit. The lavender-blue flowers are also much larger. It is ideal for rockeries, dry stone walls, on steep slopes or in tubs. Good partners are Artemisia schmidtiana 'Nana', Dianthus deltoids, Geranium dalmaticum, Heuchera, Potentilla area, Sedum spurium, Stachys discolour and Thymus. Propagation is easy by seed or cuttings.

Cardiocrinum; Liliaceae

There are three species of the Giant Lily and they are at home in the Himalayas, China and Japan. All prefer shade and moisture and are easy to cultivate, remembering the basics: Plant the bulbs shallow (the top of the bulb should only be just under the surface) in autumn into deep, friable soils (leaf litter works great) and do not let the soil dry out. They are lime-fleeing species, so plant together with other species that need acidic soils. The fruit is decorative and usually lasts through winter. Be aware of snails and slugs and leave the plants undisturbed for some years. Propagation is by seed under cold-moist stratification and separation of the bulblets also in autumn, like the planting time.

Cardiocrinum cordatum Thunb

This species comes from Japan and Sakhalin. It grows to two hundred and fifty centimetres high with up to thirty-centimetre-long leaves. The flowers are up to fifteen centimetres long, creamy-white with red-brown dots and a light perfume.

Cardiocrinum giganteum Wall

The largest species, up to three hundred and fifty centimetres tall comes from the Himalayas where it naturally grows on shady, moist but well-drained slopes. The leaves can become up to forty centimetres long and the stem can reach the thickness of an arm with good nutrition. Numerous flowers, white with reddish insides appear in late summer.

87 – Cardiocrinum giganteum
Courtesy Wikipedia

Carex; Cyperaceae

This variable genus contains around two thousand species of grasses in the cool-temperate or temperate zones of the world. There is a large choice for uses in the landscapes and Carex are long-lived and strong plants.

Carex acuta L

From Europe to Asia widespread Sedge that grows to a hundred and fifty centimetres high. This species tolerates flooding and high nutrition levels; hence it is sometimes used to control nutrients in sediment ponds. It may also be utilised to stabilise creek borders or along rivers, but is also nice around water features in the garden.

Carex arenaria L

This specialised Sedge naturally grows in poor and dry sandy soils, often on dunes or in Pine forests. It avoids alkaline soils and should be used like its natural habitat in larger-scale, natural and wild designs.

Carex humilis Leysser

A small sedge that prefers dry-warm slopes and rocky or gravelly alkaline soils from Eurasia. It flowers very early in spring and is good company in dry meadow communities with Pulsatilla, Adonis, Thymus, Globularia and Potentilla.

Carex pendula Hudson

The 'Weeping Sedge' or 'Giant Sedge' is an evergreen species from Eurasia that naturally inhabits moist forest floors and flowers in summer. It is a great structural plant in such places and best used in larger, natural designs.

Castilleja; Scrophulariaceae

This genus is named after the Spanish botanist Domingo Castillejo and contains around two hundred species. With only three exceptions, these inhabit North America and 'listen' to common names such as Indian's Brush', Fire of the Prairies' or 'Painted Cups'. Most are suited to dry and sunny places in the rockery or steppe plantings, dry meadows and the like. It is important to know that they are semi-parasitic and consequently require host plants for best performance. Propagation is by seed in winter; thankfully the young plants do not immediately require a host. Recommended hosts are grasses or other perennials that share the same natural habitat and may be inserted into the pot for cultivation. Both host and Castilleja species are then planted out together with the least possible root disturbance.

Castilleja chromosoma Nels

The 'Desert Paintbrush' originally inhabits dry, poor grasslands and prairies in North-West America, California and down to Mexico. The plant grows to around fifty centimetres high and features a spectacular glowing orange to scarlet-red flower from spring into late summer. Recommended host plants are Bouteloua gracilis, Buchloe dactyloides, Artemisia tridentate and Eriogonum umbellatum.

Castilleja hispida Benth

This species inhabits valleys and can ascend to around two thousand two hundred metres altitude in North America. A common name is 'Harsh Paintbrush' referring to the hairy cover of the entire plant. With around thirty centimetres height, it is a bit smaller than the above. Its flowers are orange and sometimes yellow, also from spring into late summer. Like C. chromosoma it requires excellent drainage and dry sun on poor soils. Host plants are Poa alpine, Festuca rubra, Koeleria cristata, Solidago spathulata, Sedum lanceolatum and Penstemon proverus.

Celmisia; Asteraceae

There are around sixty species of this Asteraceae; most are endemic to New Zealand. Some are in Australia and Tasmania. The use in the landscape is varied, but for most it would be best in rockeries or moors. They avoid calcium and apart from acidic soils require high humidity for best growth. Propagation is by seed with often erratic germination, cuttings or division are possible.

Celmisia argentea Kirk

From New Zealand, this small silvery pillow-forming species naturally grows in acidic moors but also together with other heathland plants in well-drained soils from six to fourteen hundred metres altitude. It flowers white with small, two centimetres across flower heads.

Celmisia coriaceae Hook

The largest Celmisia comes from the southern part of New Zealand where it grows in subalpine and alpine zones between seven and fourteen hundred metres altitude. The leaves are also attractive, with grey-green to silvery green on the top and pure white on the underside. The flowers are four to ten centimetres wide and pure white.

Centaurea; Asteraceae

The genus of the 'Flockenblume' (German for 'Flake-Flower' as in snowflake) is large and has approximately five hundred species. It is most common in Europe, the Mediterranean and Asia minor. There are only a few that are of interest here in the context of use in landscapes and gardens; most like well-drained soils and can tolerate drought very well. Some become woody at the base. Propagation is by basal cuttings or root cuttings, but seeds are usually prolific and germinate well in spring.

Centaurea bella Trautv

A species of rocky forests, it grows to around twenty centimetres and becomes woody at its base. The leaves are dense, grey-green to grey with pink flowers in summer. The long-lived plant is best used in rockeries and very well deserves its Latin descriptive name of bella – the beautiful.

Centaurea dealbata Willd

A strong species that offers itself to wild and natural planting designs. It grows to around eighty centimetres tall and flowers happy pink in summer. If we cut off the fruit after flowering, a second flush of flowers appears in autumn. Good partners are other strong perennials like Telekia speciosa, Aster divaricatus and Buphtalmum salicifolium. There is a gorgeous variety 'Steenbergii' with dark red flowers available that is also good for use as cut flower.

88 – Centaurea dealbata var steenbergii
Courtesy Wikimedia

Centaurea montana L

The 'Mountain Flake-Flower' lives mainly in the Alps, from the Pyrenees to the Carpathian Mountains in open woodlands or on the margins of light forests. The species grows to forty centimetres and flowers blue, sometimes light blue or white. There are good selections available like 'Grandiflora' and 'Violetta' or 'Parham'; all of them are great cut flowers.

Centranthus; Valerianaceae

The well-known 'Red Valerian' is widespread naturally throughout the Mediterranean and Southern Alps on dry slopes, meadows and open shrublands. Use in the landscape is primarily in large natural and wild designs, with appropriate maintenance ensured it is also a valuable addition to the semi-formal landscape or garden. It flowers and self-sows freely even under quite extreme conditions of drought and heat. Due to this strong character, I would not recommend it alongside delicate designs or in formal settings, but used well it can be a wonderful character species. I remember some castle ruins and their surroundings that were almost over-run by Centranthus and looked fantastic and romantic. Propagation is easy by seed.

Centranthus ruber DC

The main species of Centranthus flowering through the warmer parts of the year, its colour varies from light to deep pink and strong reds. There are two cousins; 'Coccineus', with a beautiful scarlet red and 'Albus', with white; both fall true from seed and can be recommended.

Cerastium; Caryophyllaceae

Cerastium are widespread throughout the northern hemisphere, usually on poor soils and meadows. Only a few are really suited to be used in the landscapes and gardens, they are mostly subalpine species that form little carpets or pillows and flower profusely. Suited to rockeries, dry stone walls or sandy/gravelly meadows and heath land design, they require excellent drainage, love full sun and are drought tolerant. Good combinations are Aubrieta, smaller Dianthus and Saponaria. Propagation is easy by division but if larger numbers are required, i.e. for a production nursery basal cuttings of soft tip cuttings have higher yields.

Cerastium alpinum L

This delicate Cerastium is recommended more for the collector, it is essentially tied to gravels and rocks in cultivation and because of its gentle and slow growth can be combined with Saxifraga, small Campanula and other alpines from the same habitat that would be overwhelmed by the stronger Cerastiae. It features grey-white and hairy leaves, flowering white in early summer.

Cerastium grandiflorum Waldst et Kit

Coming from Croatia, Bosnia, Serbia, Albania and Montenegro this large-flowering white Cerastium forms large, greyish mats or carpets and is best used in larger rockeries or cascading down larger dry-stone walls.

Cerastium tomentosum L

The well-known 'Snow-in-summer' originates in Italy and south-eastern Europe. It inhabits dry, exposed places and often moves into disturbed soil but disappears when shaded out by higher plants. Through garden cultivation it is now widespread. The grey-white, small leaves are felt-like and the white flowers appear in early summer. The use in the landscape is variable, best in rockeries, in dry stone walls but also a good species for tubs. Good companions are Aubrieta, small Phlox, Campanula poscharskyana, small Dianthus and Veronica prostrata.

Ceratostigma; Plumbaginaceae

These attractive perennials, sub-shrubs or small shrubs are at home in the Himalayas and the mountains of south-east Asia; some are from tropical north-east Africa. Only some are suited to cultivation in the gardens or for use in the larger landscape. Propagation is by cuttings in spring. I personally value them for their late flowering time in smaller designs and the combination of the brilliant blue together with the lovely orange-red autumn colour of their leaves.

Ceratostigma plumbaginoides Bunge

This lovely perennial, also called 'Dwarf Plumbago' is from northern China and western Tibet. It is a spreading plant with its base becoming woody and forming little thickets with elliptic leaves that turn a nice red in autumn. This species loves the warmth and is one of the few plants that also thrives in dry shade, like that of Cupressus-type conifers which often present difficult planting situations.

Ceratostigma willmottiana Stapf

The 'Chinese Plumbago' is a small shrub growing to around a metre high. It also features a brilliant blue flower late in the growing season and a very attractive autumn colour. It has a large variety of applications and I would plant it close to paths or other places where people can appreciate its beauty close as it is more delicate and does not work over larger distances.

89 – Ceratostigma willmottiana
Work in Canberra, Australia 2005

Chamomilla is now under **Matricaria**

Chelone; Scrophulariaceae

There are eight species in this genus from North America. They occupy damp places in the prairies, swamps and open woodlands, some common names are 'Turtlehead', 'Snakeflower' and 'Shellflower'. These plants should not be allowed to dry out, so plant and maintain accordingly; they survive some dry periods but become unsightly. Flower and fruit are good for the florist; the flowers appear usually in late summer. Good partners are Asclepias, tall Campanula, Eupatorium, Euphorbia palustris, Phlox amplifolia, Physostegia and the tall autumn Asters. Propagation is by seed with light variations in the colour; alternatively, soft-tip cuttings or division will do fine.

Chelone cuthbertii Small

This is the tallest Chelone with around a hundred and eighty centimetres height provided it has enough water supply. The up to three centimetres wide flowers are usually purple but can be pink or cream.

Chelone obliqua L

This species is at home in the south-eastern USA where it grows in moist to wet forests in rich soils. It gets to around a hundred and twenty centimetres with dense, deep pink to purple flowers. I would use it in the landscape as a swamp plant or along the edges of water features, but is equally suited to the moist perennial border.

90 – Chelone obliqua
Work in Canberra, Australia 2005

Chiastophyllum; Crassulaceae

There is only one species in this genus.

Chiastophyllum oppositifolium Berger

The around fifteen-centimetre-high plant comes from the western Caucasus; it is a species more suited for the collector. It requires places that are turned away from the direct sun and is ideally suited for these locations in rockeries or dry-stone walls where it sometimes is hard to find attractive plant material. The Chiastophyllum flowers yellow in summer and propagates easily by cuttings or division, seed is also easy.

91 – Chiastophyllum oppositifolium
Work in Kevockgarden, England 1989

Chionodoxa; Hyacinthaceae (Liliaceae)

In western Turkey, Crete and Cyprus grows the 'Glory of the Snow' in open wood lands, between shrubs and in heathlands. The plants enjoy loose, light soils with good drainage and flower early in the growing season, often pushing up in late snow, hence the common name. They are closely related to Scilla.

Chionodoxa forbesii Baker
Its blue or pink, white-cantered flowers stand up to thirty centimetres tall. It is a strong growing and competitive species that is well suited to be combined with early flowering shrubs like Cornus maas, Forsythia or Viburnum x botnandense.

Chionodoxa sardensis Whittall
Up to forty centimetres tall, this species comes to best presentation when left to grow into large carpets of massed shiny blue flowers under deciduous shrubs or trees.

Chrysanthemum; Asteraceae

The nomenclature of Chrysanthemum has changed significantly and consequently we only look at three main groups here, the Chrysanthemum x Hortorum, the Chrysanthemum x Indicum and the Chrysanthemum x Koreanum groups.

Chrysanthemum alpinum: find under Leucanthemum alpina
arcticum: find under Arctanthemum arcticum
argenteum: find under Tanacetum argenteum
astratum: find under Leucanthemopsis atrata
balsamita: find under Tanacetum balsamita
cinerarifolium: find under Tanacetum cinerarifolium
coccineum: find under Tanacetum coccineum
corymbosum: find under Tanacetum corymbosum
densum: find under Tanacetum densum
erubescens: find under Dendranthema zawadskii var latilobum

haradjanii: find under Tanacetum haradjanii
hosmariense: find under Leucanthemum hosmariense
leucanthemum: find under Leucanthemum vulgare
macrophyllum: find under Tanacetum macrophyllum
mariesii: find under Leucanthemum hosmariense
maximum: find under Leucanthemum maximum
millefoliatum: find under Leucanthemum millefoliatum
nipponicum: find under Nipponanthemum nipponicum
oreades: find under Tripleurospermum oreades
parthenium: find under Tanacetum parthenium
roseum: find under Tanacetum coccineum
rubellum: find under Dendranthema zawadskii
serotinum: find under Leucanthemella serotina
tchihatchewii: find under Tripleurospermum oreades var tchihatchewii
vulgare: find under Tanacetum vulgare
weyrichii: find under Dendranthema weyrichii
zawadskii: find under Dendranthema zawadskii

Chrysanthemum x Hortorum group Bailey

This group is one of the most important Chrysanthemums in Horticulture. Flowering in autumn and into winter there is a great variation of height, colour and single, semi-double or double flowers available. Both the following groups combined are considered as the Hortorum group:

Chrysanthemum x Indicum group

The Indicum group is one of the oldest ornamental plants in garden history and is already documented well over two thousand years ago in China. Likely parents of our modern Daisies are Crysanthemum morifolium, C. zawadskii, C latilobum, C. japonese, C. ornatum and C. makinoi that lead to the great variations in colour, height and hardiness. The gardener Robert Fortune sent and introduced six different colour varieties from Japan to England that formed the basis of our European Chrysanthemum cultivation. There are several thousand varieties now. Cultivation is simple for most, the plants desire rich, organic and friable soils and balanced nutrition which they reward with prolific flowers.

Chrysanthemum x Koreanum group

The Koreanum group originally consisted of very hardy, single or semi-double flowers mainly in pastel colours. A missionary in China sent in 1917 seeds, possibly of Chrysanthemum sibiricum to California. The results of the subsequent breeding is considered as Koreanum group that have been used to increase winter hardiness of the Indicum group.

A few selected from the many thousands I can recommend are:

Altgold – bronze-golden, double, fifty centimetres, late summer
Annabelle – yellow, semi-double, eighty centimetres, early autumn
Burgzinne – red, seventy centimetres, late summer
Edelweiss – white, semi-double, eighty centimetres, autumn
Goldenes Rehauge – golden, double, eighty centimetres, autumn, very frost hardy flower
Hebe – light pink, eighty centimetres, autumn
Julie Lagravere – red-brown, double, seventy centimetres, autumn
Karminsilber – purple-red, seventy centimetres, early autumn
L'Innocence – pink/white, single, sixty centimetres, late autumn, very robust
Orange Ball – orange, double, sixty centimetres, autumn
Red Velvet – dark red, seventy centimetres, autumn

Schwabenstolz – brown/red, sixty centimetres, autumn
White Bouquet – white, double, sixty centimetres, autumn

92 – Chrysanthemum cultivars
Autumn in the nursery of the Countess of Zeppelin, Germany

Chrysocephalum; Asteraceae

Chrysocephalum has been split up from the old genus of Helichrysum.

Chrysocephalum baxteri
This is a nice 'Everlasting' species growing to thirty centimetres high with hairy stems and grey-green hairy leaves. The flowers are papery and white with yellow centres in spring and summer. The plant grows in most soils in sunny positions. Cutting back after flowering is recommended. Propagate by cuttings.

Chrysocephalum semipapposum
The 'Clustered Everlasting' is a tufted perennial with fine silvery-grey leaves and erect stems to sixty centimetres tall. It has clusters of bright yellow flowers in spring and summer and requires full sun. Cutting back after flowering is good practice.

Cichorium; Asteraceae

There are eight known species of Cichorium in Europe, the Mediterranean, temperate Asia, Yemen and Ethiopia. They usually thrive on hot and dry locations and the genus comprises annuals, biennials and perennials. All carry a milky sap that may result in skin irritations in sensitive people on contact.

Cichorium intybus L
The German common name of Wegwarte', loosely translates into 'Custodian of the Path' and indicates one of the places the species is often found, along roads, paths or other marginal locations. It is widespread in Eurasia and occupies disturbed ground. The plant is quite salt-tolerant and often able to survive where other species find life too hard. The perennial is up to a hundred and twenty centimetres high with a clear blue, rarely a white or pink variation in colour. The species is important as a medicinal plant and in

homoeopathy; it is also used as a salad. In post-war Germany, it has also been used as a tea and coffee substitute. In the landscape, I would use it for its lovely blue in wild and natural designs. Unfortunately, the flowers open only during the middle of the day.

93 – Cichorium intybus
On the side of a road in Germany

Cimicifuga; Ranunculaceae

The genus of handsome perennials is at home in the forests of the northern temperate zones or in close association with trees. They should be used accordingly in the landscape; in the shade or semi-shade with high humidity and sufficient soil moisture in rich and friable soils. Astilbe and Hosta are good partners; in sunnier places, the blue of Aconitum complements these perennials well.

Cimicifuga foetida L
Eastern Europe, Siberia and Eastern Asia are home to this up to two-metre-high species. The white, candle-like flowers are beautiful placed against the dark background of the moist forests or tree groups, for best effect I would use the plant in groups rather than single specimens in natural designs of semi-formal borders.

Cimicifuga racemosa Nutt
This species comes from northern America and is often called 'Black Snakeroot', referring to its rootstock. It is more sun-tolerant than most other Cimicifuga species and may be used in warmer locations but provided there is sufficient water available. Up to two and a half metres high, the plant is very handsome with flowers up to a metre long, quite a feature in any design when it is in flower in late summer. Native Americans used it as a medicinal plant and it is still used today.

94 – Cimicifuga racemosa
Courtesy Baumschule Wegener, Germany

Cimicifuga rubifolia Kernery

A smaller species, with up to a metre and a half in height, the plant is almost strictly upright and offers itself as an architectural and structural perennial. As the above, it tolerates somewhat more sun and warmth provided it can draw on sufficient soil moisture. There is a cultivar named 'Blickfang' that can be recommended.

Cistus; Cistaceae

These mainly small, sun-loving sub-shrubs and shrubs are very useful as structural plants in a large variety of applications and produce large, attractive flowers. They are also known under the common name of 'Rock-Rose'. Propagation is best by semi-hardwood cuttings in late summer/early autumn as the shoots harden.

Cistus albanicus E.F. Warburg ex Heywood

This small, up to fifty centimetres high and wide Albanian species flowers white in late spring and early summer and has attractive evergreen foliage.

Cistus creticus

A very variable species, mostly with pink flowers, it has been used often for breeding and several hybrids and cultivars are available.

95 – Cistus creticulus ssp corsicus
Travel study, Corsica

Cistus laurifolius

Up to two metres tall with larger, dark-green foliage it also carries larger, up to ten centimetres across attractive white flowers in early spring. It is widespread around the Mediterranean and popular in horticulture.

Cistus salvifolius

The sage-leaved rock rose grows to around a metre in height with around the same spread. It features white flowers in spring and is a great structural rockery plant.

Clematis; Ranunculaceae

This large genus contains around three hundred species, perennial and woody, climbing or clumping, deciduous and evergreen. These inhabit temperate and subtropical zones of the northern and southern hemisphere and the mountains of Africa. Most species are open forest and woodland dwellers; some inhabit open places of slopes and prairies. Propagation is by cuttings or seed. In cultivation, it is important to observe slightly deeper planting to protect the growing points. Larger plants may be planted around five to seven centimetres deeper; the difference to the original soil surface may be filled with sand or gravel. Smaller plants should be planted between three and four centimetres deeper. Leaf litter is great mulch for most Clematis. This genus is a very important part of horticulture and landscape architecture. The woody climbers are amazing features in combination with fences, pergolas, trees, shrubs or any climbing aid provided to them. The smaller species are valuable for the rockery or alpinum, or structural roles in natural and wild perennial designs or in association with shrubs.

Clematis crispa L

At home in south-eastern USA and inhabiting lowlands and swamps, this up to two hundred centimetres tall, delicate Clematis is a very graceful feature plant. The bell-shaped flowers are up to five centimetres across, the petals are elegantly curved back and range in colour from bright blue, lavender or purple blue with a white throat; one of the common names is 'Blue Jasmine'. Use in the landscape in warm and wet locations and mulch thickly with leaf litter or other organic compost.

Clematis fremontii S. Watson
The 'Prairie-Clematis' originates in north-western America where it inhabits dry and poor limestone soils in full sun. It rarely grows over fifty centimetres high and features hairy stems. The flowers are formed like an urn, crimson-purple to lavender blue in summer. It is a valuable addition to rockeries or steppe and prairie plantings in combination with gravel, rocks and carpet-forming perennials.

Clematis heracleifolia DC
Out of western China and Manchuria comes the 'Trumpet-Clematis', an around eighty-centimetre-high perennial that eventually becomes woody at the base. Its nodding flowers resemble hyacinths, are three centimetres across and are usually purple-blue in late summer and early autumn. I would use it in the landscape in low to medium high wild designs, among ornamental grasses where the late flowering time is very valuable. Please do not over-fertilise this species with too much N as the plant could become 'floppy'.

Clematis integrifolia
There are two varieties, Clematis integrifolia var. integrifolia and Clematis integrifolia var. latifolia that occur from south-eastern Europe to central Russia. The main difference is the height, with var. latifolia being the taller one, around a hundred and thirty centimetres. Both varieties inhabit open forests and woodlands on heavy soils and are upright perennials, not climbing ones. Colours vary from light blue to dark purple; in cultivation, it is important to grow them in heavy soils for best development. There are some wonderful hybrids derived from Clematis integrifolia:

'Aljonushka', around two hundred and fifty centimetres tall with very large purple-pink flowers from summer to autumn, albeit it usually requires some support; 'Aromatica', around a hundred and fifty centimetres tall with four centimetres wide flowers, crimson-purple to blue-purple, also flowering from summer into autumn; 'Herndersonii', around two hundred centimetres tall, prolifically flowering with bells-shaped purple flowers from summer into autumn; Juuli, around two hundred centimetres tall with blue-purple star-shaped flowers from late summer to autumn.

Clematis recta var. recta
Coming from Europe and southern and central Russia in open woodlands, this species grows to around two hundred centimetres and flowers white, around four centimetres across and fragrant in summer. It develops beautiful seed heads that last for a long time, especially beautiful in very early or late light. There are some recommendable horticultural cultivars; 'Grandiflora' with larger flowers, 'Peveril' very prolific flowering and a hundred centimetres tall, 'Purpurea' with purple flowers. All these cultivars develop the lovely seed heads of the wild form.

Clematis tenuiloba Hitch
A wonderful species for the rock garden that comes from heavy, gravelly soils of the USA, Montana, to Arizona, Colorado to North Dakota. It is a small, up to fifteen centimetre tall plant that forms dense, gorgeous pillows with its dark purple flowers. The key to success in cultivation is to learn from its original habitat and place the plant in heavy, gravelly but well-drained soils to keep it dense and beautiful.

Clematis texensis Buckl
Texas and the south-western United States are home to this interesting climber, that grows to around three hundred centimetres, sometimes higher. The only perennial Clematis species with red flowers, it has an urn-shaped inflorescence, three centimetres long and two centimetres wide. The plant is sun and heat-loving and should be given a corresponding location in the garden or landscape with deep, rich and moist soil properties. There are several good cultivars available in the trade.

Codonopsis; Campanulaceae

The genus Codonopsis consists of around thirty species and inhabits temperate zones of central and eastern Asia, some species extend into the tropical zones of Asia. They are mostly climbing plants or of bushy habitat with a fleshy rootstock. Most of the species flower from summer into autumn and the entire plant features a predatory-like fragrance, this being the reason for the common name of 'Tiger-Bells'. Other common names are 'Bonnet Bellflower' or 'Glockenkraut', which translates into 'Bell Herb'. The most common habitats of the climbing types are open woodlands, the shrubby types we find more often in meadows, on slopes or among rocks. They should be used accordingly in the landscape or garden design. The climbing types offer themselves also to be used in association with shrubs; ideally the flowers should be at around eye level to be fully appreciated. Most species thrive best in deep, friable soil that is well-drained, but are by and large uncomplicated and easy to cultivate. Propagation is by seed; one of the things to remember is to put seedlings early on in reasonably large pots to assist with good root development.

Codonopsis clematidea Clarke

This species comes from central Asia and grows prostrate as well as upright to around a metre. All parts of the plant are hairy; the flowers are like broad bells. They are held singly or in small groups on terminal long stems and are light blue with dark nerves and a red-brown or yellow-brown throat in summer. In its original habitat, the species is part of meadow or mountain woodlands. For its use in the landscape, I would recommend wild and natural designs of tall grasses; Aquilegia, Geranium, Ligularia. The species is also suited for large natural rockeries or large dry-stone walls; large because it desires space to expand into and in this way, can develop its full beautiful potential with its abundant flower displays. The best soil for this species is rich and deep loam.

96 – Codonopsis clematidea
Courtesy Stephan Willenberger

Codonopsis lanceolata Benth et Hook
This is a climber from Japan and China that grows to around a metre. The flowers are broad bells in the lightest blue or cream with crimson dots in the throat, in late summer and autumn. It is a very nice species through its interesting colour combination and for the genus late flowering time. I would use it near paths or seating opportunities so people can admire it close.

Codonopsis ovata Benth
This is a smaller, up to thirty-centimetre-high species with striking long flower bells, bright blue with dark veins in summer. It is a very beautiful and outstanding plant for cooler locations with higher humidity as it comes from such areas in the Himalayas. The soil should be rich and deep, well drained and at neutral PH. It does not like transplanting or relocating.

Codonopsis pilosula Nannf

A tall climber, up to two metres high, from north-eastern Asia, this species features bright green flower bells in late summer. It is excellent for strong fences or smaller pergolas, but it can overwhelm smaller shrubs. The flowers are abundant and if the plant is used well can be quite a feature in larger natural designs.

Colchicum; Colchicaceae (Liliaceae)

This genus comprises around ninety species, from Europe, the Mediterranean, central Asia and northern India. The German common name means 'Timeless'. These are poisonous, spring or autumn flowering bulbous plants. They contain Alkaloids (Colchicin) that is used in medicine a well as in plant breeding. For example, we used it for the breeding of Hemerocallis; Colchicin prevents the formation of cell walls and consequently produces Polyploidy. The large autumn-flowering species prefer well-drained, loamy soils and dry summers and may be used as a small feature in the garden. There are options of planting these in meadows or grassed areas without intensive maintenance, Colchicum x agrippinum, C. alpinum, C. autumnale, C. bivonae, C. byzantinum, C. cilicicum and C. speciosum. It is imperative that the grass is not mown before their leaves have died down to receive sufficient photosynthesis. Other than this specific use, Colchicum may be part of larger rockeries or lower, natural perennial planting designs. The autumn-flowering species are best planted in the middle of summer, the spring-flowering ones best in autumn.

Colchicum autumnale Griseb et Schenk

This may be one of the best-known Colchicum, inhabiting moist meadows from Europe, Russia and the Ukraine. A distinct purple-pink, up to fifteen centimetres across flower appears from late summer into late autumn.

Colchicum cilicicum Dammer

In and around Turkey lives this lovely, large-flowered species on stony, rocky slopes, the margins of woodlands and between limestone blocks. It ascends to two thousand metres altitude. The plant reaches around forty centimetres in height and flowers in abundance in autumn.

Colchicum hungaricum Janka

Not only Hungary, but also Macedonia, Yugoslavia, Greece and Albania are home to this very small species that inhabits dry places, slopes, mountain sides or woodland margins up to fifteen hundred metres altitude. The flowers are white or pale purple and appear sometimes throughout winter and into spring, which makes it a delightful surprise in the landscape.

Colchicum luteum Baker

As the name suggests, this species is the only one that features golden-yellow flowers. Rocky mountain slopes in Kashmir, central Asia, India and Afghanistan at altitudes between eighteen hundred and four thousand metres altitude is the original habitat of this plant. The flowers appear in early spring, often in combination with melting snow.

Colchicum speciosum Stev

The Caucasus and Turkey are home to the up to twenty-five centimetres high, very attractive species that inhabits mountain meadows, rocky slopes and disturbed soils between six hundred and three thousand metres. It flowers with a pale or dark purple colour often with a white throat. There is the variety 'Album' which represents one of the most beautiful treasures available in the kingdom of bulbs.

Cononostylis; Haemodoraceae

This genus is related to the Kangaroo Paws and comes from Western Australia. There are around forty-five species and most are very desirable little rockery plants of tufted herbs and heads of woolly flowers ranging from white to yellow or pink. Cultivation is in well-drained soils in full sun. Propagation is by seed or division.

Conostylis aculeata
A tufted plant forming clumps with strap-like leaves to sixty centimetres long. Some subspecies form runners. The flowers are woolly yellow and last long in spring. A hardy and adaptable species that can be used in exposed areas.

Conostylis setigera
The 'Bristly Cotton head' describes a tufted plant growing twenty centimetres across. Yellow flowers with rusty-red tips are borne on twenty-centimetre-high stems in spring.

Conostylis setosa
Up to forty centimetres high, soft and hairy flower heads in spring are characteristic for this very attractive species. Like some roses the flowers are pink in bud and open to white. Propagation is by seed or division.

Convallaria; Convallariaceae

This small genus has only four species which inhabit mountain forests and river valleys with aged, organic soils, preferably with a thick layer of leaf litter. The PH is either neutral or slightly alkaline, except for the Asiatic Convallaria keiski which prefers slightly acidic soils. Covallaria develop best if left undisturbed for many years.

Convallaria majalis
The well-known 'Lily of the Valley' or 'Maiglöckchen' (German for May Bells) grows to around thirty centimetres high. The flowers appear in spring, in the northern hemisphere in May, hence the German common name and are highly fragrant. The plant bears red berries after pollination that are toxic.

Convolvulus; Convolvulaceae

There are around two hundred and fifty species in this genus of annual, perennial, climbing or ground-covering character. They are mainly originating from hot and dry areas around the Mediterranean and extend into sub tropic and tropic zones. Most are rather aggressive and competitive and thought must be given as to their placement. In my opinion, most are best suited to wild and natural designs.

Convolvulus althaeoides
This perennial species grows to around a metre and features pink or purple-pink funnel-shaped flowers throughout summer and autumn. It is a nice plant when used in wild, natural settings where it can grow and expand to its heart's content with its runners; it may also be handy and easy in a tub or container planting.

Convolvulus cneorum
The 'Silver Bush' from Italy, former Yugoslavia and northern Africa is an upright and up to fifty-centimetre-high perennial that becomes woody at the base. The flowers are white or pale pink, often cultivated as an annual and pot plant. Propagation is best by root cuttings in early spring.

Coreopsis; Asteraceae

In this genus, there are some one hundred and twenty species of herbaceous perennials. The German common name is 'Mädchenauge' and translates into 'Girl's Eye'. They all come from North America, inhabiting the sunny prairies with either dry or moist soil properties. Flowering time is from spring into late summer, they are valuable and long-lived perennials. Most propagate easily enough by seed; soft-tip cuttings are another option.

Coreopsis grandiflora Hogg et Sweet
From Georgia, down to Texas the large-flowered and up to eighty-centimetre-high perennial flowers through summer; it is also a good cut flower. There are some hybrids that can be recommended like 'Badengold' or 'Sonnenkind'.

Coreopsis verticillata
The around half a metre high, graceful perennial originally comes from Maryland, Florida, Alabama and Arkansas. It possesses fine foliage and flowers prolifically from summer into autumn. There are some nice hybrids like 'Grandiflora', large and with larger flowers and 'Moonbeam' with pale yellow flowers that give a special appearance in moonlight. They are great partners for other summer-flowering perennials in the semi-formal or formal border like Echinaceae purpurea, Phlox paniculata, Delphinium x elatum and Asters.

97 – Coreopsis verticillata
This picture shows the Coreopsis verticillata in the background of glass art together with Hemerocallis and Potentilla. It was taken in 2013 at the nursery of the Countess of Zeppelin; courtesy Staudengärtnerei Gräfin von Zeppelin, Germany

Correa; Rutaceae

The small genus of around twelve species of Correa essentially occur in south-eastern Australia, apart from a variety of Correa backhousiana which originates in Western Australia. Like Cistus Correa, they are not strictly herbaceous perennials but sub-shrubs and I have included them in this book for the same reason. They are fantastic hardy structural plants, complementing perennial designs. Most flower in winter with bell-shaped flowers which provides valuable colour and food source for birds in the dormant season. Correas prefer well-drained soil in dappled shade but do well in full sun provided there is sufficient reserve moisture, they are surprisingly drought tolerant. Propagation is easy by semi-hardwood cuttings.

Correa alba

This species is a rounded shrub growing to a hundred and fifty centimetres in height, with glaucous round leaves and open white flowers in winter, some flowering may occur throughout the year. The plant requires well-drained, rather poor sandy soils and full sun. It is a tough species that may be used in areas of low maintenance, as screen and structural plant. Through its foliage and white flowers, it combines well with many plants.

Correa baeuerlenii

This is a plant for shade and heavy shade in rich soils that grows to a hundred and fifty centimetres high and across. The flowers are of a somewhat curious shape with a unique calyx and resemble a chef's hat. The plant looks always neat with its foliage and is valuable for dark spots where many other plants fail or grow too leggy.

Correa pulchella

A small, very pretty shrub to fifty centimetres height with orange to pink bell-shaped flowers in winter from Western Australia. It requires well-drained soil and thrives in full sun to semi-shade, in my opinion one of the best Correas with a wide range of applications.

Correa reflexa

This species grows to a hundred and fifty centimetres and is a variable shrub with bell-shaped flowers that may be greenish yellow to deep red with yellow tips in winter. A hardy plant that requires well-drained soils and full sun to dappled shade.

There are numerous lovely cultivars and hybrids of Correa in the trade.

Correa 'Dusky Bells'

This hybrid between Correa reflexa and Correa pulchella forms a low spreading shrub to a metre high and sometimes up to three metres across. Deep pink flowers appear from late autumn throughout winter providing structure, colour and food for birds in a time when very many perennials are dormant.

Correa 'Marian's Marvel'

An excellent, more upright hybrid between C. reflexa and C, backhouseana that grows to two metres. Use the plant in shaded or semi-shaded and well-drained places and do not overfeed, otherwise the branches tend to fall outward. The flowers are pink and lime-green.

98 – Correa 'Marian's Marvel'
Author's home garden in Queanbeyan, Australia 2012

Cortaderia; Poaceae

These ornamental grasses originate in South America, New Zealand and New Guinea. Most are clumping grasses that may grow as high as four hundred centimetres with their flowers. The use in the landscape may be best as structural elements of character plants in grassed areas, they may be a bit overwhelming in subtle perennial displays.

Cortaderia selloana Asch et Graebn
This is undoubtedly the best known and most important species and comes from the steppe, the Pampas of Argentina. Full sun and lots of moisture are ideal for this grass, however it is remarkably drought resistant. The flowers are excellent for a cut-flower display and last very long. It should be mentioned that the serrated and sharp leaves can easily lead to cuts and abrasions, so do not plant close to paths and be careful when handling please.

Corydalis; Fumariaceae

There are some four hundred and fifty species in this genus. It describes annuals or perennials that inhabit Europe and expand into eastern Asia, with very many at home in China. They come in form of alpine dwarfs, carpet-forming creepers, climbing species and up to two-hundred-centimetre-high herbaceous perennials. Many species are easy and beautiful plants in association with shrubs and trees and create lovely spring scenes. Some are strong species through self-sowing and can be used in the landscape in difficult situations where other perennials struggle. Propagation is by seed and it should be as fresh as possible as their viability decreases rapidly. Division is also possible.

Corydalis angustifolia Bieb DC

This in early spring flowering species is at home in northern Iran, the Caucasus and north-eastern Anatolia. Its original habitat are woodlands and shrublands; accordingly, it should be used close to woody ornamentals. It usually flowers white, sometimes with a purple hue, occasionally creamy-yellow varieties occur from seed. It is a self-sowing species that gently occupies suitable places in natural gardens.

Corydalis elata Franch

This Chinese species grows to around forty centimetres high and flowers a little later in spring than most Corydalis. An outstanding feature is its intensely blue flowers held tightly together and making for a brilliant display. It is happy to ascend in up to three thousand metres of altitude and may also be used in rockeries and the alpinum.

99 – Corydalis elata
Meierhof, Sulzburg in Germany 1987

Corydalis flexuosa Franch

This species also comes from China where it grows in moist deciduous forests and shrublands with fertile soils. Around thirty centimetres tall, the plant starts to flower in early spring and keeps putting on displays right into late summer, therefore it is highly recommended for bringing such landscapes alive with an elf-like friendliness. There are several horticultural cultivars available.

Corydalis schanginii ssp ainae Ruksans ex Liden

A graceful species that comes from Kazakhstan where it grows in the shade of Fraxinus, Salix, Crataegus and Amygdalus forests in moist soils. Climbing up to two thousand metres, the species features yellow and white, almost orchid-like flowers in early to late spring. It should be used in the landscape in association with deciduous trees and shrubs where sufficient moisture remains in summer.

Crambe; Brassicaceae

A remarkable genus of perennials of twenty-five species with some annuals included. Most are originated around the Mediterranean or coastal western Europe and some extend into tropical Africa. They are attractive with their grey-green hairy foliage and clouds of numerous small white flowers. The plant resembles a giant Gypsophila and the German common name translates into 'Sea-Cabbage'.

Crambe cordifolia Stev

This species comes from the northern Caucasus and Iran. It lives in rocky, gravelly soils and grows to around two metres height with large, heart-shaped and rough leaves. The fragrant flowers are held well above the foliage in long terminal panicles, usually swarmed by bees in summer. The plant is best used in the landscape as a feature plant, given enough space and in front of shrubs and trees but also in larger perennial borders. Good drainage is essential.

100 – Crambe cordifolia
Courtesy Beth Chatto

Crambe maritima
A coastal plant from the shores of northern and western Europe which inhabits salty sand and gravels. It grows to around seventy centimetres and smells like cabbage. The species presents well all year round and has been used since the late Middle Ages as a vegetable. The grey leaves offer themselves as a structural element in borders or even in xerophytic designs. It combines very well with wild tulips and dwarf Iris.

Craspedia; Asteraceae

The genus Craspedia describes a small group of mainly alpine herbaceaous perennials. They are not yet widely used but have great potential in horticulture.

Craspedia canens
The 'Billy Buttons' were formerly known as C. glauca and are an herbaceous perennial from alpine areas of Australia. The plant forms a rosette of narrowly ovate, grey-green to spathulate leaves to thirty centimetres. The flowers appear in spring and summer and form globular yellow heads up to seventy centimetres high. In cultivation, the species requires good drainage and adapts to a wide range of soils in full sun. Propagation is by seed or division. Use in the landscape in informal and natural designs, rockeries and the alpinum, it may also be used in larger numbers in bedding displays.

Crinum; Amaryllidaceae

A large genus with more than a hundred and thirty species from south and middle Africa and Asia and five from Australia. The genus usually forms large bulbs and features long linear leaves. The flowers are held terminally on strong stems.

Crinum bulbispermum Milne-Redh et Schweick
This species comes from South Africa where it grows up to seventy centimetres tall and has pink, veined flowers that are highly fragrant and up to twenty centimetres wide in summer.

Crinum pedunculatum
The 'Swamp Lily' from Australia and islands north of Australia is an excellent feature plant with its up to a metre long upright leaves and white, open flowers, to ten centimetres across in summer and autumn. As the name suggests, the plant requires damp locations in full sun or part shade and looks great in association with water features. In colder areas, it requires a protected microclimate.

101 – Crinum pedunculatum
Eastern terrace perennial border, Government House in Sydney, Australia 1999

Crinum x powellii hort

This is a hybrid between Crinum bulbispermum described above and Crinum moorei. It has a large egg-shaped bulb from which up to a metre-long leaves emerge. The flowers stand around a metre tall and are pink and pendulous in late summer. The plant develops best if left undisturbed for decades. As planting technique, I recommend planting it so deep that just the top of the bulb is at the soil surface and fertilise with a balanced NPK during the growing season and add some additional potassium after flowering before the plant becomes dormant. Mulch with aged leaf litter. Propagation is easy by separation of side bulbs, but remember that the plants require some time to fully develop their potential.

Crocosmia; Iridaceae

This genus lives in South Africa and resembles Gladioli.

Crocosmia masoniorum

The up to eighty-centimetre-high plant has sword-shaped leaves and orange to orange-red flowers in summer. The flowers are good for the vase and the plant is very tough in summer-dry areas where the winters are mild. It is tough to such a degree that it may overrun weaker neighbours; therefore, I recommend using it in the landscape mainly in wild and natural plantings like steppe or prairies and among grasses.

Crocus; Iridaceae

The well-known genus of Crocus contains around eighty species from the Old World, from Portugal to China, Poland to Jordan. Most species however come from around Turkey. Most Crocus are at home in the mountains and climb up to three thousand five hundred metres altitude in neutral and well-drained soils.

Please note the well-drained aspect as this is a key for good cultivation; otherwise the genus is reasonably uncomplicated with, as almost always, some exceptions.

Crocus in grassed areas

Crocus may be used in grassed areas to great effect but provided the grass is not mown before the leaves have matured and die down. The following Crocus are well suited to be used in grass: Spring-flowering; *C. abantensis, C. flavus, C. gargaricus var herbertii, C. kosaninii, C. reticulates ssp reticulates (only in drier areas), C. veluchensis, C. tommasianus, C. versicolor*. Autumn flowering; *C. banaticus, C. kotschyanus, C nudiflorus, C. pulchellus, C. serotinus ssp salzmanii, C. speciosus ssp speciosus and Crocus vallicola.*

Crocus in the rockery

Wonderful scenes can be created with combinations of spring-flowering Crocus and other spring flowering plants like *Iris danfordiae, Iris reticulates, Iris histrio, iris histrioides, Iris winogradowii, Anemone blanda, Corydalis lutea, Erica, Chionodoxa, Scilla, Daphne cneorum, Helleborus, Primula vulgaris* but also grasses and, for example, low Phloxes etc. Add perennials or small shrubs that are effective in summer and autumn and we get brilliant displays throughout the year.

102 – Wild Crocus in Switzerland, at the Eiger mountain
Courtesy Anton Büchli

Crocus around shrubs and trees

Open, deciduous woodlands and shrubs are great places for many groups of Crocus where they will develop a lovely relationship over the years with their big brothers. It is recommended to use more spring-flowering Crocus as they will receive enough light before the shrubs and trees come into leaf. Do not be tempted to be 'too clean' and remove the leaf litter, as this provides shelter and perfect nutrition for this plant community. Mice are sometimes a problem as they like the Crocus bulbs.

Spring flowering Crocus

Crocus abantensis Herb

From the alpine meadows of north-western Turkey comes this blue flowering Crocus. It sometimes flowers when snow is still around and often grows naturally in association with Juniperus communis ssp nana and Pinus species.

Crocus aerius Herb

Mountain slopes up to two thousand five hundred metres are the home of this strongly coloured, beautiful treasure with dark blue, veined petals and a contrasting red or orange pistil. The species tolerates more moisture in summer than others as in its original habitat summer rains are frequent.

Crocus biflorus ssp biflorus

Italy, Sicily and Rhodes are home of this species that grows there in open, sunny and hot places or in very open Pine forests with sufficient light penetration. The flowers are fragrant, white, or pale purple with strong venation in very early spring.

Crocus chrysanthus Herb

From south-eastern Europe to Asia Minor grows the parent of many of our garden Crocus, in short meadows often saturated by melting snow in spring. The flowers of the species are sulphur-yellow to orange-yellow and are often one of the first signs of early spring. There are numerous cultivars available.

Crocus corsicus Vanucci

In the Macchia or dry scrublands of (guess where) Corsica grows this very beautifully purple Crocus. It ascends to two thousand five hundred metres and requires summer-dry places in rockeries or in association with dry sclerophyll shrubs or trees.

Crocus korolkowii Regel ex Maw

This species comes from northern and eastern Afghanistan, northern Pakistan, Uzbekistan and Tadzhikistan. It thrives in open, rocky or grassy places, often together with Colchicum kesselringii in altitudes of up to three thousand two hundred metres. The flowers are brilliant yellow with the outsides of the petals in a darker brown hue, a remarkable species with one of the earliest flowers in spring.

Autumn Flowering Crocus

Crocus banaticus Gay

Romania, the former Yugoslavia and the Ukraine are home to this lovely, deep-purple or pink-purple Crocus. Its natural habitat are meadows, deciduous forests or shrubs. One of its valuable qualities is its ability to push through ground covers, even Hedera and Vinca.

Crocus goulimyi ssp goulimyi Turrill

This interesting species comes from southern Greece where it lives under Olea and Ficus and around the dry-stone walls often terracing these orchards. The flowers are usually pale or deep purple-blue. There is a highly prized form, 'Mari White', with white flowers.

Crocus laevigatus Bory et Chaub

Greece and its neighbouring islands are the home of this pretty Crocus. It features a great variety in flower colour; from white, yellow, mauve or purple, with or without venation and a prominent yellow or orange pistil. Plants from Greece are highly fragrant. Interestingly, most of the plants from the surrounding islands are not, or are only slightly, fragrant. Cultivation is summer-dry rocky soils and scrublands.

Crocus longiflorus Raf

On rocky slopes, in dry grasslands and along woodland margins grows this beautiful and fragrant Crocus in Italy, Greece, Sicily and Malta. Purple and crimson-purple fragrant flowers appear from early to late autumn; this species prefers alkaline soils and limestone and is a treasure for summer-dry places.

Crocus speciosus M Bieb

The splendid Crocus is differentiated into three subspecies; ssp speciosus, ssp ilgazensis and ssp xantholaimos.

Crocus speciosus ssp speciosus

From the Crimea to the Caucasus, into northern Iran and Turkey into Greece extends the original habitat of the ssp speciosus. It is a highly valuable plant preferring neutral to slightly acidic soils and it ascends to two thousand five hundred metres. The flowers are a gentle to dark purple with lovely dark veins on the outside and a contrasting yellow or orange pistil. It populates mixed woodlands or meadows and can push through and live with ground covers.

Cyclamen; Primulaceae

This is a small but important genus with nineteen species that form tubers and are at home in Europe, the Mediterranean down to Iran and one species from Somalia. Most species prefer dappled or semi-shade and rather drier, alkaline soils. They are ideal to be naturalised or go wild under and in association with deciduous shrubs and trees like Corylus, Hamamelis and similar shrubs but also in open woodlands and forests. They combine well with sub-shrubs like Dryas, Helianthemum and Thymus.

Cyclamen coum Mill Hildebr

This smaller species originates around the Mediterranean and of the most importance is probably the subspecies C. coum ssp coum. The leaves are variable but often kidney-shaped and the flowers vary from white, light pink to deep pink in early spring and appear usually before the deciduous partners produce their leaves. If left to grow undisturbed, the plants form very beautiful and long-lived colonies.

103 – Cyclamen coum
Work in Canberra, Australia 2012

Cyclamen hederifolium Ait

Also from the Mediterranean comes this evergreen and, through its leaves, very attractive Cyclamen. Its original habitats are rocky and gravelly open forests and woodlands where the tubers can grow to around twenty centimetres. The leaves resemble Hedera somewhat but are pretty and unlike Ivy, the plant is very kind to its neighbours.

Cyclamen persicum Miller

This is the parent of the popular and well-known pot plants usually for sale in winter. The species is also from the Mediterranean and descends as far as Tunisia, where it lives in forests or in association with shrubs on alkaline soils. The pot plants live longer if kept in a cool but bright place. If used in the landscape, the species requires good drainage and warmer positions but not in full sun.

Cynara; Asteraceae

There are fourteen species with large ornamental leaves; the two that are discussed here have been in cultivation since ancient times and used as vegetable and medicinal plants. They also have a high ornamental value and their leaf shape, flowers and fruit have been used as ornament in architecture and sculpture. Propagation is by seed or division. In cultivation, a rich and loamy soil with some Calcium is best for them, even that this may be somewhat contrary to the conditions in their natural habitat.

Cynara cardunculus Cardy

From the southern and western Mediterranean and southern Portugal comes the 'Kardone'. It grows naturally on rocky, dry slopes and grasslands to a metre tall. The leaves are up to half a metre long and end in a yellow spike. Flowering time is late summer to early autumn.

Cynara scolymus

This species is cultivated since ancient times and looks like the above, but grows up to two metres with quite large, up to fifteen centimetres across, purple-blue attractive flowers also in late summer and early autumn. The leaves can grow to a metre. Apart from its use in medicine and the vegetable garden the species can be used as a highly ornamental structural perennial in larger borders, formal and semi-formal.

104 – Cynara scolymus
Work in Canberra, Australia 2014

Cyperus longus
Also called 'Sweet Galingale' this tall, up to a hundred and fifty-centimetre-high swamp grass inhabits southern Europe and extends into western Asia. It looks like Papyrus and may be used as a decorative, structural plant around larger water features, but is also very nice as a pot plant. The flowers appear in summer and autumn. Good partners are Butomus or Iris pseudacorus. Propagation is by division.

Cypripedium; Orchidaceae

The genus of the 'Slipper Orchid' or 'Frauenschuh' contains around forty-five species from North- and Middle America and Eastern Europe; some occur in Asia as well. They usually develop a creeping rhizome with upright leaves. Use in the landscape best in natural landscapes near spots where people rest, a great collector's plant.

Cyperus; Cyperaceae

This is a large genus of around six hundred species of grass that is at home mainly in subtropical or tropical areas.

Cyperus badicus Desf
A herbaceous swamp grass growing up to seventy centimetres high with nice, chestnut-brown flowers and fruit; it would be attractive around smaller ponds or water features.

Cypripedium calceolus var calceolus
This beautiful species is in Germany called 'Marien-Frauenschuh' or 'Gelber Frauenschuh' and named after the yellow colour of its large flowers. Its original habitat is Europe where it lives in the dappled shade

of deciduous forests or woodlands on alkaline soils with good drainage always but sufficient moisture during the growing season. The flowers are carried at around forty centimetres above the foliage. It is best left undisturbed and can live a very long life.

105 – Cypripedium calceolus
Courtesy Tracey Willmott

Cypripedium reginae Walt
The 'Royal Slipper Orchid' comes from North America and grows to around sixty centimetres tall. The natural habitat is the shade and semi-shade of trees and it prefers the soil to be moist always, indeed I would put it in a swampy scene.

Cyrtomium; Dryopteridaceae

The genus of the 'Sickle-Ferns' is sometimes grouped under Polystichum.

Cyrtomium falcatum Presl
This is an evergreen fern with attractive foliage that comes from China, Korea and Japan. It requires moisture and shade and can give these locations a special appearance. Use in natural and wild designs.

Dampiera; Goodeniaceae

This genus is endemic to Australia with around seventy species, most of them from Western Australia. They are herbaceous perennials and sub-shrubs of outstanding horticultural value with amazingly brilliant colours from blue to purple, yellow to red. Propagation is by seed, soft-tip and semi-hardwood cutting, some even from leaf cuttings.

Damperia alata
The 'Winged-stem Dampiera' is a multi-stemmed perennial with long, winged stems to a metre. Individual clumps can reach a metre across and the bright green stems carry bright blue flowers, woolly and grey on the outside. In cultivation, the species prefers dappled shade and good drainage, but otherwise it is an adaptable and hardy plant. Propagation is easy by cuttings or division of the clumps.

Dampiera lavandulacea

This up to seventy-centimetre-high upright perennial has conspicuously ribbed, smooth stems and bears clusters of blue flowers in late winter and early spring. It requires full sun and very good drainage; an attractive species that propagates from cuttings.

Dampiera sericantha

An almost prostrate plant to twenty centimetres, to more than half a metre across, that suckers strongly. The flowers are of a glowing bright blue and may appear throughout the year with peaks in spring and summer. It is a great plant for small designs, rockeries or containers and propagates easily by cuttings or separation of the suckers.

Daphne; Thymeleaceae

Traditionally Daphne are really shrubs and woody ornamentals. However, like Helianthemum, Lavandula and Cistus, in cultivation they have a place in perennial designs, complementing or structuring them or many other purposes. There are fifty species of Daphne and they may be small to medium shrubs or sub-shrubs that are deciduous or evergreen. The flowers are generally white, pale or dark pink in tone and praised for their fragrance and produce berry fruits. Propagation is by seed or semi-hardwood cutting; the seed needs to be freed from the flesh. All Daphne are poisonous and care should be taken when handling them.

Daphne should not be planted in places or near playgrounds where little children may be tempted to try the showy red fruits.

Daphne cneorum

This dwarf Daphne is an exceptional beauty that comes from central and southern Europe, extending to the Ukraine. It prefers open Pine forests and meadows with poor and alkaline soils. It grows to a metre wide like a high ground cover with dense foliage. The intense fragrance of its bright pink flowers in late spring or early summer is a unique experience. Good partners are smaller perennials that are not too competitive and adapt to the slowly expanding Daphne. I would use it in the landscape in rockeries or subalpine meadows in natural designs.

Dampiera; Goodeniaceae

This genus is endemic to Australia with around seventy species, most of them from Western Australia. They are herbaceous perennials and sub-shrubs of outstanding horticultural value with amazingly brilliant colours from blue to purple, yellow to red. Propagation is by seed, soft-tip and semi-hardwood cutting, some even from leaf cuttings.

Damperia alata

The 'Winged-stem Dampiera' is a multi-stemmed perennial with long, winged stems to a metre. Individual clumps can reach a metre across and the bright green stems carry bright blue flowers, woolly and grey on the outside. In cultivation, the species prefers dappled shade and good drainage, but otherwise it is an adaptable and hardy plant. Propagation is easy by cuttings or division of the clumps.

Dampiera lavandulacea

This up to seventy-centimetre-high upright perennial has conspicuously ribbed, smooth stems and bears clusters of blue flowers in late winter and early spring. It requires full sun and very good drainage; an attractive species that propagates from cuttings.

Dampiera sericantha
An almost prostrate plant to twenty centimetres, to more than half a metre across, that suckers strongly. The flowers are of a glowing bright blue and may appear throughout the year with peaks in spring and summer. It is a great plant for small designs, rockeries or containers and propagates easily by cuttings or separation of the suckers.

Daphne; Thymeleaceae

Traditionally Daphne are really shrubs and woody ornamentals. However, like Helianthemum, Lavandula and Cistus, in cultivation they have a place in perennial designs, complementing or structuring them or many other purposes. There are fifty species of Daphne and they may be small to medium shrubs or sub-shrubs that are deciduous or evergreen. The flowers are generally white, pale or dark pink in tone and praised for their fragrance and produce berry fruits. Propagation is by seed or semi-hardwood cutting; the seed needs to be freed from the flesh. All Daphne are poisonous and care should be taken when handling them.

Daphne should not be planted in places or near playgrounds where little children may be tempted to try the showy red fruits.

Daphne cneorum
This dwarf Daphne is an exceptional beauty that comes from central and southern Europe, extending to the Ukraine. It prefers open Pine forests and meadows with poor and alkaline soils. It grows to a metre wide like a high ground cover with dense foliage. The intense fragrance of its bright pink flowers in late spring or early summer is a unique experience. Good partners are smaller perennials that are not too competitive and adapt to the slowly expanding Daphne. I would use it in the landscape in rockeries or subalpine meadows in natural designs.

106 – Daphne cneorum
Travel study, Austria 1988

Daphne petraea Leybold
Naturally living in northern Italy on limestone in altitudes between seven hundred and two thousand two hundred metres, this Daphne is a multi-branched and evergreen low species at fifteen centimetres height. Flowers are pink with a cultivar 'Tremalzo' available in pure white. Great to use in small rockeries or on dry stone walls.

Darmera; Saxifragaceae

Darmera peltata Voss

A quite special American perennial species that thrives along creeks and other moist places. The plant grows to a metre high and can cover entire areas. Scaly, thick rhizomes cover the ground and from those long, serrated leaves emerge. They look a bit like shields and can become up to sixty centimetres wide, with prominent veins and lovely coppery red autumn colour. The flowers appear before the foliage and rise to eighty centimetres in spring. This is a very decorative but easy to cultivate species in all soils with sufficient moisture. They look great together with Miscanthus, Iris siberica, Rheum and other structural plants. Propagation is by division; the rhizomes can also be cut into pieces if higher numbers are required.

107 – Darmera peltata
Courtesy Gärtnerei Häussermann Stuttgart, Germany

Delosperma; Aizoaceae

The genus comprises around a hundred and forty species and originates in South Africa. They are succulent and mostly small perennial or woody perennial plants that form pillows and carpets in dry areas.

Delosperma cooperi Hook

A sub-shrub that grows prostrate and features bright red or reddish-purple flowers in arid and semi-arid areas. Use in the landscape accordingly in dry, natural zones and designs. Other good uses are for pot and container planting.

Delphinium; Ranunculaceae

Delphiniums are a well-known and almost essential element in the formal and semi-formal perennial border. There are around four hundred species; most of them occur in the northern temperate zones. They inhabit not only gardens but also dry steppe and grasslands, most garden varieties originate in mountain forests.

108 - Delphinium x 'Liberty'
Work in Canberra 2014

Delphinium for Wild and Natural Designs

Delphinium cashmerianum Royle

This is a pretty and quite tough species from the Himalayas, growing to forty centimetres in height with dark purple flowers in summer. Great to use in cooler, somewhat shadier places in the rockery. Propagation is easy by division and seed.

Delphinium grandiflorum Fish ex DC

A very beautiful but often not very long-lived perennial growing to a metre which comes from eastern Siberia and western China. The bright blue flowers are large and appear in summer, in cultivation it is sometimes treated as an annual. It is lovely used in rockeries or natural gardens and meadows with partners such as Potentilla fruticosa, Helianthemum, Oenothera missouriensis, Coreopsis verticillata and Calamintha nepeta.

Delphinium for Use in the Formal or Semi-Formal Borders and Designs

Delphinium x elatum

These hybrids usually grow tall and feature dense, candle-like inflorescences. They prefer rich, moist soils with sufficient calcium available and require generous fertiliser applications to perform at their best. They are worth every effort. Out of the huge number of great plants in a still growing line I can recommend:

Abgesang; a hundred and sixty centimetres with azure-blue with white centre; flowers late in the season
Chelsea Star; a hundred and seventy centimetres with true purple and small white centre
Cymbeline; a hundred and sixty centimetres, pink with white centre and large flowers
Finsteraarhorn; a hundred and seventy centimetres with dark blue and brown centre
Gute Nacht; a hundred and seventy centimetres with very dark blue flowers
Perlmutterbaum; a hundred and seventy centimetres, light blue with pink, centre is brown
Polarnacht; a hundred and fifty centimetres, deep gentian-blue and white centre
Purpurlanze; two hundred centimetres with purple-blue flowers
Strawberry Fair; a hundred and eighty centimetres, pink with white centre
Zauberflöte; a hundred and eighty centimetres, blue with pink and white centre, late flowering season

Delphinium x belladonna

This group consists mainly of lower growing hybrids compared to the Elatum. Recommended are:

Atlantis; a hundred centimetres, deep purple, second flowering when cut back appropriately Ballkleid; a hundred and fifty centimetres, light blue, also second flowers
Casa Blanca; a hundred and fifty centimetres, pure white, good for cut flower, falls true from seed
Kleine Nachtmusik; a hundred centimetres, gentian-blue
Völkerfrieden; a hundred and twenty centimetres, deep blue with white bee

Delphinium x pacificum

These hybrids originate in California with the aim of falling true from seed. The colours vary somewhat which is an issue, but a disadvantage is that the flower stalk is not as firm and sturdy as with the European types and falls over easily, they need to be staked. If that is considered, the following hybrids are acceptable:

Black Knight; a hundred and forty centimetres, dark blue
Blue Dawn; a hundred and eighty centimetres, bright blue with white centre, good for cut flower
King Arthur; a hundred and eighty centimetres, dark purple with white centre
Summer Skies; a hundred and fifty centimetres, light blue
Galahad; a hundred and fifty centimetres, white
Astolat; a hundred and sixty centimetres, pink

Dendrobium Find under Thelichiton

Derwentia; Scrophulariaceae

Derwentia arenaria
A hardy perennial from Australia with several stems from thirty to a hundred centimetres in height. It has a long flowering period from spring into autumn with its violet-blue inflorescences that are held in long sprays of up to thirty centimetres. It is a hardy plant and valuable for many applications from sun to semi-shade. Cut back after flowering and propagate by division or cuttings.

Dianella; Phormiaceae

The genus of the 'Flax Lilies' consists of around thirty species extending from south-eastern Africa through south-eastern Asia, Hawaii and Australasia. They all have flat, flax-like leaves and may be used as structural and textural plants in groups rather than individuals. They bear bright blue flowers up to a metre high that produce showy globular fruit. They are generally tough and adaptable plants and suitable for areas of low maintenance. Propagation is by seed or division.

Dianella revoluta Brown
This species is commonly known as the Black-anther Flax-lily, Blueberry Flax-lily or Spreading Flax-Lily is a perennial herb of the family Hemerocallidaceae found across the eastern states of Australia and Tasmania. It was first described in 1810 by Robert Brown. It has a wide range of applications in the landscape as a hardy and adaptable species for structure, foliage contrast and is well suited for moist rockeries and planting along borders.

Dianella tasmanica Hook
Known as the Tasman Flax-lily or Tasmanian Flax-lily is a herbaceous strappy perennial herb of the family Xanthorrhoeaceae, subfamily Hemerocallidoideae, found in southeastern Australia and Tasmania. It has leaves to eighty centimetres, flower stem to one and a half metres, and the berries are not edible. Blue flowers in spring and summer are followed by violet berries. Use in the landscape as the above D. revoluta.

Dichopogon; Anthericaceae (Liliaceae)

Dichopogon fimbriatus
This is a very attractive and up to eighty-centimetre-tall species with grass-like leaves and delicate, fragrant mauve flowers in summer. The plant produces tubers and is endemic to Australia. The flowers have a lovely chocolate perfume on warm days; the Aborigines use the tubers as food. The species requires full sun and adapts to a wide range of soils. I would plant it in groups and near paths of seating areas for the perfume. Propagation is by seed or division.

Dianthus; Caryophyllaceae

Across the northern hemisphere are the mostly sunny habitats of the around three hundred species of Dianthus. The majority require excellent drainage and alkaline soils. Dianthus are popular in landscape and gardens and versatile in their use, from natural, informal landscape designs to the formal gardens, pot plants or collector's items for the passionate specialist. The well-known cut flowers originate from Dianthus barbatus, D. caryophyllus and D. plumarius. The dense pillows of D. gratianopolitanus (D. caesius) are excellent in small borders or giving evergreen structure in smaller rockeries, dry stone walls or the alpinum as they look very attractive always, with the flowers of course being the icing on the cake. Natural, wild designs, heathlands or meadows may be filled with D. arenarius, carthusianorum, cruentus, deltoidus, strictus, knappii and superbus. Good partners in the heath-type design are Festuca, Verbascum, Thymus, Helianthemum, Gypsophila, Linum flavum, Potentilla aurea, Campanula poscharskyana, Artemisia schmidtiana 'Nana' and similar species. Propagation of the wild species is easy by seed, hybrids are best by semi-mature cuttings from the ripened growth of summer, some pillow-forming species can be done in winter by small divisions but attention should be paid to not have the moisture levels too high.

Dianthus arenarius

A lovely species forming a loose carpet of small, feathery leaves and white, fragrant flowers that appear from summer to autumn. Great in the heathland garden with Erica, Calluna, Edraianthus graminifolius and species of similar communities.

109 – Dianthus arenarius
Courtesy Baumschule Eggert, Germany

Dianthus barbatus

The 'Sweet William' is at home in the Pyrenees and extends into the Balkans, Russia, Siberia and China. The perennial grows to fifty centimetres and has a great colour variation in its flowers, from white to pinks and reds including almost black-red, single, semi-double or double, striped or spotted.

Dianthus carthusianorum

Named after the religious order, this beautiful Dianthus lives on sunny hills, in meadows and along rural pathways and fields. It grows to thirty centimetres high and flowers deep red from summer to autumn. I would use it in natural designs or in heathlands on dry, alkaline soils.

110 – Dianthus carthuisanorum ssp carthusianorum
Berlin, Germany 1990

Dianthus deltoides

The 'Maiden Pink' or 'Heide-Nelke' (Heath-Dianthus) is widespread through Europe and temperate Asia. It grows naturally in gravelly and dry areas or in grasslands, becomes up to fifteen centimetres high and flowers deep pink in summer.

Dianthus gratianopolitanus Vill

This species forms dense pillows with its grey-green to blue-green leaves and as such is attractive throughout the year. The flowers are mostly pink and appear in late spring to early summer. It is in horticultural terms one of the most important Dianthus, with numerous hybrids and cultivars. All require dry, well-drained and sunny locations and calcium available in the soils. Great on dry stone walls, also in tubs and containers with species from the same background.

Dianthus petraeus Waldst et Kit

A very special plant from Bulgaria, this small Dianthus has pointy, strong and dense leaves and this is the reason for its German common name of 'Igel-Nelke', which translates into something like hedgehog-Dianthus. The flowers are small, fine and of pure white. They feature an intense fragrance that is strongest in the evening. Flowering time is late in the season and the plant appears to have grown a mystic white mist across it. The plant prefers sunny and dry places but is easy to grow.

Dianthus plumarius

The 'Feder-Nelke', German for 'Feather-William' originates in Eastern Europe. It has a strong fragrance in its white or pink flowers that are finely sectioned, like the feathers of a bird. Flowering time is summer. Like in D. gratianopolitanus there are numerous hybrids and cultivars available.

Dianthus superbus
The magnificent Dianthus extends from Europe through to Siberia, Manchuria and Japan. It grows to sixty centimetres with large flowers that are highly fragrant from summer to autumn. In its area of origin, there are great variations in their appearance. Different to other Dianthus, this species loves moisture and sometimes grows to the water's edge or in swamps, but mostly in moist meadows and grasslands.

Diascia; Scrophulariaceae

This is a genus from South Africa where most species live in the mountains but with temperature ranges not much below minus ten degrees Celsius. They love the sun and reasonable moisture in the soil that should not dry out in summer. Propagation is easy by cuttings and Diascia are graceful flowering plants for perennial borders.

Diascia barberae Hook
A dense, to thirty-centimetre-high perennial with usually pink flowers. Excellent for along paths and borders or hanging over stone walls, also in pots or container plantings.

Diascia integerrima Benth
A slenderer species that grows to fifty centimetres tall with iridescent dark pink flowers. It is one of the most beautiful Diascia.

111 – Diascia cordata 'Ruby Fields
Work in Badenweiler, Germany 1992

Dicentra; Fumariaceae

Most people know the 'Bleeding Heart', a species from a genus of around twenty, originally from North America or East Asia. They have fleshy, fragile roots with lovely, fern-like foliage and most prefer shady or semi-shady places in moist soils. Combinations with Aquilegia, Epimedium, ferns, Hosta or Polygonatum are very effective and produce magic, fairy-tale scenes under and with shrubs and trees.

Dicentra eximia Torr

From the USA, the dwarf Bleeding Heart grows in heavy and summer dry soils. It is a fragile plant, up to forty centimetres high with flowers usually pink, but sometimes red or white in spring. There are several hybrids available.

Dicentra peregrina Makino

This beautiful but a little difficult to cultivate Dicentra originates in eastern Asia, Japan, Sakhalin, Siberia and Kamchatka. It grows there in sandy and gravelly soils, flowers bright purple to pink and deep red or pure white in summer. The species does not like a high organic content in the soil, so try to cultivate in gravel and sand. It does not take well to drying out or too much sun, at the same time excellent drainage is important and high light levels preferred. As with some special orchids, a careful preparation of the soil and choice of the right location is the key to success.

Dicentra spectabilis

This is the species known as the 'Bleeding Heart' with its unique pink and white, sometimes pure white, flowers in spring. It is a medium-sized perennial of up to a metre with light, lovely foliage. However, it enters a semi-dormancy in summer and the leaves turn slightly yellow. In some climates, it dies back altogether. Therefore, it should be combined with and planted behind other perennials that become effective in summer and through to autumn and winter. The plant prefers to be undisturbed for some years.

112 – Dicentra spectabilis 'Valentine'
Courtesy Ingrid Meier

Dichopogon; Lomandroideae

Dichopogon fimbriatus
The species has up to twelve leaves that are linear or lanceolate in shape and are up to sixty-five centimetres long and one to twelve millimetres wide. The racemose inflorescence is up to a metre high. This appears between August and January in the species' native range. The individual, drooping flowers range in colour from pale mauve to dark purple. The common name 'chocolate lily' alludes to the scent of the flowers which resembles chocolate, caramel or vanilla. It is somewhat frost-tender but I have grown it in a sheltered spot in Queanbeyan in Australia for many years.

113 – Dichopogon fimbriatus
Courtesy Wikimedia (reference 5199984697)

Dictamnus; Rutaceae

Dictamnus albus
A remarkable and long-lived perennial, growing to a metre with stems becoming woody as they mature. Plants have been recorded as more than a hundred years old. It is at home in the southern Mediterranean and related to the lemon. Some consider this to be the 'Burning Bush' of the Bible. Dictamnus grows naturally on sunny hills and shrublands, on poor limestone soils. In cultivation, I would use it in steppe or semi-arid natural designs; or in larger rockeries in association with white limestone. Once established, it should not be transplanted. Great partners are Iris barbata, Iris pallida, Linum flavum, Centaurea ruthenica, Acanthus spinosus, Cytisus purpureus, Cistus, Artemisia and species from a similar background. Propagation is by seed. Harvest of the stem is best when the first fruit is starting to discolour; put in large paper bags. Fresh seed germinates best – the seed requires light to germinate. Older seed benefits from cold-moist stratification. Seedlings usually need around three to four years to flower.

114 – Dictamnus albus
Courtesy Krzew Mojzesza

Dierama; Iridaceae

A lovely common name for this robust plant is 'Fairies Fishing Rod' or 'African Harebell' and the genus indeed comes from either tropical or southern Africa.

Dierama pendulum Bak

From a thick rootstock spring long, thin and grass-like leaves. Above those appears around a metre-long flowering stalk that carries nodding, bell-shaped flowers in white, pink or red through late summer.

Dierama pulcherrima Bak

This species is quite like the above but differs in the later flowering time, throughout autumn and a silvery appearance of the petals. It is a handy and tough structural plant that I would use in the informal or semi-formal perennial planting or a natural design. There are some pretty cultivars available.

115 – Dierama pulcherrima
Courtesy Angelika Kaufmann

Dietes; Iridaceae

Dietes robinsoniana
The plant resembles small flaxes with its broad, sword-shaped leaves that grow to a hundred and fifty centimetres long and are usually of a grey-green colour. White. Iris-like flowers up to seven centimetres across with yellow centres appear in spring. This is a handsome specimen plant for normal garden soils or landscape situations with sufficient moisture, it grows well in full sun or semi-shade. Propagation is by seed or division.

Digitalis; Scrophulariaceae

The genus containing the famous 'Foxglove' has around twenty-five species in western and southern Europe, north-west Africa and extends to middle Asia. They are handsome wild species, best used in natural and informal designs, but also to great effect in the perennial border, cottage garden or seasonal planting. Naturally they occur in the semi-shade or open areas of forests and woodlands; they often come up after trees have been felled or following storm damage. This indicated that they are well suited to be 'let go' and self-sow as they will occupy suitable places by themselves. Propagation is by seed (light is required) and is very easy.

Digitalis ferruginea
Coming from southern Europe and extending into Turkey and the Lebanon, this tall, up to a hundred and eighty-centimetre-high perennial (sometimes biennial) plant has yellow-red to rusty red flowers in late summer. Its leaves form a nice evergreen rosette in winter.

Digitalis grandiflora Miller

Europe, Siberia and Turkey are home to this perennial that is, unlike most Digitalis, very long-lived. It occupies grassy meadows, open areas in forests and places along shrubs and trees. The plant becomes around a metre tall and flowers through summer. Great for group or massed plantings.

Digitalis purpurea

This may be the best-known Foxglove and it comes from Western Europe, occurs in Ireland and down south into Spain and Morocco, also Corsica and Sardinia. It is a biannual plant growing to around a hundred and twenty centimetres with long beautiful flowers in shades of white, pink and red and dotted throats in spring and summer. The natural habitats are open woodlands, forest margins and meadows. It has diverse uses in the landscape and gardens, from wild, natural designs where it can self-sow to the cottage garden and perennial borders, but also great seasonal displays can be created. I remember in the Royal Botanic Gardens in Sydney I did a planting along the Herb Garden in 1996 with around three thousand Digitalis purpurea.

116 – Digitalis purpurea hybrids

Dionysia; Primulaceae

This is a special, small genus of around forty species at home in Turkey, Iran, Afghanistan, western Pakistan, Tadzhikistan and Oman. They are alpines growing on sunny, semi-shaded but mostly shady places on limestone between five hundred and four thousand five hundred metres altitude. They are sub-shrubs and form pillows or carpets. Flowering time is early to late spring with colours ranging from yellow, pink, blue, red or purple. It should be said that this is a speciality for the passionate collector, either creating small delicate rockeries or in an alpine house with the right conditions. These plants need close attention and want to be admired close.

Dionysia afghanica Grey-Wilson

As the name suggests, the species comes from Afghanistan where it grows on shady limestone rocks and under overhangs to around one thousand four hundred metres altitude. The plant features dark green pillow-forming leaves and grows to around twenty centimetres across; the flowers are up to seven millimetres, purple-blue with dark eye. Flowering time is very early in spring; it is often one of the first flowering plants in spring. It flowers abundantly and is a very sought-after species among collectors.

117 - Dionysia afghanica
Travel study, Afghanistan 1984

Dionysia archibaldii Wendelbo

From Iran comes this climber that ascends between two thousand five hundred and four thousand three hundred metres. It grows on limestone, features grey, powdery and hairy leaves and light purple-blue or pink flowers with a white eye.

Dionysia involucrata Zapr

On shady or semi-shaded limestone rocks in Tadzhikistan grows this beautiful species forming dense pillows. It flowers in spring with deep pink with white eye, sometimes pure white.

Dodecatheon; Primulaceae

This is a small genus with around fifteen species from North America. Common names are 'Shooting Star' or 'God's Flower'. They are related to Primulas and grow in moist meadows and together with shrubs and trees or rocks with sufficient water on or around them. They are delicate and small perennials for smaller natural gardens or rockeries, more for the plant collector than the landscape architect or larger designs. Propagation is by seed or by taking off roots with a growing tip.

Dodecatheon media

In meadows, open woodlands or prairies lives the 'Praise of Ohio' as this Dodecatheon is also called. It grows to thirty centimetres, with the flowers up to fifty centimetres tall and can carry over a hundred showy flowers on good specimens. The flowers appear in summer and are purple-red with yellow stamens.

118 – Dodecatheon media
Staudengärtnerei Gräfin von Zeppelin, Germany

Doronicum; Asteraceae

Most species of this genus are alpine plants; there are around thirty of them. They are popular and graceful spring-flowering plants and hold well in the vase too. They do best in loamy soils but are easy. Propagation is by division or seed.

Doronicum grandiflorum Lam

This species comes from the limestone zones of the Alps, from the Pyrenees to Corsica. The plant gets to fifty centimetres in height and has large, golden-yellow flowers in spring, one of the most beautiful Doronicum species.

119 – Doronicum grandiflorum
Courtesy Stephan Willenberger

Doronicum orientale Hoffm

From south-eastern Europe extending to Asia Minor comes this early flowering species with yellow flowers that are good as cut flowers. I would plant it in natural designs together with Brunnera, Frittilaria and Dicentra, good drainage is important.

Doryanthes; Doryanthaceae (Agavaceae)

The 'Gymea Lily' from Australia is a spectacular feature plant with up to two metres long, broad sword-like evergreen leaves.

Doryanthes excelsa

The leaves of this species form a dense, impressive clump which is a structural feature throughout the year. In cool climates, the leaves do discolour somewhat. Out of this clump of leaves grows an immense, strictly upright flower spike, up to six metres in height with bright red flowers in spring and summer. These flowers can last up to two months in the vase if the stem is cut back regularly. The leaves are also used in floral displays. I used to cut a wedge shape into their base to make it easier to arrange them. The plant requires well-drained soils in full sun. Due to its size, the plant should be used in larger landscape context, large rockeries, informal large designs. Amazingly, I find that both dry and wet designs appear to suit the species well as context. The plants need some maturity, around five to seven years to flower. Propagation is mainly by seed but division is possible, if a little awkward.

120 – Doryanthes excelsa
Courtesy Phil Bend

Doryanthes palmeri

This species is like D. excelsa described above but differs in that the flower spikes are a bit shorter and pendulous and the flowers are borne along it. Equally spectacular and its use in the landscape is the same as for the above.

Dracophyllum; Epacridaceae

The species of this genus from Tasmania are primarily used for their structural foliage in damp and wet places from shade to dappled shade. They can create somewhat surreal and fairy-tale-like scenes along water features, waterfalls and rocks and are very interesting.

Dracophyllum oceanicum
This sub-shrub grows to around two metres and has recurved linear leaves fifteen centimetres long. It has terminal flower spikes of a cream-white in spring. Naturally, this species grows along cliffs in Jervis Bay in New South Wales, Australia. I would use it in exposed situations associated with rocks. Propagation is by cuttings.

Dracophyllum secundum
This species is best in shade or semi-shaded conditions with ample moisture. It has a trailing habit and nicely colonises rocky habitats around water and should be used accordingly in the landscape. Lovely terminal flower spikes with cream or pale pink tubular flowers in spring. Propagation by seed or cuttings.

Drosera; Droseraceae

The genus of the 'Sun-Dew' is at home mainly in the southern hemisphere and inhabits swamps, moors and other wet places. Consequently, they have specialised uses, either in natural areas as described here or for the plant collector providing the appropriate habitat. Propagation is by seed or leaf cuttings.

Drosera arcturi Hook
This species inhabits swamps of the subalpine zones of New Zealand, Tasmania and south-eastern Australia but sometimes descends even to sea level. Leaves are around twelve centimetres long, the flowers are up to fifteen centimetres high.

121 – Drosera arcturi
Schopfloch, Germany 1992

Drosera rotundifolia
In Europe, northern Asia, the Lebanon, Caucasus, Japan and North America lives the round-leafed Sundew. Its leaves are almost round and feature the red dew-tipped hairs, the flowers are white, one centimetre and rise from the rosette.

Dryas; Rosaceae

A small, interesting genus with only two species of sub-shrubs that form evergreen carpets in the northern hemisphere in arctic and alpine zones. They ascend to around three thousand metres and grow in limestone or granite mountains but are very tolerant of other soils. Their use in the landscape is best in rockeries or the alpinum, draped across rocks or hanging down over them. However, one needs to be careful to select strong partners or keep them apart from more delicate ones as the plants usually grow fast and strong. The feathery seeds are very beautiful in early or late light.

Dryas drummondii Richardson ex Hook

This Dryas comes from North America where it is also called 'Yellow Mountain Avens'. From wet, sandy places at sea level to the high mountains grow the up to twenty-centimetre-high carpets of this species. The nodding yellow flowers appear in summer.

Dryas octopetala

This species is at home in the northern temperate and polar zone and inhabits tundra, meadows and mountains up to four thousand metres. It naturally grows in gravelly and rocky soils by itself or in combination with grasses, dwarf shrubs and other species of that habitat. It flowers earlier, in late spring or early summer with white upright inflorescences above dark green, leathery leaves.

122 – Dryas octopetala
Travel study, Switzerland 1993

Dryopteris; Dryopteridaceae

An important genus of around two hundred and fifty ferns, mainly distributed in the northern hemisphere but extending into Australia.

Dryopteris affinis Jenkins

The German common name translates into something like 'Gold-Scaled Fern' and it describes a pretty fern with up to a metre-long leaves. It grows on moist soils in semi-shaded places, usually in association with trees and shrubs or along creeks. The preferred soil type is loam but this is not that important, moisture is though. It appears lovely with its first leaves unfolding in spring against a dark backdrop, where it really appears to be golden. There are numerous horticultural cultivars available.

Dryopteris cristata Gray

Northern Europe, northern Asia and North America are all home to this a bit special species of moisture-loving fern. Given sufficient moisture, it adapts reasonably to more sunny locations and does well with partners like Cornus canadensis, Gaultheria procumbens and Ericaceae.

Echinacea; Asteraceae

The genus of the Cone Flower has been separated from Rudbeckia and contains nine perennials with black and fleshy roots. All are used as medicinal plants.

Echinacea purpurea Moench

The most important species of this genus is widely used and apart from medicine also produces great cut flowers and is a valuable ornamental perennial. It originates in the USA where it grows up to a metre and a half tall and flowers reddish-purple in late summer and into autumn. It can be used widely in landscapes and gardens like naturally in open woodlands or prairies but also in perennial borders or the cottage garden, it is also farmed for medicinal purposes.

123 – Echinaceae purpurea
Work in Canberra, Australia 2014

Echinops; Asteraceae

There are seventy-five species in this genus but only a few are used in landscapes and gardens. The perennials are tough, thistle-like and occupy steppes, rocky slopes and disturbed soils. The ornamental species are best shown off in exposed situations with other strong, sun and heat loving perennials like Achillea filipendulina, Inula, Gypsophila and Verbascum and combination with grasses. They are useful as cut and dried flowers, they accept any well-drained soil. Propagation is best by root cuttings or division, but seed is also possible.

Echinops banaticus Rochel ex Schrad

South-eastern Europe is the home of this recommendable species growing to a hundred and fifty centimetres height. The flowers are large and blue in summer, 'Taplow Blue' is one of the best cultivars available.

Echinops ritro

A widespread species living in the Balkans, the Alps, Turkey, the Caucasus, western Siberia and central Asia. The plant is up to a metre tall and is a bit thorny. The flowers are round, steel-blue balls and colour up already before fully ripe. The species can self-sow in the right places and is not only for natural designs but also for the more formal perennial border a special focus plant.

124 – Echinops ritro 'Veitch's Blue'
Courtesy Lambley Nursery, Australia

Echium; Boraginaceae

A very interesting, different genus from Europe, the Canary Islands, the Azores, western Asia and Africa. Most species are short-lived perennials or sub-shrubs with hairy leaves and stems. Their character suggests the use in wild, natural steppes and rockeries, they like rocky, sandy or gravelly and open soils. Bees love them! Their prominent inflorescences stand out and are very attractive, but the body of the sub-shrubs I find also very handy as structure in herbaceous borders. They are somewhat frost-tender, survive infrequent light frosts but not repeatedly hard ones.

Echium russicum Gmel

This species comes from central Europe, Turkey and extends into Russia. Its original habitat is dry heathlands, steppes and open Pine forests. The plant develops a deep taproot and features up to a metre-tall flower spikes with red-brown, sometimes white flowers.

Edraianthus; Campanulacee

Ten species from southern and south-eastern Europe represent this genus that is closely related to the Bell-Flowers. They are recommended for the rockery or alpine designs in sunny, dry locations or dry-stone walls. Propagation is by seed.

Edraianthus dinaricus Wettst

From Dalmatia in Yugoslavia comes this pretty plant with deep purple flowers in summer, the petals are more open than in Campanula.

Edraianthus graminifolius DC

This very attractive small jewel features dark, deep purple flowers and grass-like foliage. It comes from Italy, Romania and Slovenia.

125 – Edraianthus graminifolius
Courtesy Wikimedia

Edraianthus tenuifolius Waldst et Kit

This species comes from the western half of the Balkans. It has small lanceolate leaves to five centimetres and purple-blue flowers held in clusters.

Epacris; Epacridaceae

The lovely genus of Epacris resembles the south-African Erica in habit and flower with their beauty. They require well-drained soils but need ample moisture; they should not dry out. They then do well in full sun but also perform admirably in dappled shade. Pruning after flowering produces compact plants and propagation is best by cuttings of semi-hardwood in later summer. Epacris impressa was cultivated in nineteenth century England by many plant enthusiasts.

Epacris impressa
This species is in nature a straggly shrub to a metre high with pendent tubular flowers to two centimetres long throughout the year with a peak in spring. It is the floral emblem of the state of Victoria in Australia. Colours vary from white to deep red. Propagation is by cuttings, use in the landscape is in heathland designs or rockeries and birds love the nectar.

Epacris longiflora
This species describes a shrub like E. impressa but it has displays of red tubular flowers with white tips that are up to three centimetres long. The flowers are produced throughout the year. This is a very attractive plant through its long flowering period and is excellent hanging over rocks and dry-stone walls.

126 – Epacris longiflora
Courtesy John Simmons

Epilobium; Onagraceae

This genus of around two hundred and twenty species contains low ground covers, upright perennials and sub-shrubs that live in the temperate zones of the world but extend even into the arctic zones. There are views that the genus Zauschneria are included in Epilobium; this may be justified from a botanic perspective, but it needs to be remembered that from their use in landscape architecture and horticulture the old Zauschneria are quite different to all other Epilobiums. I have included them here in Epilobium with reference to their old names.

Epilobium angustifolium
The 'Narrow-leaved Epilobium' or 'Weidenröschen' (German for Little Pasture-Rose) inhabits moist places in open forests, at the margins of woodlands or disturbed land, but also follows creeks and rivers. It lives in the northern hemisphere and is a great pioneer plant able to stabilise soils along moving and still water. The perennial grows to a hundred and twenty centimetres and flowers with a very glowing

pink from summer into autumn; sometimes white forms occur. Use this plant very carefully in the landscape or garden due to its pioneer characteristics. It can overwhelm vegetatively and by seed small spaces quickly. Rather I would play to this strength by using it in large open, natural and wild landscapes and parklands of low maintenance where it can populate areas to their advantage.

127 – Epilobium angustifolium
Courtesy Klaus Mödinger

Epilobium obcordatum Gray

This American species forms carpets in subalpine and alpine zones where it lives in rocky and gravelly soils that it stabilises. It is a beautiful plant with blue flowers in late summer but needs to be given the right environment in an alpine rockery.

Zauschneria now Epilobium

This southern group of sub-shrubs is highly attractive but requires excellent drainage and a hot, sunny place, best in poor soils. Propagation is by seed or semi-hardwood cutting. As planting community, I would recommend Ceratostigma, Yucca, Cistus and similar plants from a semi-arid steppe or prairie like background. The German common 'Kolibri-Trompete' name translates into something like 'Kolibri-Trumpet' which refers to the flower shape.

Epilobium (former Zauschneria) canum ssp canum

This species comes from California where it lives on dry, rocky slopes. It is a small, multi-branched sub-shrub with grey to white felt- or silk-like foliage and deep crimson to scarlet red flowers from autumn into winter. May also be kept as a pot or container plant and it is well worth the effort!

Epimedium; Berberidaceae

The genus of the 'Elf-Flowers' is a large perennial group of around forty within the greater Berberidaceae family. They grow from Algeria to Japan, some are summer-green, some are evergreen. Epimedium are essentially forest and woodland plants where sufficient moisture is available. They cover ground densely and should be used as such; they are great weed suppressors and very lovely plants for shade at the same time.

Epimedium alpinum

This European species has been documented in garden cultivation for around four hundred and fifty years. It is best suited to cover large natural areas in combination with Omphalodes verna, Oxalis acetosella, Carex umbrosa and Asarum europeaum. Flowering time is spring with reddish-yellow flowers that stand well above the foliage.

Epimedium perralderianum Coss

This evergreen perennial comes from Algeria where it grows in forests of Cedrus, Abies numidica, Acer obtusatum, Populus tremula and Quercus species. It is a highly valuable ground cover for natural areas.

Epimedium pinnatum ssp colchicum Fisch

This species is of great importance in landscapes and gardens where many cultivars of it are being propagated. Best propagation method is horizontal root cuttings in winter that may be laid into seed trays. Golden yellow flowers appear in spring and are held well above the foliage; they do look like little elf spirits floating above a mini-forest.

Epimedium grandiflorum Morr

From Japan comes this variable species with large white, pink or purple flowers. The foliage is usually reddish-brown when it first appears in early spring and beautifully veined. The plant requires in cultivation more moisture than other Epimedium.

Epimedium elatum Morr et Decne

The unusual species from Kashmir grows up to a hundred and fifty centimetres high and has finely dissected foliage, it resembles Thalictrum somewhat and features often more than a hundred small flowers on a single stem. They are best in warm, moist conditions under trees.

128 – Epimedium x versicolour
Baumschule Häussermann, Stuttgart, Germany

Eremurus; Asphodelaceae

The genus of the 'Desert Candles' or 'Foxtail Lilies' has around fifty different species and originates in western and central Asia. They are at home in hot, dry and stony places or grassy steppes and prairies but experience a cold winter. They have an unusually shaped central bulb with fleshy, spider- or octopus-like rhizomes. That is how I will always remember them because during my apprenticeship my master took one out of the dry sphagnum moss they were delivered in and quickly held it into my face whilst wobbling the 'spider legs' around. Some are quite large and as spiders, would be truly frightening! Back to botany. Their original habitat is baking hot and dry in summer, usually without any rain, whilst the plant comes to life in spring with the moisture provided by the melting snow. If we combine this knowledge with the fleshy bulb, we come up with the best way of cultivating them. Plant the bulbs deep and in a hot and dry location that is very well drained, especially in areas of summer rainfall. In Germany, I used to build up the garden beds with Eremurus on a thick layer of rough gravel. Once planted, Eremurus do not want to be disturbed and should be left alone for many years. They do benefit from a balanced fertiliser high in potassium (K) in spring when they also want moisture. The effort put into their cultivation is well rewarded with exceptional flower spikes, the candles that start flowering from the base up and can become more than a metre with close to a thousand single flowers, very spectacular! They are great as cut flowers too. The planting community or design naturally needs to be matching these environmental conditions, plants like bearded Iris, Oriental Poppies, Paeonia lactiflora, Asphodelus, silvery Salvia and species from a similar background are great partners. One of the techniques I use is to put Eremurus a bit back behind a species that is effective in summer and autumn/winter because the Eremurus dies completely back after flowering. If a garden is designed this way, another plant then takes over the structural role. When planting place the rhizomes flat on the ground and fill in around them carefully and gently as they are fragile.

Eremurus himalaicus Baker

From Afghanistan and the north-western Himalayas comes this up to two hundred and fifty-centimetre-high species. It is one of the first to emerge and features white, veined flowers in spring.

Eremurus robustus Regel

The largest of the Eremurus comes from Afghanistan and central Asia, it grows to three metres tall and is an unforgettable sight with sometimes more than a metre long pink or sometimes white inflorescence in early summer.

Eremurus stenophyllus Baker

This smaller species is widespread through Afghanistan, central Asia, into the Iran and western Pakistan. Its habitat ascends to two thousand five hundred metres altitude and the leaves are fine with a flower spike up to a hundred and fifty centimetres tall, usually bright yellow, turning orange as it matures in summer.

129 – Eremurus stenophyllus in natural habitat
Work and study in Tajikistan

There are numerous cultivars available today, consult your local suppliers.

130 – Eremurus hybrid 'Romance'

Combined with Australian native flora in author's home garden in Queanbeyan, Australia; an unusual combination of flora but by matching growing conditions and adaptive appearance of the different species the design makes sense.

Erigeron; Asteraceae

This genus is closely related and similar in appearance to the Aster; main differences are in the finer, thinner petals. There are around a hundred and fifty species, but of greater importance in the landscape and gardens are the numerous hybrids. They are great cut flowers that often re-flower after being cut back when there is sufficient water and food available. They are best used in formal or informal perennial borders alongside Rudbeckia, Helenium, Monarda, Heliopsis, Oenothera, Phlox and Gypsophila. Ornamental grasses and flowering shrubs and small trees should not be overlooked. Propagation is best by division or soft tip cuttings taken from the first growth in spring. Parent stock can be made to shoot earlier in the greenhouse. Colour varies from purple, white, blue, pink and red.

Erigeron aurantiacus Regel
This through its orange-red flower colour remarkable species requires a well-drained and much drier spot than most other Erigeron species. It may be best used in the rockery and the alpinum.

Erigeron composites var discoideus Pursh
A delicate and pretty species flowering white with orange-yellow centre that comes from North America and lives in Greenland to Alaska. It grows to ten centimetres high and is also best used in the rockery or the alpinum.

Erigeron karvinskianus DC
From Mexico to Venezuela comes this well-known tough and prolific flowering species. The small daisy flowers are white, turning pink as they mature. It flowers from summer right into the first real frosts. Ideal for dry stone walls and informal borders, I would not use it in a delicate collection as the plant can quickly overwhelm its neighbours. It is also great in pots and baskets.

Erigeron speciosus Lindl DC

An up to sixty centimetres tall species that is at home in Alberta, British Columbia and extends down to Mexico and Arizona. The blue to purple large flowers appear in summer and last a long time. Several hybrids are available; some that I can recommend are: 'Dominator' (deep purple, sixty centimetres), 'Strahlenmeer' (purple-blue, eighty centimetres), 'Ms Beale' (bright blue, thirty sixty centimetres – great for borders and foreground), 'Försters Liebling' (deep pink, sixty centimetres), 'Rotes Meer' (red, sixty centimetres), 'Sommerneuschnee' (white, sixty centimetres).

Erinacea; Fabaceae

There is only one species in this genus:

Erinacea anthyllis Link

This dwarf sub-shrub grows, often hugging rocks, in the mountains of southern France, Corsica, Spain and north-western Africa. It occurs usually on limestone and grows to around 60cm, sometimes to a metre depending on exposure and other local conditions. It is a thorny shrub that you don't want near your favourite seat in the garden but is a great structural plant in the larger, wilder rockery. It requires full sun and a well-drained position and is a wonderful sight when in full flower, from light lavender to deep purple. Slow growing but being a great structural plant in the right design, good partners are Acantholimon, Astragalus, Ptilotrichon, Vella, Anryala, Anacyclus, Erodium, Thymus and small Iris. Propagation is by seed or semi-hardwood cuttings from autumn into winter.

131 – Erinacea anthyllis
Travel study, Corsica

Eriophorum; Cyperaceae

This genus has around ten species distributed across the temperate and arctic zones. A common name is 'Wool Grass' describing the soft white hairs that serve the fruits as wings in the wind. The plant is best used in wet, swampy heathlands or around the margins of swamps, ponds and like bodies of water in natural areas and all species avoid alkaline areas or water with a neutral or high PH.

Eriophorum angustifolium Honck

Europe, Asia and North America are home to this up to fifty centimetres tall grass that forms long, strong runners. For that reason, it is best used only in wild and natural designs where it colonises larger areas

Eriophorum latifolium Hoppe

This may be one of the most beautiful Eriophorum, it is distributed like the above. Growing to around sixty centimetres, its leaves are broader and it grows only in clumps, which makes it friendlier to use and excellent for smaller landscape or garden designs.

Eriophorum vaginatum

This pretty grass comes from the northern temperate zones, grows to around sixty centimetres and is a clumping grass without runners. It flowers in late spring and early summer and is great in small wetlands or swamp gardens with partners like Erica tetralix, Gentiana pneumonanthe or Pilularia globulifera.

132 – Eriophorum vaginatum
Courtesy Miriam Goldstein

Erodium; Geraniaceae

The 'Heron's Bill' or 'Storchschnabel' (Stork's Beak; German) contains around sixty species, most of them European or Mediterranean. They are closely related to Geranium but are less used in gardens and more planted by collectors. This is in my opinion undeserved, as a lot of these are very beautiful and long-flowering plants, for example in rockeries. Propagation is by seed, division or cuttings.

Erodium amanum Boiss et Kotschy

This species comes from Turkey and is a delicate but very long-flowering plant in the rockery. The soil should be well drained and contain gravel and loam, propagation can also be done in winter by root cuttings.

Erodium manescavii Coss

A perennial of dry grasslands, Erodium manescavii comes from the Pyrenees and is one of the longest flowering species of the genus. The crimson-red flowers appear from spring right through into autumn. The plant self-sows in the right environment and may be best used in natural and wild designs together with Pulsatilla vulgaris, Potentilla megalantha, Koeleria glauca in association with shrubs and trees and other ornamental grasses of a similar habitat.

Eryngium; Apiaceae

This genus of thistles is widespread in the temperate zones; most species come from the Mediterranean. Almost all are popular in floriculture, are excellent sources of food for butterflies and bees and can be propagated by seed or root cuttings in winter (observe polarity).

Eryngium alpinum
The Alps and mountains of Bosnia are home to this easy to cultivate Eryngium. It grows to around eighty centimetres tall and flowers steel-blue in late summer.

Eryngium planum
This species originates around the Mediterranean but extends into central Europe, Asia Minor and into central Asia. The perennial grows to fifty centimetres high with numerous blue flowers above the serrated leaves. The plant offers itself for dry steppe, heath land or rockery designs, there are strongly coloured cultivars in the trade.

Erythronium; Liliaceae

A small genus with around twenty-five species, nonetheless well known in horticulture as 'Trout Lily', 'Fawn Lily' or 'Hundszahn' (German; Dog's Tooth'. They are a typical forest and woodland dweller forming small bulbs and thrive best in the semi-shade in rich, organic soils that do not dry out in summer. Great partners are Rhododndron, Azalea and Cornus. With some patience, they may colonise places that they like and create magic scenes.

Erythronium dens-canis
Translated to 'Dog's Tooth', this small very attractive perennial grows to fifteen centimetres high in deciduous forests of Europe and Asia. It ascends to around one thousand seven hundred metres altitude and flowers pink to red, sometimes white and often darkly spotted in early spring.

133 – Erythronium dens-canis
Courtesy Miriam Goldstein

Erythronium grandiflorum Pursh

Coming from mountain forests of northern America, this species grows to sixty centimetres tall with golden-yellow flowers and brighter throat and dark red stamens from spring to summer.

Erythronium revolutum Baker

This lovely Lily inhabits the giant Redwood forests and other evergreen forests of North America where it lives along creeks and swamps. The bright pink, white or pink flowers stand up to forty centimetres high with yellow stamens in spring. This species requires more moisture, especially during spring and summer.

Erythronium tolumnense Appleg

Inhabiting Pine and evergreen Oak forests in the western USA, this species grows to thirty centimetres high and has golden-yellow flowers in spring. It is, compared to the others, a reasonably robust Erythronium and there are many beautiful cultivars and hybrids.

Eucomis; Hyacinthaceae

From tropical Africa and South Africa comes the 'Pineapple Lily', a bulbous genus of perennials with an interesting inflorescence. The plants are best grown in warm and sheltered places or in pots. Propagation is by seed or bulbils.

Eucomis bicolor Baker

The species grows in South Africa on moist grassy slopes in up to eighteen hundred metres altitude. The flowers are cylindrical, to sixty centimetres high and pale green with purple margins and flowers in autumn.

Eupatorium; Asteraceae

Around forty species are named in this genus from America, Europe and Asia. Most are perennials, some are shrubs. The perennials are very attractive and sometimes large, to around two hundred and fifty centimetres tall and best suited to natural and wild designs.

Eupatorium cannabinum

The up to two-hundred-centimetre-high perennial lives naturally in sunny, moist to wet places in forests and open woodlands, along creeks, rivers and lakes. It is a great structural plant for larger natural designs, flowering pink to copper red from late summer to autumn. Propagation is by seed (fresh is best) or early soft tip cuttings.

134 – Eupatorim cannabinum
Courtesy Miriam Goldstein

Eupatorium fistulosum Barratt

From the south-eastern USA comes this impressive perennial growing to three hundred centimetres on moist or wet soils near water. Flowering time is summer to autumn in pink and light purple. Use in the natural design as structural plant or in single stand.

Euphorbia; Euphorbiaceae

Widespread throughout the world are around two thousand species of Euphorbia. The German common name, 'Wolfsmilch', translates into 'Wolf's Milk' and refers to the acidic white sap in the plant. In some species, this sap can be strong enough to cause skin irritations in sensitive people and even allergic reactions, so please take care when pruning or taking cuttings, especially to not get anything in your eyes! Best method for vegetative propagation is cuttings from mature shoots. Take a bucket with warm water and put the cuttings into this warm water straight away; you will see that the sap dissolves somewhat off the wound, resulting in higher strike rates. Propagation by seed is in most cases easy; indeed, some Euphorbia can quickly become a problem through self-sowing. By and large Euphorbia are best suited to natural or semi-formal gardens rather than a formal border and they have often the ability to be effective in tough spots where other plants struggle, there is almost always a Euphorbia for any given environmental conditions.

The large genus of Euphorbia is here divided into four groups according to their use in landscapes and gardens:

Group 1

This group consists of herbaceous European and western Asian species that are competitive, very hardy and are often self-sowing. Their use in the landscape is consequently preferable in natural and wild designs, their competitiveness makes them suitable under and around shrubs and trees where many other perennials would not cope well with the root pressure, but also of course in steppe or heathland designs and large rockeries where they assist with maintenance; even road embankments may be stabilised with them.

Euphorbia cyparissias

This variable species is very strong and may be used together with other strong shrubs or perennials like Artemisia procera, Artemisia pontica, Ceratostigma, geranium sanguineum, Pinus and Aemone sylvestris on limestone soils.

Euphorbia epithymoides

The 'Golden Wolves' Milk' is a valuable and adaptable perennial growing to around sixty centimetres with yellow-golden flowers in spring. It is a great partner to many stronger perennials as the foliage connects and ties together different parts of a design. It tolerates full sun as well as semi-shade and works well with shrubs and trees and partners like Brunnera macrophylla, Dictamnus albus, Genista tinctoria, Lathyrus niger, Ranunculus bulbosus, Tanacetum corymbosum and bulbous plants like Tulipa. Propagation of cultivars is by cuttings, the species itself propagates easily by seed, there are several good cultivars in the trade.

Euphorbia palustris

The 'Swamp Wolves' Milk' is widespread across Europe where as the name suggests it inhabits wet zones in valleys, along creeks and rivers and even at the coast as it is moderately salt-tolerant. However, it is also capable of colonising drier areas. The plant grows to a hundred and fifty centimetres tall with lively, bright green foliage and yellow-red autumn colours, the flowers are dark yellow and appear in early summer.

Group 2

Describing Mediterranean species that are adapted to dry summers and mild winters with rainfall occurring mainly in autumn and winter. They are good pioneer plants on poor or disturbed soils, requiring good drainage but otherwise are very tough.

Euphorbia amygdaloides

The 'Almond-leaved Wolves' Milk' is an evergreen perennial where the overwintering shoots flower in the next growing season. The species is easily propagated by seed and self-sows; the cultivars obviously need to be propagated vegetatively by the cutting methods described in the introduction to Euphorbia. The plant does extremely well in shade and semi shade, even in quite dense root zones of trees and is one of the few plants ideal for such design purposes. Good partners and plant communities are Helleborus foetidus and other Helleborus, Prunus tenella, Ceratostigma and Lonicera. One of the best cultivars is 'Purpurea', with dark pink to dark red foliage that is strongly coloured in winter making it very valuable.

Euphorbia characias ssp wulfenii Radel

This subspecies is often found in garden cultivation and larger landscapes, it is a strong and tall, up to a hundred and eighty-centimetre-high evergreen perennial with blue-grey foliage. The inflorescences appear from winter into spring and the plant is of great structural value and may form the skeleton of natural planting designs. The emphasis is on natural as this plant needs control and higher levels of maintenance in a more formal setting, it also self-sows freely.

135 – Euphorbia characias ssp wulfenii

This placement of the plant shows well the structural character of the species and use in the landscape or garden as it provides a reliable body even in the dormant season of cool-temperate zones

Euphorbia x martini Rouy

A very attractive hybrid between E. amygdaloides and E. characias that is well suited to warm to hot and dry areas. Ideal for rockeries, steppe and dry heath land designs from natural to formal landscapes and gardens.

Group 3

Describing Mediterranean species from higher altitudes requiring good drainage and are generally smaller than those of Group 2.

Euphorbia glabrifolia Vis

This is a small sun-shrub from Croatia, Albania and Greece that naturally grows on stony mountain slopes. The plant gets to around twenty centimetres in height with yellow flowers in spring and summer.

Euphorbia myrsinites

A prostrate evergreen species to around twenty centimetres, with attractive leaves, which is great for dry, sunny rockeries, in dry stone walls and along paths. The plant is best for natural designs as it grows irregular and is quite variable, but in all cases, it provides an evergreen structure to a perennial planting. Good partners are Allium senescens, Sedum, Iris barbata-nana, Asphodelus and other plants of similar background.

Group 4

Describing Asian species that grow in zones with regular snowfall and require more moisture and richer soils than the other three groups.

Euphorbia griffithii Hook

This species is at home in the Himalayas, Nepal, Bhutan and southern Tibet where it grows to eighty centimetres tall. The flowers are a lovely orange-red. The plant thrives in semi-shade and moist soils where the colours are at their most intense. The cultivar 'Fireglow' is to be recommended with dark red leaves and beautiful autumn colour.

Euphorbia sikkimensis Boiss
This tall, up to a hundred and fifty-centimetre-high species has a spectacular dark pink emerging of new leaves that matures to green. The flowers are yellow in late summer. It is a very 'friendly' Euphorbia that has short runners. It is not aggressive but grows loosely in amongst other plants; it appears to 'dance' between grasses and other perennials.

Euphorbia wallichii Hook
From Iran, eastern Afghanistan, north-western Pakistan, Kashmir and Nepal comes this handsome perennial that ascends to around four thousand metres altitude. It grows to eighty centimetres with large yellow flowers and the entire plant colours bright yellow in autumn. It is a great species for semi-shade together with Astilbe, Campanula punctata, Hosta, Polygonatum and Anemone.

Ferula; Apiaceae

This is a variable genus with around a hundred and thirty species in western Asia and the Mediterranean. Some species are used in herbal medicine.

Ferula communis
The 'Giant Fennel' grows on dry slopes and becomes more than two hundred centimetres tall with very large, ornamental leaves. The plant flowers in summer but requires several years to flower from seed. It is an impressive plant that I would use in large, open spaces in natural designs and together with other Mediterranean plants.

Festuca; Poaceae

Spread across the world are around four hundred and fifty species of this genus of grasses. They are used widely in landscapes and gardens. Propagation is by division in early spring or late summer, after flowering is another option.

Festucas amethystina
A fine-leafed up to eighty centimetres tall grass that is at home in south-eastern Europe. It inhabits dry, open forests, usually in Pine & Erica communities. Flowering is in summer, the leaves are long, slightly pendulous and appear to be coated with a blue-purple tinge, in different light situations the colours change and this is the reason for the common name of 'Rainbow Grass'.

Festucas gigantea Vill
This European forest grass grows in damp to wet zones and grows to a hundred and fifty centimetres tall. The leaves are two centimetres wide and pendulous, the plant flowers in late summer.

Festucas glauca Vill
A commonly used species in landscapes and gardens, the 'Blue Grass' naturally lives in dry grasslands in south-eastern France, north-eastern Italy and extends into central Europe. It grows to forty centimetres with steel blue, thin leaves.

Filipendula; Rosaceae

A genus of medium to tall perennials from the northern temperate zones that are valuable in sunny to semi-shaded areas in borders, parks or in association with water features. 'Meadowsweet' and 'Dropwort' are names in common use for these perennials that thrive in every good garden soil and are easy to cultivate if they have sufficient moisture. Propagation is by division or cuttings in spring.

Filipendula kamtschatika Mxim

This species is highly decorative and grows to two hundred centimetres high which makes it very valuable for parks and larger landscape designs. It flowers in late summer.

Filipendula rubra Robins

The American species grows to a hundred and fifty centimetres and has lovely dark pink to red, highly fragrant flowers in summer. Great with neighbours like Iris siberica, Eupatorium, Lysimachia clethroides, Artemisia lactiflora, Carex pendula, Cimicifuga, Lythrum, Panicum and Molinia.

136 – Filipendula rubra 'Venusta Magnifica'
Gärtnerei Häussermann, Stuttgart, Germany

Filipendula vulgaris Moench

This species is coming from Europe, Asia Minor, the Caucasus, western Siberia and northern Africa where it grows on drier and sunnier places than the other Filipendula described here. It grows to around half a metre and flowers white in summer. I would use it in open, natural designs along with Aster linosyris, Aster tongolensis, Campanula carpatica, Campanula poscharskyana, Dianthus carthusianorum, Geranium sanguineum, Inula ensifolia, Melica and Prunella.

Foeniculum; Apiaceae

This is a small genus with only three species, but is nonetheless important in landscape architecture and horticulture.

Foeniculum vulgare Mill
This species originally comes from south-western Europe but is now widespread throughout Europe. It varies between biannual and perennial, grows to two hundred and fifty centimetres high with hollow stems and flowers yellow in summer.

Fragaria; Rosaceae

The genus of the strawberry has around fifty species distributed in the northern hemisphere, with one in South America. Most are evergreen perennials with long runners. Apart from their popular use as delicious fruit, their use in the landscape and garden is limited to ground cover in more natural designs, apart from the clump-forming Fragaria vesca cultivars.

Fragaria x ananassa Guedes
The strawberry has around fifteen hundred named cultivars worldwide; it may be a nice addition to cottage gardens or similar informal plant designs as a dense ground cover. It is rather competitive when sufficient moisture is available and therefore more recommended for natural designs with other strong plants.

Frittilaria; Liliaceae

There are around a hundred and fifty species of Frittilaria in the temperate zones of the northern hemisphere. There are great variations between the species and consequently the environmental conditions and optimum cultivation vary also. Most flowers show a distinct chess-board pattern, the reason why one German common name is 'Schachbrettblume' which translates into 'Chess Board Flower'. One of my Australian gardeners came up with 'Snake Flower' as it reminded her of the skin of snakes.

General cultivation techniques for Frittilaria are that their cycle starts in autumn when the new roots are formed. They should be kept reasonably moist then and not be allowed to dry out. When they start shooting in late winter to early spring, they desire more water but do not tolerate wet feet. At that time, a moderate application of fertiliser is needed, the N-K balance should be higher on the potassium. Additional food is important when the plants have been pollinated and seed is formed to avoid exhaustion of the plant. Propagation is by seed in autumn or bulbils from those species that form them; not all do. More specific cultivation techniques are in the following five groups:

Group 1: These are robust species growing in well-drained, open soils but should not completely dry out in summer. They are best used in rockeries or in association with shrubs and trees.

Group 2: These are rarer species that are more sensitive and need sheltered positions in the garden. These species also should not dry out in summer.

Group 3: These species now require a pronounced dry period for their summer dormancy, most originate in the Mediterranean or central Asia.

Group 4: North American species requiring acidic soils (PH at or below 6) and need a dry period in summer to complete their cycle for best cultivation.

Group 5: Species from north-western America that grow in acidic clay or gravel soils without or only minimal organic content, these also require summer dry dormancy.

Frittilaria alburyana Rix
North-eastern Turkey is the home of this very beautiful species with pink flowers with the chess board pattern in spring. The plant inhabits stony slopes close to the snow margins at altitudes between two thousand and three thousand metres and grows to fifteen centimetres high. Group 2 for cultivation.

Frittilaria aurea Schott

This species comes from central Turkey where it grows on rocky limestone slopes in altitudes up to three thousand metres. The plant grows to fifteen centimetres high and has pendulous, bell-shaped golden flowers with a brown or red-brown chess board pattern. This is one of the most beautiful species. Cultivation requirements of Group 2.

Frittilaria falcata Beetle

Coming from central California where it grows ten centimetres high in gravelly slopes, Frittilaria falcate has fleshy grey leaves and bowl-like flowers. Their colours are yellow-green with rusty-red dots and spots in spring. Group 5.

Frittilaria hermonis ssp amana Rix

This species hails from Lebanon and southern Turkey where it grows in altitudes between one thousand four hundred and two thousand metres in gravel and in between rocks, often in shade. The plant grows to forty centimetres tall and has bell-like yellow flowers. Group 2.

Frittilaria imperialis

The 'Kaiserkrone' German for 'Emperor's Crown' is a remarkable species that has been in cultivation since ancient times. Originally it comes from south-eastern Turkey, Iran, Afghanistan, Kashmir and Pakistan. It grows there in grassy, rocky meadows and ascends to three thousand metres altitude. The bulb can be as big as a man's fist and has an unpleasant smell. The plant grows to a metre tall with a tuft of leaves and several pendulous, orange-red flowers in spring. Propagation is best by bulbils that are formed generously if the plant has not been disturbed for a couple of years. Use in the landscape in cottage gardens, informal designs or historic gardens where applicable, the best planting time is during the summer dormancy, the bulbs should be set around thirty centimetres deep! Cultivate with generous applications of a balanced fertiliser, high in K.

137 – Frittilaria imperialis
Courtesy Stephan Willenberger

Frittilaria meleagris ssp meleagris
This species is widespread in central Europe growing in wet meadows to around thirty centimetres high. The leaves are narrow and the flowers have a very distinct chess board pattern in red-brown in spring. Group 1.

137a – Frittilaria meleagris
Work in Canberra, Australia 2014

Frittilaria michailovskyi Fomine
A very beautiful and remarkable species with nodding dark red flowers with a bright yellow skirt in spring. It comes from north-eastern Turkey and grows in gravelly slopes in altitudes between two thousand and three thousand metres. Group 3.

Frittilaria persica Baker

Iran, Iraq, Lebanon and Turkey are home to the up to a metre tall plant with bell-shaped flowers in greenish, yellow, ochre, brown or plum blue colours. The species may be set back by late frosts and sometimes the flowers are lost.

Frittilaria recurva Benth

The 'Scarlet Frittilary' comes from southern Oregon and northern California where it grows on dry hills between seven hundred and two thousand metres. The plant grows to ninety centimetres high and has narrow, pendulous orange to crimson red flowers with recurved petals and light, often yellow, chess board pattern in late spring. Group 4.

Fuchsia; Onagraceae

The well-known genus of Fuchsia comes mainly from South America; some are from Central America, New Zealand and Haiti. The species vary from small woody ground cover and shrubs to small trees. Fuchsia are not strictly perennials but, like Cistus, are mentioned here as they may complement perennial designs very well. They naturally grow in shade or semi-shade and most are tender to serious frosts but perform very well in sheltered locations or behave like perennials with the above-ground parts of the plant dying back, but the plant will come back from the roots with the warmer temperatures, hence behaving like a herbaceous perennial. Their almost continuous flowering time is a treat for any aspect of a garden or landscape design. Propagation is easy by soft tip cuttings.

Fuchsia magellanica Lam

Named after the famous explorer and first circumnavigator of the earth, this species lives in the southern and central Andes and grows upright with pendulous branches. Its natural habitat is shrublands and forest margins, where it often grows near water. The plant can become to three metres tall when not exposed to real frosts and has attractive pendulous red flowers. There are numerous cultivars.

Fuchsia regia Munz

In high altitudes, up to two thousand four hundred metres of southern Brazil live the large, up to six metres tall, Fuchsia regia. The plant comes in shrub form but can also adapt to grow like a climber into higher trees. It is reasonably frost hardy and has lovely red-purple flowers.

Fuchsia hybrids

These are hybrids crossed between the wild species, there are very many in the trade ranging from white, pink, red and purple flowers. Frost hardiness varies according to their parentage. Best used in the landscape in sheltered places and near paths or seats where visitors can admire them close.

Gaillardia; Asteraceae

A small genus of around twenty species; some are annual, some are perennial. Gaillardias are tireless flowering plants but usually do not live very long. The taller species are good for the perennial border, the dwarf varieties are best in the rockery. They partner well with Coreposis grandiflora, Erigeron, Echinacea, Salvia and grasses like Chasmanthum, Hystrix and Panicum. In cultivation, they require well-drained but rich soils, preferably lighter in properties as Gaillardia die quickly in heavier loams or clay. Propagation is by seed.

Gaillardia aristata Pursh
This species comes from Arizona, New Mexico and extends to British Columbia, it grows to sixty centimetres tall with grey-green hairy leaves. The flowers are large, yellow with red base and appear through summer and into autumn.

Galanthus; Amaryllidaceae

This special little genus of Snowdrops or in German 'Schneeglöckchen' (Snow Bells) is at home in Europe and western Asia. It contains around twenty species. They inhabit sunny or semi-shaded moist areas in between shrubs and trees.

Galanthus caucasicus Grossh
From the forests of the Caucasus comes this graceful species that grows well in shade or sun. It flowers in early spring and has grey leaves.

Galanthus nivalis
This is probably the most widespread species; it is well suited to wild and natural designs where it can develop on its own. Naturally it grows in forests, meadows and along creeks and rivers up to fourteen hundred metres altitude.
There are numerous cultivars and hybrids available, best to check with your local supplier about details.

Gallium; Rubiaceae

Worldwide are around three hundred species of annual or perennial nature, some characterise forest floors and create lovely scenes when in flower. Most are too competitive for borders or more formal settings; I would consider this genus to be almost entirely for the natural and wild designs, parklands, woodlands and similar settings.

Gallium odoratum Scop
The 'Waldmeister' (German for Master of the Forest') or 'Sweet Woodruff' is widely common from Europe to Siberia and North Africa. It grows to twenty centimetres high, flowers white in spring and inhabits mixed forests and woodlands. It tolerates deep shade and I would combine it with Anemone nemorosa, Circaea, Convallaris, Lamium, Maianthemum, Oxalis acetosella, Sanicula and shade tolerant grasses like Luzula, Milium effusum and Melica uniflora which results in fairy-tale like scenes in spring.

Galtonia; Hyacinthaceae

From the grasslands of South Africa comes this very handsome bulbous perennial. Also called 'Summer Hyacinth' the genus prefers mild winters and combines well with natural steppe or prairie designs but is also beautiful in the perennial border.

Galtonia candicans Decne
The species originates in moist meadows and grasslands from south-eastern Transvaal to western Natal and the eastern Cape provinces from sea level to around two thousand eight hundred metres altitude. The plant grows to eighty centimetres high with green-bluish leaves and flowers white with up to sixty individual flowers on a long stalk in late summer.

Galtonia princeps Decne
Also, a species from the grasslands, this smaller Galtonia grows to around fifty centimetres with more greenish flowers.

Galtonia viridiflora Verdoorn
The largest Galtonia with up to a metre tall inflorescences also grow in moist grasslands. Its flowers are bright green and are slightly trumpet-shaped and it flowers in late summer.

Gaura; Oenotheraceae

The 'Prairie-Candles' are perennial, biannual or annual species from a small genus originating in North America. Their original habitat is sunny, with gravelly or rocky poor soils and they should be used in such places in rockeries, on slopes and natural steppe and prairie designs. But they can also be used in perennial borders if the soil conditions are not too rich and wet. Gaura are very valuable through their very long flowering time and graceful, open habit.

Gaura lindheimeri Engelm et Gray
The species comes from the more southern part of North America where it lives in prairies, steppes and in open Pine forests. It is a medium perennial growing to around a hundred and fifty centimetres high, but height may vary greatly according to local conditions. I often use it in shallow, rocky soils where it grows no more than a metre tall but is appreciated for its abundant white to pink flowers that appear from late spring into the first frosts. There are numerous hybrids and cultivars available in the trade.

Gentiana; Gentianaceae

The very variable, large and interesting genus of Gentiana is represented with more than eight hundred species in the temperate zones of the world. Some are annual or biannual but most are long to very long-lived perennials. The species are listed here in alphabetical order with a reference to their botanic section as the section is indicative of their habit and habitat as well as the best possible methods of cultivation.

Section Calathianae (Ca)
These are the spring flowering Gentiana species with small basal leaves between two and three centimetres that grow best in well-drained, organic and moist soils in full sun. Propagation is by seed or division.

Section Condrophyllae (Ch)
Small-leaved Gentiana that grow in acid humus that is always moist but well-drained whilst during the growing season require soils that are almost saturated with moving water. Propagation by seed or division.

Section Cruciata (Cr)
This section of Gentaina species features opposing leaves that are up to twenty centimetres long with a basal rosette. Their flowering time is usually in summer and their cultivation is easy in most normal garden soils. Propagation is by seed.

Section Frigida (Fr)
The up to four-centimetre-long leaves appear around the stem, crowded or dispersed, flowering time is from summer into autumn. These species are by and large a bit more difficult to cultivate and need to be grown in acid humus or peat soils, either in rockeries or special perennial borders that provide this

environment. Propagation is by division in spring or cuttings that need to form viable winter buds at their base – therefore take these cuttings early in the growing season.

Section Gentiana (G)

The species in this section have large leaves, up to thirty centimetres long and crowded at the base; their roots are large and fleshy and their flowers stand up to a metre tall. They are impressive and beautiful plants for the perennial border or large rockeries; amongst them is Gentiana lutea which is used in herbal medicine. Propagation is by seed.

Section Gentianopsis (NZ)

A very variable section from Australia and New Zealand flowering most often white from early to late summer. Cultivation is best in well-drained, organic soils in full sun, they may be best for the collector and the alpinum.

Section Megalanthe (M)

The 'Bell-flowered Gentiana' have leaves up to eight centimetres long that are crowded at the base and flower from spring to summer. They are best used in rockeries or along borders and pathways; their cultivation is easy in well-drained soils in full sun. Propagation is by division after flowering or cuttings either in autumn or also after the flowering has finished.

Section Pneumonanthe (P)

The leaves in this group are up to ten centimetres long and are placed like scales along the stem. Flowering time is from summer into autumn with yellow, blue, greenish-white and sometimes pink colours. They are also good cut flowers. Cultivation is easy in acidic (they avoid calcium), well-drained soils with sufficient moisture in full sun or lightly shaded. Propagation is by seed.

Gentiana acaulis (M)

This famous species comes from the Alps and grows down into north-eastern Spain, central Italy and central Yugoslavia where it grows in acidic, moist soils in full sun. Propagation is by division after flowering or cuttings.

138 – Gentiana acaulis
Courtesy Betty Ford Alpine Gardens

Gentiana angustifolia (M)

This species now prefers limestone and alkaline soils and comes from the south-western Alps, the Jura and the Pyrenees. The flowers are very clear gentian-blue, sometimes they are ice-blue or white, it is a good cut flower and opens in cool temperatures at around 4 °C, easy to cultivate.

Gentiana asclepiadea (P)

This handsome, sometimes u to 100cm tall species inhabits mountainous regions of central Europe and extends into central Italy, the eastern Ukraine and Asia Minor. It inhabits moist, semi-shaded or even shaded areas with its strong rootstock. It is one of the most beautiful garden perennials and a great cut flower; One of my favourites, I would use it in the landscape and garden alongside ferns or in cooler perennial borders. They do not like being transplanted but propagate by cuttings.

139 – Gentiana asclepiadea
Courtesy Wikimedia

Gentiana farreri Fr)

This species comes from western China where it grows like an open ground cover. The flowers are of a very special blue inside with dark stripes on a white-yellow outside and appear from late summer into autumn. This wonderful plant requires open, well-drained soils and tolerates sun, a drier summer and neutral PH.

Gentiana lutea (G)

The 'Golden Gentiana' is a handsome plant to around a hundred and fifty centimetres, from the Alps, the Pyrenees, Carpathian Mountains and the Balkans. The roots are strong and grow to a thickness of a man's arm; they are used for medicinal purposes and to produce the popular 'Enzian-Schnaps' (Gentiana spirit), even when some producers put a label on the spirit that shows the blue Gentiana acaulis. Aside from these purposes, this Gentian is a highly valuable plant in natural or wild designs that is very long-lived. The species does not like being transplanted and is best propagated by seed.

140 – Gentiana lutea
Courtesy Miriam Goldstein

Gentian septemfida var lagodechiana (P)

A graceful, low-growing Gentian that flowers from summer into autumn with deep blue nodding bell-shaped flowers and is easy to cultivate in borders or rockeries.

Gentiana sino-ornata (Fr)

This remarkably beautiful species comes from south-western China and grows to around fifteen centimetres high. The flowers usually stand singly and are funnel-shaped, the inside is deep azure blue and the outside is of a somewhat matte blue but with five distinct purple-blue stripes. It flowers in autumn and the plant requires acidic soils with sufficient moisture. Propagation is by division in spring or cuttings in early summer, a highly recommended species.

141 – Gentiana sino-ornata
Courtesy Miriam Goldstein

Gentiana verna (Ca)

This species is widespread across the mountains of southern and central Europe, the Caucasus, Iran and western Siberia. It is a low species and stays at around ten centimetres in height. The plant grows in little carpets and can vary in colour from a deep azure blue to white or purple-red, sometimes stripes occur. It is certainly worth selecting some exceptionally good-looking ones. It is one of the most beautiful and special small perennials but requires careful cultivation in reasonably moist acidic soils that should have (in apparent contradiction) small limestone gravels mixed through. Also important is that the delicate species is not overgrown by strong neighbours. Propagation is by seed; it takes around three years from sowing to flowering.

Geranium; Geraniaceae

The genus Geranium has increasingly gained importance in landscape and garden design. There are summer-green and evergreen species with a large variety of leaf forms and flower colours. I find many Geranium extremely valuable as ground cover or complementing and 'filler' perennials between larger feature plants in borders or natural designs. Most Geraniums are associated with shrubs or trees and live in shade and semi-shade but there are many others suited to a range of habitats. For this reason, the species are listed in alphabetical order under their main habitat conditions to assist with selection and cultivation. Propagation is by seed or cuttings; my first 'professional' cuttings as an apprentice were indeed Geranium sanguineum. The German common name for this genus 'Storchschnabel' translates into something like 'Stork's beak' and refers to the shape of the fruit.

Habitat 1; Mediterranean mountain meadows

These species require balanced moisture and warmth, there are many commonly used garden perennials in this group.

Geranium x magnificum
This is a remarkably long-lived (plantings of over fifty years are recorded) hybrid perennial with attractive leaves and gorgeous purple-blue flowers in summer. The plant grows to eighty centimetres tall.

142 – Geranium magnificum
Courtesy Baumschule Eggert, Germany

Geranium renardii
This species comes from the Caucasus, has shallow rhizomes and grows to around twenty-five centimetres high. The leaves are rounded and resemble Salvia officinalis a little; the flowers are white to pink, veined and appear in summer. It is a valuable ground cover with its foliage for warm, rather sunny places in rockeries or natural open designs, but it should not be overlooked as a smaller feature plant in small groups dotted around rocks or small shrubs.

Habitat 2; Forests and woodlands

The species in this group can withstand the root pressure from trees, live in their shade and may 'go wild' in this habitat.

Geranium nodosum
Widespread in southern and central Europe this species grows to around thirty centimetres and is very well adapted to live under and with trees. The flowers are purple to light pink and appear not in great numbers but spread over a long period of time from summer to late autumn.

Geranium gracile
From north-eastern Turkey to the southern Caucasus and northern Iran grows this forty centimetres high Geranium. It has small pink flowers from summer to autumn and graceful foliage in deep shade where few other plants do well.

Habitat 3; Mountain meadows

These plants grow best in semi-shade in moist mountain meadows or in mountain forests and woodlands that do not dry out completely in summer.

Geranium psilostemon
Home in the Pontus mountains and the south-western Caucasus Geranium psilostemon. Grows to a hundred and forty centimetres high and has lovely bright magenta-red flowers with a black eye in summer. It requires sufficient moisture and rich soils; the species combines well with ornamental grasses and other tall perennials.

Geranium sylvaticum
This species originates in the mountains of southern Europe, in northern Europe it descends to sea level and it also extends into northern Turkey. The plant can be quite variable and grow in height from thirty to a hundred and twenty centimetres. The flowers are usually in shades of reddish-purple, pink or white and blue in early summer. Use in the landscape in informal, natural and wild designs, it can be cut back hard after flowering.

Habitat 4; meadows

Moist to wet soils in sunny to semi-shaded open spaces or meadows characterise the environmental conditions for this group of Geranium.

Geranium endressii
The Pyrenees are the home of this perennial with many uses in the gardens and landscapes. The plant grows to fifty centimetres tall with prostrate rhizomes and it flowers with a hard to describe pink-purple in late summer to autumn.

Habitat 5; temperate South-Pacific zone

Some very attractive species and hybrids, in both leaf and flower, come from this habitat, albeit these plants are often not very frost hardy and are thus only suited for mild climates or sheltered warmer areas.

Geranium x riversleaianum
The well-known 'Mavis Simpson' grows to twenty centimetres high and fifty centimetres across with bright pink flowers that stand above white-haired leaves from summer to late autumn, it is probably the hardiest hybrid on well-drained soils.

Habitat 6; African group

A group of plants that generally tolerates dry summers very well.

Geranium brycei
This is an interesting sub-shrub with blue-purple flowers in summer. It may be used in perennial borders and natural designs like Cistus and does best in areas with mild winters.

Geranium robustum
This is a mostly prostrate species with the shoots becoming woody as they mature. The leaves are evergreen with a silvery underside and long-lasting purple-blue flowers with white centre.

Habitat 7; American group

Most representatives of this group are best used in meadows and open woodlands on rich soils with balanced moisture levels.

Geranium maculatum
An up to seventy-centimetre-high perennial, with light pink to purple-pink flowers in late spring to early summer that may be used for many purposes in and around woody ornamentals. It requires reasonably moist soils and is suited to 'go wild' in natural designs but will not overwhelm its neighbours.

Habitat 8; Meadows

These species require light for best development and perform best in open spaces.

Geranium pratense
This widespread species inhabits meadows from northern Europe to the Caucasus, central Asia and the Himalayas. The clumping plant grows to a metre tall with large, up to twenty-centimetre-wide leaves and has white to purple-blue or even dark purple flowers from early to late summer. It adapts to a wide range of soils but prefers rich, loamy and slightly alkaline soils. There are many horticultural cultivars available.

Geranium himalayense
A carpet-forming species from the Himalayas growing to forty centimetres high and large, bright blue flowers with white, pink or red veins from early to late summer. Good to use in natural designs and in association with shrubs and trees where plenty of sunlight is available, however the plants should not dry out in summer.

Habitat 9; Asian Erianthum group

These species come from an Asian background but are like the American group in application and requirements.

Geranium erianthum
This is a variable species with attractive, orange-red autumn colouring of the leaves. The species grows to forty centimetres and flowers light purple-blue in summer. It requires rich soils in sunny or shady aspects of trees and combines well with Trollius, Camassia, Hemerocallis and similar perennials in natural, informal designs.

Geranium platyanthum

A smaller species, sometimes wrongly labelled as Geranium sinense, the plant has hairy leaves and nodding, purple flowers in early summer and is best used in meadows or around shrubs.

Habitat 10; Monsoonal forests

The cultivation requirements for this group are high summer rainfalls and the species should not be planted in the full sun or in areas with severe frost.

Geranium wallichianum

This lovely species grows to thirty centimetres and has large flowers that range in colour from white-pink to crimson and purple in late summer and autumn. The plant can climb into others by leaning its shoots into them.

Geranium procurrens

A strong growing perennial to a metre high that has a long flowering period from summer into autumn. The flowers are dark purple with a black eye. Unfortunately, this species is quite frost tender and is suited only to mild climates.

Habitat 11; Asian Sinense group

This group originates in the mountains of south-eastern Asia.

Geranium sinense

The more delicate Geranium sinense is best suited to smaller landscapes and to be admired close. It grows slowly and has dark-brown flowers that are conspicuously looking downward in late summer and early autumn.

Habitat 12; Moist meadows

The species of this group are mostly robust and strong-growing plants requiring moist or wet conditions in natural designs.

Geranium palustre

This very nice perennial features large magenta-red flowers from summer to autumn and is a very graceful plant in wet meadows and wet zones along creeks and rivers. It can climb up to two metres when it can anchor its shoots into other plants, but it is not a true climber with organs developed to climb independently.

Geranium wlassovianum

A dense, up to thirty-centimetre-high plant that comes from Siberia and north-eastern Asia. The leaves turn beautifully red in autumn with flowers of purple that appear from summer and often into the first frosts. It is a very valuable perennial in natural areas around woody ornamentals but the soil needs to be sufficiently moist during the growing season.

Habitat 13; Moist meadows of East-Asian zones

This group is in Europe also referred to as the 'Krameri group' and describes also species from moist meadows but their requirements and subsequently cultivation differs from the above described group.

Geranium dahuricum

An attractive and long-flowering species from eastern Siberia and Mongolia; other than the above described species it tolerates dry periods in summer. The flowers are pink and the plant grows to fifty centimetres high.

Geranium soboliferum

Magenta-red flowers appear from summer to autumn on this dense perennial. It adapts well to a wide range of soil properties but prefers a shaded area.

Habitat 14; Alpine Pylzowianum group

This group consists of alpine geophytes that are by and large strong growers that combine well with more open plants.

Geranium pylzowianum

A smaller perennial to twenty-five centimetres high, forming runners, that is best suited to rockeries, dry stone walls and gaps between rocks. The flowers are trumpet-shaped, pink with a green centre and appear in summer.

Geranium orientalitibeticum

From eastern Tibet comes this interesting fifteen-centimetre-high perennial. It forms runners and features bright green leaves with purple-pink flowers.

Habitat 15; European Forest margin

Geranium sanguineum

The 'Blood Stork's Beak' (translated from German 'Blut Storchschnabel') is a unique Geranium growing along dry forest margins across Europe and into Turkey and the Caucasus. The plant grows from fleshy rhizomes and forms dense carpets of leaves that usually develop a lovely orange or red autumn colour. The flowers appear over a long period of time from spring into autumn and have a deep red or magenta-red colour. I would recommend the plant as a beautiful, tough and reliable ground cover around trees and shrubs in natural designs, but I have used it also successfully in formal perennial borders as ground cover or along the edge of borders. There are numerous cultivars and hybrids available.

143 – Germanium sanguineum
Courtesy Staudengärtnerei Häussermann Stuttgart, Germany

Habitat 16; Disturbed land - Asphodeloides group

This group of Geranium occupies as a pioneer plant disturbed land.

Geranium asphodeloides

Sometimes a biannual but usually a perennial forty-centimetre-high plant that has multiple branches and is a profusely flowering species with white or light pink flowers in summer. It is at home in south-eastern Europe and extends down into the Lebanon. It works best in groups in open areas and can be combined with Salvia sclarea, Malva and Centranthus. It is self-sowing in places that it likes and when it is cut back straight after flowering the plant usually develops another set of flowers.

Habitat 17; Summer-dry mountains – Tuberosa group

Geranium tuberosum

Coming from the Mediterranean, this thirty-centimetre-high perennial forms tubers that are edible. It flowers in spring with light purple, veined inflorescences.

Geranium malviflorum

Large, fifty millimetres across purple-blue flowers decorate this perennial in spring that usually has a pronounced summer dormancy.

Habitat 18; Macrorrhizum group

The species in this group primarily grow around rocks and in dry mountain forests, that is why the German common name is 'Felsen Storchschnabel' which translates loosely into 'Rock Stork's Beak'.

Geranium macrorrhizum

An aromatic, up to half a metre high perennial which is very drought resistant. The perennial flowers with purple-red, purple, white or red flowers in early summer. In its original habitat, the species lives among rocks, shrubs and in open mountain forests. Use in the landscape accordingly in natural designs.

Geranium x cantabrigense

The hybrids of this group have Geranium macrorrhizum and Geranium dalmaticum as parents. They are mainly used in gardens for informal rockeries or formal and semi-formal smaller perennial borders. Like G. macrorrhizum it is quite competitive but can consequently be used to reduce weed incursion in lower maintenance beds. There are several nice hybrids in the trade; most are very drought resistant.

Geranium dalmaticum

This carpet-forming small perennial from Croatia grows to only ten centimetres and features pink to purple-pink or white flowers. It is best used in small rockeries, along stone features and in dry stone walls.

Habitat 19; Alpine Cinereum group

This group features subalpine and alpine species from Europe that require sunny locations with open, good soils.

Geranium cinereum ssp subcaulescens

Coming from the Balkan Peninsula, Turkey and southern Italy this only ten-centimetre-high perennial is very attractive in leaf and flower. The plant most often lives in sandy soils and sandstone country and flowers in summer with glowing deep purple flowers that have a distinct dark spot in the centre. The cultivar G. cinereum 'Ballerina' is highly recommended with its veined lovely flowers.

Geum; Rosaceae

The name 'Geum' has already been used by Pliny (Plinius der Ältere) and has a meaning of sampling, trying, testing or smelling something. There are around fifty species in this genus worldwide; most are low, bushy perennials with thick roots with some forming runners. Geum grow in a wide range of good soils that are moist but not wet and sunny or semi-shaded. Applications and use in the landscape are in natural designs as well as in more formal borders, they combine well with Achillea, Aconitum, Alchemilla, Aster, Campanula, Erigeron, Geranium, Iris, Nepeta, Salvia, Tradescantia and Trollius. They need rejuvenation every four to five years. Propagation is by seed, division after flowering or cuttings in summer.

Geum chiloense Balb ex Ser

Named after the island of Chiloe, this species is very attractive through its large, scarlet or deep blood red flowers that appear over a long period through summer. The plant grows to fifty centimetres high and prefers summer-moist meadows and dry winters, albeit it is usually short-lived and needs regular re-propagation.

Geum coccineum Sibth et Smith

This species comes from Asia Minor and the Balkans where it grows in moist meadows or along creeks and along the margins of forests with sufficient water in the soil. Geum coccineum is like the above but a lot tougher and longer-lived.

Geum x cultorum

Under the hybrid name of 'cultorum' are usually all hybrids and cultivars of Geum listed, there are very many. Some that can be recommended are: 'Bernstein' – fifty centimetres with golden yellow semi-double flowers that is long-lived and slow-growing; 'Fire Opal' – sixty centimetres with large orange-red veined flowers in late summer; 'Magnificum' – forty centimetres with bright orange semi-double flowers in summer.

Geum montanum

As the name suggests this species inhabits mountains up to three thousand metres altitude in the Pyrenees, the Alps, and Corsica and extends into western Russia and south-western Greece. The pure, bright yellow flowers are large and appear from spring to summer.

Gladiolus; Iridaceae

This variable genus is mainly known for its garden hybrids and cultivars rather than the around a hundred and eighty wild species. They are at home in Africa, Madagascar, the Mediterranean and Europe, and describe bulbous perennials with sword-like leaves and mostly funnel-shaped flowers in summer. All like full sun and well-drained, light and moderately rich soils with some loam.

Gladiolus callianthus Marais

This up to a hundred and twenty-centimetre-high perennial comes from eastern Africa and Ethiopia. The nodding white flowers have a rhomboid red venation and appear in late summer to early autumn. They are fragrant and large, up to ten centimetres across, which makes it a desirable plant in perennial borders. However, it is not frost hardy; in colder areas, I would recommend taking it into a greenhouse in winter.

Gladiolus cardinalis Curtis

Bright red flowers up to eight centimetres across are the hallmark of this species that grows to over a metre tall. The plant flowers in summer and is also not frost hardy.

Gladiolus communis ssp byzantinus Miller

This species grows to around seventy centimetres and has dark purple-red flowers with white venation in summer. It may be the most commonly used form in cultivation.

Gladiolus tristis L

From South Africa comes this tall, up to a hundred and fifty centimetres high Gladiolus. The flowers appear in summer and are creamy-yellow and fragrant at night. It tolerates mild frosts and has been used for breeding of some beautiful hybrids like 'Christabel' with butter-yellow fragrant flowers of which the first few have a contrasting purple venation and 'Corfe Castle' with yellow-greenish flowers and dark pink middle vein, this hybrid is fragrant in the evening.

144 – Gladiolus tristis
Courtesy Lambley Nursery, Australia

Glaucidium; Glaucidiaceae (Paeoniaceae)

There is only one species in this genus:

Glaucidium palmatum Sieb et Zucc

This amazing forest perennial comes from Japan, it is a long-lived perennial up to sixty centimetres high with slightly hairy, hand-shaped (palmatum) leaves that grow to thirty centimetres across. The plant requires light or semi-shade and neutral to slightly acidic rich and moist soil for best development. Use it in the landscape in special places free of competition or together with 'gentle' species like Astilbe, Hosta or non-competitive ferns. Propagation is best by seed or division only of quite old plants as the tuberous rootstock has at age started to grow apart and can be cut. The species is rarely seen so far but is most certainly worth the effort.

145 – Glaucidium palmatum
Courtesy Staudengärtnerei Häussermann Stuttgart, Germany

Glaucium; Papaveraceae

A small genus with around twenty species from Europe, northern Africa, central and south-western Asia. The plants usually invade disturbed ground in warm and dry locations and are short-lived perennials, biannual or annuals that feature attractive blue-grey leaves and distinct yellow or orange flowers. For its use in the landscape, I would suggest natural or wild designs like steppes, rockeries or prairies in warm and sunny locations. Soils should be freely draining, sandy, gravelly and poor. Choice of partners should be done carefully with the following recommendations: Bearded Iris, Eryngium bougatii, Linaria purpurea, Linaria genistifolia, Artemisia, Lychnis flos-jovis, Lychnis coronaria, Salvia pratensis and grasses like Festuca glauca and Stipa. In the rockery, we could add carpet-forming species like Dianthus noeanus, Paronychia kapela, Sedum and Thymus. In suitable places, the plants self-sow easily. Propagation is by seed and experience shows that using deep tubes has the best success rate and subsequent performance of the plants in the ground.

Glaucium corniculatum Rudolph
This Mediterranean species ascends to eighteen hundred metres altitude and is mostly short-lived. The flowers vary from yellow to orange and red are held around sixty centimetres high in early summer.

Glaucium flavum Crantz
A widespread species that usually lives only three or four years, Glaucium flavum can grow to a hundred and twenty centimetres high on better soils but lives longer on poorer soils. The flowers are yellow, sometimes more orange from spring to late summer.

Glaucium grandiflorum Boiss et Reut
From Turkey, the Caucasus, Syria and Iran and the Sinai comes the largest flowering species, up to ten centimetres in colours from dark orange to crimson red, often with dark spots. The plants grow to fifty centimetres in height.

Globularia; Globulariaceae

There are around thirty species in the genus of the 'Ball-Flower'. The name refers to the round shape of its flowers. Most of the species prefer alkaline soils and the plants have small leathery leaves. Their use in the landscape would be in rockeries or in tubs; they all need good drainage and want full sun. Propagation is by seed or semi-hardwood cuttings in late summer, note that these cuttings should be laid on the ground horizontally and pinned, the way the plants naturally grow.

Globularia cordifolia L
This dwarf sub-shrub comes from southern and central Europe where it grows in the mountains. The plant has small, three to four-centimetre wedge-shaped leaves and steel-blue round flower heads. It is a very valuable ground cover for the sunny rockery and combines beautifully with Helianthemum canum. There are two cultivars, 'Alba' and 'Rosea' with white and light pink flower heads respectively.

Globularia trichosantha Fisch et Mey
A fast-growing, carpet forming species with bright blue flowers in early summer. Its ability to over larger areas in full sun or semi-shade makes it a great ground cover for larger rockeries but it can also nicely be used along paths and borders.

Glycirrhiza; Fabaceae

The genus comprises around twenty species from the Mediterranean, Asia and North and South America where they thrive in a large range of habitats from dry to wet. Most like deep, rich soils with sufficient moisture in full sun, their use in the landscape may be best in natural and wild designs and in association with shrubs. They naturally lean on higher plants and are important in herbal medicine, the genus is also called 'Sweet wood' or Liquorice (in German 'Lakritze').

Glycirrhiza echinata L
The 'Roman Sweet wood' is a decorative perennial with its ornamental fruits and as a wild perennial, is not too aggressive toward its neighbours.

Glycirrhiza glabra L
This is the actual Liquorice plant; the rhizomes harvested in autumn provide the base raw material for the sweets. It is at home in southern and eastern Europe, western Siberia, western and central Asia and the Mediterranean. The plant grows to a hundred and twenty centimetres and forms subterranean runners. The flowers are like peas, a centimetre across and blue or light purple in colour, sometimes white. Remarkable is the sugar content of the Sweet wood; it is more than fifty times that of Sugar cane. The perennial is used in herbal medicine against colds and problems of the breathing tracts, it is also helpful against viral and other infections and relaxes cramps.

146 - *Glycirrhiza glabra*
Courtesy Staudengärtnerei Häussermann Stuttgart, Germany

Goniolimon; Plumbaginaceae

A genus like Limonium that originates in north-western Africa and extends to Mongolia. Leathery leaves indicate its adaptation to steppes, dry grasslands and rocky slopes and its species should be used accordingly and rather in natural and wild designs of these habitats.

Goniolimon speciosum Boiss

The species comes from Siberia and extends to the Caucasus mountain range, it grows to thirty centimetres with pink to purple-pink flowers in late summer.

Goniolimon tataricum Mill

This species is also known as 'Statice' and produces the well-known dried flowers for florists. The perennial grows from south-eastern Europe to central Russia in Steppes and dry grasslands. The leaves form rosettes and the flowers are ruby-red with white throat held around thirty centimetres above ground in late summer. The plant prefers summer-dry places and is commercially harvested for the dried flowers, best planting distance is fifty centimetres apart. Propagation is by root cuttings or seed.

147 – Goniolimon tataricum
Courtesy Klaus Mödinger

Gunnera; Haloragidaceae

This genus comes from the southern hemisphere and features prostrate rhizomes requiring some frost protection in areas with real frosts.

Gunnera manicata Linden

This very ornamental species from Brazil derives its decorative value from its huge, up to two metres wide leaves. It is best used as a feature plant with carefully selected location, either singly or in small groups. Soil preparation is crucial for good development and in my experience, it is best to dig a large, more than a metre deep, hole and fill it with aged compost and old leaf litter. Plant in late spring in frost-prone areas. The plant is adapted to live in moors or along creeks and in high humidity; consequently, ensure ample supply of water. In the Royal Botanic Gardens in Sydney, I planted a specimen in Government House grounds in the shade of a Ficus macrophylla with drip irrigation constantly running in summer and the specimen looked fantastic. Propagation is by division of rhizomes with heads before the plant becomes active in spring. Seed propagation is also an option and gives larger numbers of plants but naturally takes more time. Fresh seed is best.

148 – Gunnera manicata at Stourhead
Courtesy National Trust of England

Gypsophila; Caryophyllaceae

The genus Gypsophila is widespread over Eurasia and describes species from alpine habitats as well as species from dry, rocky or sandy steppes. According to their habitat they often develop strong, deep taproots for survival. Their use in the landscape is in alpine settings or rockeries and dry-stone walls and by and large they are better suited for the natural or semi-formal design.

Gypsophila paniculata L

The well-known 'Baby's Breath' or 'Hohes Schleierkraut' (Tall Veils Herb) is at home in southern Europe, the Caucasus and western Siberia. It is an up to a hundred and twenty-centimetre-high robust perennial with strong roots and grey-green leaves. The flowers are small but numerous and the plant is covered with them in late summer and into autumn. The species requires well-drained, rather poor soils. This Gypsophila combines very well with a large range of plants as the foliage and flowers blend in or 'mediate' between other plants. Bearded Iris, Allium, Crocus, Tulipa and Echinope, Eryngium, Lychnis and very many Salvia are great partners suited for the same soil conditions.

Gypsophila repens

A more alpine species that grows prostrate in limestone gravels in the mountains of Spain, France, Italy and other southern European countries. It does well in smaller rockeries or trailing down dry-stone walls; propagation by cuttings.

Haberlea; Gesneriaceae

This is an ancient genus of small plants usually growing as a rosette in sheltered rockeries or dry-stone walls facing away from the sun. They can live for a very long time and form lovely colonies in alkaline soils. Propagation is easy by cutting off rooted rosettes and even leaf cuttings; seed is another option.

Haberlea rhodopensis Urum
The around fifteen-centimetre-high species comes from Bulgaria and has hairy lanceolate leaves. It flowers in early summer with purple-blue flowers.

Hebe; Scrophulariaceae

There are around seventy-five species in the genus Hebe; most come from New Zealand, some from Australia and South America. The genus contains mainly small prostrate or upright shrubs with leaves of a leathery or fleshy texture. These plants inhabit moist temperate zones and should not be let dry out; they thrive best in PH values between six and 7.5 but tolerate more acidic soils. In cultivation, it is important to note that leaves that are shaded out die back and these branches do not recover most of the time, therefore specimens that are too closely planted tend to become bare at the base. There are many applications for them to be used; in the landscape, rockeries, along borders or as container plants. Propagation is best by soft-tip cuttings in spring or semi-hardwood cuttings in late summer.

Hebe buchananii Cock et Allan
This species is at home in New Zealand between nine and fifteen hundred metres altitude. It is a small plant and grows prostrate to around twenty centimetres high, forming pillows or carpets. Ideal for small rockeries or container plantings, this is a very hardy species.

Hebe cupressoides Cock et Allan
Also from New Zealand, this interesting species lives up to its Latin name and looks like the Cypresses; however, it is slow growing and requires many years before it reaches its height of around a hundred and fifty centimetres. Consequently, it may be used as a substitute for small conifers in rockeries or heath-land plantings, also with Rhododendron, Azaleas and other Ericaceae.

Hebe pimeloides Cock et Allan
Another 'Kiwi' (nickname of Australians for New Zealanders) is this up to thirty-centimetre-high shrub with small blue-grey leaves. Unlike most other Hebe it is reasonably drought tolerant and looks a treat in the rockery between ground covers and small carpet-forming plant species.

Hebe topiaria Moore
An up to ninety-centimetre-high, well-branched roundish plant species with grey-green leaves and white flowers in summer. This is a particularly lovely and hardy species.

Helenium; Asteraceae

Around forty species are known in this genus. Some are annual, some are biannual and most are perennial. The German name 'Sonnenbraut' translates loosely into something like 'Bride of the Sun'. Another English common name is Sneezeweed, which does not do the plant justice. Helenium are among the most beautiful and graceful flowers from summer to autumn for the perennial border and as cut flowers. Cultivation is not too hard in good garden soil but they do require sufficient moisture and a good supply of food. I would use them in the formal or semi-formal perennial border together with Phlox paniculata, Aster,

Delphinium x Elatum, Erigeron, Gaillardia, Heliopsis, Monarda, Coreposis, Rudbeckia, Solidago and higher ornamental grasses. Propagation is by soft-tip cuttings from the first growth in spring (repeated harvests are possible) or division in winter.

Helenium bigelovii Gray

This species comes from California and extends to Oregon, it grows to sixty centimetres high and features large deep yellow flowers in early summer, great cut flower.

Helenium hoopesii Gray

An American species that tolerates drier places than other Helenium, it has large bright golden-yellow flowers in late spring, I would use it in meadows or along shrubs in natural designs.

Helenium hybrids & cultivars

Many have been bred in the early twentieth century and are wonderfully attractive and long flowering plants. Some that I can recommend are:

'Moerheim Beauty' – eighty centimetres, copper-red with dark centre

'Waltraut' – a hundred centimetres, golden-brown flowers'Blütentisch' – eighty centimetres, golden-yellow with brown centre

'Coppelia' – a hundred centimetres, coppery orange'Flammenspiel' – a hundred and thirty centimetres, golden-yellow playing into brown-red

'Kupfersprudel' – a hundred and ten centimetres, velvety copper-brown, large flowers

'Rubinzwerg' – eighty centimetres, deep ruby-red, flowers profusely and for a very long time

'Waldhorn' – eighty centimetres, warm, velvety brown'Baudirektor Linne' – a hundred and twenty centimetres, velvety red large flowers for a long time

'Indianersommer' – a hundred and twenty centimetres, gorgeous brown-red

'Septembergold' – a hundred and ten centimetres, bright yellow, flowers late, profusely and very long

149 – Helenium hybrid 'Moerheim Beauty'
Work in Stuttgart, 1984

Helianthemum; Cistaceae

A genus with around a hundred and twenty species from Europe, the Mediterranean and central Asia that describes evergreen or semi-evergreen sub-shrubs. Use in the landscape mainly in rockeries, dry stone walls, gravelly slopes or steppe designs on light, dry and well-drained soils in full sun. They may also be used along and to define paths and borders. Good to combine with smaller Artemisia, Delphinium tatsiense, Gaura lindheimeri, Hieracium, Iris barbata, Iberis sempervirens, Calamintha nepeta, Geranium dalmaticum, Linum narbonense, Salvia nemorosa, Scutellaria baicalensis, Veronica incana and grasses. They are graceful plants with masses of flowers, whereas the single-flowered species do not flower if the semi-double or double ones. It is good practice to cut back straight after flowering in case they get too long and leggy. Propagation is best by cuttings in summer.

Helianthemum apenninum Mill
This is a widespread species that occurs from south-western Europe, around the Mediterranean and extends into Asia Minor. The plant grows to around forty centimetres with velvety grey to white lovely foliage and white flowers from spring into summer, there is an attractive pink-flowering form, Helianthemum apenninum var roseum.

Helianthemum canum Baumg
This small plant comes from central and southern Europe and grows to only around fifteen centimetres high with a prostrate habit. The flowers are dark yellow and appear in early summer, it is a great species for among rocks and in gravel that sometimes self-sows. It combines well with Lavandula and Phlox subulata.

Helianthemum hybrids
Recommended are:

'Album Simplex'- fifty-five centimetres, dark green foliage and white flowers

'Apricot' – thirty-five centimetres, apricot-coloured

'Ben Alder' – twenty centimetres, bright orange-red

'Blutströpfchen' – twenty centimetres, single blood-red

'Dompfaff' – twenty centimetres, grey foliage, pink-red flowers'Fire Dragon' – fifteen centimetres, grey foliage bright crimson red flowers'Gelbe Perle' – twenty-five centimetres, dark green foliage, lemon-yellow flowers'Golden Queen' – fifteen centimetres, yellow flowers, great ground cover

'Lawrensons Pink' – twenty centimetres, dark green leaves, salmon-pink flowers'Rose of Leeswood' – twenty centimetres, grey foliage, double crimson-pink flowers

'Rotkehlchen' – twenty centimetres, orange with red eye, very lovely

'Sterntaler' – fifteen centimetres, prostrate with dark green foliage and golden yellow flowers

'Supreme' – thirty-five centimetres, dark scarlet-red with dark eye

150 – Helianthemum 'Henfield Brilliant'
Work in the botanic garden Stuttgart, Germany

Helianthus; Asteraceae

The famous 'Sunflower' genus comprises around eighty species from America. Most of these are tall perennials or annuals; only a few are important for landscape architecture or horticulture. Propagation is easy by seed or division of runners of those species that form them. Use them in the landscape or garden in natural, informal designs in full sun or light shade.

Helianthus atrorubens Elliott

The 'Hairy Forest Sunflower' is at home in the south-eastern USA where it grows in dry, open forests. The plant develops long runners and grows to around a hundred and fifty centimetres tall and flowers yellow with crimson centre in late summer to autumn. As it is a strong growing and competitive species its neighbours need to be chosen carefully.

Helianthus giganteus Wats

From North America comes this species that inhabits swamps and wet meadows, true to its name the plant grows up to three hundred and fifty centimetres tall. The flowers are sulphur-yellow and appear in late summer and last into late autumn. This plant is rarely used but worth putting in larger, natural landscape designs where sufficient water is available. Great in combination with Aster x amethystine and other large perennials from wet prairies.

Helianthus x multiflorus

This hybrid has its historic origins in the Spanish palace of L' Escorial in Madrid and has produced some beautiful offspring. The original plant grows to a hundred and twenty centimetres high and has numerous single lemon-yellow flowers.

Some of its recommended children:

'Triomphe de Gand' – a hundred and sixty centimetres with golden flowers from summer to autumn

'Loddon Gold' – a hundred and eighty centimetres with large yellow flowers from summer to autumn.

Helianthus orgyalis DC

Another North-American species that stands up to two hundred and fifty centimetres tall and flowers bright yellow in autumn. It is a very decorative species that may be used in a prominent position in the prairie garden or in association with trees or buildings. Good partners are Eupatorium fistulosum, Vernonia askansana, Acogonum and tall prairie grasses. Propagation is in spring by division of its rhizomes.

Helianthus salicifolius Dietr

The 'Willow-leaved Sunflower' is widespread in the USA where it grows in dry tall prairies or meadows. The species develops strong rhizomes and grows to three hundred centimetres tall with dark yellow flowers in autumn and late autumn and requires long, warm summers for full flowering. It is an impressive ornamental species with its foliage effective for a long period of the growing season. The stems tend to become softer and fall over when the plant receives too much water, therefore use it in dry areas like its original habitat. At the nursery of Her Highness the Countess of Zeppelin we had a stand on a slope below the old potting shed. It was overlooking the village and valley below and the flowers above the valley meant for me the end of autumn, with winter about to arrive.

151 – Helianthus salicifolius

This picture from the nursery Horstmann in Germany demonstrates very well how these tall Helianthus may be used in mixed borders. They last quite late into autumn, note the first autumn colouring of the trees in the background; courtesy Baumschule Horstmann, Germany

Helichrysum; Asteraceae

The 'Straw-Flowers' have their common name describing the texture and qualities of their papery petals that grow in roof-tile fashion. Worldwide there are around five hundred species of perennials, sub-shrubs or shrubs. Many species of the genus Helichrysum have been re-named. These are found under their alphabetical name.

152 – Helichrysum macranthum
Courtesy National Botanic Gardens, Australia

Helichrysum rutidolepis
A hardy perennial plant with grey, linear leaves and yellow flower heads held at twenty centimetres height in spring and summer. Full sun is required the plant adapts to many soil types and is propagated by cuttings or division.

Helictotrichon; Poaceae

Helictotrichon sempervirens Bess ex Pilger
This is an outstanding ornamental grass of xerophytic character. The leaves are blue-grey coming from a dense clump with the inflorescence standing a hundred and twenty centimetres above. The species requires full sun and dry, stony and alkaline soils, it is therefore best suited as structural plant for rockeries and steppe designs but I have used it also in formal dry perennial borders and xerophytic plantings. Propagation is by division in spring.

153 – Helictotrichon sempervirens
Courtesy Plantes de Jardenes, France

Heliopsis; Asteraceae

The genus of the 'Sonnenauge' or 'Eye of the sun' is small with seven species, all of which come from North America. They are medium-sized perennials that are reasonably drought tolerant and produce excellent border plants and long-lasting cut flowers. They partner well with Monarda, Helenium, tall Aster, tall Veronica, Delphinium, Phlox paniculata, Erigeron and medium ornamental grasses. They require normal garden soil with sufficient nutrients in full sun and can be propagated by division in spring or autumn or cuttings in spring.

Heliopsis helianthoides var helianthoides

A medium to tall perennial from one metre to a hundred and eighty centimetres high with bright yellow flowers in summer and into early autumn, a recommended cultivar is 'Light of Loddon' that grows to a hundred centimetres and has Dahlia-like flowers in golden yellow.

Heliopsis helianthoides var scabra Fern

This variety inhabits drier areas than the above described, it has tough, hairy leaves and flowers profusely in variations of yellow, both single and semi-double forms occur. It is a parent of the following recommended cultivars:

'Goldgefieder' – a hundred and forty centimetres with large, double golden-yellow flowers
'Jupiter' – a hundred and seventy centimetres with very large orange-yellow single flowers

'Karat' – a hundred and twenty centimetres with bright large yellow single flowers, great cut flower
'Venus' – a hundred and twenty centimetres with golden yellow flowers

154 – Heliopsis 'Tuscan Sun'
Staudengärtnerei Gräfin von Zeppelin, Germany

Helleborus; Ranunculaceae

Helleborus is a genus of around twenty species that are sometimes difficult to differentiate from each other. They are at home in Europe to the Caucasus, China and Turkey where they grow mostly in forests and woodlands on alkaline soils. Helleborus form rhizomes and may be divided into those growing stems (H. Argutifolius, foetidus, lividus and vesicarius) and the Hellebores without stems. Apart from two, these are deciduous. Hellebores niger, the well-known 'Christ Rose' is in between, it is a long-lived perennial forming large clumps with decorative leaves and a long flowering period. The evergreen species forming stems are very valuable for the larger landscape and garden in association with shrubs and trees. The deciduous species are best for the natural, wild garden designs. All Helleborus love calcium and prefer reasonably consistent moisture, both drought and wet feet damage the plants. They partner well with ferns, shade grasses, Galanthus and Cyclamen and can be planted from deep shade to quite sunny places provided sufficient water is available. Propagation is by division after flowering in spring or after the summer dormancy, seed propagation is easy too and most species self-sow freely in locations with the right conditions.

Helleborus argutifolius Viv
An endemic plant to Corsica and Sardinia, formerly named H. Corsicus. The species grows in open forests and woodlands in higher altitudes and is the largest of the evergreen stem-forming Hellebores. The bowl-shaped light green flowers can stand up to a metre high above the large, dark-green hard and serrated leaves. This species requires a sunny position otherwise the stems tend to fall over.

155 – Helleborus argutifolius
Courtesy Carolyns Shade Garden

Helleborus foetidus

This European species lives in mixed forests and woodlands, around shrubs and on rocky slopes with poor alkaline soils. It is evergreen with palmate leaves, flowers in late winter to early spring with bell-shaped yellowish-green flowers and for these winter features is a most valuable plant in herbaceous perennial borders. It is adaptable to different soils and varies accordingly. Propagation is best by seed. The species does not like transplanting, but it's possible.

Helleborus niger

This plant is usually known as 'Christ's Rose', flowering in late winter in the northern hemisphere, also as 'Schneerose' (Snow Rose). Growing in mixed forests and woodlands, sometimes also in meadows in groups and has thick, leathery and evergreen leaves. The flowers may vary from white to pink, red or even apricot and green, the species is also used in herbal medicine.

156 – Helleborus niger
Courtesy Angelika Kaufmann

Helleborus orientalis Lam

From southern Europe to Turkey comes this up to fifty-centimetre-high perennial with evergreen leaves. The flowers are up to ten-centimetre-wide and vary in colour from greenish-white to white, cream, yellowish or pinkish. It is an easy plant for the natural garden, doing well in every average, loamy soil.

There are many pretty Helleborus cultivars and hybrids as the plant has been bred since the nineteenth century. One of the old and reliable hybrids between H. purpurascens and H. orientalis is 'Atrorubens der Gärten' (German for Atrorubens of the Gardens); this should not be mixed up with the actual species – H. atrorubens.

Helmholtzia; Philydraceae

Helmholtzia glaberrima

The 'Stream Lily' is an Australian native, flax-like plant up to a hundred and fifty centimetres tall. A plume-like head of small pale pink flowers is held up to two metres high above the foliage in summer. The plant is essentially a rainforest plant for damp, shady places along water features or wet rockeries. It should not be exposed to full sun and in colder zones requires a sheltered microclimate. In Canberra, it grows well in the Rainforest Gully of the botanic gardens and I have planted it in the Fern Gully in the National Zoo. The flowers are quite spectacular and the lush foliage makes it valuable as structural plants for shade and under trees. Propagation is by seed and division.

157 – Helmholtzia glaberrima
Work in Sydney, Royal Botanic Gardens

Hemerocallis; Hemerocallidaceae

The Day Lilies derive their common name from the flowers that are mostly open for only one day. However, the plant usually produces so many flowers that it appears to be an uninterrupted flowering period. The translation verbally means, 'Beauty for one day' and comes from the Greek 'hemera' (day) and 'kallos' (beauty). There are twenty species in this genus from China, Manchuria, Mongolia, Siberia, Korea, Japan and northern India. In China, Hemerocallis is also used for cooking and medicine. Most Hemerocallis are herbaceous and winter-dormant and generally tough and adaptable plants with flower colours covering almost everything except for blue.

Like Lilium, all Hemerocallis are highly toxic to cats!

Hemerocallis altissima Stout
A remarkable, up to two-hundred-centimetre-high day lily that comes from the mountains of Nanking. The leaves are around a hundred and twenty centimetres high and overwinter as a clump; the flowers appear from summer into autumn and are bright yellow and fragrant.

Hemerocallis aurantiaca Baker
This species has orange-coloured flowers that are held around eighty centimetres high in summer.

Hemerocallis citrina Baroni

From central China comes this species that has up to one metre long, pendulous leaves that feature a reddish colour at their base. The flowers appear in summer and are small, funnel-shaped and very long of a lemony colour. They are carried at a hundred and twenty centimetres high and are strongly fragrant in the evening and at night.

Hemerocallis lilioasphodelus

The 'Yellow Day lily' inhabits moist meadows and open woodlands from Europe to Japan and Siberia. It grows to eighty centimetres tall with bright lemon-yellow bell or funnel-shaped flowers that appear in early summer and remain open for up to sixty hours. The species has a strong fragrance resembling Convallaria majalis.

158 – Hemerocallis lilioasphodelus
Courtesy Klaus Mödinger

Hemerocallis middendorffii Trautv

From Asia comes this tough and long-flowering orange-coloured species that is for those reasons popular in landscape designs.

Hemerocallis hybrids

Exist in huge numbers and many come in and go out of fashion in a rather short time; for that reason, I do not recommend ones here but advise to go to the local suppliers and ask for their availability and characteristics.

Hepatica; Ranunculaceae

There are seven species and ten varieties described in the genus Hepatica. All are at home in the northern hemisphere. They resemble Anemones somewhat and thrive in forests and woodlands in shade and semi-shade. Propagation is by seed and in the right places Hepatica self-sow or employ ants for the distribution of their seed. In cultivation, the seed should be covered with sand and the pots sunk into the soil, which assists with more even temperatures as compared to pots that are in the open. They are slow to grow. In the first year, Hepatica usually only develop two cotyledons with the first true leaves appearing in the second or even third year. They start flowering in the fourth or fifth year and do not want to be disturbed or like transplanting, so choose their place carefully and then leave them alone apart from ensuring there is enough moisture, minerals and a balanced food supply. Hepatica can live for more than thirty years.

Hepatica maxima Nakai

The largest Hepatica comes from Korea where it grows in acidic soils with Rhododendron in a climate with mild and rainy summers. The flowers are up to ten centimetres across, are white, sometimes pink and have a reddish underside.

Hepatica nobilis var nobilis Garsault

This European Hepatica occurs from Scandinavia to Spain and from France to Russia. It naturally grows in deciduous forests on well-drained soils usually on limestone subsoils. The flowers are up to three centimetres and have a noble blue-purple but can also be pink or white.

159 – Hepatica nobilis
Gärtnerei Häussermann, Stuttgart, Germany

Hepatica transsilvanica Fuss

As the name suggests, this species comes from Romania where it grows in the mountains up to two thousand metres high. It flowers very early in spring with five centimetres large, blue, purple, white or pink colours.

Heracleum; Apiaceae

This is a genus of around sixty species of the northern temperate zones. The leaves and stems are hairy and may cause allergies in sensitive people. The plants grow mostly in rich soils and in association with water, indeed they may become weedy along water courses like creeks or rivers.

Heracleum mantegazzianum Somm et Levier

This tall, up to three-hundred-centimetre-high perennial comes from the Caucasus and bears handsome, huge umbellate flowers that are up to fifty centimetres across. The individual leaves are up to a metre and because of these features, the species is valued as focal point in displays. However, the plant is very competitive and may become a weed as well. There are health issues due to its irritating leave properties. If used in displays, the plant should be placed well back from paths and where people could touch it or should be substituted with other impressive species from the Apiaceae family.

160 – Heracleum mantegazzianum
Work in Stuttgart 1984

Heuchera; Saxifragaceae

This genus is named after the German physician and botanist Johann Heinrich Heucher (1677 – 1747). It originates in the Atlantic and Pacific North America and describes mainly bushy, tight perennials that are used for their evergreen foliage. They have a wide range of applications; however, drought is not well tolerated, so they need to be kept in moist environments. Good partners are Helenium, Artemisia valesiaca, Nepeta, Salvia, Erigeron, Veronica, Aster amellus, Rudbeckia, Campanula and Bergenia. Division or cuttings with a part of the older, woody parts are best propagation methods.

Heuchera abramsii Rydb

From the USA and California comes this most beautiful small species that grows in rock crevices. The flowers are held around ten centimetres high and start pure white, but then colour to a deep pink-purple. Use in the alpinum for the collector and enthusiast.

Heuchera americana

Out of forests and woodlands of the eastern USA comes this, popular for its Ivy-like foliage in horticulture, species. There are many cultivars; one of the best-known ones are 'Palace Purple' with red-brown leaves up to sixty centimetres high and white-pink flowers in summer, it was selected in Kew for formal garden borders.

Heuchera micrantha Douglas ex Lindl

This western American species occurs naturally in conifer forests, it has silvery grey marbled leaves and bears numerous pink flowers up to ninety centimetres high above the foliage in early summer. This species requires regular moisture.

There are very many garden cultivars and hybrids available, best check with local suppliers for availability and characteristics.

Hibiscus; Malvaceae

This genus is at home mainly in the warm-temperate, subtropical and tropical zones of the world and consists of small trees, shrubs and perennials. Propagation is either by seed, best fresh and kept warm; or soft-tip cuttings which will need protection in very cold areas in their first winter.

Hibiscus coccineus Walt

This species comes from warmer areas of the USA where it grows in swamps and wet meadows. It grows to three hundred centimetres tall and has outstanding glowing scarlet red flowers in autumn.

Hibiscus moscheutos ssp moscheutos

These are tall, up to two hundred centimetres high perennials with huge, up to twenty centimetre wide flowers from white to pink in colour, always with a red centre. A very attractive large perennial species for the background due to its size and because it becomes active later in the growing season than most other perennials.

161 – Hibiscus moscheutos 'Disco Belle'
Courtesy Brett Samon

Hieracium; Asteraceae

This is a very variable genus with more than 100 species, mostly form the northern temperate zones but some originate in the mountain ranges of southern India, Ceylon, South Africa and South America. Only a few, however, are of significance in landscape architecture and horticulture.

Hieracium pilosella

This interesting ten to twenty-centimetre-high species grows almost everywhere in Europe on poor soils, in dry meadows and in open woodlands. The leaves are silvery or greyish, woolly and the yellow flowers appear from spring to autumn. Due to the shape of the leaves the German nickname for this species is 'Mausöhrchen', which translates loosely into 'the little ears of a mouse'. Due to its toughness and adaptability the species is even suited to rooftop plantings or in rockeries with partners like Campanula, Dianthus, Festuca, Sedum, Thymus and other species from a sunny, dry and exposed habitat.

Hippuris; Hippuridaceae

Hippuris vulgaris

The only species of this genus is an aquatic plant of standing or slow-moving waters. The German common name 'Tannenwedel' means it looks like a small Spruce (Abies), and indeed a stand of Hippuris does look like a miniature Black Forest with a little imagination. Use in the landscape in larger water features as the species is strong growing. It stabilises mud and provides oxygen to the water. Propagation is simple by division.

Hosta; Hostaceae

This genus comprises around fifty species, mainly from East Asia. Most are perennials that form dense clumps and have thick, fleshy roots. They are primarily grown for their ornamental foliage but also possess very attractive flowers. Hosta require lots of regular moisture combined with high humidity and need to be used with sensibility in designs; they do usually well in combination with water features but still require good drainage. Some partners that experience has shown to go well with the Hostas are Astilbe, Campanula macrantha, Carex muskingumensis, Cimicifuga, Deschampsia caespitose, Epimendium, Hakonochlea macra, Hemerocallis, Geranium macrorrhizum, Lilium henryi, Polygonatum, Primula, Pulmonaria and many ferns. An ideal combination is with early flowering species like Corydalis and Scilla as they start to become dormant as the Hosta starts to become active, late in the season. Unfortunately, Hosta appear to produce snails.

Hosta fluctuans Maekawa
This Japanese species grows in the moist mountains of Monshu; it is a medium-sized plant around fifty centimetres high with light purple to purple flowers that stand ninety centimetres tall. Its leaves arise on long stems and are somewhat egg-shaped and bright green, the species is best used as feature plant singly or in small groups in perennial borders or semi-formal designs.

Hosta montana Maekawa
A widespread and variable species also coming from Japan; the plant forms dense clumps to around fifty centimetres height with an elongated, heart-shaped leaf form. The flowers are off-white and stand well above the foliage.

Hosta plantaginea Aschers
The 'August Lily' from China is a robust species around thirty centimetres tall with broad, heart-shaped leaves of a bright green to yellow-green colour. The in late summer appearing flowers are held around 60cm high, white and have a delicate fragrance at night, therefore place it in a spot where this can be appreciated. This species is more robust than most Hosta and tolerates more sun.

Hosta sieboldiana Engl
This species grows to around fifty or sixty centimetres high with large, stiff blue-grey-green leaves that are quite a feature. The flowers appear in early summer and stand only a little above the foliage. This species is a strong grower.

Hosta ventricosa Stearn
Coming from China, this species is strong and fast growing with a handsome clump of leaves up to sixty centimetres high. The numerous flowers are purple and are held at almost a metre height in late summer.

Hosta have been the subject of extensive breeding over a long period of time, therefore it may be best to check with local suppliers what is available in your area and keep in mind how to use Hosta in the landscape and garden.

162 – Hosta 'Royal Standard'
Courtesy Baumschule Eggert, Germany

Hyacinthoides; Hyacynthaceae (Liliaceae)

The 'Bluebells' are bulbous perennials that are sensitive to soil compaction. Identified are eight wild species in Europe and North Africa in habitats of deciduous forests with rich soils.

Hyacinthoides hispanica Rothm
The Spanish Bluebell grows apart from the Iberian Peninsula in northern Africa, mainly Algeria and Morocco, in forests and shady habitats. They can form impressive large stands and characterise the landscape when in flower in spring. The wild species flower colour is purple with blue stamens and it can be grown within the root zone of established trees. That is in my opinion the best way to use it in the landscape – let it grow wild and on its own and spread under deciduous trees. Mind you keep it in areas of low or no foot traffic as they do not tolerate that well. There are several lovely cultivars and hybrids available.

Hyacinthus; Hyacinthaceae (Liliaceae)

The small genus of Hyacynths describes three species of bulbous perennials related to Brimeura, Galtonia, Hyacinthella, Polyxena, Muscari and Ledebouria.

Hyacinthus orientalis
The common Hyacinth originally comes from western Asia, Turkey, Syria and the Lebanon where it grows between rocks in altitudes up to two thousand metres. The wild species is interesting for the collector, of importance for the gardens and horticulture is the numerous hybrids either as potted plants, for seasonal displays or planted in warm, sunny and mainly dry but rich soils. They are easily propagated by division of bulblets with their base cut cross-wise and then planted upside down into the soil. The whole bulb is planted as it normally grows. Unless planted in massed displays for events the Hyacinthe is a plant for small spaces like rockeries.

Hybanthus; Violaceae

Hybanthus monopetalus
This small, up to forty-centimetre-high herb has linear leaves and purple flowers held in terminal racemes. It is a great plant adaptable to full sun or heavy shade if sufficient water is available.

Hybanthus stellarioides
Bright orange flowers appear in summer on this around thirty centimetres, small herbaceous perennial. It requires moisture and warmth and seems to prefer sandy soils.

Hypericum; Clusiaceae

This is a large genus of around two thousand herbs, perennials, sub-shrubs or shrubs that is distributed mainly in the temperate and subtropical zones of the northern hemisphere. Some species are fantastic garden plants for light, sandy or gravelly soils from full sun to semi-shade. Propagation is by the fine seed or cuttings.

Hypericum calycinum
Turkey, Bulgaria, Anatolia and south-western Europe are home to this strong-growing, up to forty-centimetre-high ground cover. It tolerates drought very well but needs to be used carefully in the larger landscapes as it is quite competitive and tends to invade and overwhelm weaker neighbours, a bit like Vinca.

Hypericum coris
This up to thirty-centimetre-high alpine species is a pretty rockery plant with golden-yellow flowers in summer. It combines well with Campanula portneschlagiana, Silene alpestris, Moltkia petraea, Potentilla nitida and other plants from the same habitat.

Hypericum olympicum
At home in Asia minor and the Balkans, this rich flowering forty-centimetre-high perennial is easy to grow and ideally suited for rockeries and dry-stone walls.

Hypericum perforatum
Widespread from Europe to central China is the since old times used medicinal plant which is commercially farmed and would be used in the landscape in natural and wild designs. It self-sows freely and has become a weed in Australia.

Hypoestes; Acanthaceae

Hypoestes floribunda
This herbaceous perennial grows to around a metre and has an open habit. From late summer, right into winter mauve-pink and sometimes white flowers appear on terminal spikes. They require lots of water in a semi-shaded and sheltered, warm position and can be propagated by seed or cuttings.

Hyssopus; Lamiaceae

A genus of shrubs and sub-shrubs that is naturally distributed from the Mediterranean to central Asia in steppes and dry meadows. All Hyssopus are aromatic plants and some are used in herbal medicine and the kitchen. However, in my opinion they are also well suited to natural, wild planting designs including low maintenance spaces like traffic islands and median strips of roads. They are just as tough, decorative and long-lived as like Lavandula and Santolina. Propagation is by seed or cuttings; older plants should be cut back to rejuvenate.

Hyssopus officinalis
Widespread from the northern Mediterranean to the Black Sea and the Altai is the traditional herb and kitchen plant that has been used in monasteries for herbal medicine and is also often found in farm gardens. From there it has often spread across the landscape and is still found around castle ruins. The plant flowers pink or white in late summer.

163 – Hyssopus officinalis
Courtesy Wikimedia

Hyssopus offiinalis ssp aristata
This rich flowering species comes from the Pyrenees and Spain and has a stronger fragrance than the straight species. The dark blue flowers appear in late summer to autumn and it is very well suited for larger rockeries and as tough ground cover.

Hyssopus seravschanicus Dub Pazji

From central Asia and Turkestan comes this valuable evergreen and up to sixty-centimetre-high perennial. Its flowers are light blue or sky blue in summer and it has a dense, compact habit without any maintenance, well suited in front of roses.

Iberis; Brassicaceae

This genus describes around forty species of annuals, perennials and sub-shrubs. Most of these originate in the Mediterranean, some are from central Europe. By and large they are evergreen, dense and low-growing plants with deep green leaves, valuable for the rockery, dry stone walls or may be used as borders and along paths. They require well-drained soils in full sun, some of the higher growing species should be cut back after flowering; Iberis should not be over-fertilised as they originally come from poorer soil properties. They can cover up to a metre in a few years and propagate well by semi-hardwood cuttings taken in summer and autumn.

Iberis saxatilis Tineo

This species comes from southern Europe and extends into western Switzerland. It grows to ten centimetres and forms dense, lovely pillows that are very valuable as small structural plants in the rockery or perennial border. The white flowers appear in spring and usually a second flowering occurs in autumn.

164 – Iberis saxatilis by Visoflora

Iberis sempervirens

This species is at home in the mountains of the Mediterranean. The plant forms dark, deep green pillows with a profusion of white flowers in late spring, it flowers later than the above described Iberis saxatilis. Very valuable in many garden situations and many good cultivars are available in the trade. Propagation is by semi-hardwood cuttings in late summer and early autumn.

Incarvillea; Bignoniaceae

An interesting genus of fourteen species for the rockery or perennial border, they come from Turkestan, Tibet and China. Cultivation is in sunny or semi-shaded positions in well-drained and rich soils that should contain some free calcium. Propagation is by seed which is reasonably large and germinates erratically.

Incarvillea compacta Maxim
Tibet and north-western China are the home of this small, up to fifteen-centimetre-high species. Lovely, magenta-coloured flowers and deep red lips with a yellow throat appear in late spring and early summer.

Incarvillea delavayi Bur et Franch
The up to ninety-centimetre-high plant comes from the Yunnan and has large, up to thirty-centimetre-long leaves. The flowers are pink-red with yellowish throat and appear in summer. From all the species in this genus this is the largest and toughest, it combines well with Iberis sempervirens, Artemisia schmidtiana, Briza media, Festuca amethystine, Molinia caerulea and other species of the same habitat.

165 – Incarvillea delavayi
Courtesy Wikimedia

Inula; Asteraceae

This genus comprises around a hundred and twenty species that are spread over Eurasia, Africa and East Asia. There are some annuals but most are perennial plants, there are some shrubs also, most have yellow flowers with narrow petals; their cultivation and use in the landscape vary considerably according to species.

Inula acaulis Schott et Kotschy
A small species that grows to only ten centimetres with yellow flowers in summer. It is best used in rockeries with moist soils in full sun.

Inula conycae Meikle

A European species that grows from thirty to a hundred and twenty centimetres tall on very dry, alkaline soils. The plant characterises these landscapes and flowers yellow in late summer to early autumn. Use in the landscape in natural and wild designs like meadows, rocky slopes or large rockeries.

Inula ensifolia

The species is widespread from Eastern Europe to northern Italy and the Caucasus. It is a dense species with basal leaves that grows to eighty centimetres high and flowers golden-yellow in late summer. Its habitat are warm, dry meadows on alkaline soil. It is a valuable plant for natural and informal planting designs and partners well with Carlina acaulis, Carex montana, Campanula carpatica and Linum perenne. Propagation is by division, seed or cuttings.

Inula helenium

The 'Elecampane' or 'Echter Alant' (German for true Alant) is a tall, eighty to three-hundred-centimetre-high perennial with thickened, fleshy rhizomes that are used in herbal medicine. The flowers are large, to eight centimetres across and appear in summer.

Inula magnifica Lipsky

This handsome, up to hundred-centimetre-high perennial comes from central Asia and the Caucasus. It has large leaves, up to a metre long and large, up to fifteen centimetres across flowers of a golden-yellow colour in summer. The species requires a lot of space in the perennial border and is also good to use in association with woody ornamentals like Cotinus coggygria 'Royal Purple'.

Ipheion; Alliaceae

Ipheion uniflorum Raf

The 'Spring Starflower' is an early spring-flowering species with around twenty-centimetre-long leaves that thrives in full sun. It is easy to cultivate and forms over time small colonies that are attractive in informal perennial border designs.

Iris; Iridaceae

The genus Iris is exceptionally varied and contains around three hundred species of the northern hemisphere. They are among the most beautiful and outstanding plants for the garden and its ornament is the flower of the French Kings, the 'Fleur-de-Lys'. In Germany, it is called the Sword-Lily, named after its sword-shaped leaves and since childhood it was my personal favourite plant. One of Vincent van Gogh's most famous paintings are bearded Irises. Another common name was 'Flower of the Rainbow' referring to the amazing range of colours, colour combinations and tones. There are numerous uses in the garden and greater landscapes for Iris, from small to large rockeries and natural garden designs to manicured formal perennial borders. I remember that on the dry-stone walls of the vineyards in southern Germany, bearded Iris were thriving, retaining the often-steep slopes. This leads me to point out that in cultivation it is imperative to know exactly what Iris we do have as their requirements are as varied as the colour range. There are Iris that stand in water, Iris that need to be protected from water in summer and Iris that occupy every niche in between in terms of water use and life cycles. Soil properties and PH requirements are also very different. There are books entirely dedicated to Iris; two great ones are: *A Guide to Species Iris. Their Identification and Cultivation* of the British Iris Society and *Iris'* of Fritz Köhlein of the Ulmer Verlag. For the smaller context of this book, I would just like to stick to the simplest indication of Iris classification:

Genus Iris
Sub-genus Iris

Section Iris
Section Pammiris
Section Onocyclus
Section Regalia
Section Hexapogon
Section Pseudoregelia

Subgenus Limniris

Section Lophiris
Section Limniris
Series Chinense
Series Vernae
Series Ruthenicae
Series Tripetalae
Series Sibiricae
Series Californicae
Series Longipetalae
Series Laevigatae
Series Hexagonae
Series Prismaticae
Series Spuriae
Series Foetidissimae
Series Tenuifoliae
Series Ensatae
Series Syricacae
Series Unguicalares

Subgenus Nepalensis
Subgenus Xiphium

Subgenus Scorpiris
Subgenus Hermodactyloides

Section Brevituba
Section Monolepis
Section Hermodactyloides
Section Micropogon

There are many thousands of beautiful garden hybrids and I will never forget the sight of our Iris fields in Her Highness the Countess of Zeppelin nursery in southern Germany overlooking the green valleys of the Black Forest.

166 – Iris fields in the Black Forest
Staudengärtnerei Gräfin von Zeppelin, Germany

Subgenus Iris

Iris pallida Lam

Also called the 'Perfume Iris' due to its rhizomes having been used in perfume production, Iris pallida is endemic to northern Italy, Slovenia, Croatia and Bosnia. The plant grows to a metre tall with wide, blue-green leaves and beautiful bright, lavender blue fragrant flowers in early summer. One of the most lovely and fragrant tall bearded Irises for warm locations in the rockery, natural garden designs or the formal border. There are two variegated forms, Iris pallida 'Aurea Variegata' (Variegata) and Iris pallida 'Argentea Variegata' (Albovariegata) that are very effective throughout the year as structural plants with their foliage.

Iris pumila

As the species' name suggests this is a dwarf Iris growing to only around fifteen centimetres high. It is a variable plant with flower colour ranging from white to dark purple and yellow to blue, even pink forms are known. Flowering in early spring, Iris pumila thrives in alkaline, gravelly soils and is a specialist plant for small rockeries or the alpinum, or the plant collector and breeder.

Iris reichenbachii Heuff

This lovely dwarf Iris comes from the Balkans and grows to twenty-five centimetres at most. The flowers are quite large, yellow, sometimes with a mild brown venation and appear in spring. This is a very graceful small iris species for natural plantings.

Old bastard forms of the tall bearded Iris

Often around castles, palaces, monasteries or old farm gardens we can find old bastard forms of the tall bearded Iris, some of the best are:

Iris flavescens DC

A prolifically flowering and very tough plant with light yellow flowers in spring to early summer, this cross is nicknamed 'Peasant's Garden Iris' for its reliability.

Iris florentina

This plant is farmed in large fields in upper Italy and around Florence, hence the name. White flowers with a 'Mother of Pearl' glimmer is produced in late spring and early summer, often found in old farm gardens.

Iris germanica

There are many types of this bastard of an unknown medieval origin, the average type is around eighty centimetres tall with purple-blue flowers, brown throat venation and yellow beard.

Modern forms of bearded Iris

The best practices for the cultivation of this group are full sun, well-drained and rich, loamy and alkaline soil properties. A moderate application of fertiliser balanced in favour of potassium in spring and moisture produce best growth and flowers. The summer should be hot and dry; the rhizomes of Iris want to 'bake' in summer when the plant is in its dormancy and roots die back. The Iris rhizome can survive months of drought, even if taken out of the ground during this time of dormancy. This is also the best time for division, the rhizomes are taken out and divided; this is best done in the fourth and fifth year. In commercial production, we used the third year for division for speed so the second-year fields were used as display. In the first year after transplanting, the Iris will not flower very well. The autumn rains in its natural habitat then produce new roots and autumn leaves which provide the nourishment for the flowering in spring and summer, therefore another application of fertiliser in autumn is advised. I would recommend checking with the available suppliers for Iris according to your selection criteria, height, colour and purpose in your designs. From my personal experience with Iris I would recommend them as 'team players', not so much in the foreground but more in the middle ground behind low evergreens or species that are effective in summer and autumn and in front of taller structural plants. The reasons for this are the innate summer dormancy and dying back of leaves after the flower. For the same reason, I often combine the Papaver orientale that thrives in the same environmental conditions with the Iris.

167 – Iris barbata used in a mixed border together with Stachys byzantina and a variety of Geranium, Staudengärtnerei Gräfin von Zeppelin

Section Pammiris

Iris humilis

This is a delicate and pretty but somewhat sensitive species that grows to twelve centimetres high and prefers sandy soils. The leaves are thin and bright green, the flowers are bright yellow and appear in spring.

Section Onocyclus

This section contains some of the most wonderful albeit sometimes tricky to grow Iris. Their original habitat is Palestine, Syria, Asia Minor and Transcaucasia. Consequently, they require scorching hot full sun on rocky, gravelly or sandy dry soils. In areas with plenty of summer rain, they would have to be protected from summer moisture. Fertilise sparingly, in my experience an NPK of 4-3-7 on alkaline soils works best. The flowers are very large and often have fantastic venations that want to be admired from close.

Iris samariae

A most beautiful large-flowered Onocyclus Iris that comes from the border between Israel and the Lebanon between three hundred and five hundred metres above sea level. The flowers are up to twenty centimetres across and may be the largest in the Iris world, the plant grows to seventy centimetres tall and may be extinct in the wild. Possible sources are Iris societies or passionate collectors and obviously this plant is for plant enthusiasts.

Iris susiana

The famous 'Lady in Mourning' grows to around thirty centimetres tall, with light blue-grey flowers that are covered with a net of black-purple veins in spring. Its origins are unknown. The plant has not yet been found in the wild, it has been introduced from Constantinople (Istanbul) around three hundred and fifty years ago.

Section Regalia

These plants come from central Asia and the western slopes of the Himalayas. They are very beautiful but sensitive species that flower ahead of the tall bearded Iris. Cultivation is best in protected, sunny positions in well-drained loamy soils that are dry in summer. They are fantastic cut flowers.

Iris korolkowii Regel

This species comes from Turkestan and grows to fifty centimetres high with compact rhizomes. The flowers are narrow and high with a conical dome and white with strong, red-brown venation resembling some precious orchids. There are two known colour variations – 'Concolor' with purple flowers and 'Violaceae' which is white with purple venation.

168 – Iris korolkowii
Courtesy Miriam Goldstein

Iris stolonifera Maxim

Also coming from Turkestan, this species grows sixty centimetres high with dark-green leaves with a reddish base. The flowers are open brown-purple and steel blue tones with a blue beard in spring. One of the most colour-intense Iris.

Section Hexapogon

There are no species relevant to landscape architecture and horticulture.

Section Pseudoregelia

These species come from mountain meadows of the Himalayas. Cultivation is in positions away from the sun in normal garden soils.

Iris hookeriana Foster
Linear leaves and strong growth characterise this species which flowers vary greatly from white to purple-red in spring.

Subgenus Limniris (beardless Iris)

Section Lophiris

These species come from varied backgrounds from North America and Eastern Asia. They have in common that their original habitat has rich, moist soils in semi-shade. They are best used as small delicacies in rockeries or between heathland designs with Ericaceae like Rhododendron and the like.

Iris gracilipes Gray
This graceful plant grows to twenty centimetres with grass-like pendulous leaves that are up to thirty centimetres long. The flowers are purple-pink with dark venation.

Iris milesii Foster
From the Himalayas comes this beautiful Iris that the Chinese call 'Waterbird Iris'. Strong rhizomes produce sixty-centimetre-long bright green leaves and up to ninety twenty-centimetre-high flower stems that carry bright, reddish-purple inflorescences with dark veins. The species requires acidic soils and protection in areas with harsh winters, the leaves must remain throughout winter for the plant to be able to produce flowers.

169 – Iris milesii
Work and study in Weihenstephan, Germany

Section Limniris

Series Chinense

There are no species of significance to landscape architecture and horticulture.

Series Vernae

Iris verna
This up to fifteen-centimetre-high species comes from the USA and has sword-like dark blue-green leaves and purple-blue flowers in spring. It is very pretty but sensitive; in cultivation, it requires semi-shade and sandy, humous and acidic soils.

Series Ruthenicae

Iris ruthenica Ker Gawl

Mainly a south-eastern European species, however some occurrences are as far east as China. The plants grow to thirty centimetres high and form dense, almost turf-like carpets with their deep green, shiny leaves. Flowers of a light purple colour appear in early summer and are held in between the foliage. This is an easy and tough Iris for rockeries but also as definition along borders for its foliage.

Series Tripetalae

Iris setosa Full ex Link

This species occurs in Japan, Sakhalin, eastern Siberia, Alaska and Canada and grows to fifty centimetres tall with thin, sword-like leaves and mauve-purple falls with dark veins. The standards are tiny, flowering is in early summer. It is an easy plant but requires a lot of water during the growing season and does not like calcium.

Series Sibiricae

This group is next to the bearded Iris this most important for horticulture. They are characterised by forming strong rhizomes and dense clumps, all come from eastern Asia with the only exception of Iris siberica which extends into central Europe. All love moisture and may be used near water features, running or still.

Iris chrysographes Dykes
A Chinese species growing to fifty centimetres tall, Iris chrysographes has velvety, crimson-purple falls with golden-yellow stripes in summer. It is an exceptionally pretty species.

Iris sanguina Hornem
Coming from Japan, eastern Siberia, Korea and Manchuria, this species is flowering prolifically and grows to sixty centimetres with narrow, stiff leaves. The flowers are intense blue and the plants are tough and long-lived even in drier locations.

Iris siberica
It is a widespread species from Iran, the Caucasus, the Balkans and central and eastern Europe. Iris siberica grows to a metre high with narrow, stiff leaves and blue-purple flowers with dark veins in summer. A very graceful garden plant which is the parent of numerous hybrids, it prefers slightly acidic soils and likes cooler areas compared to the bearded Iris. It works well in larger groups with Allium schoenoprasum and other, tall Alliums, Doronicum orientale, Euphorbia polychroma, Geranium, Geum rivale, Helianthus salicaria, Lysimachia clethroides, Thalictrum, Tradescantia, Trollius and Hemerocallis.

Series Californicae

This North-American group is at home on the Pacific Coast in mountain forests. They form small clumps and are lovely, but sensitive Iris, requiring humous, acidic soils and a protected place. Moisture in spring and autumn but dry in winter and summer are keys to successful cultivation. Propagation is by seed.

Iris douglasiana Herb

A variable species from fifteen to fifty centimetres in height and flower colours ranging from white to pink and blue and tones in between, used as a breeding partner with Iris innominata, resulting in beautiful hybrids.

Iris innominata Henders

A mainly small, around twenty-centimetre-high species with narrow, grass-like leaves that comes from Oregon and extends down to northern California. Flowers are in ochre and yellow tones but vary to lavender in late spring and early summer. It is a lovely species and despite its small size used for cut flowers.

Series Longipetalae

Iris longipetala Herb

This species grows from sixty to ninety centimetres tall and features evergreen, greyish leaves and whitish flowers with purple venation in early summer. Easy to cultivate.

Series Laevigata

This series describes species with strong rhizomes and broader leaves that prefer to stand in shallow water in summer.

Iris ensata Thunb

Manchuria, Korea and Japan are home to this up to a metre tall species, with fresh green foliage and flowers from white over pink to light purple in summer. They require reasonably rich soils without calcium and lots of water from spring to late summer; during other times, they want to be a bit drier. There are numerous hybrids and cultivars available, mainly from Japan.

Iris pseudacorus L

The yellow 'Swamp Lily' is widespread from Europe to Siberia, Asia Minor and northern Africa. Its original habitats are the margins of ponds and creeks and the species should be used accordingly in the landscape. It grows up to a metre high, sometimes more, with bright green, broad leaves and yellow flowers in early summer. Note that it is a strong grower and competitive. It has been successfully used in environmental projects of water cleaning and oxygenation.

Iris versicolour

Northern America is home to the up to a metre tall plant that grows in and around swamps and features reddish-purple flowers in summer. Use of the plant is best in wet areas and in association with water features.

Series Hexagonae (Lousiana Iris)

Iris brevicaulis Raf

This species is living on meadows in the USA and is easy to cultivate. It grows to fifty centimetres high and flowers blue-purple with white marking in summer. Use in the landscape in moist meadows and larger, informal landscape and garden designs.

Iris fulva Ker-Gawl
Another species from the USA, Iris fulva stands out for the for Iris unusual colour tone of coppery orange in summer. The plant grows to eighty centimetres high and prefers light shade or semi-shade and is a swamp species.

Series Prismaticae

Iris prismatica Pursh
Growing to sixty centimetres tall, this species comes from the eastern USA and has small lavender-blue flowers. Not often in cultivation.

Series Spuriae

The 'Steppe Iris' come from eastern Europe and Asia Minor where they grow in rich soils. The plants are long-lived and prefer to stay undisturbed for a long time; they start to fully show their potential only after three or four years. They like some moisture in spring but want to be dry and 'bake' in the summer.

Iris crocea Jacq ex Foster
This species comes from Asia Minor and grows to a hundred and twenty centimetres high, stiff and upright. Large flowers of a golden-yellow colour are produced in summer. It is an outstanding yet easy-to-grow plant that should be used in natural and informal steppe and prairie designs but does also do extremely well in the perennial border.

Iris graminea L
From northern Spain to southern Russia extends the habitat of the up to forty-centimetre-high 'Plum-scented Iris'. The species forms dense, grass-like clumps with its foliage and bears purple flowers in summer that as the common name suggests, have a strong scent like ripe plums. It is a plant that is often found around old farm gardens and combines well with Thymus, Chrysogonum virginianum and Carex montana.

Iris pontica Zapalowicz
A small to medium size Iris that forms large colonies with its grass-like leaves. Flowers are large, reddish dark-blue and are held well above the foliage, like the above the species has a plum-like scent. It resembles Iris graminea but stays smaller and is best for the rockery.

Iris spuria
The species is at home in central Europe, Hungary and extends into southern Russia and has been split into several subspecies. However, the actual species are less important than the numerous beautiful hybrids that were created.

Iris spuria hybrids
These plants flower generally after the tall bearded Iris and are well suited to be used together. In cultivation, they require rich, loamy soils, moisture in spring and autumn but hot, dry summers. They prefer to be undisturbed for many years and reward good care with a spectacular display of large flowers held high in the ornamental foliage. I personally often use them behind bearded Iris and together with Paeonia, Papaver orientale, Helianthus and ornamental grasses for effect.

Series Foetidissima

Iris foetidissima
The Mediterranean and Western Europe are home to the only species of this series that grows sixty centimetres high. The foliage is broad and smells unpleasant when crushed, hence the name. The plant requires moisture and a semi-shaded location; the flowers are insignificant but the fruits are attractive for dried flower arrangements.

Series Tenuifolia

Iris tenuifolia Pall
Coming from central China, iris tenuifolia is around thirty centimetres high and has blue-purple flowers; it is mainly for species collectors.

Series Ensatae

Iris lactea Pall
The only species in this series grows to fifty centimetres with grass-like, stiff leaves and a variable flower colour from white to purple.

Series Syriaceae

The species of this series, Iris grant-duffi, Iris aschersonii and Iris masia are not of significance in horticulture or landscape architecture.

Series Unguiculares

Iris unguiculares Poir
An up to fifty-centimetre-tall species mainly from the Mediterranean; flowers are light blue or white and appear through winter in mild areas. It is a very pretty Iris that flowers when few herbaceous plants are in flower but is sensitive to harder frosts.

Subgenus Nepalensis
There are four species: Iris barbatulata, Iris collettii, Iris decora and Iris staintonii that have roots like Hemerocallis, but smaller; they are mainly for collectors.

Subgenus Xiphium
These species originate in the western Mediterranean and feature bulb-like tubers. They flower in late spring and early summer with elegant inflorescences that are highly valued in the cut flower trade but of course beautify any part of a garden. Cultivation is in full sun in aged, well-drained soils – they do require a dry summer for their dormancy. Propagation is by division of the bulbous tubers (they do form bulbils) in late summer and early autumn, a bit like bearded Iris.

Iris latifolia Voss
The 'English Sword-Lily' comes from the Pyrenees and grows to sixty centimetres tall. The wild species flowers purple-blue with a distinct yellow spot and middle line along the falls. This species requires more moisture than other Xiphium Iris.

Iris xiphium L

The 'Spanish Iris' does come from Spain and extends into northern Africa. The wild species flowers purple and is parent to the many gorgeous Iris hispanica hybrids available in white, purple, yellow and bronze colours.

Iris x hollandica (Iris Hollandica hybrids, Holländische Iris)

Many of these hybrids are in horticulture and used in cut flower production or larger landscapes as massed displays but also in gardens.

Subgenus Scorpiris (Juno Iris)

This group describes around fifty species, mainly from western and central Asia. These are bulbous plants with only few segments, requiring excellent drainage and full sun. In cultivation, care should be taken with fertilisers to keep the N-K balance in favour of the potassium. Propagation is by seed or root cuttings (!) but for that to succeed a piece of the bulbil's plate must remain with the root. This should be done in late summer and early autumn during their dormancy, the cuttings should be kept slightly above twenty degrees Celsius in clean sand for two months, then kept cool. Seed germination is erratic and can take several years, the seedlings also take some years, usually four to six before they are able to flower.

Iris aucheri Sealy

This lovely, around fifty-centimetre-tall Iris comes from rocky and gravelly soils in south-eastern Turkey, northern Iraq, northern Syria and western Iran. It grows in altitudes of up to two thousand two hundred metres and flowers very early in spring. The flowers are variable in colour, from light blue to purple and dark blue or pure white.

Iris bucharica Foster

From north-eastern Afghanistan and Tadzhikistan comes this around thirty-centimetre-high species that naturally grows on stony slopes, grassy hills and field margins in altitudes of up to two thousand five hundred metres.

Iris cycloglossa Wendelbo

Other than most iris of this group Iris cycloglossa prefers moist meadows along rivers and creeks. It is a strong plant to fifty centimetres that eventually forms dense clumps. Large flowers, lavender-blue with white centre and yellow spot, appear in late spring and are highly fragrant. This is a very valuable plant for the rockery.

Iris magnifica Fedtsch

Coming from central Asia where it grows on rocky slopes of limestone, this very beautiful species is also robust and grows up to a metre tall. It flowers in spring with a light purple but there are gorgeous pure white forms.

Iris persica L

Rocky and gravelly places in south-eastern Turkey, northern Syria and north-eastern Iraq are the home of this elegant Iris named after the ancient empire. It flowers very early in spring and requires perfectly drained, warm places. It is one of the most wonderful Iris but hard to get and keep.

Subgenus Hermodactyloides

Sections Hermadactyloides and Micropogon (Reticulata Iris)

Described in this group are six species that are interfertile and come from the Mediterranean. They are garden plants for early spring requiring very good drainage and rich, but balanced soils. Propagation is by seed or bulb division.

Iris danfordiae Boiss

A small, only around eight-centimetre-high species that grows on rocky slopes or in open conifer woodlands in altitudes of up to two thousand metres. The flowers are held at twenty centimetres and are yellow with some greenish spots and appear early in spring. Use in the landscape in warm and dry rockeries together with 'gentle', non-competitive neighbours.

Iris histrioides Arnott

This for breeding important species comes from Turkey where it grows in short meadows, on slopes or in open conifer forests. The plant grows to fifteen centimetres and features blue flowers with white and yellow markings. Can be widely used in gardens remembering the small size, quite suitable for pots and urns.

Iris reticulata Bieb

This species is widespread from Turkey to Iran, Iraq and the Caucasus. It thrives in mountain meadows, stony slopes and within shrubs; its colours vary greatly from blue, purple or almost crimson in early spring. One can create lovely scenes in combination with other spring-flowering species like Scilla mischtschenkoana, Crocus, Puschkinia scilloides, Galanthus and Narcissus. There are innumerous hybrids and cultivars available in the trade.

Iris winogradowii Fomin

From western and eastern Transcaucasia comes this beauty that grows up to thirty centimetres tall with straw-yellow flowers in early spring. It grows naturally in subalpine meadows but it is considered as an endangered species. Cultivation is best in humus, rich and consistently moist soils in cool, semi-shaded locations.

170 – Iris barbata-elatior 'Mer du Sud'
Staudengärtnerei Gräfin von Zeppelin

Ixia; Iridaceae

A South-African genus of around 50 species of small, bulbous perennials that require well-drained, aerated soils.

Ixia maculata L
Up to thirty-centimetre-long leaves that form small clumps from where orange-yellow flowers emerge in summer.

Ixia paniculata Delaroche
This is a tall species for Ixia with the foliage sixty centimetres high and up to a metre long stalks that carry yellow flowers with a red eye in summer.
There are many attractive Ixia hybrids available in the trade.

Johnsonia; Anthericaceae (Liliaceae)

This is a genus restricted to Western Australia with only around five species. They are all doing well in cultivation but only one really is of horticultural significance.

Johnsonia lupulina
The 'Hooded Lily' is a tufted plant with grass-like leaves and thirty-centimetre spike of very small flowers that are hidden by large bright pink bracts. They remain on the plant for a long period from spring to summer and are the main attraction, though I would consider and use the foliage like small ornamental grasses in the landscape. In cultivation, it requires well-drained soils with ample moisture from full sun to semi-shade. Propagation is by seed, with patience; or division in spring or autumn.

Jovibarba; Crassulaceae

This small genus of two species used to be part of the Sempervirens but has been split into its own genus. The main difference to Sempervirens is in that the flowers have a bell-shaped form with six to seven petals. Cultivation is the same; a sunny and dry spot with perfect drainage. They have been used to great effect in roof-top greenings. Propagation is easy by separation of plantlets that form on the short stolons.

Jovibarba globifera Parn
Originally this species comes from central and eastern Europe and forms small, up to two-centimetre-high rosettes with the greenish-yellow flowers standing up to twenty centimetres high above.

Jovibarba heuffelii A et D Löve
This species has large, up to twelve centimetres across rosettes but does not form stolons. Propagation is by division of the old rosettes. The flowers are up to twenty centimetres high and vary from red-brown to pale yellow.

Juncus; Juncaceae

There are around two hundred and thirty species in this genus of grass-like perennials and annuals with stiff, tube-like or flat, veined leaves. Only a few are of importance here.

Juncus effusus L

The 'Common Rush' is widespread in Europe, Asia and North America where it grows in wet, compacted places or places with constantly high-water table. It reaches eighty centimetres in height and flowers in summer. The species is valuable for revegetating disturbed, rich and wet soils where few other plants do well, I often use it along sediment ponds of nurseries to clean water of excess nutrients. They are popular in floristry including two cultivars, 'Aureus Striatus' and 'Spiralia' with lemon-yellow stripes respectively spiral leaves. Their propagation is obviously by division.

Kirengeshoma; Hydrangeaceae (Saxifragaceae)

Two species form this genus from Japan and Korea.

Kirengeshoma koreana Nakai

This species grows to an impressive two hundred centimetres and sometimes higher and features star-like, upright flowers, very attractive.

Kirengeshoma palmata Yatabe

A smaller relative from Japan, Kirengeshoma palmate reaches a hundred and twenty centimetres with large leaves and light buttery-yellow, pendulous flowers in late summer and autumn. Use in the landscape in semi-shaded, natural areas in combination with Anemone japonica, Cimicifuga, Rodgersia and ferns in moist and rich soils.

171 – Kirengeshoma palmata
Courtesy Baumschule Eggert, Germany

Kniphofia; Asphodelaceae

The genus of the well-known 'Red Hot Poker' or 'Torch Lily' is characterised by short, thick rhizomes, fleshy leaves and upright, usually strongly coloured inflorescences on leafless stems. Coming from South Africa where they have been in garden cultivation for a long time, Kniphofias are easy to grow; however, for best cultivation most require ample moisture. Naturally many of the parents of our modern hybrids inhabit moist, riparian zones; some come from moist meadows and some from more alpine habitats with stony soils with good drainage, requiring drier soils during their winter dormancy. It is best to leave them undisturbed for many years and water them well before flowering. Propagation is easy by division after flowering but as they do not like disturbances they usually require a full growing season before they flower again. Seed propagation is also not too hard and sometimes yields nice surprises.

Kniphofia angustifolia Codd
In wet grasslands of the Drakensberg (Dragon's Mountains) in altitudes of up to two thousand metres grows this species with grass-like, blue-green leaves of sixty centimetres and open inflorescences from white, yellow, orange and coral red.

Kniphofia fluviatilis Codd
Natal, Oranje Freistaat and eastern Transvaal are home to this species that grows along mountain rivers directly in the water. The flowers are orange, yellow or apricot and are held up to eighty centimetres high.

Kniphofia hirsuta Codd

A sub-alpine species from the Drakensberg, this species ascends to two thousand eight hundred metres in altitude. It features somewhat hairy leaves and fifty-centimetre-high flowers, held tightly in colours from orange, salmon to coral red or yellow-green.

Kniphofia laxiflora Kunth

Transvaal, the Cape and Natal are home to this widely used species with flowers that change from scarlet-red to crimson and pale yellow as they mature in autumn.

Kniphofia triangularis Kunth

A smaller, to forty-centimetre-high species with bright red flowers growing in wet meadows and moors in altitudes of up to two thousand metres. It is a tough species that is suitable for smaller perennial borders or natural designs.

Kniphofia uvaria Hook

This strong-growing and up to a hundred and fifty-centimetre-tall species is one of the parents of many of our modern hybrids. It flowers prolifically in late summer to late autumn.

There are numerous hybrids in a large range of colours and sizes available today.

172 – Kniphofia uvaria
Courtesy Wikimedia

Koeleria; Poacae

Koeleria glauca DC
This species comes from central Europe and extends to western Siberia. It indicates poor, dry soils and should be used accordingly, with its blue-grey ornamental leaves in dry steppe or prairie designs or together with xerophytic plants.

Koeleria vallesiana Gaudin
Southern Europe and northern Africa are home to this limestone-loving species. It grows naturally on dry, stony slopes and dry, warm meadows up to fifty centimetres high with blue-green, stiff foliage. It is well suited to xerophytic designs or roof-top plantings.

Lamiastrum; Lamiaceae

This is a small genus of five species from central and southern Europe. All of them are long-lived (different to Lamium) plants that form dense colonies.

Lamiastrum argentatum Smeijkal
The 'Silver-leaved Nettle' comes from Sicily and Italy where it inhabits forests and river margins. It is characterised by an intense silvery marking and large flowers; a reliable and easy-to-grow ground cover that forms dense carpets. It is very strong growing plant and consequently requires either other strong neighbours or is best combines with rocks, sculptures or hard landscape features like walls and paths. Another good use in the landscape would be under tall trees.

173 – Lamiastrum argentatum
Courtesy Klaus Mödinger

Lamium galeobdolon
The 'Yellow Archangel' or 'Goldnessel' (Golden Nettel; German) is widespread through middle and southern Europe where it grows in deciduous forests on reasonably dry and poor soils. It is a great ground

cover to thirty centimetres high with yellow flowers in early summer suited best to natural and wild plantings.

Lamium; Lamiaceae

There are around fifty species in the genus of the 'Dull Nettle' (as opposed to the 'Stinging Nettle', Urtica dioica). They are plants in the understorey of open deciduous or mixed forests and woodlands, some are annuals others are short-lived perennials that are easy ground covers from shade to semi-shade. Use in the landscape as a textural ground cover and contrast.

Lamium album
The 'White Dull Nettle' is widespread from Europe to western Asia and extends into the Himalayas, Siberia, Mongolia, Korea and japan. The species grows to forty centimetres and is well suited as ground cover for natural parks and areas of low maintenance as it is tolerating poor soils and neglect.

Lamium maculatum L
This species is parent to most of the horticultural cultivars and hybrids; it is at home in Europe, northern Africa, Turkey and the Iranian plateau. Naturally it inhabits forest margins, shrublands, grows along creeks, rivers and lakes and paths and fences. It flowers in from late spring to summer with red, purple or sometimes white nettle flowers and prefers rich, moist soils. It is an excellent choice of ground cover and texture plant for cottage gardens, farm gardens or formal designs and does great in combination with Aquilegia vulgaris, Doronicum caucasicum, Geranium himalayense, Thalictrum and Epimedium.

Laserpitium; Apiaceae

This genus has become more important with the increasing use of wild perennials in low maintenance and meadow-type designs. They typically characterise a plant community and are of great structural value with their foliage. The flower umbel is very attractive and works its own magic in large numbers in wild or natural designs. Propagation is by seed.

Laserpitium siler
At home in southern and middle Europe on shallow, poor soils on limestone, this species grows to a hundred and fifty centimetres tall and has large, up to a metre long, fern-like compound leaves. The flowers are up to thirty centimetres across, white and appear in summer. They are a great structural partner for many other perennials like Paeonia, Geranium and Allium. Both, leaves and flowers are good in the vase and the plant further has medicinal properties.

174 – Laserpitium siler
Courtesy Visoflora

Lathyrus; Fabaceae

This is a genus with around a hundred and eighty species from Eurasia, Asia Minor, North Africa and America. They are annuals and perennials of which some are climbing plants. Lathyrus have attractive flowers and for that reason are old garden plants. The clumping varieties are best used as soil improving ground cover in association with shrubs and trees whilst the climbing varieties are great along fences or grown into woody ornamentals. General soil preferences are for drier or slightly moist soils. Propagation is by seed or cuttings.

Clumping varieties

Lathyrus aureus Brandza
This species comes from the Black Sea, Romania, Bulgaria, northern Turkey, the Caucasus and Crimea where it grows in forests and shrublands of up to two thousand metres altitude. Around eighty centimetres high, it flowers profusely with orange-brown inflorescences in early summer, it combines well with red foliage plants like Tellima grandiflora 'Rubra'.

Lathyrus vernus Bernh

This well-known species originates in Europe, Asia Minor and Siberia where it grows in deciduous and mixed forests with moist, alkaline rich soils. It grows to fifty centimetres with deep taproots over a metre down into the soil. The flowers appear early in spring and are of crimson red colour. It is a great soil-improving plant sometimes used as green manure crop and it combines very well with Asarum, Helleborus, Lamium, Polygonatum, Pulmonaria, Smilacina and Brunnera.

Climbing varieties

Lathyrus grandiflorus Sibth et Sm

From shady places in the forests of southern Italy and Sicily comes this up to a hundred and fifty-metre-high climbing species. Its large flowers are purple with red wings and pink in summer. It is a valuable plant between small woody ornamentals, conifers or deciduous. It grows without the chance of climbing it forms a dense, ground covering mat.

Lathyrus tuberosus L

This European species extends to the Caucasus and central Asia and its tubers are edible, tasting sweet. It is a pretty and tough plant on alkaline soils that works well if it is let to climb into early flowering shrubs.

Lavandula; Lamiaceae

There are around twenty species of Lavender; most of them originate in the Mediterranean and the Canary Islands. They are essentially sub-shrubs, small shrubs that become woody at the base but stay soft and evergreen at the tips. Lavenders naturally grow in well-drained, alkaline and structured soils in full sun. They occupy steppe and prairie-like habitats. Some Lavender species, Lavandula angustifolia, L. x intermedia, L. latifolia and L. stoechas are farmed for medicinal purposes and essential oils and related products. As a medicinal plant Lavender was introduced north of the Alps in the early Middle Ages into monastery gardens. The genus has many applications in landscape architecture and garden design for its structural values, the attractive evergreen foliage and toughness. Cutting back for rejuvenation should occur either in spring before the plant becomes active or in summer after flowering; the cut needs to stay in the soft parts of the plant for best results. Good partners are Adonis vernalis, Buphtalmum salicifolium, Geranium sanguineum, Hemerocallis, Oriental Poppies and bearded Iris to name only a few as Lavenders are very versatile. They may also be forming structures of formal garden designs or medieval herb gardens.

Lavandula angustifolia Mill

The 'True Lavender' comes from the Mediterranean and extends into south-western Europe, it can climb into altitudes of up to eighteen hundred metres. It is a compact, dense plant with grey, hairy foliage and flowers that may range from blue to purple and white to pink. This species produces the Lavender oil. There are plenty of good cultivars of various sizes and flower colours.

Lavandula dentata

South-eastern Spain and the Baleares are home to the 'Toothed Lavender' that grows to a metre tall and has conspicuously serrated leaves. The flowers are light blue and whilst slightly frost tender the plant is also a great container plant.

Lavandula x intermedia

Describes the hybrid between L. angustifolia and L. latifolia with positive properties between the two parents combining toughness with rich contents of essential oils.

Lavandula stoechas Lois

This species is one of the characteristic plants of the Mediterranean Macchia. It is a small sub-shrub, around sixty centimetres high with grey, velvety foliage and lovely dark purple flowers in summer; the cultivar 'Alexandra' with large flowers is recommended.

Lavatera; Malvaceae

From Europe to the north-western Himalayas, Australia and California extends the origin of these annual, perennial or soft-wooded shrubby Malvaceae. They have attractive large flowers but are by and large somewhat frost tender and therefore need to be carefully used in good climates or microclimates.

Lavatera olbia L

This species is an up to two metres high shrub with hairy stems and silvery velvety leaves. It is parent to many cultivars and hybrids that are grown for their beautiful Hibiscus-like flowers. Use in the informal or semi-formal design and settings like cottage gardens. Some recommended cultivars are 'Kew Rose', which is particularly robust and grows to an impressive four metres or the old, reliable 'Rosea' that gets to two metres tall and flowers prolifically.

175 – Lavatera olbia 'Rosea'
Courtesy Plantes Vivaces

Lavatera plebeia

The Australian cousin of the Hollyhocks is a short-lived perennial with erect up to two metres tall stem. Large, up to twenty centimetre broad, ovate leaves and around six-centimetre-wide white to lilac flowers characterise the plant. The species prefers sunny and warm places and adapts to most soils. Use in the landscape in the background of natural settings or perennial borders, needs regular replacing and is propagated by seed.

Lechenaultia; Goodeniaceae

This genus of around twenty-six species contains some brilliant plants, mainly from Western Australia. They are semi-woody, prostrate or low-growing perennials with glowing colours and absolutely outstanding in the plant world. They can be easily propagated by cuttings throughout the year and require perfect drainage in sandy or gravelly soils in full sun. Most are short-lived or difficult to maintain in cultivation. I would always re-propagate as a standard procedure for displays. In my experience, it is best to fertilise sparingly and with a balance in favour of K.

Lechenaultia biloba

This irregular sub-shrub grows to around fifty centimetres tall with linear, succulent leaves. The flowers vary from white to a very deep blue in spring. It is an outstanding plant for rockeries, dry stone walls or tub plantings. Propagation is by cuttings.

176 – Lechenaultia biloba
Western Australia 2003

Lechenaultia hirsuta
The 'Hairy Lechenaultia' is a scrambling shrub growing to forty centimetres with bright green, rough leaves. It bears brilliant scarlet flowers in spring; a very desirable plant.

Lechenaultia macrantha
A special plant more for the passionate collector, the 'Wreath Lechenaultia' is a prostrate species forming circles. The large cream and red flowers are displayed around the perimeter of the plant and make a unique display.

Leonotis; Lamiaceae

This special little genus 'listens' to lovely common names like 'Lion's Ear', Lion's Tail', or 'Minaret Flower', for its conspicuous and highly attractive flowers in white, yellow, orange or red. They come from subtropical and tropical South Africa and are consequently not very frost hardy. One of the secrets for higher frost hardiness is to keep them hot, dry on poor soils and fertilise with a high K fertiliser in late summer onward to slow and harden the growth before cold temperatures set in. Otherwise they are a showy part of container plant displays that are moved indoors in areas with real frosts, or utilised as annual summer display, but that would be a bit of a waste considering their potential and the show they can give as mature shrubs.

Leonotis dysophylla Benth
The species grows in the Drakensberg, Natal and Cape Province of South Africa and can ascend into altitudes of up to two thousand metres. The plants reach mostly around a metre height with orange or sometimes light pink flowers from summer to autumn. Given good cultivation this species tolerates down to minus fifteen degrees Celsius frost.

Leonotis leonurus
This sub-shrub originates in Natal and Transvaal where it ascends to eighteen hundred metres altitude. The flowers are beautiful orange or orange-red and appear from summer into late autumn with the plant reaching up to two metres in height. Great pot plant.

177 – Leonotis leonurus
Courtesy Muldersdrift

Leontopodium; Asteraceae

The genus of the famous 'Edelweiss' contains around forty species that inhabit the mountain ranges of Europe and Asia. They are small to medium-sized perennials with mostly hairy leaves and small flowers surrounded by white, woolly bracts in summer. Their use in the landscape is suggested for the rockery, containers or plant communities with small and non-competitive plants in poor, alkaline soils. Propagation is by seed or division in spring.

Leontopodium alpinum ssp alpinum Cass
The original 'Alpen Edelweiss' is at home in the mountains of the Pyrenees, the Alps, extending into the Balkans. It grows in gravelly, alkaline soils in altitudes from eighteen hundred to three thousand five hundred metres. The plant grows to around twenty centimetres and is dense with beautiful white, velvety leaves and flowers. Whilst the high UV levels and exposure promote the density and beauty of the hairs and velvety appearance and plants grown in low altitudes sometimes disappoint, there are strains that do very well in low altitudes and even in more nutritious soils. These strains of course need to be propagated vegetatively. Other than that, the Edelweiss is easy to cultivate in well-drained soils and full sun.

178 – Leontopodium alpinum
Travel study, Switzerland

Leucanthemum; Asteraceae

Leucanthemum atratum DC

Formerly named *Chrysanthemum atratum* this up to thirty-centimetre-high beautiful Daisy lives in the Alps in up to two thousand five hundred metres altitude. Alkaline soils are a requirement and I would recommend this species for the rockery or the alpinum but not for cultivation in the lowlands as the plant's characteristics do not fully develop.

Leucanthemum maximum group

This is the familiar medium, fifty to ninety-centimetre-high Daisy of the gardens flowering in summer with large, up to ten centimetres across white flowers from summer to autumn. The leaves are somewhat fleshy and slightly serrated. Good in combination with Papaver orientale, Lilium bulbiferum, Delphinium and Lupinus. However, because it is a comparatively strong grower it requires some restraining over time, other than that it is very easy to grow and a graceful plant for many garden situations or the greater landscape in natural meadows. There are many cultivars and hybrids available.

Leucojum; Amaryllidaceae

This is a small genus with around ten bulbous species from Europe, north-western Africa and south-western Asia.

Leucojum vernum

The 'Snowflake' is an up to thirty-centimetre-high species that is easy to cultivate if there is sufficient moisture throughout the year. The white flowers appear early in spring and the plant is well suited to natural or informal landscapes and garden designs where it can 'go wild' and naturalise around and under shrubs and trees.

Leucophyta; Asteraceae

Leucophyta brownii syn Calocephalus brownii
The compact, rounded silvery sub-shrub is called 'Cushion Bush' by common name. It grows to a metre high and across and I would use it in the landscape as a structural or dominating feature plant for arid or semi-arid designs. Small, globular greenish yellow flower heads are around one centimetre across. The plant requires full sun and well-drained soils. Do not fertilise. In my experience, it can be integrated in a large variety of applications from rockeries, steppes or prairies to even formal applications. If kept in formal design settings, the plant benefits from regular pruning to ensure the tight, compact habit. Propagation is by cuttings without mist, otherwise they rot quickly.

179 – Leucophyta brownii
Courtesy Wikipedia

Lewisia; Portulacaceae

An American genus with fleshy, succulent-like leaves and carrot-type roots that is very showy but requires appropriate placement and good care to work well. Most flower in summer, some in autumn and the plants need acidic, mineral and rich but very well drained soils. The genus is ideal for rockeries or smaller garden beds in semi-shade and with low competition; if the environmental conditions are right the species self-sows without becoming weedy. Other than seed, propagation is by dividing side-shoots and keeping them in moist sand until well rooted; it is advantageous if a part of the old stem remains on the cutting.

Lewisia cotyledon var cotyledon Robinson
Mainly growing in mosses between rocks in cooler places this Lewisia has lovely up to forty millimetres wide flowers that range from white and yellow, pink and salmon to crimson and orange-red in summer with some after-flowering in autumn. Together with L. cotyledon var heckneri and L cotyledon var howellii it has produced many beautiful hybrids that are in the trade today.

180 – Lewisia cotyledon
Courtesy Giardin Gardens, France

Lewisia longipetala Clay

This lovely species grows in rocks and gravel in cooler, semi-shaded or shady places in California. Flowers are white to light pink and appear in early summer, this plant combines well with small ferns like Adiantum pedatum var aleuticum.

Liatris; Asteraceae

The genus of Liatris comes from North America and describes species with tuberous rhizomes and small leaves. The upright flower spikes mature from the top down and are in shades of purple-pink or deep purple and appear in summer to autumn. Propagation is by seed and the plants combine well with Echinaceae, Coreopsis, Eurybia spectabilis and ornamental grasses. I remember a design where it has been used to great effect as upright accents in a ground cover of Acaena.

Liatris graminifolia Willd

This interesting species grows in open Pine forests, prairies and dry meadows. Consequently, it would be used to its advantage in such natural or wild designs and combined with Solidago nana and small grasses.

Liatris spicata Willd

Different to the above species this plant originates in moist and even swampy meadows where it stands out with its stiff upright flower spike. This species is the most significant in horticulture and landscape architecture and has produced several cultivars that may be used in a large range of applications including formal borders.

181 – Liatris spicata
Mutterpflanzen, Staudengärtnerei Gräfin von Zeppelin, Germany

Ligularia; Asteraceae

Around a hundred and eighty species are described in the genus of Ligularia with common names like 'Leopard Plant', 'Kreuzkraut' ('Cross Herb' or 'Greiskraut', 'Methuselah's Herb'). The genus is closely related to Senecio and occupies temperate zones of Eurasia. Most flower dark yellow to orange from late summer to autumn. Ligularia may be used individually or in groups if they are given sufficient space; they are more suited to larger landscapes along creeks, ponds, rivers or moist forest margins. They are naturally good with partners that also prefer moist soils like Eupatorium, Aconitum, Geum, Leucojum aestivum and Lysimachia. Like many perennials, Ligularia show their full potential only after some years in the ground, preferably not in the full sun as their leaves tend to flop quickly in the heat even when the roots have access to sufficient water.

Ligularia dentata Hara

Japan, western and central China are home to this gorgeous perennial that inhabits moist mountain meadows and likes to hug creeks and ponds growing around a hundred and thirty centimetres tall. The flowers are up to ten centimetres across, smell like honey and are warm brown-yellow with orange centre. They appear from late summer to autumn. There are several attractive cultivars ion the trade like 'Desdemona' – up to a hundred and fifty centimetres with heart-shaped leaves and yellow flowers standing out above the dark foliage and 'Othello' – a hundred and twenty centimetres with orange-yellow flowers. Unfortunately, they are not only attractive to the human species but also to slugs and snails.

Ligularia japonica Lessing ex DC

This species grows tall, up to two hundred centimetres and features handsome large leaves. Golden yellow flowers appear in late summer and make it one of the most beautiful Ligularia, also prone to snail damage.

Ligularia macrophylla DC

Coming from central Asia, the Caucasus, northern Persia and Turkestan Ligularia macrophylla has very attractive, large leaves and bright yellow flowers in late summer. It grows to a hundred and eighty centimetres high and does well as a feature plant along water courses, flowing or still.

Ligularia przewalskii Diels

The perennial grows to a hundred and fifty centimetres tall with lovely, hand-shaped leaves on long stems. Flowers are bright yellow with red-brows centre in summer. This species does not require as much water as most other Ligularia representatives and appears to best resist snails.

Ligularia stenocephala Matsuma et Koidz

The species is widespread in Asia and grows to a hundred and fifty centimetres tall. It has heart-shaped serrated foliage and long yellow flower racemes in summer that mildly resemble Delphinium from a distance. The plant grows very large over the years and may be best used in more natural or semi-formal designs in the background.

There are some very attractive hybrids of Ligularia, like 'The Rocket' with bright yellow long racemes and palm-like leaves or 'Weihenstephan' – a hundred and sixty centimetres tall with sharply serrated, heart-shaped foliage and bright yellow flowers in summer.

182 – Ligularia x 'Little Rocket'
Baumschule Häussermann, Stuttgart, Germany

Lilium; Liliaceae

The Lilies are known in garden history and human cultivation for more than three thousand years in ancient Egypt. Mentioned later in the Bible (Matthew chapter 6) and the Koran, occasionally deified or worshipped, some species of the genus Lilium have certainly become a symbol for our spiritual and physical relationship with flowers. With some Lilies like Lilium martagon, the 'Goldwurtz' (Golden Root) it was tried to produce gold. Other Lilies like Lilium candidum (the only true Madonna Lily') came to symbolise purity and chastity, or Mary herself, with its pure white flowers. More realistically Lilies are used in herbal medicine and for cooking and few would not love it for the beauty they bring into our gardens and lives.

The genus Lilium describes more than a hundred bulbous species of perennial plants ranging in height from twenty to more than three hundred centimetres. They live in a large diversity of habitats, from acidic to alkaline, from sandy to rich soils but the soil properties almost always have excellent drainage and are airy. Lilies thrive in the entire northern temperate zone and extend into the subtropics. There are different approaches to classify a system into this diversity, a bit like for Iris, but I would like to keep it as simple as possible for this book, looking at the practical applications for landscape architects and garden designers.

There is one extremely important aspect of Lilium and other Liliaceae (including Hemerocallis) to be considered that I must mention:

All parts of these plants are highly toxic to Felidae, cats!

Please do not grow them when you have cats or know cats could be visiting the garden. The toxin targets the renal tubular epithelium leading to renal failure and even very little doses of exposure can be lethal!

Martagon section (1)
Describes the 'Turk's Cap' form of Lilies with their petals curved strongly back and their pistils and stamens strongly protruding.

American section (2)
Liliums of North America

Candidum section (3)
Describes Lilies from Europe and the Caucasus

Oriental section (4)
The Liliums of Japan

Asiatic section (5)
Describes species from Asia and eastern Asia

Trumpet Lily section (6)
These are the Lilies with trumpet shaped flowers from China and southern Asia.
Lilium dauricum used to be in its own section but is now considered to be part of the Asiatic section; the above numbers are allocated accordingly in alphabetical order.

Lilium amabile (5) Palib
This lovely species is at home in Korea on gravelly, loamy and volcanic soils of well-drained grasslands. It grows to around ninety centimetres tall and has pomegranate-red flowers with dark spots and chocolate-brown stamens (they do not taste like chocolate though). It flowers in summer and works beautifully in heath-type designs.

Lilium auratum (4) Lindl
The famous 'Golden-Rayed Lily' of Japan is one of the most gorgeous Lilies and grows in its homeland between grasses, in gravel, between open shrubs in volcanic soils. The species ascends to fifteen hundred metres altitude. The bulb is roundish and of a yellow colour and produces a strong, impressive plant of up to two hundred centimetres in height. The flowers are white with a golden-yellow middle band and crimson-red spots in late summer. In cultivation, the plant requires even temperatures and humidity and slightly acidic and aged soils. The bulb should be planted quite deeply, between twenty and twenty-five centimetres and in my experience, some sand and gravel mixed evenly into the soil profile are beneficial. In a good Lily soil, one should be able to push the hand in as deep as the elbow; this gives, if not literally taken, still a good idea about the desirable friability.

183 – Lilium auratum with Anigozanthos
Author's home garden, Queanbeyan, Australia 2014

Lilium bulbiferum ssp bulbiferum (3)
The 'Fire Lily' (Feuer Lilie, German) used to be widespread in the subalpine regions of Europe, the Alps, the Pyrenees, the mountain ranges of central Europe, northern Italy, south-eastern Europe and from Corsica to Scandinavia. Unfortunately, it has become quite rare. Its habitats are gravelly or stony soils, grasslands and in shrublands on well-drained porous, loamy soils, both with alkaline and acidic PH in altitudes of up to two thousand metres. The bulb is white, to ten centimetres across and produces an up to a hundred and twenty centimetres high, strong stem with up to twenty flowers, from chrome yellow over orange to orange-red, sometimes beautifully spotted or flamed in summer.

Lilium callosum (5) Sieb et Zucc

Eastern Asia is the home of this graceful Lily that grows in meadows and open shrublands in sandy, organic soils. A thin stem emerges from an almost ball-shaped bulb and reaches around a metre. It carries strongly recurved reddish flowers that are finely dotted with black spots on the inside.

Lilium canadense (2)

The 'Meadow Lily' grows from Canada along the eastern states of the USA down to Alabama on drier, well aerated and drained and mildly acidic, loamy soils. Its habitats are meadows and open woodlands. The species grows to an impressive two hundred and fifty centimetres in height and bears up to twenty clear yellow, pendulous bell-shaped flowers in summer. It is an interesting species for the natural landscape as well as formal perennial borders or cottage garden designs.

Lilium candidum (3)

This is the true 'Madonna Lily' or 'White Lily' (notwithstanding that there are plenty of other white Lilies that people tend to call Madonna Lily). The plant has a long-standing history in gardens and has been depicted in art, secular and ecclesiastical. Originally the species comes from south-eastern Europe and extends down to Turkey, Syria, the Lebanon and Israel. It grows in summer-dry loamy soils from sea level up to high into the mountains. The bulb is oval, white and to ten centimetres across. An impressive, up to two-hundred-centimetre-tall stem develops from strong, mature plants and bears racemes of up to twenty-five funnel-shaped white and strongly fragrant flowers in summer. The plant retains a dense cluster of leaves throughout winter, one of the easy characteristics of identification. One of the important aspects of cultivation is that this species is different in the planting depth: it needs to be planted very shallow, with the bulb just under the soil surface and just covered.

184 – Lilium candidum
Work in Canberra, Australia 2014

Lilium carniolicum ssp carniolicum (3) Bernh ex Koch
A mainly mountainous species, Lilium carniolicum and its subspecies grows in rich meadows and between rocks. The plant grows to around a metre tall and carries the 'Turk's Cap' type, deep red and fragrant flowers in early summer.

Lilium ciliatum (3) Davis
Open woodlands and meadows in altitudes from fourteen hundred to two thousand five hundred metres around the Black Sea are the home of this up to a hundred and sixty-centimetre-high Lily. In cultivation, it prefers well-drained, rich and moist loamy soils in cooler locations. The species combines well with Rhododendron and other Ericaceae and Astilbe with its creamy-white to sulphur-yellow flowers in summer. The flowers are held in pyramidal fashion and look great against a dark background like Taxus baccata.

Lilium davidii (5) Duch ex Elwes

This species comes from China where it grows in mountain meadows and along the margins of moist woodlands and forests; it ascends to three thousand five hundred metres altitude. The bulbs are used as food. As ornamental plant, it delights with attractive growth to two hundred centimetres and elegant 'Turk's Cap' type crimson or scarlet-red flowers in late summer.

Lilium formosanum (6) Wallace

On mineral soils between grasses, shrubs and trees thrives this white Lily with its funnel-shaped fragrant flowers in late summer and into autumn.

Lilium hansonii (1) Leichtl

The 'Pagoda Lily' comes from Korea, where it grows in open shrublands in rich volcanic soils. The plant has a flat, yellowish bulb and reaches a hundred and fifty centimetres with its orange-yellow flowers in summer. It is a beautiful Lily that offers itself to many different applications, just not in the full sun.

Lilium harrisianum (2) Beane et Vollmer

From northern California comes the impressive 'Sunset Lily' or 'Red Giant' as it is called in its original habitat. The strong, rhizotomous bulb produces an up to three hundred centimetres tall stem that carries often thirty or more large yellow, merging from the inside to yellow, orange and red on the outsides of the petals. The species may be used to its advantage in large perennial borders with very rich, moist soils and requires in cultivation cool feet or light, dappled shade. It flowers in summer.

Lilium japonicum (4) Thunb

A Lily that grows naturally in cool Rhododendron and Bamboo slopes of Japan. It has small, whitish bulbs that produce thin, up to ninety-centimetre-high stems with light mauve-pink fragrant trumpet-shaped flowers in late summer. This species should be used in more natural or informal designs and like its original habitat. It does not tolerate heat or drought well.

Lilium kesselringianum (3) Mishsch

This special Lily originates in western Transcaucasia growing in subalpine meadows and mountain forests between fourteen and eighteen hundred metre altitudes. The yellowish, oval bulb produces a hairy stem of around a hundred and twenty centimetres in height. It bears up to ten large bell-like flowers up to fifteen centimetres across in a pyramidal order. The colour is ivory-white to canary-yellow with crimson spots and lines in summer. Cultivation is not that easy and requires loam or clay soil of a consistent friable structure that should be dry in late summer and autumn. It is a very beautiful Lily that should be displayed as an individual or only together with subtle partners as its beauty would be lost in larger plantings. Propagation is best using the scales of the bulb.

Lilium leichtlinii (5) Hook

Growing in moist meadows and between shrubs in up to two thousand metres altitude, this lemon-yellow Lily comes from Japan. The flowers are of an elegant 'Turk's-Cap' shape and the recurved petals are delicately spotted in late summer. Cultivation is recommended in well-drained loam covered with a layer of aged humus.

185 – Lilium leichtlinii
Author's home garden, Queanbeyan, Australia 2014

Lilium martagon (1)

This is the species originally called 'Turk's Cap' with its common name. It inhabits Eurasia from Portugal to Siberia, northern Mongolia and the southern Caucasus. In saying that, it may be hard to find it as the species has been decimated severely for a long period of time and people with knowledge of natural stands may be advised to keep it a little bit quiet. Mostly thriving on alkaline soils but also appearing in other places, the plant naturally lives in deciduous forests and shrublands, meadows and subalpine slopes up to two thousand three hundred metres altitude. The bulb is yellow and oval carrying a strong, up to two-hundred-centimetre-tall stem. The flowers and buds are often somewhat woolly or hairy and carried in racemes of around twelve to twenty but up to a hundred and thirty flowers have been known. The colour can vary strongly from pink to purple-pink and white and varying spots, from very small to large, sometimes even almost without spots. The plant has a strong fragrance and flowers in summer.

185 – Lilium martagon in natural habitat
Courtesy Otfried Preussler, Laufen, Germany

Lilium pardalinum (2) Kellogg

The 'Panther Lily' comes from the USA where it lives in moist areas and along the margins of rivers. Its original habitats are drier in summer and may be even inundated in winter. The plant forms a strong, rhizomatous bulb up to fifteen centimetres across. The tall, strong stem may get to three hundred centimetres in height under good conditions and can carry up to fifty 'Turk's Cap' flowers in orange-red to crimson-red on long stems in summer. This is a very valuable and quite tough species for aerated, moister soils in natural or wild designs or in larger, less formal perennial borders. Propagation is by scales.

Lilium pomponium (3)

This wonderful red Lily originates in the western Alps where it grows in sunny or semi-shaded limestone slopes with grasses, shrubs and small trees. The bulb is glassy, white, round and pointed. The flowers are held in a slender pyramid and are bright, shiny scarlet red with darker spots in the Turk's Cap shape. In cultivation, it is beneficial but not necessary to have alkaline soils properties; the plant tolerates neutral soils well if a good structure is ensured. The soils should be allowed to be dry in late summer to simulate its natural habitat where the mountain sides often 'bake' under the late summer sun.

Lilium pumilum (5) DC

The 'Coral Lily' is widespread in Asia, Siberia, Mongolia and Korea. It thrives in dry, sunny slopes in sand or gravelly loam. The flowers are held around eighty centimetres high and are in shiny scarlet, caramel or yellow with the Turk's Cap shape in early summer. This is a delicate, elegant Lily for the rockery or xerophytic plantings where excellent drainage is guaranteed.

Lilium regale (6) Wilson

This spectacular Lilium from China was introduced between 1903 and 1910 by Ernest Henry Wilson. It features a round, wine-red bulb with fleshy scales and can grow to a hundred and fifty centimetres high. The up to twenty-five flowers are held outward like the spikes of a wheel and are radiant white with yellow throats. The species possesses an irresistible fragrance. It grows in all better garden soils and has many applications; I have combined it with Delphinium, Papaver orientale, Phlox paniculata, Paeonia and even Anigozanthos and Blandfordia to great effect. Propagation is by its scales.

Lilium rubellum (4) Baker

The 'Otome Yuri' (Girl's Lily, Japanese) lives in the mountains in altitudes between two hundred and two thousand metres between shrubs, grasses and in woodlands in aged lava. In its original habitat, there is a reliable cover of snow in winter, a warm, rainy summer and dry autumn. Given similar conditions in the garden, this species is a delight but requires some patience for full development. It flowers light pink with yellow stamens and a lovely fragrance in early summer.

Lilium superbum (2)

The 'Swamp Lily' from the USA is very widespread where sufficient moisture is in the rich, loamy soil. The plant can reach up to three hundred centimetres and is impressive and beautiful with its Turk's Cap flowers in colours ranging from orange-yellow to crimson red or warm brown in late summer. It combines well with Phlox paniculata, Trillium, Hepatica, Asarum and other plants of the forest but can also form colonies of its own. I would use it in natural or wild landscape and garden designs due to its size; more in the background in moist areas or alongside water features. It is hostile to calcium and unfortunately popular with rodents.

Lilium wardii (5) Stearn

This wonderful beauty comes from Tibet where it grows together with Eagle Ferns and shrubs under conifers between fifteen hundred and three thousand metres altitude. The broad, creamy bulb has red spots and is up to five centimetres across. The stem interestingly first grows laterally up to almost half a metre and forms bulbils on the way; then it grows upward and flowers at a height of up to two hundred centimetres with Turk's Cap deep pink flowers on horizontally held stems in late summer. I would use it in natural or semi-formal planting designs in semi-shaded places among Rhododendron and other Ericaceae, and together with Cimicifuga and Thalictrum, creating elf-like scenes. Almost forgot that the species possesses a wonderful fragrance!

Lilium wilsonii (5) Leichtl

A robust Lily from Japan with a white, round bulb that grows ninety centimetres tall with bowl-shaped, large flowers to fifteen centimetres across in red-orange with a yellow central stripe. It flowers in late summer and would be ideal to use in natural and wild designs.

Lilium hybrids

Asiatic hybrids
Probably the most important group of hybrids between L. amabile, L. bulbiferum, L. concolor, L. dauricum, L. davidii, L. leichtlinii, L. maculatum, L. lancifolium and L. wilsonii. This group is easy to cultivate in a well-drained, rather lighter soil.

Martagon hybrids
Mainly crosses between L. martagon, L. hansonii, L. tsingtauense and L. medeloides. This group prefers planting in autumn and is usually slow to establish, sometimes only flowering after the second year of planting. They want rich and somewhat heavier, alkaline soil and patience.

Candidum hybrids
They do not play a large role in the gardens, some hybrids are L. x testaceum, a chance seedling between L. candidum and L. chaldedonicum (Isabellen-Lilie).

American hybrids
Hybrids are mainly between L. harrisianum, L. pardalinum, L. humboldtii, L. parryi, L. kelloggii, L. bolanderi, L. nervadense and L. pitkinense. They usually require some care and sandy-loamy soil properties with either a mild summer or lightly shaded locations with higher humidity, a bit like Rhododendron.

Longiflorum hybrids
Breeding in earnest has only recently really started and made also use of cross-breeding with Asiatic hybrids.

187 – Lilium longiflorum, in the background Acanthus mollis
Restoration Work in Canberra, Australia 2014

Trumpet or Funnel Lilies

They were created from crossings between L. regale, L. sargentiae, L. leucanthum, L. brownie, L. wallichianum and L. henryi. They have standard requirements and thrive well in good, well-drained garden soils. It is advantageous to surround the bulb when planting with a layer of sand and best planting depth is usually between ten and fifteen centimetres.

Oriental hybrids

L. auratum, L. japonicum, L. rubellum, L. speciosum, L. alexandrae and L. noblissimum are the main parents in this group. They require very well-drained, acidic soils with a high organic content and sufficient nutrient. A sufficiently long 'ripening' period in autumn is required and the plants should neither be cut down nor transplanted too early for best results.

Limonium; Plumbaginaceae

This is a genus of low to medium perennials with worldwide distribution along coasts and on steppes. They are suited to extremely dry and hot, sunny places. Many are well known as dried cut flowers; the Statice. Propagation is by seed or root cuttings in winter.

Limonium latifolium Kuntze
Widespread in steppes and grasslands from southeastern Europe to Russia, L. latifolium grows to a hundred centimetres tall. It flowers from early to late summer with light purple spikes that are often used in dried flower arrangements. Use in the landscape in natural or semi-formal dry or xerophytic perennial designs; they do well in combination with Artemisia, Eryngium, Elymus, Asphodelus, Eremurus and bearded Iris. A great cultivar is 'Violetta' which needs to be propagated vegetatively.

Limonium vulgare Mill
The common Limonium originates around the Mediterranean where it grows on salty, wet meadows, sandy or clay soils. The flowers are forty centimetres high and blue-purple in late summer to early autumn. This species may be used in difficult places including vegetating salty locations or places exposed to sea spray.

Linaria; Scrophulariaceae

There are around a hundred and fifty species in this genus, mainly from the northern hemisphere and the Mediterranean where they thrive in dry, rocky places. Most are perennials, but there are some annuals and sub-shrubs. By and large they are better suited for natural and wild designs as given the right environmental conditions, they may become invasive and too competitive for more gentle neighbours.

Linaria alpina Mill
From the central and southeastern mountains comes this with around ten centimetres, low-growing and short-lived perennial which prefers gravelly, rocky environments. The purple-blue, sometimes pink or white flowers usually have an orange throat and appear from summer to early autumn. Though short-lived it self-sows and colonises natural rockeries nicely.

Linaria triornithophora Willd
Central Spain and Portugal are the home of this attractive species with the largest flowers in the genus. It thrives in dry places between shrubs and rocks and grows to sometimes a hundred and thirty centimetres tall. The flowers are purple with a contrasting orange throat, often though short-lived it is well worth growing in natural designs and as the above self-sows in the right conditions but without becoming weedy.

Linum; Linaceae

Around two hundred species of annuals, perennials, shrubs and sub-shrubs of Linum populate the temperate and subtropical zones of both hemispheres. Their use in the landscapes and gardens are mainly in rockeries, steppes and dry heath designs in sunny positions with well-drained, porous soils. Propagation is by seed or cuttings from non-flowering shoots from late spring to late summer.

Linum arboreum
Crete, Greece, Rhodes and south-western Anatolia are home to this shrub that grows to fifty centimetres high. It is a dense plant with golden-yellow flowers that I would use as structural plant in medium to large, natural rockery designs. However, it needs mentioning that it prefers mild winters and is not well suited to areas with real frost.

188 – Linum arboretum
Study in Greece

Linum hypericifolium Presl

This species comes from the Caucasus and is a robust, up to eighty-centimetre-tall plant with pink, darkly veined flowers. It is a showy species suited to larger rockeries or dry-stone walls; low strike rate with cuttings.

Linum marginale

This up to sixty-centimetre-tall species is at home in temperate Australia and New Zealand. It bears open blue flowers on branching stems and is adaptable.

Linum narbonense

In open shrublands and dry meadows and grasslands lives this beautiful, up to fifty-centimetre-tall Linum species. The flowers last a long time and are of a lovely blue; there are two cultivars I would recommend, 'Six Hills' and 'Heavenly Blue' both obviously propagate from cuttings.

189 – Linum narbonense
Staudengärtnerei Häussermann, Stuttgart, Germany

Linum suffruticosum ssp salsaloides Rouy
A very profusely flowering Linum that comes from the limestone soils of the Alps from Spain to France. It grows to twenty-five centimetres and forms dense carpets with white flowers.

Liriope; Convallariaceae

This genus originates in eastern Asia, the plants usually form grass-like carpets, the reason for the common name of Lily-Turf. They like mildly acidic soils and warm, semi-shaded locations.

Liriope graminifolia Baker
From thin rhizomes emerge up to sixty-centimetre-long evergreen leaves and light mauve-pink to white flowers in late summer.

Liriope muscari Bailey
China is the home of this species forming dense clumps of up to sixty-centimetre-long leaves (old name was Ophiopogon muscari). The plant requires good, rich and acidic soils to produce dark or light purple to white flowers. Use in the landscape may be together with evergreen smaller woody ornamentals like Skimmia, Sarcococca, Ilex, Taxus and Viburnum, ferns and Epimedium. There are numerous cultivars in the trade, best check with local suppliers.

Lissanthe; Epacridaceae

Lissanthe rubicunda
The 'Peach Heath' is a rounded sub-shrub of fifty centimetres with slightly prickly foliage and white to pale pink or red bell-like flowers in spring. Use it in the landscape in scattered small groups in heathlands where some shade is present and other heaths like Erica or Calluna do not perform well. Requires good drainage and propagates by cuttings best in late summer.

190 – Lissanthe rubicunda
Esperance, work in Western Australia

Lithodora; Boraginaceae

This small genus of around ten species originates in the Mediterranean. They are mostly evergreen dwarf shrubs with blue, purple or white flowers. Propagation is best by cuttings of non-flowering shoots in late summer.

Lithodora diffusa Johnst
This around fifteen-centimetre-high dwarf shrub comes from south-western Europe. It has glowing Gentian-blue flowers in early summer and requires acidic, well-drained soils. Use in the landscape in small rockeries and sheltered locations.

191 - Lithodora diffusa
Work in Badenweiler, Germany

Lithospermum; Boraginaceae

A genus of around fifty species that inhabit the northern hemisphere. Flowers are mainly blue, purple, yellow or white; propagation is best by root cuttings buried around two centimetres deep and observing polarity.

Lithospermum purpureocaeruleum

This interesting species used to 'listen' to the old name of Buglossoides purpureocaerulea. In my experience, it is one of the best ground covers and elegant solutions for the difficult drier areas in tree root zones where not many plants thrive. Its natural habitats are sunny, open shrublands and Oak forests with dry, alkaline soils. It naturally grows together with Geranium sanguineum, Anemone sylvestris and Euphorbia amygdaloides and I would use it accordingly in the landscape. Propagation is best using semi-matured tip cuttings.

Lobelia; Campanulaceae

The well-known genus of Lobelia (Lobelie, Cardinal Flower) is large and contains around three hundred and seventy species. Only a few though are used in garden designs and fewer still in the greater context of landscape architecture. Most Lobelia are associated with moist to wet areas around water features or swampy zones and should be used so.

Lobelia cardinalis

From the eastern North America comes the 'Cardinal Flower' that thrives in wet meadows or along creeks and rivers. The plant grows to a hundred and twenty centimetres tall and flowers in glowing red in late summer and into early autumn. Unlike many plants from wet areas it is not very competitive and requires gentle neighbours and partners. The gorgeous red is quite unique and worth the effort. Use in the landscape in wet and consistently moist zones and together with small Hemerocallis, Deschampsia caespitose, Lysimachia clethroides, Lythrum virgatum, Tradescantia, Primula, Veronicastrum virginicum, Molinia caerulea and Lilies from similar habitats.

Lobelia siphilitica

This robust Lobelia is easy to cultivate and grows to around eighty centimetres tall. Like L. cardinalis it comes from eastern North America. The flowers are light blue or white and appear from late summer into autumn.

Lobelia trigonocaulis

This trailing plant does well in heavy shade and moist conditions. Lovely to fall over rocks or dry-stone walls, it is propagated by division.

Lobelia splendens

From Mexico comes this species that is like L. cardinalis and grows to around a hundred and twenty centimetres in height. It has produced some beautiful cultivars like 'Queen Victoria' flowering scarlet red with dark foliage. Unfortunately, it is only suitable for areas with mild frosts or a warm microclimate.

Lomandra; Xanthorrhaceae

The so-called 'Mat Rushes' are hardy and attractive foliage plants for texture. There are around fifty species in this genus and they can be easily grown from seed.

Lomandra hystrix

This species is a large, tufted plant with arching, bright green leaves up to a hundred and thirty centimetres long. Flowers appear in early summer and are held within the foliage. A great foliage texture plant for landscapes with lower levels of maintenance it is also a great binder for erosion-prone soils, i.e. along banks, they tolerate some inundation. Propagation is by seed.

Lomandra longifolia

This variable, tussock-forming species reaches seventy to eighty centimetres. It has narrow, strap-like leaves and showy, perfumed flowers in summer. A very tough plant suitable for road embankments but also in mixed, large natural landscape designs.

Lotus; Fabaceae

The genus describes perennial and annual species, usually flowering prolifically and often used as annuals or pot plants.

Lotus australis
This rounded sub-shrub grows to fifty centimetres and has pale pink flowers. It requires full sun and good drainage but is often only short-lived. Propagation is by scarified seed.

Lotus corniculatus
Growing in meadows and grasslands, this species is very variable between lying flat on the ground and reaching up to fifty centimetres in height. The flowers are yellow and appear from late spring into late summer. In horticulture, several cultivars are of significance that are propagated by cuttings.

Lupinus; Fabaceae

Most perennial Lupins are at home in North America where they grow in moist, neutral to slightly acidic soils. Propagation is mainly by seed, only with very valuable selections it is worth propagating by basal cuttings.

Lupinus arboreus Sims
The 'Tree Lupin' comes from the western USA and California. It is an evergreen shrub reaching three metres and silvery, hairy foliage. The flowers are sulphur-yellow, lavender or blue. They tolerate frosts down to around minus ten degrees Celsius. Use in the landscape in wild, semi-formal or natural areas together with Buddleja, Ceanothus, Ceratostigma and Cercis siliquastrum; the species may be allowed to form its own communities in wild designs and self-sow.

Lupinus perennis
This perennial species comes from eastern North America where it mainly grows on sandy soils in open forests. It reaches eighty centimetres in height and has blue flowers in late spring and usually an after-flowering in late summer.

Lupinus polyphyllus Lindl
The parent of most of our familiar garden lupins originally comes from western North America and Canada. It was introduced into Europe in the 1890s. The plant reaches a hundred and fifty centimetres height in good conditions with up to sixty-centimetre-long blue, pink or white flower racemes.

Lupinus polyphyllus hybrids and cultivars
Hybrids between L. perennis, L. arboreus and possibly some annual species, as well as selections and cultivars, between them form the group of garden lupins that is familiar and used in many of our garden designs. Most breeding took place in England in the twentieth century; probably the best known are the 'Russell' Lupins of George Russel that came into the trade in 1937. Use of Lupins in the landscape and gardens should be done with thought as they tend to leave a gap after flowering, therefore I would recommend avoiding the temptation of massed displays in perennial borders and mixed displays, unless of course it is just a seasonal Lupin display. In my experience, it is, like with many other plants that are dormant for some time, advantageous to combine them with perennials or shrubs that are effective and taller after the flower of the Lupins. Examples could be Aster ericioides, Aster novi-belgii, Phlox paniculata, Helenium cultivars and Rudbeckia fulgida 'Goldsturm'

Luzula; Juncaceae

These grass-like perennials have flat leaves and are important mainly for their foliage under and with woody ornamentals, but also in meadows or heathlands.

Luzula nivea DC

This species is at home in open mountain forests with moist soils from north-eastern Spain, central France and extending into central Italy. It grows to twenty-five centimetres with white flowers held at around forty centimetres above the attractive foliage. They combine well with Hamamelis mollis, Rhododendron hirsutum, Erica and a variety of ferns.

Luzula sylvatica Gaudin

This European forest and woodland grass (sylvatica – forest-dwelling) is a lovely texture plant to use under trees and shrubs where sufficient moisture is ensured. The plant grows with its foliage up to thirty centimetres and its flowers in spring eighty centimetres high. The species tolerates root pressure and deep shade like few other plants, it combines well with Euphorbia amygdaloides, Dryopteris and Polystichum ferns.

Lychnis; Caryophyllaceae

There are eight species in this small genus related to the Carnations.

Lychinis calcedonica L

The 'Calcedonican Lychnis', 'de Croix de Jerusalem' ('Cross of Jerusalem') or 'Brennende Liebe' ('Burning Love') is essentially a Russian species. The leaves are elongated, hairy with glowing vermilion red flowers held above in summer. The colour is very intense and unusual, one of the reasons why it has become quite popular. The species is best used in the full sun, alkaline soils and rather dry locations, in rockeries, steppe designs or informal and formal borders.

Lychnis coronaria Dest

From south-eastern Europe to Asia Minor and the Himalayas ranges the habitats of the 'Rose Campion' or 'Coquelourde des Jardin' which are sunny, dry and poor soils of steppes, meadows and prairies. The whole plant is of a velvety, hairy grey texture with the deep crimson red, sometimes pink or white, flowers held above in contrast. Use in the landscape in natural, wild designs, rockeries or steppe and prairie plantings where it often self-sows nicely.

Lysimachia; Primulaceae

From Eurasia, North America and South Africa come around a hundred and fifty species of perennials or small shrubs of Lysimachia.

Lysimachia ciliata

This robust North-American perennial is a beautiful wild species when used in moist soils in front of or between open shrubs and around water features. It grows to a hundred centimetres and has bright yellow flowers that partner well with Lythrum salicaria and Eupatorium species. Propagation is by cuttings or division.

Lysimachia clethroides Duby

Japan, Korea and China are home to this attractive, up to a metre tall plant that develops rhizomes on moist, heavier soils. The flowers are white in late summer and as the above combines well with woody ornamentals in informal, natural or wild designs or the cottage garden rather than the formal perennial border.

Lythrum; Lythraceae

The 'Loosestrife' or 'Weiderich' is a typical genus of wet zones around water, running or still and describes around thirty perennial species and some sub-shrubs.

Lythrum salicaria L

The 'Purple Loosestrife' is at home in the northern temperate zones and South Australia. It grows in moist to wet meadows, along ditches and in moors. It is a very valuable perennial in combination with water features of all kinds as it flowers for very long periods; the butterflies like it also. A strong grower, it partners well with Iris pseudacorus, Lysimachia ciliata, Iris laevigata and Tradescantia. There are some nice cultivars in the trade, these need to be propagated by cuttings from the first shoots in spring to early summer; the pure species comes easily from seed.

Lythrum virgatum L

This widespread species extends from Eastern Europe to western Asia and grows to a hundred and twenty centimetres tall. Its original habitat are swampy meadows and ditches where it flowers deep red in summer. Use in the landscape in informal, natural and wild designs in wet areas or along water features.

Macleya; Papaveraceae

This genus describes special perennials from eastern Asia; one of their common names translates to 'Feather Poppy'. They are tall perennials with a yellowish, milky sap and handsome foliage. Mature plants provide a gorgeous background for other perennials or could be a feature plant in front of walls or trees. Propagation is by division of roots or root cuttings in the dormant season.

Macleya cordata Willd

Knowledgeable use of this tall, up to three metres high perennial is paramount to success. Use it as a background in large, robust plant designs, on its own as feature in front of walls, buildings or with trees. It can also be a good structural screen. Due to its strong-growing nature it tends to invade and overrun the average perennial border via its strong, aggressively growing root system. Its main features are the large, palmate leaves that are of a blue-greyish, green tone.

192 – Macleya cordata
Baumschule Häussermann, Stuttgart, Germany

Macropidia; Haemodoraceae

Macropidia fuliginosa syn Anigozanthos fuliginosa
The famous 'Black Kangaroo Paw' has Iris-like grey-green leaves to fifty centimetres. The branched flower spike is up to eighty centimetres and has green tubular flowers to six centimetres with strongly recurved petals. The flowers and stems are covered with dense jet-black hairs. The plant is an excellent and outstanding feature, also popular in floristry. It requires a sunny warm spot in well-drained soils. Ensure a mild microclimate as the flower spikes can be damaged by late frosts.

193 – Macropedia fuliginosa
Courtesy Wikipedia

Macrozamia; Zamiaceae

I have included the ancient genus of Macrozamia here as representative of the cycads for their structural and ornamental value in the designed landscape. Most Macrozamia develop attractive dark green fern-like leaves that grow to a metre or two outwards from a trunk. This trunk is subterranean in some species; in others, it can stand up to five metres tall. They are fantastic rockery plants or may characterise lush or dry perennial plant designs in larger landscapes. To develop their beauty, they do require sufficient space. The seeds are toxic and therefore Macrozamia should not be planted where little children, animals or curious tourists have access. The Australian Aborigines used it as a food source after thorough washing removes the toxic compounds.

Macrozamia communis
This species does not usually develop a trunk but appears almost like a very impressive dark fern. The common name is Burrawang. Best grown in well-drained soils in dappled shade, the plant is adaptable to a wide range of conditions and uses in the landscape. Easily propagated by seed.

194 – Macrozamia communis
Courtesy Brett Samon

Macrozamia riedlei

This large plant grows a trunk to two metres and features large leaves up to two metres long. It is an impressive structural feature plant that can dominate large landscapes or gardens. Good drainage provided it can be grown in full sun or semi-shade. Originally from Western Australia.

Malva; Malvaceae

Malva alcea

This species is widespread in Europe and the Mediterranean where it occupies open meadows and disturbed ground. The plant grows to a hundred centimetres and bears pink, large flowers from summer into early autumn. Often found in cottage gardens.

Malva moschata

A smaller Malva with up to fifty centimetres height, Malva moschata inhabits drier meadows. It flowers from late summer into early autumn with light pink flowers and the entire plant smells like musk.

Malva sylvestris

Along roads and pathways, walls and ditches grows this up to one-hundred-centimetre-tall perennial that prefers warmer locations. Flowering from early summer until autumn, the species has been used in herbal medicine as a tea for treating coughs and colds since the Middle Ages.

Mandragora; Solanaceae

The mystic 'Mandrake' or 'Alraune' and its roots has been attributed many magic properties; it even played a role in one of the *Harry Potter* movies. Some of the reasons for the mysteries surrounding it since the Middle Ages were that it was growing under gallows and its fleshy roots sometimes resemble a human shape (with some imagination). The Mandrake as a perennial is a pioneer plant that very often invades disturbed ground and ground was disturbed when gallows were erected, which may be a possible explanation. An important fact is that the plant is highly toxic. It has been used as an anaesthetic for surgery in ancient times but the risk of death from respiratory failure is high.

Mandragora officinarum L

Widespread in the warmer parts of Europe, the Mandrake sits usually flat on the ground with the flowers sessile within the leaves. It is not so much an ornamental perennial as it is a species for medicinal herb gardens or botanical collections.

Meconopsis; Papaveraceae

The genus of the 'Blue Poppy' or 'Himalayan Poppy' contains around fifty species. They are at home in Eurasia and the Himalayas, reaching altitudes of up to six thousand metres. Their habitats are open forests, meadows and rocky slopes. As can be derived from their origin, most Meconopsis thrive in a cool, humid environment and reasonably poor soils. In my experience, in cultivation they do well in lower altitudes in dappled shade and well-structured and drained, loamy sands or sandy loams of a neutral or only slightly acidic reaction. Humble amounts of a N-K balanced fertiliser and drier periods in late summer and autumn, to harden them off before winter. They should be kept reasonably dry in winter to prevent fungal infections. Propagation is best by seed in very sandy mixes and it is important to keep the plants actively growing in cool conditions and plant out before the growing season ends. Use in the landscape as feature in cool, shady places together with Ericaceae and Primulaceae.

Meconopsis betonicifolia Franch

This species comes from the Himalayas, Tibet, eastern Myanmar and Yunnan where it lives in altitudes between three thousand and four thousand five hundred metres. Open forests and moist meadows in sandy soils are the original habitat of this perennial with fleshy-woody roots. The hairy plant grows to a hundred and fifty centimetres tall and carries around eight centimetres wide, slightly nodding flowers of the most royal sky-blue and golden-yellow contrasting stamens. It grows easily in open, well-drained soils in light shade and with higher than average humidity; the right microclimate is a key to joy with this species.

195 – Meconopsis betonicifolia
Travel study, Himalaya

Meonopsis grandis Prain

In stony, gravelly slopes between three thousand and five thousand six hundred metres thrives this gorgeous perennial that forms a branched tap-root for survival. The species develops up to a hundred and twenty-centimetre-high stems that carry usually four deep blue to purple, up to twelve centimetres across flowers in summer. In cultivation, they require a porous loam and humus in light shade and high humidity. Over the years they can develop amazing and unforgettable displays of flowers. They combine well with Rhododendron, Azalea and Primula. Propagation is by seed or division; division is best in spring as soon as the leaves develop, the young shoots without roots that are broken off are placed in a sand/peat mix and kept moist. I found a mist-propagation unit, like for soft-tip cuttings, works well.

Meconopsis integrifolia Franch

At home in north-eastern Tibet, western Kansu, Sichuan, north-western Yunnan and north-eastern Burma in altitudes between three thousand and five thousand five hundred metres, this handsome Meconopsis makes a great display even when not in flower with its grey-green rosettes of soft-haired leaves. Dew drops or water droplets in high humidity make the entire plant a shining jewel. The species grows to eighty centimetres high and features large up to twenty centimetres across shiny yellow flowers in summer. Young seedlings require sufficient space and when planting any designs these monocarpic species it should be remembered that after fruit had been formed the space will be vacant again.

Meconopsis nepaulensis DC

The 'Satin Poppy' from Nepal and Sichuan thrives between three and six thousand metres altitude. It is another monocarpic species with rosettes of leaves held through winter and a deep taproot. It can reach an impressive two-hundred-and-fifty-centimetre height on heavy soils. The rosette of leaves is very decorative and the blue, sometimes white flowers grow to ten centimetres. Despite its size, the species does not want a lot of food; indeed, over-fertilising can quickly lead to death in winter. It combines beautifully with Rhododendron and other Ericaceae against a backdrop of evergreen trees.

Meconopsis regia Taylor

This large, up to two-hundred-centimetre-tall Meconopsis lives in central Nepal between four and five thousand metres. Its leaves may reach forty centimetres and are held on stems and covered with white-yellowish hairs. The flowers are yellow, sometimes red and up to fifteen centimetres across.

Melissa; Lamiaceae

This is a small genus of three species of aromatic herbs.

Melissa officinalis L

This widespread species originally comes from the eastern Mediterranean, the Caucasus and south-western Siberia but due to its toughness and adaptability to various soil types, has migrated out from the gardens and is found almost anywhere. The perennial forms short runners and grows to around eighty centimetres with small white flowers in early summer. It was known as a medicinal plant already in 960 in Arabia, from where it was introduced into Spain. The most important ingredient is an essential oil, Citral, which produces a pleasant lemon scent. It is interesting that plants from dry locations in northern region produce more oil than those in southern regions. The production of true Melissa Oil is labour intensive. The medicinal Melissa tea is calming, relaxing and works against cramps as well as stimulating for the hydrologic cycle of the body and it helps against bacterial infections. In cultivation, Melissa prefers cooler places and adapts to many soils. Propagation is by seed unless it is one of the variegated forms that needs propagating by division or cuttings.

Mentha; Lamiaceae

The Mints have been used since ancient times in herbal medicine. The genus comprises around thirty species and numerous hybrids through cultivation. They are perennial, aromatic herbs with runners above or below the soil surface; most mints are at home in moist or wet soils. There are three main medicinal groups of Mentha; the first contains mainly Menthol, the second Carvon and the third Pulegon. Of importance in ornamental horticulture are Mints as strong ground covers that combine with other strong partners or shrubs. They and their varieties with coloured leaves are also popular as pot or hanging basket plants, as well as for supplementing cut flower arrangements. The name of the Mint comes from the Greek myth told by Ovid that the nymph Minthe, a daughter of Kokytes, was transformed into this plant.

Mentha x piperita

The hybrid between M. spicata and M. aquatica has spread throughout the world. The plant grows to fifty centimetres and has mauve to purple flowers. The species contains commercial quantities of Menthol and can also be used in dried form. Provided there is sufficient moisture in the soil Mentha piperita adapts to almost any soil type and can indeed become invasive in designs. Therefore, I would recommend the Mint for displays in herb and medicinal gardens where either the time to control it is available or the plant is contained within a pot or container, paving or ornamental stone walls. There are numerous coloured cultivars available in the trade.

Mentha pulegium L

Widespread throughout the greater Mediterranean, this swamp plant inhabits flooding zones of rivers and lakes. It forms strong underground runners and is highly aromatic with purple flowers. The species is known as a medicinal plant since ancient times and documented by Dioskorides. It is used as disinfectant and for the preservation of drinking water on ships during long sea voyages. In cultivation, the plant prefers wet locations, the cultivar 'Pennyroyal' has been successfully used to grow a fragrant, low and dense carpet. This cultivar needs to be propagated vegetatively by cuttings.

Mentha spicata Hudson

The 'Spearmint' probably originates in France and upper Italy but has spread in the wild through cultivation and garden escapees. This Mint grows reasonably well in drier climates and produces a pleasant tea.

Mentha suaveolens Ehrh

This round-leaved species is also called the 'Apple Mint' and is well suited as ornamental plant in the gardens for its large and soft-haired foliage. The flowers are mauve and it has a very fruity fragrance, therefore it invites being planted near paths or seating where it may be appreciated.

Mertensia; Boraginaceae

The genus of the 'Blauglöckchen' (little blue bells) contains around fifty very variable species from Eastern Europe, Asia, Afghanistan and North America. They range from dwarf alpine rosette-forming perennials to tall forest dwellers and pioneer plants of the sea margin. Their cultivation naturally varies according to their habitat; alpine species grow in well-drained gravelly soils, forest species in rich, deep humus soils and species of the sea margin in pure sand or mostly sand mixed with a little loam and humus. Use in the landscape in rockeries, shady forests and woodlands together with Waldsteinia fragaroides, Podopyllum peltatum, Astilbe, Polygonatum, ferns and similar plants. Propagation is by seed (fresh is best) or division.

Mertensia ciliata Don

The 'Fringed Lungwort' from North America is a beautiful species for the large rockery or semi-shaded situations in open woodlands or at the margins of forests. Naturally it grows in open woodlands and reaches eighty centimetres in height with pink-budded light or deep blue flowers held in open racemes.

Mertensia pulmonarioides Roth

This species inhabits moist lowlands near forests and rivers where it grows to sixty centimetres. The lovely bell-shaped sky-blue flowers with their pink buds appear in spring. The plant withdraws after flowering, therefore it would be advantageous to combine it with other species that are effective from summer onward.

Milligania; Astelaceae (Liliaceae)

Milligania densiflora

A plant from alpine areas of Tasmania, this species requires ample moisture, rich soils and some shade, more so in hotter lowland areas. It is a tufted plant with thick, tapered leaves to thirty centimetres. The flowers are white, to two centimetres across and are held in branching stems. It is a great plant for the cooler rockery, the alpinum or along water features. Propagation is by seed and is requiring cold-moist germination or also by division. One can create very special magic moods in the landscape with it.

196 – Milligania densiflora
Courtesy Jenny Simmons

Mimulus; Scrophulariaceae

The genus of Mimulus with common names such as 'Monkey Flower' or 'Gauklerblume' (Harlequin Flower) is around a hundred and fifty species wide and originates mainly in western North America, temperate zones of South and Middle America, Africa, Asia and Australia. They are annuals or perennials for moist to wet locations and shrubs for normally drained places in the landscape.

Mimulus cardinalis Dougl ex Benth
The 'Scarlet Monkey Flower' comes from western North America where it grows in moist soils. It is a perennial but often only cultivated as an annual; it gets to seventy centimetres and has scarlet red flowers from spring to autumn. Use in the landscape in informal designs or cottage garden type designs for the long flowering period.

Mimulus cupreus Dombrain
This attractive but mostly short-lived perennial comes from Chile. Growing to around thirty centimetres, the flowers appear in late summer and colour from golden yellow to copper red with darker spots. Recommended for the rockery where it can self-sow if the conditions are right.

Mimulus guttatus Fish ex DC
Also, a species from western North America, this wetland perennial inhabits the water's edge. It flowers throughout the summer with golden-yellow inflorescences, albeit through strong growth and self-sowing it can suppress weeds as well as wanted species in that habitat and even in drier areas.

Mimulus hybrids
There is a large variety of beautiful Mimulus available; I would recommend using them more like annuals or bedding plants for their brilliant, playful colour.

Minuria; Asteraceae

Minuria integerrima
An Australian native plant this perennial has glabrous leaves to fifty centimetres long. White daisy flowers appear from winter through to spring. Adaptable to most soils the plant does best in full sun and benefits from pruning back after flowering for rejuvenation. Propagation is most efficient by cuttings.

Minuria leptophylla
This smaller daisy forms a small cushion to ten centimetres high. Lilac-blue flowers appear for most of the year and make this little perennial a great filler plant and a valuable addition to many landscape situations. Propagation is best by cuttings. The plant prefers full sun and good drainage.

Miscanthus; Poaceae

Miscanthus are rhizome-forming perennial grasses of up to four hundred centimetres in height. There are around twenty species recognised but this is notwithstanding further botanical investigation. Naturally they grow on moist slopes or in lowlands and flat areas and are happy with poorly aerated soils and little food. Use in the landscape as ornamental grasses and structural plants. Personally, I value their foliage and fruit that often lasts through winter and looks fascinating when coated with frost or snow. It is important to remember that Miscanthus become active late in the season, therefore it is advantageous to combine them with either evergreen or species that are effective early in spring. Examples for the latter would be geophytes like Allium, Ornithogalum, Frittilaria, Tulipa, Narcissus and the like. Another approach would be to interplant with perennials like Geranium sylvaticum, other Geranium or Thermopsis villosa and Doronicum pardalinum which populate the surface through winter. Cutting back of the old foliage should be very late and after winter, as the clumps of old leaves form a great shelter for many little animal souls.

Miscanthus purpurascens Anderss
This Siberian species has, as the name suggests, a reddish autumn colour of its foliage that can be extremely attractive in good clones. It is a tough plant except for the fact that it does not like drought, so plant in places where sufficient moisture is guaranteed.

Miscanthus (Triarrhena) sacchariflorus Benth
The 'Silberfahnengrass' (Silver banner grass) comes from Asia and grows to a hundred and fifty centimetres in height. They are eventually considered as a genus of their own '*Triarrhena*'.

Miscanthus (Eumiscanthus) sinensis Anderss
A clumping species which, with its great variety of cultivars, plays within the genus the most important role in horticulture and landscape architecture. The plants with their foliage texture and long-lasting flowers may be used in formal, informal, natural or wild designs in many applications. I used them in natural, large sweeping landscapes in Europe and even in a formal seasonal display as focal points in Government House Grounds in Sydney in the summer of 1997.

Miscanthus sinensis group

Out of the large number of cultivars I would like to recommend some exceptional ones in the following list where two numbers indicate average height; the first number the height of the clump of foliage and the second, the height of the flowers.

'Adagio', a hundred/a hundred and fifty; 'Africa', sixty/a hundred with beautiful red foliage; 'Goldfeder', a hundred and eighty/two hundred and twenty; 'Poseidon', two hundred/two hundred and fifty; 'Silberfeder', a hundred and seventy/two hundred and twenty; 'Variegatus', a hundred and twenty/a hundred and fifty.

Moltkia; Boraginaceae

This small genus of eight species is closely related to Lithospermum and features a long flowering time from spring to late summer with an outstanding blue. Their use in the landscape is mainly in rockeries, containers and dry-stone walls. Propagation is by seed or cuttings.

Moltkia petraea Griseb

This attractive species originates in the mountains of south-eastern Europe and central Greece, where it grows to two metres tall. It is a wonderful plant if excellent drainage and full sun are ensured. Modest amounts of a balanced fertiliser contribute to a long life of many decades and the plant rewards good cultivation with an abundance of lovely blue flowers from spring to late summer.

Monarda; Lamiaceae

'Horsemint', Wild Bergamot', 'Beebalm' or 'Indianernessel' are common names for this genus of around sixteen annual or perennial species. They are generally easily cultivated and graceful, long-flowering plants for perennial borders, cottage gardens or natural designs in association with woody ornamentals. They combine well with Aconitum, Aster dumosus and A. novi-belgii, Astilbe, Campanula macrantha, Cimicifuga, Delphinium, Heliopsis, Lysimachia, Phlox paniculata, Rudbeckia fulgida var sullivantii 'Goldsturm', Veronica longifolia and others. Propagation is best by division or cuttings from the first growth in spring.

Monarda didyma L

In moist forests of the USA lives up to a metre tall perennial with a very pleasant Melissa fragrance. It is used to produce tea and as parent for breeding the red flowering ornamental hybrids used in horticulture. The flowers are scarlet red and appear from summer through to autumn.

Monarda fistulosa L

This North American species grows to a hundred and twenty centimetres high and has whitish, mauve of reddish flowers from late summer to early autumn. Use in drier locations.

Monarda hybrids

The ornamental hybrids originate from the species have mainly been bred in the Netherlands. Some recommended for their qualities are: 'Adam' – a hundred centimetres and cherry red; 'Balance' – a hundred and twenty centimetres and salmon pink; 'Cambridge Scarlet' – a hundred and twenty centimetres and dark scarlet red; 'Comanche' – a hundred and eighty centimetres and deep pink with a very long flowering time; 'Maiden's Pride' – eighty centimetres and white; 'Mohawk' – a hundred and seventy centimetres and strong purple; 'Sioux' – a hundred and sixty centimetres and white with pink overtones; 'Squaw' – a hundred centimetres with large orange flowers.

197 – Monarda hybrid
Courtesy Wikimedia

Murdannia; Commelinaceae

Murdannia graminea

This tufted, grass-like perennial features lovely mauve-purple flowers on branched, up to fifty-centimetre-tall stems. The plant is widely distributed in Australia, from Western Australia, Northern Territory, Queensland and New South Wales, with the New South Wales selections obviously best adapted to cooler climates. Propagation is by division of the tuberous rootstock or by seed.

197 – Murdannia graminea
Courtesy Noosa Native Plants, Australia

Muscari; Hyacinthaceae (Liliaceae)

The 'Grape Hyacinth' describes a genus of around thirty species, mainly from the Mediterranean and south-west Asia. Muscari thrive in sunny to semi-shaded locations in drier and well-drained soils. They do well in tree root zones where they can create pretty scenes; the bulbs should be planted in autumn.

Muscari armeniacum Baker
This species comes from south-eastern Europe and extends to the Caucasus where it thrives in grassy, rocky slopes. It is quite variable with the flowers bright blue to purplish, sometimes white forms occur. It is a plant best used in wild or natural designs where it can colonise at its leisure or along paths where its strong tendency for expansion is controlled by hard landscape fabric.

Muscari aucheri Baker
Originating in subalpine meadows of Turkey M. aucheri is like the above but is somewhat more user-friendly in that it is not so competitive.

Muscari azureum Fenzl

Well-drained but moist subalpine grassy meadows are the home of this light to bright blue Muscari species. It flowers early in spring and is best used in rockeries together with Draba aizoides, Cyclamen coum, Iris danfordiae, Iris reticulata, Iris pumila, Tulipa, small Narcissus and Dryas suendermannii.

Myosotis; Boraginaceae

The 'Forget-Me-Not' or 'Vergissmeinnicht' is one of my earliest childhood memories with its friendly and humble flowers. The species come mainly from Europe and Siberia; however, there is a group that originates in New Zealand. There are around fifty annual, biannual or perennial species with blue, pink or white flowers of moist to wet places near creeks, in forests or in grassy meadows.

Myosotis australis var macrantha

This interesting yellow flowering species comes from New Zealand (australis translates here into southern lands). It self-sows well and the lovely yellow flowers in spring are held above brown foliage.

Myosotis scorpioides L

The old name Myosotis palustris (Sumpf-Vergissmeinnicht, German – Swamp Forget-me-not) tells us that this species is at home in most and wet places mainly in meadows and following water courses. It is an up to forty-centimetre-high perennial with sky-blue flowers with white throat and yellow-orange eyes. Use in the landscape in natural designs near and around water features together with Leucojum vernum, Iris pseudacorus and Iris laevigata.

198 – Myosotis scorpioides
Salzburg, Austria, courtesy Herbert Porstmeier

Myosotis sylvatica Ehrh ex Hoffm

As the Latin description suggests, this species is at home in forests and woodlands and from there has been introduced into gardens. As above, the plant is suggested for natural and informal designs where it can be 'let go'. It was the first plant I learned to identify as a child.

Narcissus; Amaryllidaceae

The botanic name of Narcissus for our Daffodils comes from a myth of ancient Greece: Narcissus was a hunter, the son of a river god named Cephissus and a nymph named Liriope. He was very beautiful and handsome but also exceptionally proud and arrogant, to such a degree that he disdained those who loved him. The goddess Nemesis noticed this behaviour and disapproved. She attracted Narcissus to a pool, where he saw his own reflection in the water and fell in love with it, not realising it was merely an image. Unable to leave the beauty of his reflection, Narcissus drowned. The around fifty plant species of the genus come from Europe, mainly the Mediterranean and describe bulbous perennials flowering in spring or autumn. Narcissus species have been in cultivation for a very long time and are regarded as heralds of spring. They have greatly differing requirements on cultivation; most though pefer sunny or lightly shaded locations with moisture. As with all bulbous perennials it is important to leave the foliage alone and let it die back naturally as the plant requires the photosynthesis after flowering for the future.

Narcissus bulbocodium L

The 'Hoop Petticoat' originally inhabits open woodlands and shrublands in dry or moist soils of south-western France, Spain, Portugal and North Africa. The bulb is small, to two centimetres, and white. The flower stands at around twenty-five centimetres and is in shades of yellow and appears from very early spring to late spring. In cultivation, the species requires sun and well-drained soils that should not completely dry out in summer. They are lovely in a rockery, but also work together with Rhododendron and Erythronium, Gentiana acaulis and Crocus.

199 – Narcissus bulbocodium
Courtesy Miriam Goldstein

Narcissus minor L

From northern Spain and the Pyrenees comes this up to twenty-five-centimetre-high trumpet Daffodil. It lives in meadows and in between shrubs in moist soils and flowers very early in spring; use in the landscape in natural designs in rockeries together maybe with early flowering, smaller perennials like Phlox subulata, Aubrieta and Alyssum.

Narcissus poeticus L

Widespread in mosit meadows and grasslands throughout Europe and extending to southern Russia is the 'Poet's Narcissus' or 'Dichter-Narzisse'. The white or cream flowers are held up to fifty centimetres high. In the cut-flower trade, Narcissus poeticus var recurvus are most commonly used. In cultivation, they prefer not too sunny spots but adapt to full sun if sufficient soil moisture exists. They are great in natural and wild designs and can just be let go and colonise larger informal landscape designs.

Narcissus pseudonarcissus L

This is the 'Wild Daffodil' or 'Trumpet Narcissus' or 'Osterglocken' (German for Easter Bells) which describes old cultivated forms of uncertain origins. There are numerous subspecies described but for this book, these botanical differentiations are not significant. What is significant are its uses in the landscapes and gardens which covers a wide range of applications. Formal bedding displays, natural landscapes and wild meadows, cottage and farm gardens or perennial borders may be home to this Narcissus. Just remember, unlike most tulips that come from a summer-dry habitat, daffodils should not completely dry out in summer.

Narcissus hybrids

The numerous hybrids of Narcissus are categorised into many divisions; these are:
Division 1: Trumpet Narcissus (Osterglocken) – spring flowering garden plants
Division 2: Large-flowered Narcissus – spring flowering cut flowers and perennial border plants
Division 3: Small-flowered Narcissus – spring flowering garden and meadow plants
Division 4: Double-flowered Narcissus – use according to size and strength in rockeries or garden
Division 5: Triandrus hybrids – late springflowering for garden and rockery in drier locations
Division 6: Cyclamineus hybrids – early spring flowering, long-flowering hybrids for cool and moist locations, suited for Rhododendron plantings
Division 7: Jonquilla hybrids – fragrant, late spring flowering hybrids for sunny, warm, well aerated and drained garden beds and rockeries
Division 8: Tazetta hybrids – late flowering multi-flowering hybrids for warm places
Division 9: Poeticus hybrids – late flowering
Division 10: Wild species as described in the introduction into the genus
Division 11: Split Korona hybrids – Narcissus with cut or split flower, often long-lived garden plants and popular for floristry

Nasturtium; Brassicaceae

The 'Watercress' is a very small genus of only two species associated with water and frost tender, in cold climates cultivated as annuals.

Nasturtium officinale Hayek

Thin rhizomes produce heart-shaped leaves and white flowers that stand up to eighty centimetres tall from early to late summer. The species prefers fast-flowing creeks and springs. The plant has been cultivated since the seventeenth century for its high content of Vitamin C.

Nelumbo; Nelumbonaceae

The Lotus is at home in North Amrica and Asia in waters that do not freeze through.

Nelumbo lutea Pers
The American Lotus reaches a hundred and fifty centimetres with its bright to dark green, up to thirty centimetres across leaves. The leaves are coated with a water repellent layer of cells and the light sulphur-yellow flowers appear in late summer. The plant requires very warm and sheltered locations and planting should be in a loamy soil around twenty centimetres deep. In areas with frosts that would freeze the water to this depth, the plants need to be either sheltered in water containers in a glasshouse or sunk in pots into deeper water levels to achieve protection.

Nelumbo nucifera Gaertn
The Egyptian or Indian Lotus extends down to north-eastern Australia where it grows in shallow flooding zones. The stems and blue-green leaves are held up to two hundred centimetres high and contain a milky sap. The leaves may reach up to sixty centimetres in diameter and the white and pink flowers may be up to thirty centimetres across; they are produced from late spring to late summer. Use in the landscape in warm, sheltered water features and be mindful that in good conditions the plants can be very competitive.

200 – Nelumbo nucifera
Work in Sydney, Australia 2000

Nepeta; Lamiacae

Around a hundred and eighty species are described in the genus of the 'Catmint'. Most are low to medium perennials with grey-green or green serrated and aromatic foliage. Use in the landscapes and gardens in sunny, dry places in rockeries or dry-stone walls, but they have also been successfully used as partners to roses. They attract bees. In relation to cats, I must say that my cats are indifferent to Nepeta but love Valerian. Propagation of good clones is by cuttings.

Nepeta cataria ssp citriodora

Widespread in Europe and Asia Minor, this subspecies possesses a lovely lemon scent. It grows to around eighty centimetres high with lively green foliage and white flowers from late summer to early autumn. Use best in natural, wild designs in groups and along paths where the aroma may be appreciated. Soils should be reasonably rich, well-drained and alkaline. It has been a popular plant in old farm gardens.

Nepeta x fassenii Bergmann ex Stearn

This hybrid is from the parents N. racemosa and N. nepetella, grows in dense clumps of hairy leaves and is very valuable through its long flowering time from early summer to late autumn. Apart from this blue form there is a white variety 'Alba' with white flowers available, both benefit from being cut back after the first flush of flowers. The plant reaches around fifty centimetres.

Nepeta grandiflora Bieb

From the Ukraine and the Caucasus comes this up to a hundred centimetres high purple-blue flowering Catmint. This species prefers moist soils and an average supply of nutrients; it is well suited to perennial borders and larger landscape designs.

201 – Nepeta grandiflora
Courtesy Beth Chatto

Nepeta nepetella L

Sun and drought loving, this small, thirty-centimetre-high Catmint originates in the Iberian Peninsula. The foliage is an attractive grey with light blue flowers. It combines well with bearded Iris and Euphorbia in rockeries and natural garden designs.

Nepeta racemosa Lam

The parent of many of our garden cultivars originates in the Caucasus and the northern Iran. The plant grows to around twenty-five centimetres and is easy. They are long-lived in the right places and graceful in the garden with its long-lasting flowers. Some recommended cultivars are: 'Karen's Blue' – silver-grey foliage and dark blue flowers, 'Porzellan' – grey foliage and porcelain blue flowers, 'Snowflake' – pure white flowers. 'Six Hills Giant' – fifty centimetres with lavender blue flowers and 'Walker's Low' – sixty centimetres with dark mauve flowers, stands out even from a distance.

Nepeta subsessilis Maxim

A very handsome and gorgeous tall Catmint with a hundred and twenty centimetres height, which resembles with its leaves the Stinging Nettle (Urtica dioica) but is much more pleasant to the touch. The large, up to three-centimetre dark purple flowers last for months starting in summer. This would be a great partner plant for the formal perennial border with Phlox, Helenium, Delphinium and Rudbeckia in sunny to semi-shaded soils with sufficient moisture and nutrient available.

Nomocharis; Liliaceae

The genus Nomocharis comes from the mountains of Asia where its species live near the snow margins. They are bulbous perennials comparable to Frittilaria and Lilium; albeit require attention in cultivation and are therefore recommended more for the passionate plant collector. The requirements are cool, semi-shaded places with high humidity (a bit like Meconopsis) and slightly acidic, humus-rich soils that need to be well drained and aerated. They usually do well among Rhododendron, in areas with severe frosts and without snow cover they need protection in winter.

Nomocharis aperta Wilson

This up to eighty-centimetre-tall perennial comes from western China and features large, up to 10cm across light or darker pink flowers. They appear in summer and have chestnut-brown spots radiating out from the centre, very beautiful.

Nomocharis pardanthina French

Growing to around ninety centimetres, Nomocharis paranthina has nodding or upright white or light pink flowers with reddish-brown or chestnut-brown spots in the centre in summer.

202 – Nomocharis pardanthina
Courtesy Beth Chatto

Nymphaea; Nymphaeaceae

Nymphaeaceae are aquatic perennials that are at home mainly in the sun and shallow water, between thirty and fifty centimetres but some species descend to two metres depth and more. They are magnificent feature plants for still water gardens and, whilst originally from subtropical and tropical areas, may be successfully cultivated in cooler climates. In cold areas, I would recommend keeping them in large containers in moist sand and over-winter them in the glasshouse or orangeries. The long-stemmed, shield-shaped leaves swim on the water's surface. The beautiful flowers are in many shades of white, pink, red and blue, but care needs to be taken in selecting the right species for the applicable environment and depth of water. Propagation is by cutting the active buds from the rhizomes, tip cuttings or side-shoots. Propagation by seed is best done by harvesting the swimming seeds into a water container that is kept cool, below ten degrees Celsius. The seeds swim only for a day or two, so good observation is required to 'catch' them. In my experience, it is best in cool climates to then embed the seeds in washed gravel and have the water level covering gravel and seed.

Nymphaea alba

This white Nymphaea is very widespread from the cool-temperate zones, in Europe as far north as North Africa, Syria, Asia Minor, Australia, Siberia and Mongolia. In Germany, it is a protected species. The flowers are fragrant and the species is a strong grower, therefore not recommended for small water features. Ideal water depth is between a hundred and a hundred and fifty centimetres, but it grows into shallow (forty centimetres) and deep (three hundred centimetres) water.

Nymphaea caerulea

Its original habitat is likely to be Egypt and northern Africa, but the plant has been spread already in ancient time to India and Thailand through trade. The reason for this was the species mild narcotic (sedative) properties, the plant is also known as the 'Sacred narcotic lily of the Nile' or the 'blue Lotus', however it is not closely related to the true Lotus, Nelumbo nucifera.

203 – Nymphaea caerulea
Courtesy Beth Chatto

Nymphaea odorata Ait
This species is at home in America, New Foundland and grows down to Mexico and Guayana. It is a plant of still or very slow-flowing waters and as the name suggests, the flowers are highly fragrant. Ideal water depth is between sixty and eighty centimetres. The parent of many hybrids, it has a variety, Nymphaea odorata var gigantea which grows in depth of over a hundred centimetres and tolerates shade better than most other species.

Nymphaea tetragona Georgi
This small Lake-Rose is widespread in several continents from North-America to Europe, Russia and northern Asia. It bears small, white flowers for a long time and due to its size and restrained growth, is suitable for small water features.

Nymphaea hybrids
For the fabric of landscape architecture and horticultural applications, the numerous hybrids are of more importance than the species. I chose to select only a very few from the huge number of lovely plants according to colour. As always, local availability may dictate choice.

'Amabilis' – this outstanding hybrid is peach-red with a long flowering period and beautifully formed inflorescences; ideal water depth is a hundred and fifty centimetres.

'Attraction' – large, crimson-red very attractive flowers are the feature of this strong growing hybrid, ideal water depth between eighty and a hundred and twenty centimetres.

'Comanche' – a smaller hybrid for shallow water depths between thirty and fifty centimetres. The flowers change colour from ochre-yellow to apricot, orange and deep red.

'Escarboucle' – deep glowing red flowers of up to twenty centimetres characterise this large-leaved hybrid. As an added benefit, the flowers stay open for longer than most others. Water depth a hundred and twenty centimetres and deeper.

'Fritz Junge' – a rich and very long flowering peach-pink hybrid from Hameln in Germany that thrives in water depths of a hundred to a hundred and twenty centimetres.

'Glorie du Temple-sur-Lot' – bred in 1913, this highly attractive plant features huge white flowers with up to a hundred petals. They somewhat resemble a blushing Chrysanthemum, opening with light pink and as they mature, changing to white. Ideal water depth between sixty and eighty centimetres.

'Gold Medal' – a more modern breed (1991) that is highly recommended for its large, clear golden-yellow flowers. It is a strong grower best cultivated in eighty centimetres of water.

'James Brydon' – this reliable, cherry-red and round-flowered hybrid was bred in 1899 and is highly valuable for medium-sized water features in fifty to sixty-centimetre depth.

'Marliaca Rosea' – white flower petals with a pink base characterise this older (1887), reliable hybrid. It does well where many other Nymphaea struggle but a very strong grower, ideally cultivated in depths of eighty to a hundred and twenty centimetres.

'Perry's Black Opal' – a very dark red flower which darkens as it matures. One of the darkest hybrids available; however, the term 'black' is somewhat exaggerated

'Peter Slocum' – a gorgeous, large-flowes strawberry-pink and fragrant hybrid that is best cultivated between a hundred and a hundred and twenty centimetres depth, strong growing.

'Sulphurea Grandiflora' – large yellow flowers made this hybrid from 1880 a very sought-after Lake Rose that holds its flowers above the water surface. Sometimes called 'Sunrise' it grows best between sixty and a hundred centimetres.

'Wow' – a very attractive, glowing dark-red Nmphaea that can be seen from far away. Hardy and reliable, even though the glowing colour appears tropical.

Oenothera; Onagraceae

Almost all the around two hundred species come from the New World, some have colonised Europe and Australia. Most are rich-flowering, hardy annual, biannual or perennial species with a colour range from light yellow to dark orange. Some species flower only at night, hence the German common name of 'Nachkerze' which translates into something like 'Night Candle'. I would use them in the landscape as conspicuous mass flower in sunny, hot and rather dry aspects of informal designs. Propagation is by seed, division and cuttings.

Oenothera fruticosa

The between thirty and seventy-centimetre-high plant comes from the USA where it flowers in late summer. Good to use in prarie designs or cottage gardens.

Oenothera macrocarpa (O. missouriensis)

This very attractive ground cover grows to only around twenty-centimetre height and features large, canary-yellow flowers for a long period from spring to autumn. They are excellent trailing on and down dry-stone walls and in rock gardens.

204 – Oenothera macrocarpa (former missouriensis)
Courtesy Wikimedia

Oenothera pilosella
A species from the prairies of the Mid-West of the USA, this species is valuable through pure yellow flowers and wine-red rosettes of leaves in winter. Good partners are Rudbeckia deamii, Sporobolus heterolepis, Andropogon gerardii.

Oenothera speciosa Nutt
During flowering this species is visible from a large distance through its large, light pink, fragrant flowers. It prefers light, warm locations and sun. Its robust nature makes it a good partner to Yucca in informal prairie or steppe designs or the large rockery.

Olearia; Asteraceae

This medium-sized genus of around a hundred and eighty species occurs in Australia, New Guinea and New Zealand. They are called Daisy Bushes for their abundant displays of flowers and most are essentially sub-shrubs, becoming woody at the base. They benefit from regular pruning or what I like to do in natural settings; let them self-sow and colonise suitable places as they please. Easily grown and propagated by cuttings.

Olearia ciliata
This excellent ground cover is a small sub-shrub to around thirty centimetres. Also called 'Fringed Daisy Bush', it bears light blue flowers in late winter and spring and is well suited to rockeries. Propagated by cuttings.

Olearia frostii
This attractive shrub grows to around sixty centimetres and has somewhat woolly leaves. An abundance of white to blue, large flowers with yellow centres appears in spring. It is at home in alpine areas of Victoria, Australia and propagated by cuttings.

Olearia magniflora

The 'Splendid Daisy Bush' is an open shrub to around a metre and has taken its name from the large, showy purple flowers that are produced for most of the year. It requires good drainage and full sun and is highly valuable for its almost never-ending flower display. It can tie designs together if spread in natural, irregular groups around rockeries, heathlands or dry meadows.

Olearia phlogopappa

Another great Olearia, this is an erect shrub to a hundred and fifty centimetres with greyish leaves. Well-drained soils in full sun or in sunny spots in open woodlands or Mallee, it is a graceful plant for natural designs. Either prune after flowering or let the plant self-sow and rejuvenate itself in the landscape.

205 – Olearia phlogopappa
Author's home garden, Queanbeyan, Australia

Omphalodes; Boraginaceae

This genus, like Myosotis, the Forget-Me-Not, comprises around twenty-five species from the Mediterranean to Asia.

Omphalodes cappadocica DC
Widespread from the western Caucasus to Asia Minor, this small species grows to fifteen centimetres. It flowers purple in spring and is suited for the informal rockery.

Omphalodes verna Moench 1794

This valuable ground cover is very well suited to places under shrubs and trees where sufficient moisture is present. It forms pretty and reliable colonies in the natural garden and will gently expand without becoming weedy.

Ophiopogon; Convallariaceae

These stemless perennials come from East Asia and are also known as Mondo-Grass or Lily-Turf.

Ophiopogon japonicus Ker-Gawl

The name 'Mondo-Grass' was termed in the USA for this species from Japan, Korea and China. It forms dense colonies with short rhizomes and grows up to thirty centimetres high with dark green foliage. The flowers are greenish-white to light purple and appear in late summer. The plant prefers shade and moisture.

Ophiopogon planiscapus Nakai

This up to fifty-centimetre-tall species from Japan is with its cultivar 'Nigrescens' often used as a foliage contrast to yellow foliage or flowers. It prefers warm, moist places in semi-shade and combines well with Hosta.

Origanum; Lamiaceae

There are around thirty-eight species of Origanum that are grouped in three sections; Amaracus, Majorana and Origanum. Planted together in the garden often leads to the development of hybrids. Requirements for cultivation are well-drained and alkaline, rather poor soils in full sun.

Origanum amanum Post

From the Amanum mountain range in Turkey comes this very beautiful species; a creeping sub-shrub to twenty centimetres. The flowers are a glowing crimson in summer. There is an excellent pure white form in cultivation. Please keep all O. amanum rather dry.

Origanum laevigatum Boiss

This is an up to seventy-centimetre-tall sub-shrub from the mountains of Turkey and Cypres. It flowers with a deep purple-pink tone in late summer. A selected seedling from Germany is 'Herrenhausen' which is a bit smaller, up to sixty centimetres and has very dark sepals which make for a lovely background in floral arrangements.

Origanum x majoricum Cambessedes

The hybrid of O. majorana and O. vulgare ssp virens originates in Spain. This infertile plant is very often used in herb production and needs to be propagated by early cuttings in spring.

Origanum rotundifolium Boiss

Growing in slightly acidic, well-drained gravelly soils from north-eastern Turkey into Russia, this small delicate sub-shrub is highly decorative. I recommend using it in smaller rockeries or let it trail over dry-stone walls.

206 – Origanum rotundifolium
Work in Badenweiler, 1993

Origanum vulgare L

The very variable species is widespread in Europe, Asia Minor, Iran, the Himalayas, Siberia and Taiwan. Depending on its origin it may be ten or fifty centimetres high with pink flowers. There are many ornamental cultivars available. In herbal medicine, the Origanum vulgare ssp hirtum is used which originates in Corsica, Italy, the Balkans, Asia Minor, Iran and Pakistan. This subspecies is fresh green and possesses a much stronger flavour; this is what is most often used in cooking (Pasta, Pizza).

Ornithogalum; Hyacinthaceae

This genus of bulbous perennials is at home in the Mediterranean and North Africa. Most species are easy plants for informal designs in the rockery or along the margins of woodlands.

Ornithogalum magnum Krash et Shiskin

Out of dark green leaves emerges a pyramidal inflorescence with numerous pure white flowers that stands up to ninety centimetres tall. It is also a good cut flower. In the garden, it may be combined with Paeonia, Iris germanica, Papaver orientale and Artemisia.

Ornithogalum narbonense L

This species comes from the Mediterranean and extends down into north-western Iran. The plant has an up to a hundred and twenty centimetres tall stand of flowers, white with a green stripe in the centre of the petals in early summer. It is best suited to warm, sunny and well-drained places in natural designs like rocky steppes.

Ornithogalum umbellatum L

The 'Star of Bethlehem' grows from Israel to North Africa, Syria, the Lebanon and Europe. It is a smaller species of up to thirty centimetres height with star-like white flowers with a light green stripe. I would recommend it for natural and wild designs along woodland margins or in similar association with large trees.

207 – Ornithogalum umbellatum
Courtesy Miriam Goldstein

Osmunda; Osmundaceae

A small genus of around twelve species of cosmopolitic ferns. The plants look ancient, like from the Age of Dinosaurs and may be best used as structural plants in wild and natural designs and need to be given sufficient space to develop their natural form.

Osmunda regalis L

The 'King's Fern' prefers very moist, semi-shaded or shaded places under trees like Alnus. It is remarkable also for its glowing fertile leaves. The single leaves may be a hundred and fifty centimetres and, more in mature specimen and old plants, are truly impressive features.

Osteospermum; Asteraceae

From Africa comes this genus of around forty-five species of sub-shrubs, perennials and annuals with prostrate to upright habits. The genus has been intensely used and worked with in horticulture resulting in profusely flowering hybrids.

Osteospermum barberiae Norlindh
This is a perennial species with a broad growth habit to fifty centimetres height. Irregularly serrated leaves and dark purple petals with a darker underside are featuers of this plant. It is parent of many horticultural cultivars and hybrids in the gardens.

Oxalis; Oxalidaceae

This large genus of around eight hundred species mainly originates in South Africa, South and Central America. They are predominantly perennial species but with some sub-shrubs. There are two main uses for the landscape, one as ground cover in shady areas and secondly, as collectors' specimens in the rockery, the alpinum or a pot. Cultivation for the shady forest species is in ruch acidic soils from semi to full shade. The alpine species require well-drained, gravelly and acidic soils.

Oxzalis acetosella
This forest-dwelling species is at home in deciduous as well as conifer forests. It can thrive in very low light situations. The plant grows to fifteen centimetres with mostly white or light pink flowers, sometimes veined. It needs to be used carefully in wild or natural designs as it is very competitive and expands rapidly.

Oxalis adenophylla Gill
This species grows in open, rocky places in the alpine zones of Chile and western Argentina. It is a small plant, growing to ten centimetres, with lovely flowers in shades of pink.

Ozothamnus; Asteraceae

Ozothamnus obcordatus
This species is a sub-shrub in the family Asteraceae and native to the states of Queensland, New South Wales, Victoria and Tasmania in Australia. It grows to 1.5 metres high and has obcordate, broad-elliptic obovate leaves which are six to fifteen millimetres long and three to six millimetres wide. These have tips that bend backwards and are shiny and green on the top and covered with grey hairs underneath. The flowers are bright yellow and may have potential in commercial cut flower production. I would use it in the landscape in heathland designs or mixed borders.

208 – Ozothamnus obcordatus
Author's home garden, Queanbeyan, Australia

Pachysandra; Buxaceae

A small genus of five species that originate in eastern Asia and eastern North America.

Pachysandra procumbens Michx

Coming from eastern North America, this reliable and valuable ground cover for shady areas stands at around thirty centimetres. It is evergreen with small, fragrant brown-white flowers. Propagation is by cuttings; division is possible but not economic.

Pachysandra terminalis Sieb et Zucc

At home in deciduous forests and woodlands of Japan and China, this species is a popular evergreen ground cover but requires the right conditions of rich, slightly acidic and moist soils in semi-shade of deciduous trees.

Paeonia; Paeoniaceae

There are around thirty-five species of Peonies, perennials and shrubs. The perennial species feature fleshy tuberous rhizomes and grow from around thirty to two hundred centimetres. Peonies flower in spring and early summer and retain their foliage into autumn, which is a very valuable feature. They are slow to grow and establish but long-lived and highly valuable garden plants. Choose their planting spots carefully as they do not like being disturbed and transplanted. They combine very well with a huge range of shrubs, trees and other perennials but require sufficient space to develop and show their full potential. Propagation is mainly by division which is sometimes a bit tricky due to their entwined fleshy root system; little tricks of the trade are to either wash most of the soil out with water, or let it dry out and gently shake some of it out. Divisions must have at least two healthy active buds. Only some of the Officinalis group regenerate well from parts of their root system. Usually it cannot be expected that divisions flower in the year after propagation; like many slow-growing plants they require an establishment phase. When planting, the buds should be five centimetres under the surface of the soil; planting too high or deep cause difficulties for the plants and long delays before good growth develops. Pure species may be propagated by seed, or of course we use seed propagation when breeding. The large, thick-skinned seeds of Paeonia require cooling treatment for germination. It helps if the seeds are lightly nicked or sanded or even gently hit with a rubber mallet. I recommend starting the cooling treatment straight away after harvesting; store the seeds in moist sand in the cool room at around four degrees Celsius. Do check regularly and once germination has commenced sow. In cultivation, Peonies require heavy, rich soils that retain some moisture even in hot summers but nonetheless need to be well-drained. PH should be between five and six and as always, very good and thorough soil preparation is the foundation of all growth and rewards the effort for many years. For commercial cut flower production, I recommend planting the individuals around fifty centimetres apart and the rows at a metre's distance from each other, this results in dense, self-supporting rows that do not require staking. Harvesting is in the budding phase. Moderate amounts of a balanced fertiliser in early spring and late summer are good.

In the following listing, horticulturally important Paeonia are grouped.

209 – Paeonia suffruticosa
Restoration Work in Canberra, Australia 2013

Wittmanniana group
Paeonia mlokosewitschii Lomak

This plant was found near the small town of Lagodech in the Caucasus by the forester E.D. Mlokosewicz, hence the name. The species grows to around seventy centimetres and flowers golden-yellow in spring.

Paeonia wittmanniana Hartw ex Lindl

This is another species from the Caucasus, it grows to ninety centimetres with flowers that start yellow, and then the colour fades to yellow-white when fully open until they are almost pure white before falling.

Cambessedesii group
Paeonia cambessedesii Willk

This smaller, up to fifty-centimetre-high and a bit sensitive species comes from the Balearic Islands. Deep pink flowers stand above dark green foliage in early summer.

Mascula group
Paeonia mascula Mill

This is a larger, up to ninety-centimetre-tall plant that comes from southern Europe and extends down to North Africa. It has carrot-like roots with wide leaves that are hairy underneath. The flowers are up to fifteen centimetres across and a strong crimson red, unfortunately they do not usually last long. The plant is very pretty and has been in cultivation since the Middle Ages.

Obovata group
Paeonia obovata Maxim

In mountain meadows of China grows this up to sixty-centimetre-high species. The flowers are white to deep pink and appear in late spring to early summer.

Lactiflora group
Paeonia emodi Wall ex Royle

A Himalayan species growing in altitudes between fifteen hundred and three thousand metres. Pretty white, nodding ten-centimetre flowers, often held in groups, appear in early summer. The plant requires acidic soils.

Paeonia lactiflora Pall

This up to a metre tall species originates in Tibet, China and Siberia. It was described in 1788 by Pallas as Paeonia albiflora. The parent of many of our garden hybrids descends from the Chinese forms introduced into West Europe in the nineteenth century.

Peregrina group
Paeonia peregrina Mill

Italy, the Balkans and southern Romania are home to the up to 90cm tall plant. The flowers are up to twelve centimetres wide and usually deep red, sometimes white.

Officinalis group
Paeonia officinalis L

From France, Hungary and Albania comes P. Officinalis which grows to sixty centimetres. The flowers appear in early summer and are clear red and up to fifteen centimetres wide. There are several good cultivars in the trade.

Clusii group
Paeonia clusii Stern

This is a rare species from Crete that is only thirty centimetres high. Flowers are to ten centimetres and white, sometimes light pink. A collector's item.

Tenuifolia group
Paeonia tenuifolia L

In dry meadows of south-eastern Europe, Asia Minor and the Caucasus grows the 'Net-leaved Paeony', the name is derived from its finely sectioned foliage. Up to fifty centimetres high, the plant flowers in shades of a strong red.

Anomala group
Paeonia anomala L

The around ninety-centimetre-tall plant extends in its origins from eastern Russia to central Asia. The flowers are to ten centimetres across and have shades from pink to reddish purple.

Paeonia lactiflora hybrids

These hybrids require rich, mineralic loamy soils with sufficient calcium. Best planting time is late summer/early autumn, just before the new roots start to develop. Best planting depth is for the buds to be between three and five centimetres below the surface. There is a huge number of great hybrids available, some recommended:

'Alice Harding' – eighty centimetres, buttery white, late flower
'Angelika Kaufmann' – sixty centimetres, light pink, early flower
'Bowl of Beauty' – eighty centimetres, Fuchsia-red with creamy-white centre
'Dragon's Nest' – eighty centimetres, strong red, golden stamens
'Edulis Superba' – eighty centimetres, rich pink, fragrant
'Felix Crousse' – eighty centimetres, dark wine-red with silvery shine, late flower
'Festiva Maxima' – eighty centimetres, white with pink spots, fragrant early flower
'Granat' – seventy centimetres, strong, pomegrenade-red with golden stamens
'Jan van Leeuwen' – ninety centimetres, white, robust
'King of England' – eighty centimetres, crimson red
'Mandaleen' – ninety centimetres, silvery pink, fragrant, early flower
'Marechal Mac Mahon' – seventy centimetres, deep cherry-red, late and prolific flower
'Ruth Clay' – ninety centimetres, dark red, prolific flower
'Top Brass' – eighty centimetres, light pink, huge double and fragrant flowers

Panicum; Poaceae

The 'Switch Grass' is a genus of tropical, subtropical and warm-temperate zones with creeping rhizomes or clumpy-growing species. Some may reach four hundred centimetres in height; they are ornamental grasses for warm places with rich, moist soils.

Panicum virgatum L

This is probably the most important species for landscape architecture and horticulture. It comes from central and eastern North America and extends to Mexico. The handsome plant reaches two hundred centimetres and flowers in late summer. In cultivation, it requires good nutrition, moisture and warmth. In my experience, it is advantageous to let the old foliage stand right through winter and only cut back in early spring. These perennial feature plants can provide structure in winter and look amazing when covered in hoar frost or snow. There are several cultivars and hybrids in the trade that differ in flower and colour of their foliage.

Papaver; Papaveraceae

The Poppies are a very variable and diverse genus of around a hundred annuals and perennials. Most are at home in the 'Old World' of Europe and temperate Asia but a few occur in North America. They are bringing colour into the landscapes, P. nudicaule and P. orientale. The larger species are best used in the perennial border, informal and natural designs whilst the smaller ones are well suited for rockeries and the alpinum. In my experience, it is important to place Papaver with thought to their life cycle; for example, most P. orientale die back after flowering for the duration of their summer dormancy and form new leaves with autumn rains and cooler temperatures. Therefore, I would use it not in the foreground, but behind partners that become visually effective after the Poppies' flowering time, such as late Chrysanthemum. However, it needs to be ensured that there is sufficient space and sun exposure for the Papaver to thrive and develop their full potential – they are adapted from their original habitat to 'bake' in hot dry summers with no or minimal rainfall. Propagation is by seed for annual species and by root cuttings for perennials like P. orientale. The best time to do this is winter, or once the plants have died back after flowering in summer.

Short pieces of root will suffice but polarity needs to be observed and they should not be over-watered. They do not like transplanting and usually require an establishment period of a year before they start to flower well, so please be patient – it is worth the effort.

Papaver bracteatum Lindl

This species comes from Turkey, the Caucasus and Iraq where it grows on steep, rocky slopes in the full sun but with some moisture in the soil. The plant reaches a metre and has blood-red flowers with black spots in late spring.

Papaver nudicaule ssp nudicaule L

The well-known 'Iceland Poppies' come from arctic and subarctic zones of Asia and North America. They grow in gravelly soils of slopes or steppes in altitudes of up to four thousand metres. The plant reaches forty centimetres and flowers in spring. The natural colours are in shades of yellow. There are numerous hybrids in the trade covering a large range of colours from strong contrasts to gentle, pastel shades. In the landscape, they are usually treated as annuals but may live two years. Easy to grow and the gorgeous colours make them popular for a large range of applications.

Papaver orientale L

At home in northern Iran, Armenia, the Caucasus and Asia Minor, P. orientale thrives in alkaline, well-drained and gravelly soils. It is an up to ninety-centimetre-tall perennial with deep, fragile taproots; I remember that at the nursery of Her Highness the Countess of Zeppelin we experimented for some time with special 'Poppy pots'; very deep pots that suited the development of this taproot. They were a bit like the tubestock pots for Australian native plants developing taproots like the Eucalypts. The wild form of P. orientale has scarlet-red flowers, sometimes with large black spots. It is summer-dormant and should only be divided or transplanted in that time. Many cultivars and hybrids were created in the nursery of Helen von Stein-Zeppelin, the trade marks of our Poppies were clear colours, with strong stems and harmony between the height of the plant and size of the flower.

210 – Papaver orientale
Restoration Work in Canberra, Australia 2013

'Aladdin' – ninety centimetres, glowing red with black spots, early and very large flower
'Catharina' – eighty centimetres, strong salmon-pink with black spots, early flower
'Helen von Stein' – eighty centimetres, gentle pink with dark red spots and wavy petals
'Perry's White' – eighty centimetres, pure white with black spots
'Rosenpokal' – eighty centimetres, deep, rich rose-pink
'Sindbad' – a hundred and ten centimetres, glowing orange-red with a little white
'Spätzünder' – seventy centimetres, clear red with black spots, flowers very late
'Türkenlouis' – eighty centimetres, fringed, glowing red flowers with black spots

Papaver somniferum

The Opium poppy is the species from which opium and poppy seeds are derived. Opium is the source of many narcotics, including morphine (and its derivative, heroin), thebaine, codeine, papaverine, and noscapine. The Latin botanical name means the 'sleep-bringing poppy', referring to the sedative properties of some of these opiates. The opium poppy is the only species of Papaveraceae that is an agricultural crop grown on a large scale. It is also valuable for ornamental purposes and is often found in gardens, sometimes in the wild. Poppy seeds of Papaver somniferum are an important food item and the source of poppy seed oil, which is healthy edible oil that has many uses.

211 – Papaver somniferum purple selection
Restoration Work in Canberra, Australia 2013

Paradisea; Asphodelaceae

The 'Lily of Paradise' is a small genus of only two European species. The flowers are bell-shaped and appear in late spring and early summer; their use in the landscape wold be mainly in the perennial border in well-drained soils in full sun. Propagation is by seed, they are good cut flowers.

Paradisea liliastrum Bertol
The thirty to fifty-centimetre-high species grows predominantly in the Alps. It has ivory-white flowers, up to twenty on a single stem.

Paradisea lusitanica Samp
From the mountians of Portugal and central Spain comes this valuable species. In cultivation, it requires well-drained, sandy or gravelly soils.

Passiflora; Passifloraceae

More than four hundred species of Passiflora are described. Most of them are from tropical, some are from subtropical and temperate America. Some more are from tropical Asia, Australia and Polynesia. Generally, they are climbing shrubs with a few perennials among them. Their flowers are often quite amazing and brilliant. Passiflora caerulea bears the common name of Passion Flower for the comparison with the sufferings of Christ in the Christian religion. Cultivation is best in warm, sheltered areas with rich, deep soils in full sun. In colder areas, it is recommended to protect the root zone with thick mulch. Use in the landscape is in association with woody ornamentals, on fences, as climbing screen or on pergolas. Propagation is by cuttings; the pure species of course can be done by seed.

Passiflora caerulea L

The well-known 'blue Passion Flower' originates in South America, Brazil, Paraguay and Argentina. It is a climbing shrub that becomes a perennial in colder zones as the shoots die back in the frost and the roots, with the ability to re-shoot, survive. The flowers are up to nine centimetres across with a sweet scent and appear from summer and into autumn. There is an ivory- white, beautiful variety named 'Constance Elliott'.

Passiflora incarnata L

Hailing from the USA, this species is an important medicinal plant. The flowers are blue with purple stripes in late summer and autumn. With some protection in colder areas, it can live for many years as an ornamental or in medicinal plant collections.

Patersonia; Iridaceae

There are around seventeen species of this interesting Iridaceae, distributed in Australia and South-East Asia. Most of their showy flowers last only for hours but a succession of bud's results in a very nice display. Most species form clumps of strap-like leaves to around thirty centimetres. Propagation is usually easy by seed. All Patersonia require full sun and excellent drainage to be at their best.

Patersonia occidentalis

Flat leaves to forty centimetres and long flowering stems to eighty centimetres characterise this species. Rich purple flowers appear in spring and summer, great to plant in groups but also scattered in rockeries, prairies or dry meadows.

212 – Patersonia occidentalis
Author's home garden, Yass Australia

Patersonia sericea

Hairy leaves to around fifty centimetres and deep violet flowers with golden-yellow stamens are features of this species. Easily grown from seed.

Patersonia umbrosa var. xanthina
A stiff upright species with yellow flowers from Western Australia. This plant likes dappled shade and the pure yellow flowers stand out nicely, suitable for underplanting of Mallee Eucalypts.

Pelargonium; Geraniaceae

There are around two hundred and eighty species in this genus, mainly from South Africa. They are related to, but are not true Geranium. These plants prefer warmth and sun and require good drainage to thrive and reward with prolific flowers. Propagation is easy by cuttings.

Pelargonium endlicherianum Fenzl
The species grows in dry limestone soils of Armenia, north-eastern Turkey and northern Syria. It forms clumps with short, fleshy stems and flowers deep pink with dark red veins, an outstanding plant.

Pelargonium quercetorum Agnew
Thriving in limestone rocks and gravel in south-eastern Turkey and northern Iraq, this species is somewhat like the above but taller, up to a hundred centimetres. It is a handsome plant for hot, dry areas in combination with rocks or a house wall.

Pennisetum; Poaceae

Eighty species of perennial and annual grasses that inhabit dry and sunny or shady places of warm-temperate or tropical zones. Propagation is by division in spring.

Pennisetum alopecuroides Spreng
The 'Fountain Grass' comes from Japan, China, Indochina, Polynesia and western Australia. It grows in dense clumps and up to a hundred and fifty centimetres tall, the leaves are up to twelve millimetres wide and coloured golden-yellow to brown in autumn. The flowers are dark to reddish purple, silvery white panicles and appear in late summer; they are held into winter. It is a very attractive ornamental and structural grass for a wide range of uses.

Pennisetum orientale Richard
This graceful, smaller grass is at home in central Asia, the Caucasus and north-western India. Dense clumps of leaves to forty centimetres carry numerous pinkish to silvery-white panicles for a very long time. This long flowering time makes the plant valuable for smaller garden designs in warm, well-drained places.

Penstemon; Scrophulariaceae

The genus of more than two hundred and fifty species is mainly at home in North America and Mexico, with one species from north-east Asia. These perennials are attractive and popular summer flowering plants, often used in perennials borders. They partner well with other perennials in the formal border as well as in natural or wild designs and do well in the rockery. Most prefer light, well-drained and slightly acidic soils. They are generally short-lived, however, but easily propagated by cuttings.

Penstemon acaulis Williams
This pillow-forming small perennial comes from the western USA. It produces large blue flowers on short stems, very pretty.

Penstemon barbatus Roth
This up to a hundred and fifty centimetres tall perennial comes from Mexico. It features crimson red, sometimes white, pink or purple flowers in late summer and is one of the parents of many beautiful hybrids.

Penstemon cardwellii Howell
A smaller, up to twenty-centimetre-tall, gorgeous plant with large, crimson-pink to mauve-purple flowers.

Penstemon digitalis Nutt
Up to a hundred and fifty centimetres tall, this species has white to pink or light purple flowers in summer and late summer.

Penstemon grandiflorus Nutt
The 'Large Beard Tongue' comes from the USA and extends down to Texas. The plant grows to a hundred centimetres tall with up to thirty-centimetre-long inflorescences, pink to blue.

Penstemon heterophyllus Lindl
From California comes this warmth-loving species that reaches a hundred and fifty centimetres and becomes woody at its base. The flowers are azure blue from summer to autumn.

Penstemon pinifolius Greene
An interesting small shrubby species that resembles Erica is this up to thirty-centimetre-high plant. The leaves are small, like needles and the flowers are orange-red in late summer. It combines well with Erodium reichardii, Ibris saxatilis, Satureja spicigera, Onosma stellulata and Phlox subulata in the rockery.

Penstemon teucrioides Greene
From Colorado comes this dwarf species to ten centimetres that impresses with a glowing blue in summer; a great plant for the small rockery.

Penstemon hybrids
These hybrids are valuable as summer flowering partnes in formal and informal designs with Coreopsis grandiflora, Geranium dalmaticum, Delphinium, Aster, Lilium and Euphorbia. In cultivation, they require good drainage but other than that are quite easy when not over-fed with too much N; some recommendations:

'Agnes Lang' – eighty centimetres, raspberry-red with white throat (1869)
'Blue Spring' – thirty centimetres, gentian-blue in early summer
'Lena Sherba' – thirty centimetres, white, very beautiful

'Osprey' – eighty centimetres, dark purple large flowers

Perovskia; Lamiaceae

This genus describes medium to tall perennials that become woody at their base. The flowers are usually small, blue and appear in late summer. These plants are valuable for hot, dry places together with other steppe or semi-arid partners. Propagation is best by cuttings with glasshouse plants producing best results.

Perovskia abrotanoides Karelin
This sub-shrub grows to fifty centimetres and comes from central Asia. Its flowers are purple in late summer; the leaves resemble small feathers.

Perovskia atriplicifolia Benth
From Afghanistan to western Tibest grows this up to a hundred and fifty-centimetre-tall species with white, felty stems, grey-felty serrated leaves and blue flowers in late summer.

Perovskia x superba
The hybrid between P. abrotanoides and P. atriplicifolia jas purple-blue flowers and in my experience works well in small, informal groups in dry rock gardens.

Petasites; Asteraceae

This small genus of around twenty species describes essentially swamp plants or plants from the margins of ponds and creeks. In the right conditions, they grow strongly and require a lot of space, therefore they may do best in natural or wild designs.

Petasites fragrans Presl
These plants grow to thirty centimetres high with heart-shaped leaves. The flowers are pink-white and have a scent like Vanilla; they are suited for the vase. The species flowers in winter which makes it valuable but it requires a mild climate.

Petasites hybridus Gaertn
This species has been renamed from P. officinalis. It describes an up to thirty-centimetre-high plant during flowering time that forms large colonies in swampy areas. The leaves emerge after flowering and can become up to a hundred centimetres high. It is best to use only male plants in large areas where they can 'go wild', or alternatively restrict their root movement with some hard fabric. This way they become very impressive. Propagation is by division of the rhizomes that are laid five centimetres under the surface.

Peucedanum; Apiaceae

Peucedanum cervaria Lapeyr
This European species extends into the Ukraine. The plant grows along sunny margins of woodlands and in open, dry forests on alkaline soils. The stems are up to a hundred and fifty centimetres long and carry white, between fifteen and thirty flowers in umbels. Using it in the landscape the plant combines well with Panicum virgatum, Coronilla coronata, Geranium sanguineum, Allium carinatum, A. christophii and Paeonia.

Peucedanum officinale L

These handsome plants originate in central and southern Europe where they grow in poor, alkaline soils in open woodlands. The stems develop to eighty centimetres with yellow flowers in late summer. They are good structural plants in natural designs.

Phlomis; Lamiaceae

This variable genus typically features flowers arranged in a whorl from yellow, white, purple or purple-pink. Most are sub-shrubs that develop into handsome structural plants in areas of mild winters.

Phlomis fruticosa L

The 'Jerusalem Sage' is a Mediterranean sub-shrub up to two hundred centimetres tall with grey to whitish, felty leaves. The flowers are glowing yellow in summer; these plants are quire a show when in flower and at other times they provide great structure. Use in the landscape in dry, sunny places in the perennial border or natural steppe and rockery designs.

Phlomis leucophracta Davis et Hub

From rocky slopes of Turkey often in association with oaks comes this sub-shrub with yellow to rusty-brown flowers. There are two selections; 'Golden Janissary' with yellow hairy and 'Silver Janissary' with white hairy leaves. Between P. leucophracta and P. lycia is a hybrid named 'Goldmine' that shows great potential.

Phlomis russeliana Benth

This perennial species is at home in conifer and deciduous forests of Turkey in altitudes of up to eighteen hundred metres. The plant grows to a hundred and fifty centimetres tall and has two-coloured, cream and golden-yellow flowers from early summer to autumn. This species was also wrongly known as P. samia.

213 – Phlomis russeliana, in the background Salvia argentea, Lychinis calcedonica
Used as structural plant, Restoration Work in Canberra, Australia 2013

Phlomis taurica Hartwiss ex Bunge

From the Crimea and the Caucasus comes this valuable, rich-flowering species. It is a perennial to fifty centimetres high with Malva-pink flowers in summer. In its original habitat, the stems are broken off by the autumn winds and the seed is thus dispersed. It is recommended to combine some autumn-flowering species to it.

Phlomis tuberosa L

Central and south-eastern Europe, Turkey, Iran, central Asia and China are home to this widespread perennial. Naturally it grows on dry slopes, steppes and dry meadows. It should be used in the landscape in a similar way in natural or informal designs. The plant reaches a hundred and fifty centimetres and has purple-pink flowers in summer. It is a very variable species and the tubers are edible after cooking.

Phlox; Polemoniaceae

The genus with seventy species is widespread in North America with one in Siberia. Most are perennials with some annuals among them. The tall Phloxes are usually perennial and become slightly woody at the base; they are magnificent summer-flowering plants for the perennial border. The low Phloxes are mostly spring-flowering with some real jewels among them. The first Phloxes were bred in Europe in 1728. Except for the small, low and alpine Phloxes, the tall plants require rich, deep soils with good drainage and a lot of moisture. Propagation is easy by soft-tip cuttings in spring or root cuttings in autumn.

Phlox adsurgens Torr et Gray

The evergreen or Periwinkle Phlox is a beautiful low ground cover for semi-shaded or shaded areas. The flowers appear in spring to early summer and are white, purple and pink. This species combines well with Corydalis, Aquilegia and small ferns. Propagation is by cuttings or rooted shoots.

Phlox x arendsii (Arendsii hybrids)

The group of hybrids between P. divaricata and P. paniculata was created by Georg Arends in Germany. The group is distinguished through rich, early flower displays on tall Phloxes. If the old flowers are pruned back in time, a second flowering occurs in autumn. They combine well with Tiarella, Trollius, Tellima, Asarum, Viola and grasses in natural designs and are highly valuable in the perennial border.

'Anja' – fifty centimetres, glowing red
'Hilda' – sixty centimetres, white with pink eye
'Lisbeth' – sixty centimetres, purple with bright centre
'Susanne' – sixty centimetres, light pink with red eye

Phlox bifida ssp bifida

The 'Sand Phlox' inhabits sandy and gravelly soils and suits many applications in rockeries or dry-stone walls. The flowers of the wild subspecies are mainly lavender to lilac, some are white. The roots need to have a chance to go down deep into the soil to survive summer heat and drought. There are some very attractive hybrids:

'Blue Form' – large blue flowers
'Frohnleiten' – gentle light blue with dark centre
'Mina Colvin' – pure white

Phlox divaricata ssp laphamii Wood

In open woodlands from Georgia to western Texas lives this fragrant Phlox, sometimes referred to as 'Sweet William'. The flowers range from purple to crimson. It possesses an amazingly beautiful fragrance which is strongest in the evening. In cultivation, it requires a lot of water in spring with drier summers on rich, loamy or sandy-loamy soils. They combine well with tall perennials and woody ornamentals where not too much exposed to root pressure and competition.

Phlox douglasii Hook

From Oregon to Montana and into Canada comes this small, almost grasslike ground cover. It prefers heavy, rocky and dry soils and grows to twenty centimetres. In late spring and early summer, the plant is entirely covered in lovely flowers from lavender, white to light or darker pink.

Phlox paniculata L

This gorgeous species originates in North America where it grows in open woodlands in rich soils and near rivers. It is a perennial with short, thick rhizomes that often reaches two hundred centimetres. The flowers are in shades of light to dark purple, lilac, white, pink and with or without a different centre. The 'Summer Phlox' is the parent of very many of those magnificently flowering Phloxes we admire in perennial borders, flowering from summer into autumn. In cultivation, they require rich, moist soils from full sun to light shade. Propagation is by soft tip cuttings in spring, division or root cuttings in late autumn. It is a plant for the perennial border where it gets the time and attention it needs to develop its full beauty and has the right background and partners. I often combine the Phloxes with Delphinium, Coreopsis, Physostegia, Helenium, Rudbeckia and Chrysanthemum. I usually position the latest Chrysanthemum in the foreground to have its structure throughout the year and the flowers when most other herbaceous plants have already gone into dormancy. Some highly recommended cultivars and hybrids:

Phlox paniculata 'Elisabeth'
Restoration Work in Canberra, Australia 2013

'Bornimer Nachsommer' – a hundred and thirty centimetres, salmon pink with crimson eye, late flower
'Düsterlohe' – a hundred and twenty centimetres, dark, deep purple, early flower
'Flamingo' – eighty centimetres, strong pink with dark eye, intermediate flower
'Fliedertraum' – eighty centimetres, lilac with white eye, late flower
'Kirmesländer' – a hundred and forty centimetres, white with red eye, late flower
'Pax' – eighty centimetres, pure white, late flower
'Ronsdorf' – ninety centimetres, glowing red, early flower

215 – Phlox paniculata used in mixed border
Courtesy Beth Chatto

Phlox speciosa ssp speciosa

This is a small shrubby Phlox that grows to fifty centimetres. It is at home in altitudes between three hundred and two thousand three hundred metres from Sierra Nevada to Arizona. The flowers are crimson to white and have a very nice perfume. This is a special plant for the rockery with heavier soils that can dry out in summer. Propagation is a little tricky and works best with early soft cuttings in spring before the flower buds form.

Phlox subulata ssp subulata

The 'Pillow-Phlox' originates in the north-eastern USA and forms dense pillows of narrow leaves. The fragrant flowers are up to fifteen millimetres and come in shades of red, pink, lilac and white, occasionally with distinct eyes. When the plants bloom in spring, they are just covered in flowers. The plants can be used in a large variety of applications from the rockery and dry-stone walls to borders of perennial plant designs. Propagation is easy by cuttings or rooted shoots. There are numerous lovely cultivars and hybrids available in the trade.

Phragmites; Poaceae

This is a small genus of only three species of cosmopolitan grasses for shallow water.

Phragmites australis Trin ex Steud (1841)

The over two-hundred-centimetre-tall species is of significance in natural and wild designs along water courses where it provides a valuable biosphere. It provides raw material for food and buildings; there are some cultivars with variegated foliage like 'Variegatus'.

Phuopsis; Rubiaceae

Phuopsis stylosa Jacks
The only species of this genus is closely related to Asperula and somewhat similar. Growing as ground cover of up to thirty centimetres height, the plant is valuable for natural and informal designs, borders or retaining walls. The flowers appear in summer and are slightly fragrant; it is a strong grower and requires strong partners.

Phygelius; Scrophulariaceae

There are two species in this small genus from South Africa, which is commonly called the 'Cape Fuchsia'. They are small, upright sub-shrubs with long curved flowers that are pollinated by nectar-eating birds. The plants require warm, sunny places with well-drained but not too dry soils; in their original habitat, they sometimes follow the moist soils along creeks. Propagation is by cuttings.

Phygelius capensis Mey
This species grows to around a hundred and fifty centimetres tall with egg-shaped leaves and flowers in broad, pyramidal panicles. The inflorescences are coral-red with a yellow inside; these plants usually flower profusely from summer into autumn. Use in the landscape in many applications from borders to rockeries, formal or informal.

Physalis; Solanaceae

Worldwide there are around eighty species of Physalis, most of which come from the warm-temperate zones of America. They are annuals and perennials; of significance in horticulture is only one species.

Physalis alkegengii
This 'Lantern Flower' grows to eighty centimetres on moist, slightly alkaline soils. It is important to note that it is quite invasive and therefore needs to be placed carefully. Possible uses in the landscape are for wild, natural designs, together with other strong partners or in combination with woody ornamentals that restrict its growth via root pressure. The glowing red balloons are valuable in giving colour to the garden through autumn and into winter. They are also popular with florists, fresh and in dried form.

216 – Physalis alkegengii
Courtesy Beth Chatto

Physostegia; Lamiaceae

Some common names for this genus are 'False Dragon Head', 'Obedient Plant' or 'Gelenkblume', which all refer to the flowers, which may be moved into a different direction and stay there. The plants have creeping rhizomes, flower in summer to autumn and prefer moist to almost wet soils.

Physostegia virginiana Benth
From North America comes this up to one hundred and thirty-centimetre-high species. It flowers light mauve-pink or pink in late summer and stand upright. Good partners are Aster dumosus, Erigeron, Monarda, Veronica longifolia, Salvia pratensis, Veronicastrum virginicum, Molinia arundinacea, Sorghastrum, Panicum virgatum and many more. Uses in the landscape are in the perennial border, formal and informal and cottage garden scenarios, also in more natural design contexts.

Pimelea; Thymelaceae

There are around a hundred species of this genus at home in Australia, New Zealand, New Guinea and Timor. They are evergreen, low to medium shrubs with very attractive flowers. However, some are slightly tricky in cultivation. The key to success, as almost always, is to know where the species comes from and what environmental conditions it is adapted to. Most are from well-drained, rocky and gravelly soils that are not too dry. Consequently, the rockery or alpinum are suggested uses in the landscape. Propagation is by seed, which is very fragile or by cuttings, calculate for around eighty per cent strike rate only in most cases.

Pimelea prostrata Willd
This species from New Zealand grows from sea level to altitudes of up to eighteen hundred metres. It is a creeping, sometimes half upright plant with bright green leaves that feature a bluish shine.

Pimelea sericea-villosa Hook
These dense plants grow on well-drained, airy but reasonably moist soils. The flowers are white and appear in late spring to early summer.

Pimelea treyvaudii
This very showy Pimelea grows to around sixty centimetres with elliptical, grey-green leaves and white flowers with creamy bracts are held in terminal heads. Requires well-drained soil in dappled shade and propagates easily by cuttings.

217 - Pimelea treyvaudii
Restoration work in Canberra, Australia 2012

Platycodon; Campanulaceae

The 'Balloon Flower' is widespread in Manchuria, North Korea and Japan. It is a variable, geophytic perennial with a white, carrot-like rootstock.

Platycodon grandiflora DC

Growing to around eighty centimetres on heavy, but well-drained soils, the flower resembles before opening a little hot-air balloon, hence the common name. Once open, the flower is greenish-blue on the outside and sky or azure blue on the inside, sometimes pink. Use in the landscape in association with low to medium shrubs, maybe together with Achillea, Potentilla nepalensis and P. atrosanguinea. There are several varieties and hybrids available.

218 – Platycodon grandiflorum
Courtesy Missouri Botanic Gardens, United States

Pleione; Orchidaceae

This is a small genus of terrestrial orchids with pseudo-bulbs that sit on top of the soil surface rather than in the soil as with most other terrestrials.

Pleione limprichtii Schlecht

This lovely orchid comes from Tibet and western Sichuan. One common name is 'Tibet orchid'. The pseudo-bulb is dark green and a pointed egg-shape. The longish leaf has a strongly formed nervatur. The slightly nodding flowers are strong pink or purple-pink and white on the inside, with orange-brown dots in spring. The plant is hardy, during the growing season it wants to be kept moist but needs to be kept dry during dormancy. The soil should be well-drained and in semi-shade.

Poa; Poaceae

This large genus of more than five hundred species has gained some significance in landscape architecture and horticulture for environmental and ornamental values. The range of their original habitats is varied as are consequently their uses in the landscape. In my personal experience, I use them in natural and wild designs as larger ground covers and to structure grasslands, prairies or shrublands. However, I have also used them very successfully in more formal settings as ornamental grasses; for example, the soft clumps of Poa labillardieri are very reliable as structure in small horticultural designs but also in the larger scale of big landscape settings.

Poa badensis Haenke ex Willd

This species from south-eastern and central Europe is an indicator of dry soils. It enjoys warmth and sun, grows in dense clumps and features slightly bluish foliage. Use in the landscape to colonise cracks in dry stone walls, rockeries, paving and it is also well suited for greening of roofs where only a thin layer of soil is available.

Poa chaixii Vill

The 'Forest Panicle Grass' (translated from German) is at home in Europe where it grows in poor soils with changing moisture levels. For the genus, it features broad, up to ten-millimetre-wide leaves and long fertile shoots up to a metre, carrying a thirty-centimetre-long panicle. It is a great foliage contrast plant for natural designs and partners like Geranium oxonianum, Geranium sylvaticum, Digitalis purpurea and the like.

Poa labillardieri

A great tussock-forming grass with narrow, greyish leaves. It forms plume-like heads of flowers and is very hardy. It can be used almost anywhere in the landscape, from erosion control along roadbanks to underplantings of Eucalypts and as structural texture plant in natural designs. It is very popular in my back yard with my cats as they tunnel under the leaves and find perfect little hiding places.

Podolepis; Asteraceae

Podolepis jaceoides

These perennial forms rosettes with its up to twenty-centimetre-long leaves. Above these rosettes stand up to eighty-centimetre-tall, yellow, five centimetres wide flowers. Best grown in full sun, use in the landscape in meadows or informal perennial designs, propagates by seed.

Podophyllum; Berberidaceae

A genus of south-east Asia and Atlantic North America with thick, horizontal and poisonous rhizomes. Out of these rhizomes emerge hand-shaped leaves and stems that bear flowers in shades of pink. All species require sufficient moisture. Propagation is by division in late summer or early spring or seed which is best used fresh, immediately after ripening.

Podophyllum hexandrum Royle

This beautiful plant from the Himalayas grows naturally in open woodlands and forests with enough light penetration. The white to light pink flowers are held singly above the unfolding leaves. The large, chicken-egg sized fruits are red. The plant is very decorative in foliage and flower.

219 – Podophyllum hexandrum
Courtesy Beth Chatto

Podophyllum peltatum L

From North America, this species forms large colonies and possesses big, bright green leaves to thirty centimetres. It is essentially a forest plant requiring more shade.

Polemonium; Polemoniaceae

The genus of the 'Jacob's Ladder' contains around twenty species of low to medium perennials and some annuals. Their use in the landscape is usually in natural and wild designs with the small species suited more to the rockery.

Polemonium caeruleum

This widespread species has numerous variations and subspecies living from central Europe to North Asia and in western North America. The plant grows to eighty centimetres in moist soils along rivers and creeks, moist meadows and disturbed soils and is ascending into higher altitudes. The flowers appear from spring into summer and aree sky blue.

Polemonium grandiflorum Benth

From the mountains of northern Mexico comes this up to forty-centimetre-high species. The flowers are up to forty millimetres wide and can vary from sky blue to yellow. It avoids alkaline soils and is somewhat rare but quite beautiful.

Polygonatum; Convallariaceae

There are around thirty-five species of the 'Solomon's Seal' that are widespread across the temperate zones of the northern hemisphere. Some exceptions are a few tropical species that are at home in the mountain forests from Guatemala to Panama, that reach up to an amazing seven metres. Most Polygonatum are forest dwellers, requiring shade and moisture and form thick, fleshy rhizomes that flower from spring into early summer. They are well suited to colonising large gardens or parks in the shade of their trees. Quite a few species also colour up nicely in autumn and have conspicuously decorative berries. Good partners are Cimicifulga, Hosta, ornamental grasses, ferns and Astilbe; it needs to be ensured though that the Polygonatum are not overwhelming weaker neighbours. Propagation is easy by division in spring or autumn, seeds are slow to develop. By and large Ploygnatum also develop slowly as a plant and require several years to show their full beauty but are strong and reliable.

Polygonatum biflorum Ell

The only North American species grows to a handsome two hundred and twenty centimetres. The leaves are grey-green and slightly hairy, the up to two centimetre long flowers are held in groups of three to eight. The plant is valuable for large parks and gardens and creates and elf-like mood.

Polygonatum hirtum Pursh

In eastern and south-eastern Europe, P. hirtum colonises drier margins of woodlands and forests. It is a variable plant that usually reaches fifty centimetres in height and flowers in late spring. This faster growing Polygonatum is suited for sunnier and drier places than for almost all the other species; a good, tougher 'landscaping plant'.

Polygonatum x hybridum

The cross between P. multiflorum and P. odoratum is a handsome reliable garden plant; probably the best-known variety is 'Weihenstephan'. The plants develop to ninety centimetres and have broad leaves. The cream, up to 2.5centimetre long flowers appear in late spring and early summer; pictured in the introduction chapter.

Polygonatum multiflorum All

This species is widespread from Europe to Asia, Siberia and the Himalayas. It grows to eighty centimetres and prefers the cool shade of forests and woodlands. Flowers are white and appear in spring. There are some nice cultivars in the trade.

Polygonatum odoratum Druce

The fragrant 'True Solomon's Seal' extends from southern Europe to Siberia, China and Korea. The variable species is most comfortable in the forest or woodland, with the European variety preferring Oak and Pine forests. The fragrant flowers are held singly or in pairs. The plant grow to sixty centimetres. Although the plant by and large originates in moist, cool areas it adapts remarkably well to drier, sunnier places.

Polystichum; Dryopteridaceae

This is a larger genus of ferns containing more than two hundred species; recently the genus Cyrtomium has been included here. They are cosmopolitan ferns, only absent from tropical lowlands. They are large to very large ferns that can inhabit rich soil as well as rocks. Most are evergreen.

Polystichum aculeatum Roth

A European species that can be recommended for its toughness and adaptability as it thrives in more exposed areas than almost all the other Polystichum. It creates a natural, gentle feel to a landscape if used in smaller or larger groups.

Polystichum setiferum Woynar

This cosmopolitan species grows in a wide range of conditions, from forest floors and open woodlands to rocks and in dry stone walls. It is a large, evergreen fern with up to a metre long leaves. It does require milder winters and prefers, in summer, higher humidity. It forms perfect small ferns in the axils of its leaves that can be used for propagation.

Potentilla; Rosaceae

Quite a large genus with around five hundred species, mainly at home in the northern temperate zones. They do extend into the arctic zone and inhabit high mountains. Many are evergreen, but there are also semi-evergreen and deciduous species with a colour range predominantly in the yellow but reds, whites and pinks are represented also. Potentilla occupy very diverse habitats and consequently are used in the landscape accordingly. There are alpines, species from prairies and dry meadows with poor soils, rock steppes but also, plants that do best in rich soils and can be a superb partner in the perennial border. Almost all of them prefer full sun or at least sun for most of the day.

Potentilla alba
In warm places of Central and Eastern Europe lives the white-flowering Potentilla. It thrives in rocky or grassy loam soils and reaches thirty centimetres in height. Wild and natural plant communities of the steppe or prairie are good applications for this species.

Potentilla atrosanguinea Lodd 1825
From the western Himalayas hails this around half a metre tall species with dark-red, brown-red or chestnut brown flowers. It is well suited for the use in perennial borders or as grouped partner in natural designs and flowers in summer.

Potentilla auea L
The 'Golden Potentilla' is at home in altitudes of between twelve hundred and three thousand five hundred metres, in southern and central Europe. It grows as a dense mat with ten to thirty centimetres height, preferring moisture in spring and drier summers. The large golden-yellow flowers appear in summer. This is a great species for the edges of borders or the rockery.

Potentilla palustris Scop
As the name suggests, this species is at home in wet and swampy places and is in nature often found along creeks. The plant forms dense colonies and is best used in natural or wild designs where such a reliable ground cover is desired.

Potentilla x cultorum
There are very many lovely hybrids of Potentilla with single, semi-double and double flowers. Check with local suppliers for availability.

Primula; Primulaceae

One of the horticulturally most important genus, Primula or 'Key-flowers' (German/Schlüsselblumen) contains around six hundred species. They are botanically divided into thirty-seven sections; for this book I have selected species to cover various aspects of their use in gardens and landscapes and briefly described the most important sections of the genus. As one can imagine such a large and varied genus presents species with a wide variety of requirements in cultivation. From swamps and moist, shaded woodlands to sunny and dry limestone rocks, almost every habitat is represented. In the following listing, I have briefly described the sections and their requirements and the (for this book) selected species have their section reference number in brackets.

Section Auricula (2)
This section contains twenty-four European species and describes small, low perennials with fleshy or leathery leaves that inhabit crevices in rocks. Propagation is mainly by seed, division is possible after flowering but usually yields low numbers.

220 – Primula auricular
Courtesy Miriam Goldstein

Section Parryi (4)
These plants thrive in well-drained, rich and acidic soils in full sun or semi-shade. Propagation is best by seed; however, if some of the roots are exposed to sunlight they will develop into individual plants, just a slow and work-intense method suited more to the passionate plant collector than commercial production.

Section Primula (5)
These are described in more detail in the part following the section descriptions.

Section Cortusioides (10)
Easy to grow in any good garden soil in sun or semi-shade if the soil is not compacted. They are excellent for colonising wild and natural designs as they tend to self-sow in locations that suit them.

Section Reinii (14)
Difficult to cultivate Japanese mountain Primulas that require good drainage.

Section Petiolares (20)
There are many varied species in this section; some are herbaceous and some are wintergreen with leaves held for protection around the buds on the ground. Requirements in cultivation are a semi-shaded to fully shaded location and dry winters. Propagation is best by fresh seed.

Section Proliferae (Candelabrae) (21)

In soils of humus and loam and semi-shaded or shaded locations with plenty of moisture during the growing season, the species of this section thrive easily. Good drainage is still important and the recommended use in the landscape is in groups of natural designs in the shade.

Section Sikkimensis (22)

Cultivation of these perennials is in moist, sunny or lightly shaded locations. Especially the smaller representatives of this section are not very competitive and are easily supressed by strong neighbours, so please combine carefully.

Section Crystallophlomis (Nivalis) (24)

Some, like P. chionantha and P. sinpurpurea are easy to grow in sunny places. However, most species of this section are a bit trickier in their requirements. Well-drained soils and rather dry winters in well-aerated soils are needed; even then individual plants are often short-lived so I would treat them a little like biennials. Propagation is by seed and division after flowering.

Section Aleuritia (Farinosae) (29)

Moist, well-drained humus soils in full sun or part shade are cultivation requirements for these species. Naturally they grow in moist, shady places near rocks or follow creeks; these are also places recommended for their use in the natural landscape or garden.

Section Denticulatae (34)

Most of these species are easy to grow in moist to wet soils; rule of thumb is that the more sun, the more water they want.

Section Capitatae (35)

These summer-flowering Primulas require loose, rich and well-drained soils in partly shaded, cool areas.

Section Muscarioides (36)
These species are a little harder to grow and often short-lived. They desire moisture during the growing season but need to be quite dry in winter. Aged and well-drained soils are important; drainage may be improved by adding gravel or sand.

Species descriptions
Primula alpicola (22) Stapf
An up to fifty centimetres tall species from south-eastern Tibet, with flowers in summer that vary from white to purple. Good partners are Cimicifuga, Dicentra, Hosta, Lythrum, Polygonatum, Thalictrum and Epimedium.

Primula auricola (2)
The 'Golden Primula' grows naturally in cracks and crevices of limestone rocks or in moist alpine meadows of the Alps. It features large, fleshy blue-green leaves that appear to be covered with white powder. The yellow flowers stand around twenty to twenty-five centimetres high and possess a lovely fragrance. In cultivation, it requires alkaline loamy soils mixed with humus in a lightly shaded place.

Primula bulleyana (21) Fort
From north-western Yunnan and south-western Sichuan comes this up to one-hundred-centimetre-tall, gorgeous plant. Large, irregularly serrated leaves clump on the ground and the stalk carries many orange-yellow to orange-red flowers held in quirls in summer.

Primula cortusioides (10)
A plant from mountain forests of the Ural and the Altai, this species grows to thirty centimetres and is profusely flowering with shades of pink in spring. Use in the landscape in natural designs and let it colonise by itself.

Primula denticulata (34)
The 'Ball Primula' or 'Drumstick Primula' flowers in spring and as the name suggests, in a ball-shaped cluster of white, pink, red or shades of purple. It is at home from Afghanistan across the Himalayas to western China. There are many good cultivars and hybrids in the trade. It combines well with Bergenia, Ajuga, Caltha, Onmphalodes, Pulmonaria, ferns, Doronicum orientale, Waldsteinia, Luzula sylvatica and other Primulas of the same section.

Primula elatior (5) Hill
The 'Oxlip' or 'Forest Primula' is at home from Europe to central Asia and has several subspecies spread across its distribution. It is parent of very many of our old and modern garden hybrids and, for many people, synonymous with the Primula as such. They are sometimes also called P. polyantha. In cultivation, they all require moist, cool and rich soils; the straight species is also suited to colonise wooded parks or natural gardens and landscapes.

Primula florindae (22) Wand
This horticulturally important species comes from south-western Tibet and listens, to the common name of 'Bell-Primula'. Large, up to twenty-centimetre dark-green and shiny leaves and up to eighty sulphur-yellow flowers in summer distinguish the plant. Hybrids also come in many variations of red and brown. Good partners are Astilbe, Carex morrowii, Cimicifuga, Dicentra, Clematis integrifolia, Hosta, Polygonatum, Thalictrum dipterocarpum and Tiarella.

Primula hirsuta (2) All

A typical rock-dweller on crystalline mountains of the Alps and eastern and central Pyrenees, P. hirsuta lives in altitudes between two thousand two hundred and three thousand six hundred metres. It flowers in spring with up to thirty individual flowers in shades of pink to red, sometimes with a white eye, rarely entirely white. In cultivation, I would use the species in the rockery where good drainage is ensured.

Primula prolifera (21) Wall

This up to eighty-centimetre-tall species originates in the Yunnan. The handsome plant flowers golden-yellow in spring and the numerous, almost bell-shaped inflorescences are held in six to eight quirls.

Primula Pruhonicensis group

The origins are somewhat obscure, but the Primulas of this group were likely hybrids from parents like P. juliae, P. vulgaris and P. elatior and possibly others. They are all grouped under this term and are essentially very valuable spring-flowering Primulas with a wide range of colours from red, purple, pink and white. They combine well with Anemone nemorosa, Brunnera, Carex plantaginea, Epimedium, Hepatica, Heuchera, Omphalodes verna, Pulmonaria and Tiarella in natural designs. However, they can also be used effectively in formal seasonal displays. It is best to check with local suppliers as the range is vast.

Primula x pubescens (2) Jacq

Since at least 1582, this is the Primula of the gardens, documented and known. P. auricula x P. hirsuta have produced innumerable hybrids and forms. Most must be vegetatively propagated by cuttings, division or in-vitro fertilisation.

Primula sieboldii (10) Morr

Japan, Korea, Manchuria and eastern Siberia are home to this plant that usually lives in swampy meadows and is very variable. It grows to around thirty to forty centimetres and the flowers range from white, purple to pink or red in colour in late spring or early summer. In Switzerland, I have seen it beautifully used as border around garden beds. Good partners are Anemone sylvestris, Aquilegia, Corydalis lutea, Dicentra eximia, Mertonensis, Polygonatum, Thalictrum minus, Tiarella Viola and ferns.

Primula veris (5)

Formerly also known as P. officinalis, this species is very widespread from Europe to Siberia, Asia Minor and central Asia. It grows in open woodlands, in sunny meadows and prairies. It comes in many variations but by and large is a smaller plant with buttery-yellow flowers with orange spots in the throat. It is ideally suited to wild and natural designs, grasslands, prairies and the like. However, if there is a mowing programme in place it needs to be ensured that the plants have a chance to ripen and shed their seeds.

Primula vulgaris (5) Huds

The 'Primrose' originates in western and southern Europe where it lives in open woodlands, semi-shaded forest meadows and shrublands, where sufficient ground moisture is available they also grow in full sun. A vast range of hybrids and forms has found their place in the gardens and it is probably one of the best-known plants.

Prostanthera; Lamiaceae

The 'Mint-bushes' of Australia are included here in similar aspects as, for example, Lavandula or Cistus. Only one species though is completely winter-hardy outside its natural Australian distribution; the others need attention to a mild microclimate in winter. Apart from informed placements and requiring sufficient moisture, Mint bushes are fabulous plants that are covered in flowers, providing structure in natural plantings or borders and have lovely aromatic foliage.

Prostanthera cuneata Benth

This dwarf shub growing to a metre comes from Tasmania and south-eastern Australia. The pure species has white flowers but there are clones with shades of purple and even light pink in the trade. Use in the landscape along borders and as a small structural plant. It is a beautiful little species that delights with its fragrance, especially if you brush up against it.

Prostanthera ovalifolia

An erect or spreading shrub that is outstanding in flower in spring, when the entire plant is just covered with a rich purple. The plant grows to a bit over two metres and prefers somewhat cooler and moist places in the garden. It tolerates full sun when sufficient water is available. Propagation is easy by soft-tip cuttings.

Prunella; Lamiaceae

The small genus of Prunella contains around seven species of the northern hemisphere. They are prostrate ground covers, adaptable and reliable even for some extremely exposed locations like green roofs or old tree stumps. They make good border plants or suit the need for large ground covers in parks or larger landscapes. I would not recommend them for smaller gardens as they also self-sow and can be quite competitive. Propagation is by division, seed or cuttings.

Prunella grandiflora Scholler

Europe, central Russia and the Caucasus are home to the up to forty-centimetre-high plant. It flowers blue in summer and grows naturally in poor soils of meadows, around shrubs and trees on alkaline ground. It is valuable through its dense habit and once established is almost weed-proof.

Pseuderanthemum; Acanthaceae

Pseuderanthemum variabile

This around thirty-centimetre-tall perennial listens to the nice common name of 'Pastel Flower', which refers to the gentle light pink to lilac tubular flowers of spring and summer. Like the related Acanthus mollis, it should ideally be cultivated in shade or semi-shade in rich, moist soils where it is a graceful, long-lived sociable plant. Root cuttings in winter or division of the creeping rhizome make for easy propagation.

Pteridophyllum; Papaveraceae

Pteridophyllum racemosum Sieb et Zucc

The only so far known species of this genus describes a plant with leaves like Blechnum that carries pretty, bell-shaped flowers held in loose racemes in summer. Use in the landscape in the dappled shade of trees in rich, well-drained soils in places where its delicate beauty may be appreciated. Propagation is by division.

Pterocaulon; Asteraceae

Pterocaulon sphacelatum

This interesting herb from Australia grows to around a metre tall and is strongly aromatic. It features two centimetres wide globular heads of pale pink flowers. The aromatic leaves have a strong fruity fragrance and can be used to treat head colds. It requires sun and well-drained soils and benefits from being pruned back after flowering. In my opinion, not so much a plant for the ornamental garden or landscape, it could be integrated in medicinal gardens or part of wild landscapes.

Ptilotus; Amaranthaceae

This is a special, medium-sized genus of around ninety species, with one exception endemic to Australia. Most of these come from the semi-arid zones of the northern part of the continent and have great horticultural potential, as well as should be used more widely in larger landscapes. Excellent drainage and full sun are necessary as it is obvious from their original habitat.

Ptilotus drummondii

Pink, fluffy cylindrical or globular flower heads in spring are the outstanding feature of this small, up to thirty-centimetre-high herb. Originally from Western Australia, it requires excellent drainage and grows best in sandy, gravelly soils. Despite the poor soils in its original habitat, in my experience it responds very well to moderate amounts of fertiliser balanced along an NPK or around 4-0.3-6 or similar proportions. Great for dry areas or as container display plants.

Ptilotus exaltatus

The tall 'Mulla Mulla' is an erect perennial with large, woolly tapering heads of lilac-purplish grey flowers held around sixty centimetres high in spring. It is a spectacular plant for rockeries, prairies or steppes and other semi-arid designs. Excellent drainage, full baking sun and sandy and gravelly soils are essential. Fertiliser should be kept in favour of K, otherwise the plants tend to fall over once the full weight develops in the flowers. In ideal conditions, the plants sometimes self-sow but in general I would recommend to regularly re-propagate, either by seed, accepting usually poor germination, or tissue culture where this facility is available.

221 – Ptilotus exaltatus
Courtesy Kings Park, Perth Botanic Gardens

Ptilotus nobilis

The 'Yellow Tail' is a tall, upright perennial to eighty centimetres with yellowish-green flowers that can grow to twenty centimetres long and are quite impressive. Cultivation and propagation is the same as for the above P. exaltatus.

Ptilotus obovatus

Rounded, silvery-grey woolly leaves characterise this compact sub-shrub. Also called 'Cotton Bush', it bears small globular pink and grey flower heads on branching stems in spring. One of the hardiest and most adaptable Ptilotus, it has a wide range of horticultural and landscape applications and I often use it in dry heathland, steppe or prairie designs but also in informal dry perennial borders, together with Europeans like silvery Artemisia, bearded Iris and the like.

Pulmonaria; Boraginaceae

The 'Lung-Wort' or 'Lungenkraut' (German) is a genus of around twenty species at home in Europe. These are usually flat-growing ground covers with hairy leaves and flowers that range in colour from red, purple, white, blue or pink. They are valuable early flowering perennials for the semi-shade, with sufficiently moist soils in association with woody ornamentals.

Pulmonaria angustifolia
France, Germany and Scandinavia are the main areas of distribution for this species. It thrives in open forests, shrublands or meadows. The flowers are of a glowing azure blue and stand around thirty centimetres tall.

Pulmonaria officinalis L
The true Lung-Wort is at home from the Netherlands and Sweden down to Italy and Bulgaria. It grows in mixed forests on moist, rich and alkaline soils. Its flowers start pink and mature to purple-blue and appear in early spring.

There are many hybrids and strains of Pulmonaria in the trade – check with local suppliers.

Pulsatilla; Ranunculaceae

This special genus of Ranunculaceae occurs mainly in the temperate to arctic regions of the northern hemisphere. One of the features of these perennials are the silvery hairs that cover most of the plant and give it a magic appearance, especially in early or late light. Their requirements vary greatly and many need experienced hands to be successfully cultivated. Specifics are with these species I have selected and listed here. Propagation is best by seed or root cuttings.

Pulsatilla grandis Wender
This species comes from central Europe where it grows in alkaline dry meadows and conifer forests in higher altitudes. The flowers are large, up to ten centimetres across and come in light to dark purple, sometimes pink-purple and rarely white. They have a conspicuous coat of silvery or golden brown fine hairs. Flowering time is early spring. It is an outstanding plant for the rockery.

Pulsatilla montana Mill
The 'Berg-Küchenschelle', German for 'Mountain Cow's Bell' extends from Switzerland to eastern Romania in dry, rocky alkaline meadows of higher altitudes. The flowers are nodding and dark purple, sometimes pink or whitish. Given good drainage the plant is easy to cultivate in full sun.

Pulsatilla rubra Delarbre
This reddish flowering Pulsatilla is spread through central Europe and the Iberian Peninsula. It is easy to cultivate and long-lived. The species is also used for breeding the red tones into other Cow's Bells.

Pulsatilla vulgaris Mill
England, western France, Sweden and the Ukraine are habitat for the common Cow's Bell. The plant grows to sixty centimetres tall, with dark to light purple flowers. Use in the landscape in the rockery; best close to paths or garden seats where people may admire the amazing beauty of this species close.

222 – Pulsatilla vulgaris
In natural environment on limestone

Pycnosorus; Asteraceae

Pycnosorus globosus syn Craspedia globosa

The 'Billy Buttons' are an Australian native perennial with lovely, silvery showy foliage and up to eighty-centimetre-tall, erect flower stems with globular yellow flower heads in spring and summer. It is a robust perennial, accepting many soils and great for many applications from alpine rockeries, informal meadows to the formal perennial border. It propagates easily from seed.

223 – Pycnosorus globosus
Author's home garden, Queanbeyan, Australia 2012

Ramonda; Gesneriaceae

This is a small and very special genus of plants that in its origin and evolution dates to the Tertiary. Ramonda are small and evergreen plants with rough, wrinkly and hairy leaves growing in rosettes. They require sheltered, almost vertical places in the rockery that are not exposed to the sun. In such locations, they gently colonise the rockery, self-sow and can become several decades old. Combined with small ferns they can create magical scenes that appear to be from another time of our earth. They are quite drought resistant but as I said, the locaton needs to be chosen or constructed very carefully, it really is worth the effort. Propagation is by seed, division or leaf cuttings.

Ramonda myconi Rchb

The limestone ridges of the Pyrenees are home of this jewel. It grows around twenty centimetres high, with very ornamental leaves and light purple-blue flowers in late spring or early summer. There are light pink and even white varieties. This is probably the most important species for use in the collector's garden.

224 – Ramonda myconi
Work in Badenweileer, Germany 1992

Ranunculus; Ranunculaceae

The 'Buttercups' are a large genus of around four hundred species from all over the world. For this book, I have selected according to their relevance for landscape architecture and horticulture. There are annual, biannual and perennial species for the rockery, the wild and natural garden, water plants, plants for the shade and the groomed perennial border. They are all poisonous. Propagation is mainly by division; seed is also good but best when used fresh after harvest.

The widespread species grows up to a hundred and twenty centimetres in height and is a prolific and long-flowering plant for the border. It requires loamy soils; in lighter ground, it ages very quickly.

Ranunculus alpestris

This is a typical mountain plant, getting to only around fifteen centimetres. Naturally it lives throughout middle European mountains and the Alps and Pyrenees, on limestone. The flowers are brilliant white and appear in spring. Use in the landscape in shadier and moist places in the rockery or the alpinum.

Ranunculus aquaticus L

A water plant for depths between a hundred and a hundred and fifty centimetres, Ranunculus aquaticus is a hardy and pretty species. It is best used for larger, still water features or flowing water in natural or wild designs.

Ranunculus gramineus L

Originating in the western Mediterranean from Portugal, Spain and Italy to central France this fifty-centimetre-tall species thrives in dry meadows. It is a very valuable plant for natural designs, heath gardens or the rockery and alpinum. The glowing yellow flowers appear in early summer and the plant becomes then dormant after the seeds have ripened.

225 – Ranunculus gramineus
Courtesy Stephan Willenberger

Raoulia; Asteraceae

Dense, mat or pillow-forming species that occur in New Zealand, Australia and Tasmania, some are from New Guinea. The leaves are usually tightly packed like tiles around the stems, with terminal small flowers. They are sensitive to being wet in winter, therefore cultivation is necessarily in well-drained soils. In summer, they like to have some ground moisture but object to high temperatures. In my experience, a cool rockery in light shade and sheltered by open trees works well. They are somewhat special in their use in the landscape and more for the collector who desires to create scenes or themes in the rock garden.

Raoulia australis Hook

This species comes from the southern island of New Zealand where it growns from the valley floors to the montane zone. It forms dense mats and has silvery-grey foliage and yellowish flowers in summer.

226 – Raoulia australis
Used in a natural rock garden setting

Ratibia; Asteraceae

This is a small genus of around seven species from the prairies of North America and Mexico. One of the common names is 'Prairie Coneflower', which describes a bit the prominent inflorescence. They are very well suited to sunny borders, gravel gardens or meadows. They can withstand drought and heat but also wet conditions and develop deep taproots. Good partners are Aster erioides, Aster laevis, Coreopsis verticillata, Liatris, Penstemon digitalis, Salvia azurea, other Salvias and ornamental grasses with a similar prairie or steppe background.

Ratibia columnifera Wooten et Stande

Growing up to eighty centimetres tall, the plant flowers yellow, red or purple-brown from summer to autumn. It is also a good cut flower.

227 – Ratibia columnifera
Courtesy Wikipedia

Rheum; Polygonaceae

The Rheum, Rhubarb is a small genus of around twenty species, of which only few are of significance in the landscape and in horticulture. Most are large, decorative perennials with thick, fleshy rootstock and large leaves. Most Rheum prefer rich, deep and most soil in full sun to semi-shade. They may be used as foliage feature plants on their own in grass, near water or in combination with rocks. Many species have strong red shoots and impressive flowers. Unfortunately, many go into a state of semi-dormancy after flowering, therefore good placement is important.

Rheum alexandrae Batalin
From China, Tibet and Sichuan comes the 'King's Rhubarb'. It reaches a hundred and fifty centimetres on rich, moist soils of higher altitudes and flowers in early summer, with hanging infloresences that are protected from monsoon rain by large bracts. In cultivation, this plant requires cool acidic soils with sufficient moisture throughout the year, but nonetheless good drainage a bit like Meconopsis. Propagation is by fresh seed.

Rheum palmaticum L
Near rivers and in open, moist forests in China, Yunnan and Sichuan grows the Chinese Rhubarb. It is an impressive plant becoming up to two hundred and fifty centimetres tall and large, up to fifty centimetres wide palmate leaves. The flowers are creamy-yellow and develop into reddish-brown fruits.

Rheum rhubarbarum L
Manchuria and eastern Siberia are home to this species, one of the parent of our edible Rhubarb. The plant grows to a hundred and fifty centimetres tall and has heart-shaped, over fifty-centimetre-wide leaves of a grey-green colour. It flowers in early summer.

Rhodanthe; Asteraceae

Rhodanthe anthemioides syn Helipterum anthemioides
This attractive perennial has glaucous leaves and grows to around fifty centimetres. White everlasting daisy flowers are borne in summer. The plant requires good drainage and sun but otherwise is tough and easy to use in the landscape and gardens. Trailing over dry-stone walls, scattered in groups around rockeries or meadows, this species is reliable and graceful in many applications. Propagation is best by cuttings, there are quite a few horticultural cultivars in the trade.

Rhodiola; Crassulaceae

A genus of around fifty species that has been split up from Sedum. They are easy to grow and occupy special niches as in roof tops, dry stone arrangements or rockeries. All require full sun and adapt to almost any soil; only wet feet are not tolerated.

Rhodiola rosea Scop
This alpine species is widespread around the mountains of the world. It does require some moisture in summer, different to Sedum which can dry out almost completely. Use in the landscape between rocks or in tubs and containers.

Rhodohypoxis; Hypoxidaceae

There are six species in this genus from South Africa. They all come from areas with summer rainfall and adapt well to many conditions if they are given acidic, well-drained soils and a lot of water during the growing season. Propagation is best by division during the growing season.

Rhodohypoxis baurii Nel
In moist places near rocks, in moors and along water courses grows this parent of many horticultural hybrids. The flowers in spring to early summer range in colour from white and pinks to red.

Rodgersia; Saxifragaceae

These strong perennial species come from Japan, China and Korea where they grow in warm areas of high rainfall in mountain forests. They need a lot of water but at the same time, well aerated soils and do not like wet feet. Their use in the landscape is primarily as foliage feature plants in the shade or semi-shade. The rule of thumb is the more sun they get, the more water they need. They grow and develop slowly but eventually require a lot of space.

Rodgersia aesculifolia Bataal
China is the home of the chestnut (Horse-chestnut) leaved Rodgersia that thrives in moist forests and along rivers and creeks from twelve hundred to three thousand two hundred metres altitude. The flowers reach to a hundred and eighty centimetres with the foliage forming a handsome landscape feature.

Rodgersia pinnata Franch
Along rivers and creeks of China grows R, pinnata in altitudes between two thousand two hundred and three thousand five hundred metres. The foliage is dark green and shiny to fifty centimetres height, the pink to red-pink flowers rise to a hundred and twenty centimetres in summer.

Rodgersia podophylla Gray

From Korea and Japan comes this Rodgersia that inhabits moist mountain forests. The leaves stand around eighty centimetres tall and the creamy-yellow flowers develop to a hundred and thirty centimetres height in summer. The young leaves are reddish-grown to bronze before they green up when maturing.

Rodgersia Henricii hybrids

The straight species has almost no significance in the landscapes and gardens but there are some lovely hybrids in this group that deserve attention. 'Elegans' – grows to a hundred and fifty centimetres, pink-red flowers and red fruit; 'Elfenbeinturm' – two hundred centimetres with ivory-white flowers that have a vanilla fragrance (great feature plant); and 'White feathers' with light green foliage and feather-like white flowers.

Romneya; Papaveraceae

This is a small genus of perennials and sub-shrubs from California and Mexico. The plants grow to around two hundred and fifty centimetres tall and have strong, deep yellowish taproots. Their prominent feature is large, up to fifteen centimetres across white flowers with golden stamens. They are very drought hardy and love the full sun and exposure. I would recommend use of the plants more in wild and natural rock gardens, in dry stone walls or steppe and prairie plantings than in the perennial border. This is because the roots have a strong tendency to colonise large areas and possibly overwhelm weaker partner plants in a structured border. In saying this, I have sometimes used them very successfully in more informal, dry perennial borders where their wild nature is welcome and in summer can tie the design together. Propagation is best by root cuttings in winter. It is important to observe polarity; the thickness of a pencil is about right; usually active buds of the next growing season are already visible.

Romneya coulteri Harv

Often called 'Californian Tree Poppy' or 'Coulter's Matilija Poppy', this species comes mainly from Mexico and California'. Rather than a tree, it is a mostly a straggly sub-shrub of around two metres that dies back in winter. The amazingly beautiful flowers are fragrant and appear in late summer to early autumn. I often combine this species with evergreen, silvery or white-leaved plants that structure the design throughout the year and the Romenya then adds its flowers to the design.

228 – Romneya coulteri
In natural environment, California, United States

Roscoea; Zingiberaceae

The 'Ginger Orchids' describe a small genus of around twenty species with fleshy roots from Kashmir to China. They prefer semi-shade and a sheltered, warm microclimate; they are somewhat frost-sensitive in colder areas. Like many Gingers, they spread strongly when the conditions are right for them. Propagation is by division or seed.

Roscoea auriculata Schum
This up to fifty centimetres high plant lives in open forests and meadows. It features flowers in many shades of purple and is a graceful, easy plant for natural designs or the border.

Roscoea cautleoides Gagnep
Growing in meadows and open woodlands, this species is smaller, to thirty centimetres. Flowers range from purple-pink to white and there are several cultivars available.

Rosmarinus; Lamiaceae

The well-known Mediterranean sub-shrub may be divided into four species. They are mostly upright, hardy and evergreen sub-shrubs with aromatic foliage.

Rosmarinus lavandulaceus Balansa
This species is mainly prostrate and develops into mat and pillow-forming excellent ground cover. The light blue flowers appear in spring but unfortunately these plants require a mild winter and are not reliable in colder areas.

Rosmarinus officinalis
The Rosemary can grow to two metres tall with foliage of a grey-green colour. It is known in cultivation since ancient times. Used extensively in the kitchen, cosmetics and in herbal medicine, it is also a highly valuable structural feature plant in formal or natural garden designs. One of the important details of cultivation is to not over-feed Rosmarinus; they are used to poor, light and well-drained soils. They do not do well in cold areas (below ten degrees Celsius) with wet winters.

Rubus; Rosaceae

The genus of around two hundred and fifty species contains mainly shrubs and few perennials; it is quite a cosmopolitan group of plants. Easy to propagate by seed or cuttings.

Rubus arcticus
From northern Europe extending into arctic North Asia and North America comes this only twenty-centimetre-high perennial. I find it an attractive reliable ground cover for wild and natural designs. It flowers pink throughout summer, without a peak time and features a gorgeous autumn colouring of the leaves. The plant requires acidic soils but other than that it is easy and colonises semi-shaded places well.

Rudbeckia; Asteraceae

The 'Coneflowers' or 'Sun-Hats' (German for Sonnenhut) have been named by Linné in honour of his teacher, Olaf Rudbeck. It describes a genus or around thirty species with annuals and perennials. The perennials are medium to tall plants with strong stems and prominent yellow flowers. They are great to use in the groomed perennial border for the striking display of flowers but some are also suited to informal and natural designs.

Rudbeckia fulgida Att
This variable species from North America can be anything between forty and a hundred centimetres in height. It develops short runners and has gorgeous golden-yellow flowers with a distinct black or dark purple-brown cone in late summer. In cultivation, they require sufficient moisture and rich soils to be at their best.

229 – Rudbeckia fulgida
Used as structural plant at the reflecting pond in Cranbrook Gardens
Courtesy Beth Chatto

Rudbeckia fulgida var deamii Perdue

A very rich flowering species from Indiana that grows very well in drier conditions compared to the above. It may even be used in steppe or prairie plantings, a graceful and valuable plant.

Rudbeckia fulgida var sullivantii

A tall and handsome plant mainly for the moist, perennial border with rich soils, this species can grow to a hundred and twenty centimetres in height. Its main feature is the up to twelve-centimetre-wide, golden-yellow flowers with their black cone in summer. If we cut back straight after flowering and the autumn is warm enough, there is a good chance of a second flowering. The cultivar 'Goldsturm' is highly recommended.

Rudbeckia laciniata

In wet places of North America thrives the 'Long Henry', a perennial up to two hundred centimetres in height. It flowers from summer to autumn with light yellow, often nodding inflorescences. They are easy to grow but personally I would recommend them mostly for the background of cottage gardens, farm gardens or natural areas due to their size and because they often flop over. They partner well with tall Aster.

Rudbeckia nitida Nutt

Also growing in wet or at least moist areas with heavy soils, this up to two-hundred-centimetre-tall perennial could be more widely used in larger gardens or parks. The ten centimetres wide yellow flowers in summer have petals that are slightly curved. This species goes well with Eupatorium fistulosum, Inula magnifica, Aconitum carmichaelii and tall Asters. They also combine well with moisture-loving shrubs and are good cut flowers. The plants propagate easily by division.

Rumex; Polygonaceae

There are around a hundred and twenty species of Rumex inhabiting the northern temperate zones. Most are perennial species but there are some sub-shrubs as well. Most thrive in loamy, rich and moist soils. Use in the landscape is primarily in natural or wild designs, meadows and rockeries.

Rumex patientia L
The 'English Spinach' is an old garden plant that ca reach up to two metres. It flowers in late summer and features large, up to forty-centimetre-long leaves.

Rumex scutatus
This is another old herb plant that was already known in the kitchens of the Roman Empire. The plant grows to fifty centimetres and prefers alkaline soils but is quite adaptable. Flowering time is from spring to autumn; the cultivar 'Silver Shield' has somewhat silvery and fleshy leaves.

Ruscus; Ruscaceae

The small genus of 'Butcher's Broom' or 'Mouse Thorn' extends from Western Europe to the Caspian Sea, Madeira and north-western Africa.

Ruscus aculeatus L 1753
This up to a hundred and twenty centimetre tall sub-shrub is very drought hardy and accepts poor soils in full sun to almost full shade. Therefore, it is a valuable plant for difficult situations where low maintenance is required. It flowers in spring but of more importance are the very decorative red berries that are carried for a long time.

Ruta; Rutaceae

A small genus of around eight species with aromatic and decorative foliage. Most species come from around the Mediterranean, Eastern Europe or south-west Asia. They inhabit dry, sunny and rocky places and should be used accordingly in rockeries, steppe plantings or even for the greening of roofs.

Ruta graveolens L
This strong sub-shrub is an old herbal medicinal plant and has also been widely used for its ornamental foliage. The plant gets to around eighty centimetres and requires full sun and poor soils in cultivation. The off-yellow flowers appear from late spring to late summer. The leaves can be chewed (slightly bitter taste) and are excellent against headaches but should not be used during pregnancy. In the landscape, I would recommend it as a structural plant in rockeries, in natural steppe or Mediterranean designs or dry heathlands. And of course, in the herb or medicinal garden.

Sagittaria; Alismataceae

This mainly tropical and temperate genus is represented with around twenty-six species in America and Eurasia. These grow along rivers and into standing water to around fifty centimetres depth and are very decorative perennial plants for this purpose. Propagation is in winter by division of the dormant tubers.

Sagittaria latifolia Willd
This variable species grows best in shallow water depths of around twenty centimetres. It is a highly decorative plant with arrow-shaped leaves to thirty-centimetre-long and creamy-white flowers with yellow

stamens that stand on an up to a hundred and twenty centimetres high stalk. Good partners are Pontederia cordata, Butomus umbellatus, Typha laxmannii and Iris pseudacorus.

Salvia; Lamiaceae

The Sages are a large genus of more than seven hundred species of the warm-temperate and temperate regions of the world. Most are aromatic perennials, sub-shrubs or shrubs with a large range of colour in their flowers. The foliage alone may be quite striking like in Salvia argentea, the 'Silver Sage'. The content and composition of etheric oils varies greatly and is best known in the medicinal Sage, S. officinalis, which is also used in the kitchen. The use of Salvias in the landscape is varied; most are ideal for natural or wild rockeries in the full sun where they can also self-sow. Very many are also a great addition to the groomed perennial border, the semi-formal or cottage garden however. As always, it is important to know the characteristics of the species and use and manage them accordingly. Informed placement and wise use in the landscape are better than a lot of hard work against the forces of nature. Propagation of Salvias is by seed, cuttings including root cuttings or division.

Salvia argentea L

The Silver-leaved Sage comes from southern Europe, the Mediterranean and North Africa. The round, large leaves are covered by dense, silvery woolly hairs which give the plant the characteristic white-silvery appearance. The flowers are white with yellow lips and appear in summer. It is an amazing foliage plant, especially in the early morning with dew on its leaves. Important is to remove/cut back the flower stalk after flowering early, otherwise the plant dies back and disappears. I often use it together with silvery Artemisia and other grey, white or silvery plants and white limestone rocks in dry borders, rockeries or associated with dry-stone walls.

230 – Salvia argentea
Used in dry border together with Rosmarinus 'Blue Lagoon' and Yucca glauca

Salvia azurea var grandiflora Benth

This up to a hundred and fifty-centimetre-tall species originates in the USA and extends south into Texas. The foliage is grey and somewhat velvety which contrasts beautifully with the pure blue flowers from late summer to autumn. The plant requires warm, sunny spots.

Salvia glutinosa L

Widespread in open forests and shrublands from Europe to Himalayas this is the only yellow flowering Sage. The plant grows to a hundred centimetres and is well suited to natural and wild designs associated with trees or shrubs. It is long-lived and graceful in the right environment with partners like Alchemilla mollis, Aster divaricatus, Brunnera macrophylla, Campanula persicifolia, Clematis montana, Centaurea montana, Meconopsis cambrica, Stachys grandiflora, Thalictrum aquilegifolium, Aquilegia vulgaris and Waldsteinia geoides. Just let go wild after establishment, these combinations under and around trees can create magic, elf-like scenes.

Salvia nemorosa L

The 'Steppe Sage' or 'Heath Sage' grows in dry meadows and heathlands in central, southern and eastern Europe, in elevated altitudes ascending to montane zones. The actual wild species is of lesser importance than its many hybrids and cultivars. These are valuable and long-flowering plants, mostly with shades of purple. I have used them in a wide variety of applications from wild and natural designs, semi-formal plantings to formal perennial borders. Their compact low habit invites use in the foreground and in swaths around taller perennials like Achillea filipendulina 'Coronation Gold', Aster tongolensis and A. amellus, Centaurea macrophylla, Coreposis verticillata, Echinops ritro, Scabiosa caucasica, Verbena and ornamental structural grasses like Molinia arundinacea, Sesleria autumnalis and Stipa species.

231 – Salvia nemorosa
Used in semi-formal setting on top of retaining wall together with Heuchera, Phlox paniculata, Paeonia and Coreopsis

Salvia officinalis L

The Garden Sage is naturally widespread in Europe and the Mediterranean where it grows in dry meadows, heaths and steppe-like grasslands. The plant can reach a hundred centimetres and features grey, felt-like leaves and purple, sometimes pink or white flowers from late spring to summer. This old medicinal plant also has, through its evergreen foliage, structural qualities. It is widely used in the kitchen as a herb; however, moderation is recommended as there is evidence of detrimental effects on the liver in areas where S. officinalis is used very extensively.

Salvia patens Cav

A wonderful species for hot, dry borders and rockeries that comes from Mexico. The plant reaches sixty centimetres with hairy leaves and large blue flowers from summer into late autumn. It is a species for areas with milder winters, not much under ten degrees Celsius.

Salvia pratensis L

The 'Meadow Sage' is at home in Europe and prefers alkaline, drier soils and is a pioneer plant for disturbed ground. The species grows to sixty centimetres and flowers blue in late spring, with a distinct second flowering time in autumn. I would use the plant in the landscape in wild and natural designs and plant communities, together with Achillea millefolium, Leucanthemum, Campanula glomerata, Centaurea scabiosa, Sanguisorba minor, Trifolium pratense and grasses.

Salvia sclarea L

Dry, rocky locations of Europe, the Mediterranean and Asia Minor are the preferred environmental conditions for the Clary Sage ('Muskateller Salbei' - German). It is a very beautiful species for many dry, hot places in the landscape and gardens, the flower stalk reaches well over a metre and carries an abundance of light purple to purple-pink flowers in summer. The individual plant is usually biannual but if the conditions are right the species self-sows freely without becoming weedy.

232 – Salvia sclarea
Used as feature plant in semi-formal setting, in the background Alchemilla mollis

Salvia uliginosa Benth

A quite different species to the above is the 'Bog Sage' from South America. As the common name suggests, this handsome, up to two metres tall plant thrives in moist to wet conditions. The sky-blue flowers with a white spot appear from late spring and often into autumn. The plant, however, tends to fall over, therefore I would use it primarily in natural designs in the background, not in formal settings.

Salvia verticillata L

The up to eighty-centimetre-tall species prefers alkaline soils and is primarily used in wild or natural planting designs. It is a strong growing and quite 'weed-resistant' plant from which now several nice hybrids and cultivars are available.

Sambucus; Caprifoliaceae

Mostly shrubs and trees from the temperate and subtropical zones, the twenty-five species of Sambucus are represented with a few perennials. I remember a lovely tale out of the Germanic mythology that makes the shrub Elderberry (Sambucus nigra) a home to benign female spirits. These spirits protect the house next to the Elderberry; therefore, never remove an Elderberry growing near your home.

Sambucus ebulus L

This dwarf Elderberry extends from Europe down to North Africa, Asia Minor and into Iran. The plant varies greatly according to the available moisture; in dry soils it remains a ground cover, often no more than thirty centimetres high, whilst in places with sufficient water the species grows to a hundred and fifty centimetres tall. The white to light pink fragrant flowers appear in summer and develop into black, berry-like fruits. It is an old medicinal plant that has been documented in use in Germany since 1305. Although a very decorative plant, its use in the landscape is limited because of its competitive nature. It is suitable only for large, natural and wild landscapes or for stabilising slopes where this strong growth is of advantage. Hard to remove once planted.

Sanguisorba; Rosaceae

Around fifteen species represent the genus Sanguisorba in the temperate and cool-temperate zones of the northern hemisphere. Shades of white, pink or red flowers stand above lovely ornamental foliage that resembles Sorbus. Being generally strong growers, they are valuable plants for wild and natural designs, near water courses or in meadow situations but equally good for perennial borders. Whilst they are adaptable to a wide range of soils they do require sufficient moisture. Good partners in the natural designs are Astilbe, Geranium pratense, Filipendula, Cimicifuga, Bistorta amplexicaulis and ornamental grasses like Molinia arundinacea.

Sanaguisorba armena Boiss

A handsome perennial to a hundred and fifty centimetres with grey-green compound, serrated leaves. S. armena from north-eastern Turkey and Armenia to the Caucasus. It flowers in summer with pink-red and is a long-lived remarkable feature plant. Soils should be moist and rich and the location can be from semi-shade to full sun.

Sanguisorba officinalis L

This up to a hundred and twenty-centimetre-tall perennial is at home from Europe to Asia on moist and rich soils. The flowers stand in elongated heads and are blood red in summer. There are some nice cultivars in the trade like 'Arnhem', a hundred and forty centimetres with glowing deep red flowers and 'Pink Tanna', a hundred and twenty centimetres with nodding, pink flowers.

Sanguisorba tenuifolia Fisch ex Link

A species that follows water courses of wet zones of meadows, S. tenuifolia reaches a hundred and eighty centimetres and is a handsome feature plant. The late flowering time in autumn makes it valuable for many applications from formal to wild; the cylindrical flowers are dark red and may be standing upright or pendulous.

Santolina; Asteraceae

There are eight species of Santolina at home around the Mediterranean of the 'Saint's Herb' or 'Cypress herb'. These are evergreen and often strongly aromatic sub-shrubs with green to grey or silvery fine foliage that I personally value as structural component in borders, along dry-stone walls or to soften up harsh architectural contours. Flowering time is summer, the individual flowers are small. These plants are adapted to poor, well-drained soils. I would not recommend placing them alongside gross feeders like roses as the plants then become 'overweight' with the surplus nutrition and fall apart, or require intense care and regular pruning back. A gentle pruning back after flowering is recommended and like with most sub-shrubs, stay in the soft parts of the plant; if pruning is done too hard into the old woody parts there is a chance of dying back. I like using them alongside plants with the same requirements and life cycles, like silvery Artemisia, where their foliage complements each other, bulbs, Gaura lindheimeri, Eremurus species, Cistus, small Iris, alpine Dianthus and similar plants. Propagation is easy by cuttings.

Santolina chamaecyparissus

From Spain to France, from Italy to the Balkans and the West Mediterranean Islands grows this well-known species. It is a dense up to sixty-centimetre-high aromatic sub-shrub with grey-silvery foliage. The plant is documented in cultivation since 1573, it is a reliable long living structural plant that is well suited to herb gardens, borders, steppe or heath designs, rockeries, or even in formal seasonal displays.

233 – Santolina chamaecyparissus
Used as border, Restoration work in Canberra, Australia 2014

Santolina pinnata ssp neapolitana

The 'big brother' of S. chamaecyparissus differs in the larger size, up to eighty centimetres and the foliage colour of a grey-green colour, as well as a fruity aroma. The flowers are light yellow and give a rich display. Same rule applies; please do not over-feed these plant types otherwise they fall apart, do not live as long and flower less.

Santolina rosmarinifolia ssp rosmarinifolia
Dark green foliage is the distinct difference to S. chamaecyparissus. This species also flowers more profusely. However, as I mentioned in the introduction these plants are best in a structural role and the flowers are more like the icing on the cake, not the main role, in its use in the landscape.

Saponaria; Caryophyllaceae

Saponaria is a genus of around fifty mostly herbaceous perennials with a few annual species among them. It is by and large a Mediterranean genus of pillow-forming or medium plants growing in full sun and apart from S. officinalis, best suited for dry stone walls or rockeries. Propagation is by seed or cuttings.

Saponaria lutea
The limestone soils of the Alps are home to this very beautiful, up to ten-centimetre-high jewel. The flowers appear in summer and are of a darkish sulphur yellow and despite its small, delicate appearance this species is long-lived and tough. I like 'sprinkling' them around limestone dry walls in full sun.

Saponaria ocymoides L
The variable plant thrives in open forests as well as in exposed mountains of Spain, France, Italy, Switzerland and extends down to North Africa. It grows to thirty centimetres and may be prostrate or upright with red, pink or sometimes white flowers from late spring to autumn; this long flowering period makes it a valuable addition to many well-drained rockery or garden situations.

Saponaria officinalis
Other than most other Saponaria this species is at home in moist meadows, shrublands or follows riparian zones. It grows to seventy centimetres and has pink flowers from summer to autumn that have a sweet scent.

Sarracenia; Sarraceniaceae

These perennials come from North America where they are known as 'Pitcher Plants'. They are up to a hundred and twenty centimetres tall with hollow leaves that are filled with water to trap insects for additional nutrition. They are specialised plants requiring acidic soils in moor or swamp settings.

Sarracenia flava L
This species has yellow flowers and the up to a hundred-centimetre-long leaves often also have yellow veins; a common name is 'Yellow Trumpet Pitcher plant' after the flowers.

234 – Sarracenia flava
Courtesy Stephan Willenberger

Satureja; Lamiaceae

This small genus of around thirty species describes small, aromatic perennials or annuals. Most flower very profusely and late in the growing season which makes them valuable for rockeries, dry stone walls or tub plantings. Bees swarm all over the plants that just keep flowering. Naturally they grow in poor, alkaline soils.

Satureja montana L

A plant widespread from southern Europe to the Crimea, S. montana develops to seventy centimetres in height and is a reliable species for the rockery.

Satureja spicigera Boiss

The Caucasus, Turkey and Iran are home to white flowering small Satureja. It combines well with small Artemisia, Iris, bulbs like Crocus and Tulipa and should be partnered with evergreen structural plants as this species becomes active only late in the growing season.

Sassureja; Asteraceae

There are more than two hundred species in this genus that is predominantly alpine and montane by nature. They are small to medium-sized rosette-forming perennials, a few are annual. Essentially, they are plants for the collector and the passionate gardener as they are specialised and require expertise and attention. As they usually come from high altitudes they do not take well to hot summers.

Sassureja alpina DC
In stony meadows, dwarf heath and exposed ridge lines thrives this species from Europe to Russia, Asia and including North America. The plant grows to thirty centimetres with dark-green or grey-green leaves that are covered in spider-web like hairs. The flowers are purple and appear in summer.

235 – Sassureja alpina
Courtesy Anton Büchli

Sassureja pygmea Spreng
This dwarf is beautiful but difficult to cultivate in lower altitudes. It requires gravelly, alkaline soils and gets to ten centimetres with purple-blue flowers in summer.

Sassureja stella Maxim
From the Himalayas and north-western China comes this rare alpine jewel. It flowers rich and beautifully with sessile, purple-blue flowers and pink venation. Propagation is by root cuttings, best just after the plant goes dormant.

Saxifraga; Saxifragaceae

This large genus of around three hundred and eighty centimetres species carries the German common name (translated from Latin) of 'Steinbrech', which means 'breaking stones'. When observing the plants growing wild in nature, we find that they most often occupy small cracks or crevices in rocks and fill them completely, spilling eventually out over the stone. Therefore, they appear to have broken open the stone, hence the name. Species are of mainly small to dwarf, at the most medium size plants and are mainly alpine. Flowering time spreads across the growing season, from just after the snow has melted right into late autumn. Very many have exquisitely ornamental rosettes that we can admire throughout the year; covered in hoar frost they look splendid. Use in the landscape as small treasures for intensely cultivated areas where they can be admired closely, or for plant collectors. Cultivation requirements differ greatly and are here given with the species. Propagation is often easy by careful division; however, some must be propagated by seed as there is no other option, like some of the monocarpic section Lingulata.

Section Lingulata (Silver-rosette Saxifraga, crusty Saxifraga)

This section is characterised by rosettes composed of longish, tongue-shaped and calcium-crusted leaves. These rosettes die after flowering; some species, however, develop runners as the 'mother' rosette dies and the tips of these runners can form new rosettes. The monocarpic species, though, die back without runners or side-shoots formed and this is the reason why these must be propagated by seed. These species are brilliant foliage plants, beautiful throughout the seasons and the flower is of a very elegant beauty.

Saxifraga crustata Vest

The eastern Alps homes this graceful species with blue-green leaves that are strongly crusted with calcium spots. The numerous flowers are creamy white and develop on a raceme up to forty centimetres long. Full sun and poor, alkaline soils are important requirements for cultivation but otherwise this species is easy.

236 – Saxifraga crustata
Travel study Switzerland

Saxifraga longifolia Lapeyr

On the limestone rocks of the Pyrenees and in Eastern Spain in altitudes of up to two thousand five hundred metres grows this remarkable Saxifraga or 'Stone Breaker'. It forms a very dense rosette of stiff, symmetric long leaves up to around twenty centimetres. The flower stalk can be to eighty centimetres tall and may carry up to a thousand single flowers. It is a truly remarkable and fantastic plant and rightly called the 'King of Saxifraga'. Cultivation requirements are vertical or near vertical rock features that face east into the morning sun. These plants die completely after flowering, so it is essential to protect and collect the fruit and very fine seed that are formed. My first personal memory of this plant is during my apprenticeship where my master had a collection of Saxifraga.

Saxifraga paniculata Mill

This is an arctic-alpine species that extends in its habitat from Spain to the Caucasus, arctic Europe and North America. According to this widespread habitat, the species does vary quite a bit, but by and large the plants have sharply serrated, small grey-green leaves and an abundance of white flowers in late spring. I have included it here because of its attractive habit and easy cultivation. There are many lovely cultivars in the trade, best to check with local suppliers.

237 – Saxifraga paniculata
Courtesy Wikipedia

Section Porphyrion (early spring Saxifraga with subsections Kabschia, Engleria and Oppositifoliae)

Most of these species form low, dense pillows or mats that are attractive throughout the year and flower very early in spring, sometimes within the snow. They partner well with Aubrieta taurica, Campanula cochleariifolia, Gentiana acaulis, Iberis saxatilis, Iris reticulata, Linaria, Primula glaucescens and small, gentle Sempervivum and Sedum species and cultivars. In cultivation, they prefer in my experience excellent drainage but good moisture, some shade or places that slope away from the full summer sun and gravelly, rather poor soils; do not over-fertilise, please. Propagation is by rosette-cuttings either straight after flowering or in early autumn. I would recommend keeping the young plants in the glasshouse for the first year.

Saxifraga burseriana L

From the eastern Alps comes this species that is specialised for life in the cracks of sandstone or limestone rocks that face away from the sun. The plant forms attractive grey-green pillows and flowers pure white. It is one of the very first and most lovely heralds of early spring.

Saxifraga oppositifolia L

The 'Red Stone Breaker' grows all around the arctic regions but also is represented in the Pyrenees, the Alps and the mountains of Bulgaria. Interestingly, it thrives in alkaline as well as in acidic soils. It grows in rocks, on mountain walls and in gravel and loamy slopes where no strong competition is present. The glowing red flowers appear immediately after the snow melts.

Section Saxifraga (Dactyloides, Moss Stone-Breakers)

The species of this section are soft-leaved rosette plants that do not die back after flowering and develop runners and side-shoots. Thus, they form low, dense and evergreen pillows, softening up rocks or stone walls. This makes them valuable and attractive throughout the seasons and they have been popular in horticulture for a long time. In cultivation, they require cool, shady locations, or at least places that face away from the sun. They look especially pretty with frost covering their rosettes. Propagation is easy by division or rosette cuttings which are best taken in late autumn, put in sandy soils and kept in a cold glasshouse over winter. In garden situations, they combine well with Alcemilla hoppeana, Campanula, Dicentra eximia, Dodecatheon, Epimedium, Primula, Viola, small ferns and gentle shade grasses.

Saxifraga x arendsii
Georg Arends bred the first hybrids that are still current today. The flowers range from white over pink to deep red tones. They are excellent for delicate little garden scenes, for graves or even in massed display.

Saxifraga cuneata Willd
A beautiful pillow-forming plant with leathery, shiny dark-green rosettes from the western Pyrenees and northern Spain. The species flowers white in summer and features greyish calcium secretions along its leaves in autumn. It tolerates more sun than the other species of this section, an attractive and reliable plant.

Section Gymnopera (Robertsoniana, Shade Stone-Breakers)
Evergreen species with runners that require shade and are easy to cultivate. They are valuable as ground cover, tub and grave plantings.

Saxifraga hirsuta
The 'Rough-leaved' or 'Hairy Stone Breaker' lives in the Pyrenees, northern Spain and south-western Ireland. In cultivation, it requires moisture and humus-rich soils and flowers white, a reliable low ground cover.

Section Irregulares (Diptera)
The species of this section are forest plants from eastern Asia that require humus-rich soils, moisture and semi-shaded or shaded locations.

Saxifraga cortusifolia Sib et Zucc
This species is among the latest to flower white in the growing season. It comes from Japan, Korea and Manchuria. They are very beautiful next to autumn Gentians.

Saxifraga stolonifera Meerb
At home in China and Japan this species grows to thirty centimetres and has white flowers with red spots. It is a great ground cover and even sometimes used as indoor pot plant.

Section Trachyphyllum
These are evergreen flat ground covers that grow somewhat turf-like.

Saxifraga aspera

On granite rocks of the Pyrenees and the Alps grows this species and forms bright green pillows. The flowers are creamy-yellow in late summer. In cultivation, the plant requires acidic, gravelly soils that are well-drained but do not dry out and a shady location. More a species for the plant collector.

Scabiosa; Dipsacaceae

Scabiosae are at home in the Mediterranean, Europe and Africa. They are annual or perennial plants and sometimes sub-shrubs. Their terminal flowers range from white, blue, purple, pink to yellow, mostly from summer to autumn. In cultivation warm, rather dry locations and they are valued as nectar plants for bees. Propagation is by seed, division is somewhat inefficient and can be done only with larger, older plants but basal cuttings are another option.

Scabiosa caucasica Bieb

This up to eighty-centimetre-tall Scabiosa is as the name tells at home in the Caucasus. The plant features grey-green to dark green leaves and large, up to eight centimetres across flowers from summer to autumn. The colour ranges from white, red, pink to purple in the various cultivars. This species is just about only represented in cultivated forms in the gardens and landscapes. Use in the landscapes from natural rockeries to formal border settings in dry and sunny places with soils preferably loam or sandy loams. Good combinations are Dianthus gratianopolitanus, Helianthemum, Anthemis ticntoria, Lychnis coronaria, Salvia nemorosa, Artemisia, Thymus and bearded Iris.

238 – Scabiosa columbaria
Courtesy Beth Chatto

Scabiosa graminifolia L

The 'Grass-leaved Scabiosa' is an interesting sub-shrub from Spain, France, Italy, Switzerland, the Balkans and Marocco. On hot, dry and poor soils it develops into an up to eighty-centimetre-tall, rounded sub-shrub. The leaves are grasslike with a silvery underside and the flowers vary from light purple to pink. I find it a most valuable plant for natural designs and hot and dry places like dry stone walls or rockeries, where it proves to be a very long-living, graceful plant with a sustained flowering period.

Scabiosa ochroleuca L

This yellow flowering perennial comes from central and eastern Europe where it lives in sandy or loamy, warm and dry poor and alkaline soils. It often lives only two or three years but if the environmental conditions are right it self-sows gently and stays in the location. Up to eighty centimetres tall, the flowers are yellow and appear in late summer to autumn. Based on the character of this plant I would suggest using it primarily in natural or wild designs.

Scaevola; Goodeniaceae

This genus of around eighty species is mainly Australian, with a few representatives in the Pacific Islands. They are shrubs or perennials with generally large leaves and small flowers. Their main uses in the landscape or horticulture are as evergreen ground cover or hanging basket plants.

Scaevola hookeri Muell ex Hook
This prostrate species is at home in Australia from Victoria, New South Wales and Tasmania. Its habitat are alpine and subalpine zones on soils with sufficient humus in full sun or part shade. The flowers are fan-shaped and range from white to light purple.

Scaevola microphylla
This low spreading herb grows around thirty centimetres high and eighty centimetres across. It is an excellent ground cover for well-drained soils in the sun. Fan-shaped blue flowers are produced through spring and summer.

Scaevola striata
This suckering perennial has an outstanding cultivar 'Pink Perfection' and is a lovely basket plant or trailing over dry-stone walls.

Schizachyrium; Poaceae

The genus of the 'Bearded Prairie Grass' has been botanically separated from Andropogon.

Schizachyrium scoparium Nash
This species is widespread in North America from Quebec to Alberta and Florida to Arozona. It is a tight clumpy grass to a hundred and twenty centimetres with stiff upright leaves that are green to bluish and often with a reddish tone during the growing season. The flowers become silvery in autumn and are very decorative. I included this ornamental grass here also for its structural value in winter. It retains its body throughout the dormant season and looks beautiful in hoar frost or when covered in snow. Use in natural steppe or prairie gardens, rock gardens or in the formal border, a lovely grass.

Scilla; Hyacinthaceae

The medium-sized genus of the 'Star Hyacinths' contains around ninety species. They come from Europe, Asia and South Africa and describe bulbous perennials.

Scilla bifolia L
The 'Alpine Squill' is a smaller plant, to thirty centimetres with star-shaped blue, purple, sometimes pink or white flowers in spring. They are at their best around deciduous shrubs or trees on alkaline, moist soils where they form lovely colonies together with Primula, Anemone nemorosa, Corydalis and Hepatica.

239 – Scilla bifolia
Courtesy Klaus Mödinger

Scilla peruviana L

In moist, meadows lives this up to thirty-centimetre-high plant with a large bulb that should be planted rather shallow. The flowers are deep purple-blue or white and appear in early summer. Avoid areas with harsh frosts.

Scutellaria; Lamiaceae

This cosmopolitan genus is represented with more than three hundred species. They are perennial plants or sub-shrubs and mostly of a low habit, valuable as summer-flowering species for rockeries or dry-stone walls in full sun. The taller species are also suited for the perennial border. Propagation is by seed, division or cuttings.

Scutellaria alpina ssp alpina
This up to forty-centimetre-high ground cover is widespread in central and southern Europe, from Spain to Greece and Romania. It grows on alkaline rocky, gravelly slopes and flowers purple in summer.

Scutellaria incana Spreng
From dry, open forests of North America comes this up to one hundred and twenty-centimetre-tall perennial. The plant flowers late with light blue, which makes it valuable for the perennial border, especially because the grey fruits are also attractive.

240 – Scutellaria incana
Used in natural setting

Sedum; Crassulaceae

A large genus with over three hundred species, Sedum plays an important role in landscapes and gardens. Most are perennial plants with succulent leaves but there are also some annuals and sub-shrubs. They are common all around the northern hemisphere with some species extending to Mexico and central Africa. They are easy to cultivate and are well suited to semi-arid and arid, hot and dry places. I remember from my apprentice days that we used to cut stem pieces and leaves off by the kilo and sell them for cheap but effective and attractive rooftop plantings. As with many plants from a desert-like background, do not over-fertilise Sedum or rather, do not fertilise at all. They will find sufficient sustenance in just about all well-drained soils and look and flower much better that way. Use in the landscape is in many applications from natural rockeries, dry stone wall to structural borders and even strictly formal succulent displays and plant sculptures.

Sedum acre L

The 'Wall Pepper' (translated from German 'Mauerpfeffer') is a low, evergreen plant with succulent small leaves that have a slightly hot taste, hence the common name. It is a tough species that may be used as turf substitute in hot dry places or to go wild around rockeries, dry stone walls and on roofs. The flowers are yellow in summer. They combine well with Alyssum, Armeria maritime, Campanula carpatica, Festuca cinerea and F. glauca, Hieracium pilosella and Thymus.

Sedum cauticolum Praeg

Growing on rocks in Japan, this around fifteen-centimetre low plant has prostrated stems and blue-grey succulent leaves with reddish-purple margins and is an attractive structural groundcover. They flower pink to red from late summer to autumn.

Sedum floriferum Praeg

A ten-centimetre low reliable ground cover that comes from north-eastern China. The plant forms a dense carpet on poor dry soils where most other ground covers would fail and flowers profusely in summer. The cultivar 'Weihenstephaner Gold' is particularly recommended with its golden yellow flowers.

241 – Sedum floriferum 'Weihenstephaner Gold'
Work and study in Weihenstephan, Germany

Sedum kamtchaticum Fish et Mey

Kamtchatka, Sacchalin and Japan are the home of this up to twenty-centimetre-high species. It has a thick, woody rootstock and upright stems. The orange-yellow flowers appear in late summer and even after flowering the star-like fruits are very decorative.

Sedum spectabile Bor

From Korea and Manchuria originates this for horticulture important Sedum. The species gets to sixty centimetres tall with fleshy rootstock and grey-green serrated leaves on upright, smooth stems. It prefers loamy, richer soils than most of the small Sedums and partners well with Lavandula, Malva, Salvias and Stachys byzantinum.

Sedum telephium ssp telephium

This larger, upright Sedum comes extends from Europe to Siberia. It grows to forty centimetres and is a bit smaller than the above S. spectabile. The leaves are opposite, blue-grey and make this plant a structural feature for most of the growing season. It flowers in autumn with reddish-brown terminal inflorescences. Probably best known in horticulture is the hybrid 'Herbstfreude' (Autumn Joy), a cross between Sedum spectabile and S. telephium that reaches fifty centimetres and resembles, with its flat flowers, Achillea. Propagation is by division, cuttings or leaf cuttings.

242 – Sedum telephium 'Herbstfreude' (Autumn Joy)
Courtesy Staudengärtnerei Gräfin von Zeppelin, Germany

Sempervivum; Crassulaceae

A genus of around sixty species, describing succulent rosette plants that usually form colonies. Their origins are found in the Pyrenees, the Sierra Nevada, the Blakans, Asia Minor, the Caucasus and Iran. These plants survive extremes of drought, heat and famine. They are ideally suited to colonise dry stone walls, rockeries or rooftops. Over time they can create the loveliest miniature landscape scenes. Propagation is easy by division or seed.

Sempervivum arachnoideum L

One of my favourite Sempervivum, this species comes from the Pyurenees and Carpatia. It forms small to medium sized reddish-brown to greenish rosettes that are densely covered by hairs, as if they had been spun over by very busy small spiders. The flowers are rose-red and appear in late summer.

243 – Sempervivum arachnoideum in flower

244 – Sempervivum arachnoideum 'Standsfieldii' with non-flowering rosettes. During the fertile phase of the plant the spiderweb-like growth recedes

Sempervivum tectorum L
The 'House Leek' forms large, up to twenty centimetres across green rosettes, often with reddish tips. It is at home in the Pyrenees, central Europe and extends to the Balkans. Probably most garden cultivars or hybrids are descendants of this straight species. There are very many of these and it is best to check with local suppliers.

Senecio; Asteraceae

This is a very large genus of Asteraceae containing more than three thousand species that in many diverse forms, live all over the world. They are annuals, biannuals, perennials, climbers, sub-shrubs and shrubs and some medicinal plants are amongst them. The species discussed here I have selected for their usefulness in rockeries, the alpinum and natural garden designs. Propagation is by seed and division.

Senecio aureus L
The 'Golden Ragwort' comes from North America where it grows up to eighty centimetres tall in moist to wet meadows. It is a nice species for natural and wild designs.

Senecio cordatus Koch
A plant of the Alps, this Senecio becomes to a metre tall in moist zones of meadows of higher altitudes. The yellow flowers of late summer combine well with Aconitum napellus. This species is well suited to natural designs with sufficient space.

Senecio ovatus Willd
Growing in open forests in montane or subalpine zones this up to a hundred and fifty-centimetre-tall species is a beautiful perennial and valuable for its late flowering period. The flowers are yellow and fragrant and appear from late summer into late autumn. The plant is best suited to large parks or natural landscape designs with sufficient moisture throughout the year where it can develop its own life and self-sow. In open Fagus sylvatica forests, it partners with Digitalis purpurea, Galium odoratum, Luzula species, Melica nutans and Mercuria perennis.

245 – Senecio ovatus
Courtesy Karin Feldmann

Senna; Caesalpiniaceae

Most representatives of the genus Senna are tropical shrubs and trees, but there are some perennials and sub-shrubs in the temperate zones of North America. In garden, cultivation of importance is Senna hebecarpa which is sometimes mixed up with Cassia marilandica. Senna require warmth and sun and are often somewhat frost tender when young. They are suited as feature plants or as summer-flowering partners of perennial borders.

Senna hebecarpa Irwin et Barneby

These plants live alongside rivers and creeks and in open forests of the USA, from Massachusetts to Tennessee. They grow to a hundred and thirty-centimetre-tall with up to twenty-five-centimetre-long compound leaves that fold together after dark. Dense flower racemes of up to thirty individual yellow inflorescences with black stamens appear throughout summer.

246 – Senna hebecarpa
Courtesy Karin Feldmann

Serratula; Asteraceae

Europe, the Mediterranean and eastern Asia are home to the genus of Serrattula which comprises around seventy species. These represent the Daisy family with purple, pink and crimson flowers, sometimes white. Their use in the landscape is primarily in natural and wild designs where they are valuable for their later flowering time from summer to autumn. Their cultivation is easy in any average soil from sun to semi-shade and they also propagate easily by seed or division.

Serratula lycopifolia Kern

This species grows to a hundred centimetres tall and is widespread in the southern Alps. The flowers appear in summer, they are around three centimetres across and of a light purple colour. The plant is of interest as they are in symbiosis with ants, which protect the flowers and harvest the nectar. I would use this species for larger, natural and wild designs like meadows.

Serratula seoanei Willk

A valuable plant for the larger, natural rockery is this up to thirty-centimetre bushy species. The flowers start to appear in late summer and the plant keeps going right into late autumn with its purple-pink colours between the rocks. The longer the plant is left undisturbed the more beautiful it becomes. Good partners are low, silvery Artemisia, Micromeria thymifolia, Nepeta, Satureja montana, Thymus and Iris.

Seseli; Apiaceae (Apioidae)

Seseli gummiferum Pull ex Smith

On the Limestone Mountains of the Crimea, the Taurus Mountains and the Aegean grows this around sixty-centimetre-high perennial. The white flowers are held in umbels and appear in late summer. The compound leaves are decorative and make the plant of structural value in dry stone walls or natural rockeries.

Seseli montanum L

The 'Mountain Fennel' grows from Spain to the Balkans and is a clumpy perennial with blue-green compound leaves to eighty centimetres tall. The white to light pink flowers appear for a long period from summer to autumn. They are well suited for dry locations together with the larger Sedum, Sesleria nitida, Aster sericeus, Asphodelus albus, bearded Iris and Artemisia.

247 – Seseli montanum
Courtesy Annerose Dilger

Sesleria; Poaceae

This genus of grasses is widespread from Europe, western Asia, North Africa and the Balkans. It describes clumpy grasses, mostly with blue to grey attractive foliage that is of structural value. These grasses are drought hardy and the stiff leaves retain their structure even in period of extreme heat and extended drought. Propagation is by seed and division, best in spring.

Sesleria autumnalis Schultz

At home from Italy to the Adriatic Sea and Bosnia this up to sixty-centimetre-tall grass loves the sun, heat and dry alkaline conditions. The blue-green plants are attractive through most of the year and are of great structural value in many applications from natural to formal designs. They flower in autumn, hence the species name.

Sidalcea; Malvaceae

From North America come around twenty-five species of Sidalcea or 'Prairie Hollies'. They grow mostly on well-drained loamy, humus-rich soils that are low in alkalinity. In cultivation, they require of course similar conditions and heavy soils should be avoided. Their use in the landscape is mainly in perennial borders as valuable conspicuous summer flowering plants but also in larger, natural or wild designs of prairie or steppe character. Propagation is by seed or division for cultivars.

Sidalcea malviflora Gray

This up to a hundred and twenty-centimetre-tall species originates in Oregon and California and stands out for its large purple-pink flowers in early summer. The plants prefer drier places and it is beneficial to cut them back after flowering, they also make good cut flowers. There are several nice cultivars like 'Elsie Heugh' with light pink flowers, 'Party Girl' with crimson-pink flowers and 'Rosanna' with rose-red flowers. These need to be propagated by division.

248 – Sidalcea malviflora 'Rosanna'
Courtesy Baumschule Horstmann

Sidalcea neomexicana Gray

An up to one hundred centimetres tall, hairy plant which stands out for its abundant pink, sometimes white flowers. This rich flowering, prominent species is highly recommended for steppe or prairie planting designs.

Silene; Caryophyllaceae

The variable genus of Silene comprises around four hundred species that are distributed all around the world. There are only a few clumpy or pillow-forming species that are of significance in the landscape and gardens, where they are recommended for use in rockeries or natural designs. Propagation is by seed, divisions or cuttings.

Silene alpestris Jacq

An alpine species from the Pyrenees, the Balkans and Carpatian Mountains Silene alpestris grows to around fifteen centimetres and forms loose pillows. It is a pretty, small plant for the rockery and dry-stone wall where it is valuable through its late flowering time from summer into autumn. The flowers are white or pinkish; the species requires excellent drainage but is otherwise adaptable to a wide range of soils.

Silene maritima With

This species is widespread around the coasts of Western Europe. The leaves are grey-green and the flowers are white with a distinct balloon-like calyx and appear in summer. Propagation is by seed or division.

Silphium; Asteraceae

Around fifteen species of Silphium come from eastern and central North America. They are mainly tall perennials that are suitable as feature plants or in loose groups together with other tall perennials. Good partners are Helianthus, Andropogon gerardii, Asclepias exaltata, Eupatorium, Miscanthus, Phlox amplifolia and others.

Silphium laciniatum L

This tall, up to three hundred and fifty-centimetre-high species is also called 'Compass Plant'. The yellow flowers are held in loose racemes and the foliage that lasts well into winter makes this a valuable large feature plant. It partners well with Baptisia, Panicum virgatum, Rudnbeckia fulgida and Schizacharyium.

249 – Silphium laciniatum
Courtesy Klaus Mödinger

Sisyrinchium; Iridaceae

There are around ninety species in this genus that describe clumpy perennials that are suited to rockeries with sufficient moisture. Propagation is by seed or division.

Sisyrinchium angustiolium Mill
The 'Blue-Eyed Grass' from North America is an up to twenty centimetres high species that grows in a dense clump of narrow, dark-green leaves. The purple-blue flowers have a yellow throat and appear in early summer. The species self-sows gently in the right environment of a well-drained but moist rockery and

partners well with Achillea ageratifolia, Allium moly, Gladiolus communis, Linum flavum, Saxifraga paniculata and Ranunculus gramineus.

Sisyrinchium striatum Sm

At up to eighty centimetres, a taller species, S. striatum comes from Argentina and Chile. The stiff upright flower stalks bear cream or pale-yellow flowers along their length in summer. The plant is a great addition to larger rockeries or perennial borders.

250 – Sisyrinchium striatum
Courtesy Plantes Vivaces

Smilacina; Convallariaceae

This genus of around twenty species resembles Polygonatum and for that reason one of the common names is 'False Solomon's Seal'. It is a genus of the forest and woodland that is long-lived and features terminal white flowers and decorative berries. They are great in natural and wild forest and woodland designs for soils that should be rich in humus (leaf litter) and not be too dry. Propagation is best by division in spring. Seed is possible but takes a long time.

Smilacina racemosa Desf

In open forests and woodlands of North America grows this up to ninety-centimetre-tall perennial. The up to fifteen-centimetre-long flower panicle is yellowish-white and has a fragrance comparable to Convallaria. Green to red berries appear after pollination. Use in the landscape near water features or n association with ferns or ground covers, it is a great structural plant for wooded areas.

Solanum; Solancaecae

The large cosmopolitan genus of the 'Night Shade' is represented with over fifteen hundred species. A majority originates in tropical South America, there are annuals, perennials, sub-shrubs shrubs and trees as well as climbing species. Their flowers vary from white and yellow to blue and purple. Their fruits are fleshy berries. Many species are cultivated as ornamentals, vegetables or medicinal plants. Almost all species are poisonous in most parts of the plant, whereas the ripe edible parts of the plant lack the toxic alkaloids; these are removed during the ripening process.

Solanum dulcamara L

The 'Bittersweet Nightshade' is widespread throughout Europe, North Arica and western Asia to India, Japan and China. It is a climbing or prostrate sub-shrub, up to eight metres long or tall with light purple flowers. The fruits are berries that turn red after ripening. All parts of this plant are poisonous so the use in the landscape is restricted to botanical species collections and controlled displays. It should also be remembered that this, like many Solanaceae, has a strong tendency to become weedy, both with its underground runners as well as birds spreading the seed.

Soldanella; Primulaceae

The delicate species of the 'Alpenglöckchen' (German for 'Little Bells of the Alps') are mostly plants for the collector of Alpines. They are small alpine perennials or forest plants with rounded leaves and frilled flowers. These are either tube-like with short frills and carried individually on stalks (Tubiflores) or funnel-shaped with long frills and carried in multiples (Crateriflores). According to their origins they are suited to sunny, but cool and moist rockeries and moors with acidic soils or in shady areas in association with trees. They are a little tricky in lower altitudes but achievable; I had Soldanella alpina flowering well in the lowlands of south eastern Australia, ensuring cooler conditions by placing them near running water.

Soldanella alpina L

The mountains of Europe from the central Pyrenees to the Black Forest and Calabria are home to this little, to fifteen-centimetre-high jewel. Naturally the species grows in moist to wet and poor soils in subalpine or alpine zones ascending to three thousand metres. The flowers are strongly frilled, deep purple, light purple, light blue or even white in spring. Always keep moist and cool but with a lot of sun in cultivation.

Soldanella montana Willd

This species is at home in shady and moist forests of the Italian Alps and mountians of Bulgaria and central Europe. The plant grows to thirty centimetres in height and flowers purple in early summer. Easy to cultivate in moist, shaded areas under trees and shrubs but needs to be kept in acidic soils, it does not tolerate alkalinity.

251 – Soldanella montana
Travel study, Switzerland

Solidago; Asteraceae

There are around a hundred species of Solidago in the northern hemisphere, mainly in North America with a few exceptions in Eurasia and South America. They grow in prairies, along riparian zones and follow roads. Most are medium to tall clumpy perennials with dense roots that become woody in some species. Main flowering times are summer and autumn and the predominant colour is yellow. Their use in the landscape is in natural and rockery gardens with some of the modern hybrids also well suited to perennial borders. Propagation is by division and cuttings.

Solidago caesia L

From eastern North America comes the 'Blue-Stem Goldenrod'. This species grows to ninety centimetres tall and flowers yellow in autumn. In natural planting designs, it combines beautifully with Ceanothus, Caryopteris, Liatris and Echinacea purpurea.

Solidago canadensis L

A widespread species in North America, Solidago canadensis thrives along rivers and in moist meadows. The plant grows strongly and to a hundred and fifty centimetres tall and flowers from summer into autumn. It has a strong tendency to occupy vacant spaces like a pioneer plant and should therefore be used only in larger natural or wild landscapes where this is of benefit to the design.

252 – Solidago canadensis
In this picture, the Solidago is combined with Lythrum salicaria and Salvia uliginosa
Restoration work in Canberra, Australia 2014

Solidago culteri Fern

This valuable small, up to forty-centimetre-high and late flowering species is well suited individually or in small groups for the rockery. Good partners are small and medium bearded Iris, Festuca ovina, F. cinerea, Aster amellus, Aster sedifolius 'Nanus' Cistus for structure and Helianthemum.

Solidago rugosa Mill

This very decorative and tall, up to and over two hundred centimetres, species may be used as a feature on its own or complementing larger perennial borders in the background. The dense, golden yellow flowers appear from summer into autumn and are suited for the vase.

Solidago hybrids

These are better suited for the garden and smaller landscape designs than its wild cousins. Most have S. canadensis and S. shortie in their genes but they are still all strong growers and have their genus' tendency to spread by rhizome and seed.

'Goldwedel' – sixty centimetres, large, glowing yellow flowers in early summer; if cut back after flowering a second flowering will reliably occur in late summer/early autumn. 'Laurin' – forty centimetres, compact rockery plant with deep golden yellow flowers in autumn; 'Septembergold' – eighty centimetres, glowing golden yellow flowers throughout autumn

Sowerbaea; Anthericaceae (Liliaceae)

Sowerbaea juncea

This tufted perennial has rush-like thirty-centimetre-long leaves and umbels of purple, vanilla-scented flowers held around forty centimetres above the foliage. The scent gave the plant the nice name of 'Vanilla Lily'. It requires a damp position with most of the day in the sun, propagation is easiest by division but I would try seed as well.

Stachys; Lamiaceae

The around three hundred species of this genus are distributed in the temperate zones. They are usually shrubby, upright perennials with opposite leaves and terminal flower spikes.

Stachys byzantina Koch

Named after the ancient empire of Byzantium, the Eastern Roman Empire that fell after the capital Constantinople was conquered in 1453 and the city subsequently became today's Istanbul, this species is probably the horticulturally most important one. It comes from the Caucasus, northern Iran and the Crimea. The ornamental grey-silvery felty leaves are its main feature, the small pink flowers appear in summer. I like using this plant as a reliable ground cover and to frame structural plants in sunny, dry and hot places. It is very efficient in softening up architectural fabric like walls or paths. What worked well for me is to swing this ground cover around structural plants like Artemisia, Cistus, Lavandula, Phlomis and the like in dry borders and then complement this body with conspicuous flowerers like bearded Iris, Eremurus, Papaver orientale, dry Lilium and others.

253 – Stachys byzantina
Courtesy Stephan Willenberger

Stachys macrantha Stearn

This dense up to fifty-centimetre-high perennial forms reliable clumps in sun or semi-shade that are effective in formal borders as well as in natural scenes. It has large, crimson-pink flowers in late summer held above the heart-shaped, wrinkled leaves. Turkey, Iran and the Caucasus are home to this species that combines well with Alchemilla epipsila, Aquilegia, Buphtalmum salicifolium, Calamintha nepeta, Hemerocallis, Campanula latifolia and ornamental grasses like Calamagrostis, Deschampsia, Helictotrichon and Lasiagrostis. The cultivar 'Superba' is highly recommended and needs to be propagated vegetatively.

Stackhousia; Stackhousiaceae

Stackhousia pulvinaris
This beautiful rock-hugging plant forms a prostrate mat to forty centimetres across with light green, small linear leaves. Yellow-cream star-like flowers are produced in abundance in spring. In cultivation, it requires rich soil and moisture in cool places, ideal for shadier rockeries or dry-stone walls.

Stackhousia spathulata
This small herbaceous perennial grows to thirty centimetres with bright white flowers borne in spring, slightly resembling Iberis. Good drainage and sun are required, it adapts to most soils. Propagation is by cuttings or division.

Stenanthium; Melianthaceae

This is a small genus of only five species in North America and Sachalin.

Stenanthium gramineum Morong
The 'Feather Bells' from North America is at home in open, rocky woodlands with sufficient moisture and neutral to acidic soils. It grows to a hundred and fifty centimetres and has grass-like, stiff leaves and up to sixty-centimetre-long flower spikes of creamy-white to reddish fragrant flowers in late summer.

Stenanthium occidentale Gray
In mountain meadows, open woodlands and wetlands of northern America lives this very beautiful plant. It grows to around sixty centimetres with up to thirty-centimetre-long leaves held in a basal rosette. The flowers are or a warm brownish crimson. The species requires a long time to establish and develop its full potential but its well worth it.

254 – Stenanthium occidentale
Courtesy Pacific Bulb Society

Sterlingia; Proteaceae

Sterlingia simplex
This nice little sub-shrub grows to around twenty centimetres with grey-green leaves. It produces pale yellow flowers on thirty-centimetre-long stems in spring and would be a nice addition to sunny, hot rockeries with perfect drainage and sandy or gravelly soils. Propagation is best by basal cuttings of young shoots.

Sternbergia; Amaryllidaceae

This is a small genus of nine bulbous species ranging from Turkey and Spain to Kashmir and Israel. Their use in the landscape is best in the rockery in warm, sunny and sheltered sites in soils that are well-drained.

Sternbergia clusiana Spreng
The species extends from Jordan over Iran and Israel into Turkey and has the largest flowers of the genus with up to ten-centimetre wide bright yellow or greenish-yellow colours in autumn. The grey-green leaves appear after flowering.

Sternbergia lutea Spreng
The 'Common Sternbergia' or Lily of the Fields (translated from German "Lilie des Feldes") is widespread from Spain to Iran and Russia. Its habitats are dry, rocky places among shrubs and ascending to a thousand metres altitude. The golden-yellow flowers appear in autumn and stand to twenty centimetres above glossy green leaves. As use in the landscape I would recommend natural designs, warm places in rockeries, along dry-stone walls and scattered among smaller shrubs with autumn coloured foliage.

255 – Sternbergia lutea
Courtesy Wikimedia

Stipa; Poaceae

A genus that is represented almost all over the world. These grasses are clumpy perennials up to a handsome two hundred and fifty centimetres tall. Also named 'Feather Grasses' the genus is divided into two sections according to appearance and use in the landscape.

Section Lasiagrostis (Achnaterum)

Stipa calamagrostis Wahlenb (Achnaterum lasiagrostis)

This species is at home in southern and middle Europe where it grows in mountain valleys, on rocky or gravelly soils, up to a hundred and twenty centimetres tall. It flowers in summer with long-lasting yellowish-white inflorescences that mature into a warm yellow-brown. In my opinion, it is one of the most valuable ornamental grasses and is also a great structural plant. There are several good cultivars that need to be propagated vegetatively and best by division in spring. Keep warm.

Section Stipa

The species of this section are at home in sunny, hot and dry places and they should be used in the landscape accordingly. A particularity of these plants is that they are highly ornamental when in flower but their general appearance after flowering is very poor. As a consequence, I usually combine them with structural plants that are effective throughout the year and plants that develop their prime later than the section Stipa, a little bit like planting evergreen shrubs like Cistus and late flowering Chrysanthemums with bearded Iris and oriental Poppies.

Stipa gigantea Link

This impressive, up to two hundred centimetres tall grass comes from Portugal and southern Spain. The leaves are to fifty centimetres high and the flowers appear in summer. It is a magnificient grass, especially when planted elevated and in places where the sun shines through.

256 – Stipa gigantea in Beth Chatto's corner
Courtesy Studengärtnerei Gräfin von Zeppelin, Germany

Stipa pulcherrima Koch

The 'most beautiful' (translated from Latin) Feather Grass is widespread in its habitat from central Europe to Russia, central Asia, Iran and Turkey. It colonises even the driest places, in cracks of rocks in the baking sun and this is the way to use it in the landscape. The plant grows to a metre high and flowers in summer.

Stylidium; Stylidiaceae

This mostly Australian genus contains some hundred and ten species. They have a unique pollination method that gave the name 'Trigger Plants' to this group of plants. The anthers and stigma are combined into an irritable organ known as column. When an insect alights on the base of this column, it reacts like a trigger and hits the insect on its back and in this way transfers pollen to the insect, which acts as a pollinating vector between plants. They prefer warm, sunny and well-drained locations.

Stylidium adnatum

The common 'Beaked Trigger Plant' is a small clumping perennial with whorls of bright green linear leaves on erect stems. In spring and summer, terminal sprays of pale pink flowers are produced. They are lovely rockery plants and can colonise the landscape nicely without becoming weedy. Propagation is by seed.

Stylidium bulbiferum

This perennial species forms circular mats fifteen centimetres high and thirty centimetres across with its stolons. The flowers are red, pink or white and appear in spring. This is an attractive plant for moister areas in full sun of smaller rockeries, propagation is by division or seed.

Stylidium graminifolium

This tufted plant is grass-like with variable flowers from pale pink to deep magenta and are held between twenty and forty centimetres high. Propagation is by seed. Use in the landscape as the above species or in heathland or meadows in natural designs.

257 – Stylidium graminifolium
Courtesy Swinburne Image Bank

Stylophorum; Papaveraceae

There are around five species in this genus from East Asia; one is at home in North America. The plants carry a yellow sap and flower yellow to orange in spring and summer. Their use in the landscape is recommended as attractive partner along the margins of woody ornamentals, in shady borders or in large rockeries. Propagation is by seed or division. Snails can be a problem.

Stylophorum diphyllum Nutt
The 'Wood Poppy' comes from North America and is at home in moist forests and woodlands. The species grows to fifty centimetres and has fragile stems carrying up to five centimetres wide golden-yellow flowers.

Stylophyllum lasiocarpum Fedde

From East and Central China comes this species that grows within shrubs or in forests and woodlands. The individual plants are up to thirty centimetres high and around fifty centimetres across with flowers in summer. The roots of these plants are used in herbal medicine.

Stypandra; Phormiaceae (Liliaceae)

Stypandra glauca

This variable perennial is a tufted plant with long, leafy stems up to a metre. It bears blue flowers with protruding yellow anthers in slender sprays. Use in the landscape in small groups like ornamental grasses in slightly shaded positions and drier soils, they are suitable for places under open trees. Propagation is best by division and the plants benefit from removal of the old stems after flowering.

Swainsonia; Fabaceae

This fascinating genus of perennial plant species is usually short-lived and they are sometimes cultivated as annuals. They are brilliant plants and worth putting effort into. Key points in my experience are selection of ideal, baking hot positions, reflected heat, excellent drainage and open, gravelly and sandy soils.

Swainsonia formosa

The famous 'Sturt's Desert Pea' is a trailing plant of up to around two metres with brilliant, scarlet-red flowers with glossy black boss on erect peduncles. It is an endemic Australian plant, at home in semi-arid zones of Western Australia, the Northern Territory, Southern Australia, New South Wales and Queensland. Other than for displays I would use the plant in larger rockeries. I build the bed up, starting with a foundation of rocks (railway base is great, reasonably cheap and easily available) and on top of this layer I mix gravel, sand and loam and a little humus, with slightly alkaline properties. Either direct-sow after hot water treatment or pre-grow the seedlings in biodegradable cells that are planted out with the least root disturbance possible. In such rockery beds in Queanbeyan, near Canberra, plants have survived and flowered for several years despite experiencing repeated frosts. Some nurseries offer grafted plants and this gives great results in less ideal conditions. Propagation is otherwise by seed. I have successfully done cuttings but the success rate is low and the cuttings require excellent conditions and a highly experienced hand. Fertilise moderately and with a balance favouring K.

258 – Swainsonia Formosa
Courtesy Alice Springs Desert National Park, Australia

Swainsonia galegifolia
This gorgeous perennial grows to a metre tall with arching stems of pinnate leaves and bears sprays of large pea flowers in spring. The colour can vary from deep red to white, pink and mauve-pink. In cultivation, give plenty of sun but this species is very forgiving compared to S. formosa and accepts a wide range of conditions, excepting waterlogged situations. Some pruning back of old stems in late winter rejuvenates the plants.

Symphytum; Boraginaceae

The genus of the Comfrey contains around thirty-five species that live from Europe to North Africa and extend into western China. They are upright or flat-growing perennials with fleshy roots and mostly hairy, yellowish, blue or purple nodding flowers. The species are great for large, natural designs where sufficient moisture is present throughout the year. Propagation is by seed, division or root cuttings.

Symphytum azureum Van Hall
An around thirty centimetres high and fast-growing species that forms underground runners. The very lovely sky-blue flowers that appear in spring gave the name to the plant. It is a great ground cover for under shrubs and trees or together with large and robust, structural perennials with its nice, fresh-green foliage in natural designs.

Symphytum caucasicum Bieb
As the name suggests, this species originates in the Caucasus where it grows in moist places and along watercourses. It forms strong underground runners and develops to around sixty centimetres in height. The pure blue flowers stand above the foliage in summer. Use in the landscape only in wild or large, natural landscape designs, in light shade or full sun where moisture is present all year round. This way the plant forms a perfect, weed-free ground cover; it is one of the few plants that can overcome even strong weeds.

Syphytum grandiflorum DC

Also from the Caucasus, this species is less competitive but should still be used only in association with woody ornamentals or very strong, robust structural perennials in natural designs like English landscape designs of the nineteenth century. The flowers are buttery yellow in spring and are held above the around thirty-centimetre-high foliage.

Symphytum officinale L

The 'Common Comfrey' is at home from Europe to Siberia where it grows in moist meadows and in shady, moist margins of forests and woodlands. It is a clumpier growing plant and can get to eighty centimetres tall. The flowers are in a wide range of shades from purple, crimson or yellowish-white. It is an old medicinal plant that used to be in almost every home and farm garden, used against inflammation, wounds and bruises and internally, assisting the gastro-intestinal tract.

259 – Symphytum officinale
Courtesy Homöopathische Gesellschaft Badenweiler, Germany

Talinum; Portulacaceae

Around fifty species of Talinum are widespread, mostly in subtropical and tropical zones of the northern and southern hemispheres, however the below described representatives are hardy in cool-temperate zones also. They are little perennial plants or small sub-shrubs for small rockeries or tub and container plantings in full sun and with excellent drainage. Their flowers range from white, pink to red and purple. Propagation is easy by cuttings or seed.

Talinum brevifolium Torr

The mountain steppes of Arizona, New Mexico and the western USA are home to this flat growing, fleshy perennial. Attractive crimson-pink flowers appear in summer. The plant is rather small, therefore use in tubs or containers or along the crests of smaller dry-stone walls where it can trail down and will not be overgrown.

Talinum spinescens Torr

Naturally this species grows in high altitudes in the western USA together with Artemisia tridentata, Erigeron linearis, Eriophyllum lanatum, Erigeron poliospermus, Allium acuminatum, Astralagus purshii, Eriogonum douglasii, Lewisia rediviva and other plants that love sun and drought. As the name suggests, the plant has little thorns. It grows to only twenty centimetres and produces crimson-purple flowers from summer into autumn.

Tanacetum; Asteraceae

Tanacetum argenteum Willd

This special sub-shrub with its white-silvery foliage originates in Asia Minor. The plant essentially requires the hottest and driest conditions like on fully exposed dry-stone walls to thrive and develop its full potential. The small, yellow flowers in summer are not significant; it is a structural foliage plant for hot, dry rockeries or natural steppe designs.

Tanacetum cinerariifolium

Coming from Eastern Europe, this around forty-centimetre-tall species has grey-green foliage and bright white flowers through summer. It is also cultivated to produce an insecticide but has ornamental value for the garden on dry stone walls and as cut flower. Propagation is by seed or basal cuttings.

Tanacetum coccineum Grierson

Formerly known as Chrysanthemum coccineum or 'Coloured Daisy' (translated from German 'Farbige Margarite'), this species comes from the Caucasus, Armenia and Iran. It thrives there in mountain meadows and as the name suggests, can have a wide range of colours from white, pink to red variations. The flowers are held around fifty centimetres high on long stems which make the plant popular for cut flowers and in perennial beds. It is an adaptable plant for most soils but does not live long in heavy, poorly drained soils.

Tanacetum haradjanii Griersoon

This small sub-shrub is quite special in its demands on superb drainage and sandy, gravelly soils in full sun but rewards the effort with highly attractive white, felty foliage and stems. I would use it in tubs, containers or small dry-stone walls.

261 – Tanacetum haradjanii
Courtesy Angelika Kaufmann

Tanacetum vulgare
An over one-hundred-centimetre-tall plant with fern-like sectioned dark-green foliage that is widespread from Europe to the Caucasus and Armenia to Siberia. It flowers with small yellow inflorescences in late summer and the entire plant is aromatic. It is an old medicinal plant that can be found in many places. It is essentially a strong wild plant and should be used in wild or large natural designs; it is less suited to subtle garden designs. I have successfully used in it larger landscape designs for stabilising of slopes and embankments.

Telekia; Asteraceae

Telekia speciosa Baumg
This is a very handsome and impressive foliage plant for semi-shaded places with sufficient moisture. The species extends from the Alps to the Balkans, the Caucasus and Asia Minor. It exceeds two hundred centimetres in good locations and the large, serrated leaves are slightly hairy. The flowers are yellow and up to six centimetres across, appearing in summer. It is a plant for natural or wild designs and carefully chosen locations with a sheltered microclimate and they perform well in association with water features or creeks.

261 – Telekia speciaosa
Courtesy Frieder Rothmund

Tetratheca; Tremandraceae

This is a small Australian genus of around twenty species of mostly sub-shrubs with pink to purple flowers. The flowers have a black centre which lead to the common name 'Black Susan'. However, most species have pendulous flowers like bells and the centre is not easily seen. They are mostly plants for dappled shade and well-drained soils under trees. Propagation is best by semi-hardwood cuttings from late summer to autumn.

Tetratheca ciliata
This species is a variable sub-shrub to around a metre high with abundant white to pink flowers in winter and spring. Due to this flowering time when there is usually not much colour in the gardens, this is a valuable plant for the natural garden.

Tetratheca thymifolia
As the name suggests, this species has thyme-like to fifteen-millimetre short leaves. The plant can be recommended for its rich white to deep pink flowers which can be produced right through the year under good conditions.

262 – Tetratheca thymifolia
Courtesy Gondwana Nursery, Australia

Teucrium; Lamiaceae

Around a hundred species of Teucrium inhabit the temperate and warm-temperate zones of the world. They may be perennials, sub-shrubs or shrubs and are well suited to rockeries and natural designs where they are important as structural plants. All require well-drained soils, preferably alkaline and they thrive in sun or shade. Propagation is by cuttings; best are semi-hardwood cuttings for the shrubs and sub-shrubs, or division or layering if only small numbers are required.

Teucrium chamaedrys L
This species thrives everywhere in Europe and extends into Russia and North Africa and Iran. It is a plant of dry meadows or rocky steppes and grows also in association with shrubs and trees on alkaline soils. It is essentially a deciduous plant but in warmer climates, retains the foliage through winter. Up to thirty centimetres high, the plant forms strong runners which may colonise dry stone walls or rocky slopes very well. The crimson flowers appear in late summer followed by a short vegetative period. When the growth of this period matures and starts to harden, it is in my experience the best time to strike cuttings. Good partners are Geranium sanguineum, Coreopsis grandiflora, Iris barbata, bulbs and drought tolerant grasses.

Teucrium montanum L
This lovely Mediterranean species also prefers alkaline soils in dry meadows, gravelly or rocky soils of higher elevations as the name suggests. It is a flat growing ground cover with grey-green rosemary-like foliage and whitish-yellow to yellow flowers from summer to autumn.

Teucrium polium L
A sub-shrub that grows to around fifty centimetres, woolly foliage and white, red or yellow flowers which listens to the common name of 'Mary's Herb' (Marienkraut – translated from German). Planted together in larger groups in hot, sunny rockeries or other very dry natural landscapes like heathland designs they can create stunning sceneries.

Teucrium scorodonia L

Contrary to the above T. species, this plant prefers acidic soils. It is at home in central Europe, northward to southern Norway, east to Poland and south to North Africa, where it lives in heathland communities and in mixed forests and woodlands. The species develops to around eighty centimetres and flowers light yellow from summer to autumn. As in its natural habitat, I would use this plant in heathland designs together with Erica cinerea, Erica vagans, Calluna varieties and use as dominating structure Cytisus shrubs, for example Cytisus x kewensis, Cytisus purgans and Cytisus x praecox planted in irregular groups.

Thalictrum; Ranunculaceae

This medium-sized genus of Ranunculaceae contains around a hundred and forty species of northern temperate zones and the tropical zones of South America, Africa and Indonesia. They are mostly clumpy perennials ranging from small, dwarfy species to very large plants.

Thalictrum aquilegifolium L

The up to a hundred-centimetre-tall perennial inhabits moist or wet meadows and woodlands from Europe to Siberia and Japan. The foliage strongly resembles Aquilegia as the name suggests. The light purple to purple-pink flowers appear to float like little butterflies above the ground in late spring and give the plant a happy, loose and relaxed mood and therefore I would use it in natural, wild woodland scenes, together with Trollius, Geranium pratense, Hemerocallis lilioasphodelus and Aconitum napellus. Propagation is best by seed in spring after a cool-moist stratification.

Thalictrum delavayi Franch

An Asian species ranging from East Tibet to West China, this elegant perennial grows to around a hundred and fifty centimetres in good conditions. It has a slightly pendulous appearance and flowers with a light, lovely purple pink colour in late summer. Planted among shrubs and trees in irregular groups this gorgeous species makes the natural woodland scene magic and look like hundreds of little elves are dancing together.

264 – Thalictrum delavayi
Courtesy Baumschule Horstmann, Germany

Thalictrum rochebrunnianum Franch et Sav

This impressive species grows to two hundred and fifty centimetres in height and is, with its foliage, as structural plant very ornamental right into late autumn. The flowers appear in late summer and range from a light lavender to white. There is a highly recommended cultivar 'Lavender Mist' in the trade with purple flowers and golden-yellow stamens that like the straight species, is best used in small irregular, natural groups for structure.

Thelionema; Phormiaceae (Liliaceae)

Thelionema caespitosum syn Stypandra caespitosa

This tufted plant with grass-like leaves resembles a miniature flax somewhat. It grows to thirty centimetres and bears blue, star-like flowers to two centimetres on slender, branched stems in spring. It is easy and requires well-drained soils in full sun or light shade and is propagated by division.

Themeda; Poaceae

The, for horticulture important species of the genus of Themeda are at home mainly in the temperate and warm-temperate zones of East Asia, Africa and Australia. They describe ornamental grasses, some up to three hundred centimetres in height.

Themeda japonica Willd
This outstanding and drought-hardy species becomes active late in spring, later than many perennials and should therefore be combined with early effective partners. The plant grows in dense clumps with up to a hundred and twenty centimetres high foliage that changes to a gorgeous reddish colour as the late summer progresses. It requires warmth and sun and I would recommend using it as a structural plant in small groups. Propagation is by division in spring or seed in winter. I remember that the seeds were very popular with mice, so it may be worth investing in a protective cover for them.

Themeda triandra (former T. australis)
This is a perennial tussock-forming grass widespread in Africa, Australia, Asia and the Pacific. In Australia, it is commonly known as kangaroo grass. In eastern and South Africa, it is also known as red grass. Use in the landscape in natural and wild designs as a structural plant and for the lovely seed heads.

Thermopsis; Fabaceae

These perennials are related to and like Lupins in their appearance and use in the landscape. The around thirty species come from North America, North India and North-East Asia and most of them form runners. Also like the Lupins they have deeply penetrating taproots and can be used on heavy clay soils as well as in light and sandy environments. I would recommend them mainly for natural and wild designs but they are also suited to semi-formal or cottage garden settings.

Thermopsis divaricarpa Nelson
Hailing from the USA, Wyoming, Colorado and Utah the 'Golden Banner' has striking golden-yellow flowers in summer and grows to around sixty centimetres. The species ascends to the montane zone and grows in open forests as well as meadows.

Thermopsis mollis Curtis ex Gray
The probably largest species in this genus grows to a hundred and fifty centimetres in height and is at home in the south-eastern USA. The flowers are of a lively yellow in summer.

Thermopsis rhombifolia Nutt ex Richards
This species tolerates dry conditions better than the other representatives of this genus. It grows naturally in sandy to loamy soils in open, mixed woodlands and open meadows. The yellow flowers appear in early summer and stand at forty centimetres.

Thomasia; Sterculiaceae

Thomasia pygmaea
A low, spreading ground cover to twenty centimetres high that resembles a larger Thyme a little. This sub-shrub stands out with its abundant pink, cupped flowers in spring and early summer. Needs well-drained soil in full sun or dappled shade and is great in the rockery or trailing down over dry-stone walls.

Thymus; Lamiaceae

There are around three hundred and fifty species of Thymus. Most of those are aromatic perennials, sub-shrubs or shrubs extending from temperate Europe to Asia. This is an almost irreplaceable genus for gardens and landscapes with numerous species, subspecies and hybrids. Without trying to cause offence, I found that some of the names of plants offered in the trade may be questionable. However, regardless of botanic terminology they are highly valuable for many places and uses in horticulture and their suitability may be judged by simply looking at them closely. The species and subspecies that form mats are fantastic ground covers, structural plants for heathlands or may form beautiful colonies in dry stone walls or rockeries. Most are very drought hardy and tolerate a wide range of soils except for heavy, poorly drained and wet grounds. I would also recommend in terms of nutrition either not to fertilise at all or to feed only sparingly and low in nitrogen. They can be a great partner and structure for small bulbous plants and of course, Thymus vulgaris is almost a necessity in the herb and medicinal garden. Other than these suggestions I can recommend combinations with Alyssum montanum, Anaphalis triplinervis, Antennaria, Anthemis marshalliana, Anthericum, Dianthus deltoids, Dianthus gratianopolitanus, small Campanula, Dryas, Helianthemum species, Iris pumila, Origanum, Scutellaria baicalensis, Sedum, Sempervivum, Sesleria caerulea, Coreposis verticillata and small ornamental grasses. Propagation is easy by division or cuttings; I found autumn the best time, when the plants slow down and start to prepare for winter.

Thymus cherlerioides Vis
This small, mat-forming species is at home in the mountains of the Crimea and the Balkans. It grows prostrate, to ten centimetres and flowers purple in late summer. It is a beautiful plant for the rockery or to colonise dry stone walls.

Thymus x citridorus Schreb
The natural cross between Thymus vulgaris x Thymus pulegioides originates in southern France. It is an upright small sub-shrub growing to thirty centimetres with highly fragrant, lemon-scented foliage and light pink flowers in summer. It has many cultivars mainly grown for their foliage, some selected examples are:
'Argenteus' – fifteen centimetres; white variegated foliage, light pink flowers
'Doone Valley' – ten centimetres; yellow-green foliage, purple flowers
'Silver King' – twenty-five centimetres; grey-silvery variegated foliage with intense lemon scent

Thymus praecox Opiz
The around ten-centimetre-high species is fast-growing and suitable for green roofs, heathland designs or low meadow plantings on poor, shallow soils and flowers pink in early summer.

Thymus pseudolanuginosus Ronn
This special Thyme forms large, dense grey mats and gives large rockeries or dry stone walls a distinct character. To me it almost looks like magic, bewitched landscape as it often covers even large rocks entirely. Small bulbs and Campanula are great partners.

Thymus serpyllum L
The variable, usually only around ten-centimetre-high species is an old medicinal herb and used and recorded already in the Middle Ages. It thrives on dry, acidic and sandy soils but is not too fussed about higher PH levels. Good combinations are with Achillea, Alyssum, Antennaria, Anthericum, Anthemis, small Campanula, small Dianthus, Helianthemum, small Iris and bulbs. It should be noted that the plants can be overcome by strong competitors, therefore place and combine thoughtfully. There are many lovely cultivars available, I can recommend:
'Atropurpureum' – five centimetres high; crimson-red flowers

'Coccineus' – five centimetres high; reddish foliage and bright red flowers
'Purple Beauty' – around 10 centimetres high, also a ground cover with purple-pink flowers

Thymus vulgaris L

This old medicinal and spice plant has been in cultivation since ancient times around the Mediterranean and is recorded north of the Alps at around 1100 AD. It is found in kitchen and herb gardens of monasteries, schools and of course, private gardens. Its origin is the western Mediterranean down to southern Italy where it grows usually in colonies in dry, rocky meadows and Macchias. The plant gets to around thirty centimetres in height and is a highly aromatic sub-shrub. The flowers are light purple to pink, sometimes almost white. Aside from its medicinal and culinary properties, Thymus is also a highly valuable ornamental plant with many applications in the gardens and landscapes. I often use it as a subtle but very effective structural plant to form informal natural soft rockeries or heathland designs. I would combine them with Helianthemum, Cistus, small and large bearded Iris, ornamental small grasses and of course Origanum, Rosmarinus and Lavandula. From walking the beautiful landscapes in the Mediterranean, I still vividly remember the lovely clouds of scent emanating from the Thyme heathlands and imagined I would just keep walking around there for the rest of my life.

264 – Thymus vulgaris in the wild
Italy, 1990

Thysanothus; Anthericaceae (Liliaceae)

This is a small and varied genus of perennials, named 'Fringed Lilies' in Australia after their petals with long, fringed margins. They range from tufted, grass-like plants to tuberous perennials and weak climbers. They are easily grown from seed but vary considerably in their requirements. They appear to be attractive to snails.

Thysanothus juncifolius

This freely flowering species rewards good cultivation for most of the year, with lovely purple inflorescences that individually last only a few hours but are produced so frequently that it appears as if the plant is almost continuously in flower. It has short, grass-like leaves and requires full sun with plenty of moisture.

Thysanothus patersonii

This is a weak climber growing from a tuberous rootstock to around eighty or ninety centimetres. It also flowers over a long period and requires full sun and well-drained soils. Use in the landscape in natural or wild designs or larger rockeries where the plant may climb into structural shrubs or rocks.

265 – Thysanothus patersonii
Courtesy Tracey Simmons

Thysanothus tuberosus

A grass-like species that develops a tuberous root system and holds its flowers around twenty centimetres high. It flowers from spring to summer and requires sunny, well-drained locations. Propagation is by seed or division.

Tiarella; Saxifragaceae

This small genus of around four species originates in North America, with one representative from East Asia. Their use in the landscape is mainly as a tolerant and social ground cover for shady and semi-shady places, with sufficient moisture among woody ornamentals. They are valuable because of their social nature as they complement other plants of this habitat without crowding them out. They have mostly evergreen foliage, sometimes with lovely autumn colours and an abundance of white or pink flowers in spring. Great partners are Corydalis, Sanguinaria, Hosta, Polygonatum, Smilacina, Uvularia, shade-tolerant grasses and ferns.

Tiarella cordifolia L

In moist, rich soils of mountain forests of North America lives this well-known species which forms large and dense carpets with its runners. The plant grows to thirty centimetres and prefers slightly acidic soils covered by the fallen leaves of the deciduous shrubs and trees they naturally live under.

There are numerous nice horticultural cultivars that are mostly derived from crossing T. wherryi and T. polyphylla; best check with local suppliers.

Trachelium; Campanulaceae

The Trachelium are an interesting genus of Campanulaceae originating in the Mediterranean and the Balkans, where they thrive on limestone soils.

Trachelium jacquinii Boiss
A valuable late flowering plant from the mountains of Greece, Bulgaria and Rumelia. It is a great addition to dry rockeries or dry-stone walls and should be planted into rock crevices. It develops to twenty centimetres and flowers light blue from late summer to autumn, a time when many other rockery plants are not in colour. Good combinations are low Artemisia, Helianthemum, small Iris and grasses. Propagation is by seed or cuttings and best done in spring.

Trachystemon; Boraginaceae

Only two species represent this genus and only one is relevant in cultivation.

Trachystemon orientalis Don
An excellent, large-leaved ground cover for larger landscapes or parks that is reliable and after establishment, just about weed-free. The species comes from eastern Bulgaria, northern Turkey and the western Caucasus, where it grows in moist Beech forests (Fagus sylvatica) and along rivers and creeks. It ascends to around a thousand metres altitude. Its main feature is the large, to thirty centimetres long, heart-shaped leaves; the flowers are blue, held at around forty centimetres and are developed before the leaves in early spring. Propagation is easy by seed, division or root cuttings (best in winter).

Tradescantia; Commelinaceae

An American genus of around a hundred species, describing upright or prostrate plants from cool-temperate to tropical zones. They are easy to grow and a good complement for summer plantings of strong partners in informal or natural, moist settings. Hemerocallis, Iris sibirica or Miscanthus are such examples. I would recommend keeping Tradescantia in 'wilder' designs as they can become weedy and dominate and even suppress weaker partners, but are not structurally effective for a significant part of the year. Propagation is by cuttings or division.

Tradescantia x andersoniana Ludwig et Rohweder
The parents of the numerous garden hybrids are T. virginiana, T. ohiensis and T. subaspera. Their flowering time is predominantly from summer into autumn and they are robust plants. In cultivation, I recommend cutting them back regularly after flowering as they produce new flowers and this also reduces self-sowing, which can become a problem. Wild seedlings usually have blue-purple to white-pink tones.

Tricyrtis; Tricyrtidaceae (Convallariaceae/Uvulariaceae)

Of the 'Toad-Lily' there are nineteen species from the Himalayas extending to Japan, Korea and Taiwan. 'Krötenlilien' (German for Toad-Lily) are best planted in spring into acidic, rich and well-drained soils of semi-shaded or shaded habitats. They become active very early in spring and are therefore sensitive to late frosts. These plants are best used as precious highlights or collector's items that are valuable through their sometimes very late flowering time. Propagation is by seed with cold-moist stratification necessary, division in spring or cuttings in summer. Commercially, I found this to be the most efficient method.

Tricyrtis formosana Baker

This handsome plant comes from Taiwan and develops to a metre or more in good conditions. The flowers are white, often with a crimson hue and red spots; the flowers appear over a long period from summer into late autumn.

Tricyrtis hirta Hook

The 'Hairy Toad-Lily' from Japan also grows to around a metre, with a slightly pendulous habit. Flowers are white with purple spots in autumn. There are some cultivars like 'Alba' with white flowers and purple-grey anthers and 'Variegata' with an upright habit and a golden band along its leaves.

Tricyrtis nana Yatabe

The 'Dwarf Toad-Lily' is, as the name suggests, only around fifteen centimetres high with yellow flowers and lovely spotted leaves that are a feature in themselves. For the collector. The USA and Japan have developed a selection of hybrids and cultivars, best to check with local suppliers for availability.

Trillium; Trilliaceae

An interesting genus of around fifty species with a selection of common names like 'Wood Lily', 'Birthroot', 'Wake Robin', 'Toadshade', 'Dreiblatt' (Three-Leaf) and 'Wachslilie' (Wax Lily) and possibly more. North America, Camtchatka, Japan and the Himalayas are home to this upright forest perennial from five to eighty centimetres in height. As a forest plant, the genus thrives in cool, light to deep shade and rich, deep and lightly acidic soils formed by deciduous trees. They are of a unique beauty and worth every effort to cultivate them, even when it takes some years for them to develop their full beauty. They require water, especially in spring and sometimes require some extra iron in case the soil is closer to a neutral PH. In newly constructed landscapes, I would recommend waiting, with the introduction of Trillium, until the structure of a new landscape has established. Propagation is traditionally by division in autumn but this method of course is slow and yields low numbers. In-vitro propagation may prove commercially the most efficient method. Seed is possible but requires patience; germination often takes place between three and seven years. Using perfectly fresh seed is best; often germination starts straight away. Together with Corydalis, small Hosta and ferns or all by themselves, Trillium can create magical scenes where one can imagine fairies, forest nymphs and elves floating amongst their foliage and flowers.

Trillium album Freemann

The 'White Toadshade' or Freemann's Trillium is an outstanding beauty under open trees and shrubs that combines well with Snowflakes and Corydalis. It lives in mixed forests and in the proximity of rivers in loamy soils. It grows upright and to around sixty centimetres, with broad leaves that start in sping with dots that then fade as the growing season progresses. In spring, the flowers are large with petals up to eight centimetres in length and three centimetres wide, of a waxy-white to yellowish white, at the base pinkish. On warm days, there the plant has a wonderful rose perfume with Rose/lemony scent.

Trillium kurabayashii Freemann

This strong growing Trillium develops to around 60cm with ornamental spotted foliage that in itself is a feature. It originates in the USA, from coastal areas of Oregon to California, the Klamath Mountains and extending to the Sierra Nevada. The sessile flowers vary from dark crimson to yellowish green, appear in early summer and have an amazing scent resembling pineapples and oranges. I would highly recommend this species as it combines well with Rhododendron and tolerates competition in the root zone well. Often lovely seedlings appear in established plantings and delight with surprise colour combinations.

Trillium luteum Harbison

The 'Yellow Trillium' thrives in open deciduous forests of the USA from North Carolina to southern Kentucky. It grows to forty centimetres, with the young foliage being strongly spotted; as the leaves mature the spotting fades. The flowers vary from lemon yellow to greenish yellow with yellow stamens in early summer. In the Smoky Mountains National Park, they grow together with Trillium grandiflorum, low and high Phloxes, Lilium and Hepatica under Liriodendron tulipifera, fragrant Magnolia and the beautiful Cornus, creating stunning scenes worth trying for friendly parkland designs, wider landscapes or large gardens.

266 – Trillium luteum
Courtesy Pacific Bulb Society

Trillium recurvatum Beck

From moist forests and slopes to the dry highlands of the USA comes the 'Prairie Trillium' that unlike many Trillium, thrives in neutral to slightly alkaline soils. It is an upright perennial to fifty centimetres with horizontal foliage and sessile flowers that vary from a dark chestnut brown to crimson and yellow colours in early summer. This species I would recommend more for the collector to create very special garden rooms with partners like Cypripediuum, Dicentra, Primula, Hosta, Thalictrum and ferns. As it is obvious from such combinations, these scenarios require intensive maintenance.

Trillium rivale Watson
A very attractive small Trillium for shady rockeries that combines well with small ferns and Selaginella; this species also comes from the USA. Naturally it grows on grassy slopes, Pine forests and woodland margins in a range of soils from most to dry. The flowers vary from white to pink, sometimes feature nice spots and light-yellow stamens. It flowers in spring.

Trillium simile Gleason
There is only a small natural habitat of the 'Sweet White Trillium' in North Georgia and North Carolina. The plant thrives in deciduous forests where there is a lot of light penetration before the leaves of the trees appear. The species grows to fifty centimetres and features attractive large, creamy-white flowers with clearly visible nervatur in spring. The flowers exude a pleasant, fine apple-like scent.

Trillium sulcatum Patrick
This very beautiful plant comes from the southern parts of West Virginia to Kentucky and Georgia to Alabama and after its areas of distribution, is also called 'Southern Red Trillium'. It prefers cool, moist forests with neutral to slightly acidic soil properties. The species is moderately large, up to seventy centimetres with horizontal leaves and large, variable flowers from dark red-brown to crimson, yellow or white, very often with attractive stripes in early summer. I would use it in the landscapes and gardens for smaller or larger natural woodland scenes, maybe together with Dicentra, Hepatica, Jeffersonia diphylla, Thalictrum, Acquilegia, Podophyllum peltatum and Viola.

Tritileia; Alliaceae

A genus from western North America, Tritileia are fantastic cut flowers. The different species occupy greatly varying habitats and consequently have very different requirements in cultivation. They are bulbous perennials and combine well in plantings with summer-flowering species of rockeries of steppe and prairie designs; examples may be Anaphalis, Liatris spicata, Anthemis, Hieracium, Geranium sanguineum and G. cinereum, Yucca, Sedum, Cistus and the like.

Tritileia ixioides Greene
From Pine and Oak forests of the USA and California comes this lovely species that thrives in sandy soils and ascends to around fifteen hundred metres altitude. The flowers grow to eighty centimetres and are yellowish with a dark central stripe in summer. I would recommend its use in the landscape in natural designs of rockeries or open parks and woodlands, much as in its natural habitat but also as supplement for perennial borders.

267 – Tritileia ixioides
Courtesy Stephan Willenberger

Trollius; Ranunculaceae

The genus of Trollius derives its name from ancient German and translates loosely into 'round as a ball'. This describes well the shape of most of its species' flowers. Trollius are at home in the cool-temperate to cold zones of the northern hemisphere, there are around thirty species of low to medium perennials. They are plants of moist to wet meadows and prefer medium to heavy soils, the more sun they receive, the more water they need. Given their requirements are met they are graceful, long-lived plants ideally suited for colourful borders, or wet to swampy areas in parks and greater landscapes that can be 'let go'. Great partners are Aster, Anchusa, Astilbe, Brunnera, Campanula persicifolia, Dicentra, Filipendula, Geranium, Geum, Hosta, moisture-loving Iris, Myosotis, Primula and Thalictrum. Propagation is by division straight after flowering or in late winter (just before first growth), by dividing the mother stock into small sections with at least two growing points. Seed is possible with straight species and requires cold-moist stratification.

Trollius asiaticus L

From the cold spheres of actic Siberia, central Asia, northern Mongolia and north-western China comes this very variable species that is characterised by its glowing orange flowers. The up to eighty-centimetre-tall plants live in the Tundra, in forests, meadows and in the subalpine zones of mountain ranges. Ideally a plant for natural and wild places, I would recommend using it in heathlands, steppes and other wild designs.

Trollius chinensis Bunge

From Russia to China extends the home of this up to hundred and twenty-centimetre-tall species. The flowers are from four to sixty centimetres across and come in shades of orange. Special to this species are the honey leaves that keep growing during the flowering and can become up to four centimetres long, making the entire flower structure very ornamental. There is a variety, 'Imperial Orange' that can be grown true from seed and is very beautiful and long flowering. All these plants require moisture and rich nutrition.

Trollius europaeus L

The Europaean representative extends form the Polar region down to the Mediterranean and to Siberia where it grows in wet meadows, along rivers, in open deciduous and mixed forests and the Tundra. In southern Europe, it grows almost exclusively in the mountains. The plants grow to ninety centimetres in height and flower in early summer with round, yellow ball-like flowers. There is a great cultivar 'Superbus' with larger, glowing yellow flowers but it is often hard to get.

Horticultural cultivars and hybrids of Trollius

Starting around 1830 many breeds and selections of Trollius were developed, some recommended examples:
'Byrne's Giant' – ninety centimetres with large, pure yellow flowers in early summer
'Etna' – seventy centimetres with dark foliage and flat, glowing yellow flowers in early summer
'Golden Monarch' – seventy centimetres, slow growing but beautiful with glowing flowers
'Hohes Licht' – ninety centimetres, slow growing but developing to gorgeous plants
'Orange Globe' – eighty centimetres, a great reliable classic with golden-orange flowers

Tulipa; Liliaceae

Central Asia is the original home of the Tulips, bulbous perennials with some species forming runners. There are around one hundred species naturally and innumerous cultivars and hybrids in cultivation. Tulips require sun and warmth, very good drainage and two distinct periods of dormancy, one in winter and one in summer when the plants need to 'bake', as this is the way of life they have adapted to. In long-term garden and landscape cultivation, it is important to leave their foliage and let it die back naturally, as this is the time when the plant harvests and stores energy for the next flower. Nutrition should be in favour of K in the N-K balance as with most bulbous plants. Use in the landscape is mainly in two different ways; one is the massed formal bedding display, mainly of Tulipa hybrids and cultivars and the other is the informal use of Tulipa species in natural and wild designs. The actual art of bedding display I would like to discuss in a separate book. Here, I will list some species for use in informal designs and only refer to the classes of Tulipa used in formal bedding displays. In saying that, these hybrids and cultivars can of course be used ad libitum in any garden design and the wild species alike in formal displays. I intend to refer to these purposes merely as an historic observation.

Tulipa acuminata Vahl ex Hornem

The 'Horned Tulip' is known in cultivation since the seventeenth century, from Turkey. The plant grows to fifty centimetres with short, blue-green leaves with a slightly wavy margin and long, pointy flowers that range from bright red to yellowish in late spring.

Tulipa clusiana var chrysantha Sealy

From northern Afghanistan comes this twenty-centimetre-high subspecies of the 'Lady Tulip'. The petals are deep yellow inside with crimson red outside, flowering in spring and performing well in the long-term in landscapes and gardens.

Tulipa humilis Herb

A small, 'cute' Tulip from sourth-eastern Turkey, north-western Iran, northern Iraq and Aserbaidschan, this species grows to only ten centimetres high. The flowers are held upright already in the bud and are purple-pink with a yellow base. They almost look like small Easter eggs and appear very early in spring. I would use it in small rockeries or natural, small dry perennial borders.

Tulipa kaufmanniana Regel

On rocky slopes of the mountains of Central Asia thrives this twenty-centimetre-tall plant. The foliage is blue-green with wavy margins and the flowers are creamy-white with a dark yellow base and crimson-red stripes on the outside of the petals in early spring.

Tulipa praestans Hoog

Tadchikistan, Central Asia and Pamir are home to this pure red Tulip with black stamens. It grows naturally in open woodlands and on slopes with deep soils to around forty centimetres. I would recommend it for its endurance over the years in many garden situations, rockeries, but also in steppe and prairie settings.

Tulipa saxatilis Sprenger

From the beautiful island of Crete and from western Turkey comes this twenty-centimetre small species. It has delicate light purple-pink flowers, the buds are nodding and it has a lovely fragrance in early spring.

Tulipa sylvestris L

The 'Forest-Tulip' is widespread through Europe and around the Mediterranean where it grows in open woodlands, meadows and is often found in vineyards. The plant gets to thirty centimetres with the bulb forming runners. The flowers are yellow with a greenish hue on the outside of the petals. The flowers range from nodding to upright but all have a nice fragrance.

268 – Tulipa sylvestris
Courtesy Wikipedia

Tulipa hybrids and cultivars
These are divided into different classes, I have listed these classes here but for the innumerous varieties I would check with available suppliers, as they often change as fashions come or go.

Class 1: Single and early Tulips; from twenty-five to thirty-five centimetres in height and with single, small flowers of all colours

Class 2: Double early Tulips; twenty-five to thirty-five centimetres in height, with double and early flowers which includes the 'Murillo' varieties of 1860, fragrant, from white to pink

Class 3: Triumph Tulips; medium Tulips flowers small, single and appearing after the early Tulips, often cultivated for the cut flower trade

Class 4: Darwin Tulips; long stems from fifty to seventy centimetres with single, large flowers, long-lived in garden cultivation

Class 5: Single, late Tulips; usually long, up to sixty-five-centimetre stems with medium-sized, single flowers that appear late in the season (late spring)

Class 6: Lily-flowered Tulips, from forty to sixty-centimetre-long stems bearing single flowers in all colours with the petals turned outward resembling small Lilies, they flower intermediate to late in the season, excellent for garden use or perennial border

Class 7: Fringed Tulips; intermediate to late flowering types with fringed petals

Class 8: Viridiflora Tulips; thirty to fifty-centimetre-high late flowering Tulips with partially green petals, more suited for special locations in rockeries or as individual features

Class 9: Rembrandt Tulips; available today are mostly recent historic varieties with strongly expressed stripes caused by viral infections. The actual historic Rembrandt Tulips were strongly flamed Tulips but deliberately bred, not caused by a virus

Class 10: Parrot Tulips; single flowers in all colours with the petals held wide apart, most flower late in the season, they are more a curiosity

Class 11: Double late Tulips; usually long-stemmed late varieties, double flowers

Class 12: Tulipa kaufmanniana hybrids; varieties originating from crossing with T. kaufmanniana, height to around twenty centimetres with star-like flowers and very early flowers, often with crimson-red base or markings, great to use in the rockery, in tubs or small borders, less suited to massed displays

Class 13: Tulipa forsteriana; crosses with T, forsteriana with stems between thirty and fifty centimetres and very large flowers, best in small groups in rockeries or borders

Class 14: Tulipa greigii; crosses with T. greigii, twenty to thirty centimetres, often multi-coloured and late flowering; the foliage is also attractive, many applications

Class 15: Wild Tulip species

The history of Tulips goes back at least a thousand years when they have been cultivated in the Persian Empire. They 'migrated' only at around the sixteenth century to Europe; the first use is documented privately in Germany in 1550 and the Botanic Gardens in Leiden in 1593. It soon became clear that sandy soils are best suited for their cultivation and the area between Leiden and Harleem in Holland grew famous for its massed displays of Tulips. The time of the 'Tulipomania' when incredible sums of money were paid for bulbs was between 1630 and around 1637.

Typha; Typhaceae

This small genus of around fifteen species is almost cosmopolitan and includes plants of wet meadows, swamps, riparian zones and other wet places. The thick rhizomes carry upright stems with long leaves and brown spadixes which are popular in dried flower arrangements.

Typha angustifolia L

A widespread species extending from Europe to Asia and North America. It lives in water depth between twenty and sixty centimetres and grows to around two hundred centimetres tall. This very competitive plant is best used in large landscapes as erosion control and pioneer pant, it is not well suited for the garden.

Uvularia; Uvulariaceae

The only four species consisting genus of Uvularia is named 'Merry-bells' or 'Trauerglocken' (Mourning Bells) after its pendulous bell-shaped flowers.

Uvularia grandiflora Smith

Originating in North America from Quebec to Minnesota, Oklahoma and Georgia this species grows to sixty centimetres in height. It requires rich soils and naturally lives in mixed forests. The dark yellow flowers appear in late spring to early summer. It is a very slow growing and extremely valuable plant for woodlands, under trees in parklands or for shady, natural garden designs.

Valeriana; Valerianceae

The genus Valeriana contains around two hundred annuals, perennials, sub-shrubs and shrubs in Eurasia, South Africa, temperate North America and the Andes. The thickened taproots have a strong scent, but the entire plant and all its parts are scented. Their uses in landscapes and gardens are as medicinal plants or specimen plants for collections in the rockery, alpinum or historic herb and medicinal display gardens. The tall species may also be used and are beautiful in lightly shaded woody areas or perennial borders. Most Valeriana prefer moist to wet soils but do well in drier locations in average garden soils. The smaller species are best used in rockeries or the alpinum. Except for V. celtica and V. dioica that are hostile to alkaline soil conditions Valeriana require calcium and do well in gravelly soils and rock crevices. Propagation is by seed (requiring light for germination), division or cuttings.

Valeriana alliariifolia Adams

Asia Minor, Greece, the Balkans and the Caucasus are home to this very beautiful species for moist, natural garden designs. The plants grow to ninety centimetres and flower pink to whitish pink in summer. In their natural habitat, they are in communities with Aruncus dioicus, Dactylorhiza, Geranium psilostemon, Brunnera macrophylla, Tanacetum macrophyllum, Petasites and Symphytum and these are obviously great partners in the designed gardens as well.

Valeriana alpestris Stev

This lovely Valerian comes from wet meadows and moors of the Caucasus and north-eastern Turkey where it ascends to the subalpine zones. This species grows to sixty centimetres and has ball-like, bright sulphur-yellow flowers in summer.

Valeriana officinalis L

The well-known medicinal plant or common Valerian is widespread from Europe to Asia and has been introduced to North America. Naturally inhabiting moist but also drier alkaline meadows, wet lowlands, moors, open woodlands and riparian zones. The plants grow to a handsome one hundred and fifty centimetres on rich soils and have fragrant, white to light pink umbels. It is a variable species and has been documented in cultivation before 1500 AD for use of its roots; propagation is best by seed (requires light).

269 – Valeriana officinalis
Courtesy Henriette Kress

Valeriana supina Ard
This wonderful dwarf Valerian coming from gravelly, alkaline slopes of the central Alps grows to only fifteen centimetres. It has gorgeous light to dark pink flowers in spring and is a great addition to small rockeries or dry-stone walls.

Valeriana tuberosa L
From Russia to the Mediterranean, we can find this species adapted to drier meadows and rocky slopes. The plants grow to forty centimetres and have light pink flowers with a delicate fragrance in spring. A great plant for the natural, drier rockery or wild meadows and in between shrubs and trees.

Velleia; Goodeniaceae

Velleia paradoxa
This perennial from Australia grows to twenty centimetres high with flowering stems standing around fifty centimetres. The flowers are yellow and appear in spring and summer. The plant needs well-drained soils in a sunny position and self-sows but does not become weedy. I would use it in natural designs or rockeries as a pleasant filler.

Veratrum; Melianthaceae

The around fifty species of Veratrum are usually found in montane meadows and whilst most are disliked in nature as strong and competitive poisonous perennials, it can be a very impressive display feature in the larger rockery or the alpinum. Deep, rich and heavy soils are best, good partners are Ligularia, Smilacina, Trollius, ornamental grasses and ferns. Propagation is quickest by division, seedlings require a long time to fully develop. The dried flowers are great for arrangements in the vase.

Veratrum album L
From the mountains of Eurasia comes this up to two-hundred-centimetre-tall perennial with elliptic leaves and impressive, up to sixty centimetres long, white to greenish-white flower displays in late summer.

270 – Veratrum album
Courtesy Wikipedia

Veratrum nigrum L
The dark brother of the White False Hellebore is an elegant, up to a hundred and twenty-centimetre-tall perennial which can be used in many applications in large rockeries or natural montane displays but also in the less formal perennial border. The flowers are dark crimson and appear in late summer. This species requires more moisture and does well together with Primula, Ranunculus, Aconitum, Trollius in heavy soils.

Verbascum; Scrophulariaceae

The 'King's Candle' (Königskerze, German) contains well over two hundred and fifty species of mostly tall biannual and less frequently perennial plants or sub-shrubs. The biannual species form a rosette of basal leaves in the first year, out of which in the second year, after a cool dormant phase, the flowers emerge. Most species love drought and sun-baked, well-drained soils. Use in the landscape in natural tall heath, meadows or steppes or the larger rockeries, where they stand out with their imposing structure and long flowering period. As always, the key to successful designs is the knowledge of the plant's characteristics and behaviour in the environment. Verbascum may also become weedy through self-seeding. Propagation is by seed or root cuttings for the perennial species.

Verbascum bombyciferum Boiss

This very handsome, up to two metres tall 'Silky King's Candle' (Seidenhaar Königskerze, German) comes from western Asia Minor. The entire plant is covered with dense, white felty hair, hence the common name. The flowers are held on a straight upright stalk and are sulphur-yellow in late summer. The plant is best used as a feature and structural plant in natural rockeries, dry heath and steppe designs with well-drained, sandy soils that bake in summer. It is sometimes known in the trade as 'Polarsommer'.

271 – Verbascum bombyciferum
Courtesy Baumschule Horstmann, Germany

Verbascum densiflorum Bertol

This large-flowered species is widespread throughout Eurasia, as far north as south-eastern Sweden and as far south as North Arica. Generally, it occupies moderately dry, rocky or gravelly soils in a large variety of habitats and is a pioneer plant on disturbed soils. It is a biannual, therefore requiring regular repropagation unless the plant is 'let go' to colonise and find its own existence in natural and wild designs. Flowering time is summer to autumn, the large flowers are beautiful.

Verbascum nigrum L

The 'Dark King's Candle' extends from eastern Siberia, Scandinavia to Spain, Italy and the Balkans. It is often found along paths or roads in dry, sunny locations and ascends into the montane zone. The species grows to around a metre with felty, green leaves and features up to three to five centimetre wide, crimson-purple flowers in summer.

Verbascum phoeniceum L

Named after the ancient empire of the Phoenicians, a maritime trading culture, this species is a smaller perennial with crimson flowers. It is a smaller plant, ranging from thirty to a hundred centimetres in height and inhabiting disturbed ground, dry meadows and steppes with deeper soils. Its natural origin extends from south-eastern Europe to central Russia, Asia and to Iran. It flowers earlier than most other Verbascum in late spring and is a beautiful, usually long-lived plant for natural garden designs.

Verbascum wiedemannianum Fish et Mey

From dry heathlands and mountain steppes of north-eastern Turkey comes this up to one hundred and fifty-centimetre-tall species. Historically it has been used in the nineteenth century and was sometimes erroneously termed V. phoeniceum. It has larger, up to four centimetres wide, dark, crimson-purple flowers, usually with a white centre and flowers in late spring. The foliage is almost white and velvety and a feature. Jim Archibald collected the seed under number JCA 982950 of what is today in the trade under V. wiedemannianum. Propagation is not as easy as with other King's Candles; the plants are not self-fertile and the seeds often germinate erratically. In my experience, it is best to sow the seed fresh after harvest in early autumn and be patient. Otherwise, in larger-scale displays they are often able to self-reproduce and in this natural way make for the most beautiful displays.

Verbascum hybrids

There are many Verbascum hybrids available, mainly from crosses with V. phoeniceum. By and large they are short-lived and should be propagated by root cuttings, which in my experience is a nice exercise for winter in the shelter of the glasshouses when other work has slowed down.

'Boadicea' – a hundred and eighty centimetres; copper-coloured flowers with purple centre
'Cotswold Queen' – a hundred and twenty centimetres; golden-yellow large flowers with scarlet stamens
'Golden Bush' – fifty centimetres; multi-stemmed, rounded with bright yellow flowers
'Mont Blanc' –ninety centimetres; white flowers
'Silberkandelaber' – a hundred and fifty centimetres; silvery-white rosette, yellow flowers, true from seed

Verbena; Verbenaceae

The genus Verbena comprises around two hundred and fifty perennial species, sub-shrubs and shrubs in the tropical and temperate Americas. Some are used as annuals in displays but these are usually not hardy enough to be considered as perennials for this book. The species described here are perennials and suited for natural and wild designs in our gardens and landscapes.

Verbena bonariensis L

This tall, up to a hundred and eighty-centimetre perennial sustains itself usually through self-sowing over the years. It brings a lovely crimson-purple colour into natural and informal gardens.

Verbena hastata L

The 'Blue Verbena' or 'Simpler's Joy' is widespread in North America where it grows in swamps and wet meadows and follows creeks and rivers. Up to a hundred and fifty centimetres tall, it has small blue-purple, white or pink flowers from summer to autumn. It is very nice spread and let go in natural landscape designs for wet places, is valuable through the very long flowering period.

Vernonia; Asteraceae

This is a large genus with around a thousand species from annuals to trees. It occurs around the world in temperate to tropical zones with most important perennials coming from North America.

Vernonia arkansana DC

This tall, up to three hundred centimetres growing perennial lives in open, moist woodlands following rivers. Flowers are reddish purple with up to nine held in a wide, impressive corymb of twenty centimetres or more. A recommendable cultivar is 'Mammoth' growing up to around two hundred and twenty centimetres. Use in the landscape for informal large, moist areas in parks.

Veronica; Scrophulariaceae

Around three hundred annual or perennial species populate the genus Veronica, most of which live in the northern temperate zones, many in the mountains. Some botanists divide this genus into Pseudolysimachion and Veronica. For our purposes, this is not so significant, therefore I have listed all those I can personally recommend here under Veronica. The medium and high species are well suited to be used in perennial borders and the natural and wild garden. Many of these species are valuable because they flower late with the rarer blue tones and are quite hardy and adaptable in most average garden soils. The low, pillow-forming species are best used for their beauty in the rockery, dry stone wall or the alpinum.

Veronica allionii Vill

Growing in dry alpine low meadows on acidic soils this evergreen Veronica is one of my favourites for rockeries or dry-stone walls. It covers quickly large areas, is valuable for its evergreen, leathery foliage, adapts to full sun or semi-shade and has lovely, deep blue flowers in summer.

Veronica cinerea Boiss

The habitat of this species are gravelly, rocky limestone slopes of altitudes between thirteen hundred and two thousand eight hundred metres. The plant forms carpets of up to forty centimetres with its woody roots and prostrate, white felty leaves that are the main feature of this species. The flowers are dark blue to purplish and appear in summer. Great for rockeries and combines very well with bulbs.

Veronica formosa
This tufted perennial grows to around eighty centimetres tall with dark green elliptical leaves; sometimes it can reach up to two metres in good conditions. Light blue flowers are borne in sprays in spring and early summer. It adapts to a wide range of conditions from sun to shade but performs best in sun, use in the landscape like tall Aster.

Veronica fruticosa L
From the high limestone mountains of central and southern Europe comes this sub-shrub. I like using it as a structural plant for the alpinum and rock garden where it is valuable through its evergreen foliage. The flowers are light pink with dark veins and appear in great numbers in summer. Easy to grow, the species combines well with Arabis pumila, Androsace, Draba, Chrysanthemum haradjani, Iberis saxatilis, Potentilla caulescens, Globularia cordifolia, Saxifraga paniculata and low Phoxes.

Veronica gentianoides Vahl
The Caucasus, north-western Iran and central Anatolia are the home of this moisture-loving perennial. It grows to eighty centimetres in open woodlands and open, moist meadows and ascends to three thousand six hundred metres altitude. The flowers are held in up to twenty-centimetre-long racemes and are usually light blue, sometimes white in early summer. I would use this plant in the perennial border and larger rockeries in sunny or semi-shaded locations. I would recommend cutting it back after flowering.

Veronica liwanensis Koch
A very beautiful sub-shrub and ground cover to around ten centimetres with blue flowers through summer. It comes from Turkey and the Caucasus and grows in open, rocky places and sunny places of open Picea forests.

Veronica longifolia L
This is a very variable species from forty to a hundred and twenty centimetres in height, growing in moist places of Europe, Siberia and East Asia. Flowers are usually blue in late summer. It is parent to many valuable garden cultivars and hybrids:
　'Blauriesin' – eighty centimetres; strong growing and with glowing blue flowers
　'Pink Damask' – eighty centimetres; pink flowers
　'Schneeriesin' – eighty centimetres; white flowers

Veronica officinalis Mill
This widespread species grows in meadows and forests of Europe, Siberia, North America, north-western Iran, Anatolia and the Caucasus. The plant is around thirty centimetres high and flowers light purple to blue, with darker venation from spring to summer. Use in the landscape for wild scenes along woodlands.

Veronica prostrata L
This beautiful, lawn-forming ground cover is valuable for heathlands, rockeries or open meadows on dry soils in full sun. Its natural home are dry meadows and open Pine forests ascending to the montane zone. It is great in community with Helianthemum canum, Globularia cordifolia, Artemisia and stronger bulbs.

Veronica sachalinenis Yamaz
Dense purple-blue flowers in late summer are the mark of this plant that is best used in constantly moist soils in natural and wild designs along water features.

Veronica spicata L
One of the most beautiful but not very often used Veronicas is the around forty-centimetre-high 'Heide-Ehrenpreis'. It thrives only on dry, well-drained and sandy soils in full sun. Great for small dry perennial

borders, heath gardens or steppes it flowers pure blue from summer into autumn. Propagation is by division and stem cuttings. There are many horticultural hybrids and cultivars derived from V. spicata.

Veronicastrum; Asteraceae

This small genus of ten species inhabits the northern hemisphere from the Himalayas to Japan with one species from North America.

Veronicastrum sibiricum Pennell
This medium to tall perennial varies between eighty and a hundred and fifty centimetres in height. It flowers profusely with long, terminal purple-pink summer flowers and fruits that are attractive through winter. This plant can be used in many applications like in perennial borders but also as feature group planting with ornamental grasses, Iris spuria, Anthericum ramosum or Lilies.

272 – Veronicastrum sibericum
Planted in moist soil in a natural setting with Betula in the background

Viola; Violaceae

The around four species and subspecies of the genus Viola are distributed worldwide. It was the first plant I could identify and name as a child. Most Viola are annuals or biannuals, but there are perennials and sub-shrubs as well. Violas are divided into sections according to their flower form.

Section Dischidium (D)
These are cleistogam perennials, V. biflora and V. crassa.

Section Melanium (M)
Also, perennials, the plants of this section are often short-lived; the lateral petals are pointed up, colours are usually between blue, white or yellow. This section contains the well-known pansies popular in massed displays.

Section Viola (V)
These are mostly long-lived small perennials with open flowers from purple, blue to white and yellow.

Section Xylosinum (X)
Perennials or sub-shrubs with open, red-purple or yellow flowers.

'Rosulata' Viola species
These are species from the cold and dry steppes of the high Andees. They are plants for the collector and require special conditions and intense care in cultivation, usually a glasshouse where the conditions of their habitat are simulated.

Cultivation of Viola is very varied and ranges from extremely easy to highly sophisticated. For this book, I have listed here only easy species.

Viola aetolica (M) Boiss
This is a small, cute little plant for the rockery with two-centimetre-wide yellow flowers and sometimes red standards in spring. It self-sows but is not weedy.

Viola alba (V) Besser
Growing in open woodlands in warm, collin zones this species is up to fifteen centimetres high and forms runners. The flowers of spring are around two centimetres, white or light purple and fragrant.

Viola betonicifolia (V) Muell
This Australian species grows to around twelve centimetres with nodding, purple, light purple or white flowers in late summer.

Viola canina (V) L
A plant of the colder, moister areas of Europe, Asia and Camtchatka and extending as far north as Greenland. A lovely, wild little Viola for moist and wet zones in natural designs.

Viola cazorlensis (X) Gand
From gravelly, alkaline soils of south-eastern Spain comes this intensely crimson coloured Viola. It flowers in late spring and is ideal for the small rockery or in dry stone walls build with limestones.

Viola cornuta (M) L
The German common name 'Hornveilchen' loosely translates into something like 'horned Pansy' describing the around one-and-a-half-centimetre long spur of the flowers. They appear throughout summer and are of a strong purple. This species is important for breeding in horticulture and has produced many nice cultivars and hybrids. All these are easy and graceful, long-flowering plants for the natural rockery.

Viola lutea (M) Huds
This large-flowered Viola is at home in central and western Europe where it grows in montane to subalpine meadows and in between rocks. The flowers are up to four centimetres, yellow or purple, sometimes bicoloured in summer.

Viola odorata (V) L
The 'Fragrant Pansy' is widespread in Europe and around the Mediterranean. It is a plant mostly for shade and around trees and shrubs. The early spring flowers are dark purple and highly fragrant. There are quite a few nice cultivars and hybrids in the trade. They have been grown historically for the small vase but most historic plants have disappeared, apart from some traditional nurseries in England, France and Germany where they have been preserved. It may be one of the best known and most popular plants.

Viola tricolour (M) L
This very variable species grows from three to forty centimetres high and has an extremely long flowering period from early spring to autumn. The flowers are purple, blue, yellow or variegated with these colours. It is at home in Europe, western Siberia, Asia Minor, the Mediterranean and Africa.

Viola x wittrockiana (M) L
These are the well-known garden pansies that often form seasonal displays in parks or municipal areas and are just as often part of domestic plantings.

Vitaliana; Primulaceae

One species with several subspecies forms this small genus. They are related to Androsace and grow mostly on acidic gravelly soils of the Alps, the Pyrenees and in central and southern Spain in altitudes between one thousand seven hundred and three thousand five hundred metres. Best grown in well-drained slopes facing east, they are long-lived, graceful rockery plants that are less susceptible to fungal diseases than Androsace. Propagation is best by cuttings in late summer, seed requires cold-moist stratification.

Vitaliana primuliflora Bertol
Over rocks and on gravel this species develops dense pillows but when grown in grassy terrain they form large mats. The plants flower golden yellow in spring.

Wahlenbergia; Campanulaceae

The around a hundred and twenty species of annual or perennial plants are widespread, many of these in the southern hemisphere.

Wahlenbergia gloriosa Lothian
At home in subalpine zones of Australia, this plant usually has deep purple flowers in summer. They are best cultivated in slightly acidic, moist and well-drained soils mixed with humus and gravel or sand in full sun. They are often short-lived.

273 – Wahlenbergia gloriosa
Courtesy Gregs Indigenous Landscapes

Wahlenbergia stricta

The 'Native Bluebell' of Australia grows along paths and roads and what looks to me in often incredibly harsh, exposed conditions. It forms clumps, grows to forty centimetres and delights with fine, light blue flowers in spring and summer. I often use it in natural and wild landscapes and scatter small groups of them around so they can over the years self-sow and colonise where they want to be. I have never been disappointed with the results.

Waldsteinia; Rosaceae

This small genus contains six species and is also known as 'False Strawberry', which I find is an apt name. They are creeping small perennials and flower from spring into early summer. Use in the landscape as evergreen ground cover or to form colonies in the habitats woodland and forest, maybe together with Epimedium, Lamium and Lamiastrum, Pahysandra, Symphytum and Tiarella. They require moisture but otherwise they are extremely easy to grow and reliable. Propagation is by division.

Waldsteinia fragarioides Tratt

This American species grows to twenty centimetres and spreads through underground runners. Reliable and strong growing ground cover for natural and wild designs under trees and in parks. Due to its strong nature, it should not be partnered with delicate species.

Waldsteinia ternata Fritsch

From central Europe to eastern Siberia and Japan extends the home of this around fifteen-centimetre-high plant. This species is more suited to drier conditions and is sometimes used for planting on graves. The large yellow flowers appear in spring.

Watsonia; Iridaceae

Around eighty species from South Africa and Madagascar populate this genus. Cultivation is best in well-drained soils in full sun.

274 – Watsonia borbonica at Devils Peak
Courtesy Wikimedia

Watsonia densiflora Baker

An up to one hundred and fifty centimetres tall, strong and clumpy plant that holds its flowers in dense racemes. They are pink and flower from summer into autumn, the plants are usually hardy down to minus fifteen degrees Celsius.

Watsonia watsoniana Oberm

This species grows to a metre and has yellow flowers that are painted with darker brown stripes.

Wulfenia; Scrophularicaeae

These special plants are relicts from the Tertiary period like Ramonda. They are long-living rosette plants with strong, thick rhizomes and blue, white or pink flowers. Pretty but not spectacular plants, more for the collector of interesting plants than the landscape architect or gardeners in charge of large landscapes or parks. Wulfenia do not like free calcium in the soil and require lots of humus and light shade. During the growing seasons from spring to summer they like lots of moisture but in autumn and spring they become sensitive to too much water, so always plant in well-drained sites that are best faced away from the summer sun.

Wulfenia carinthiaca Jacq

In the south-eastern Alps and Austria lives this species in moist meadows of altitudes between fifteen hundred and two thousand metres. The plants form wide clumps and have up to thirty-centimetre-long, deep blue flowers in late spring. Good partners are Rhododendron ferrugineum, Veratrum lobelianum, Aposeris foetida and Athyrium filix-femina and Trollius europaeus, there is a great white form 'Alba' in the trade.

Wulfenia orientalis Boiss
From Asia Minor comes this very beautiful Wulfenia. It grows to around fifty centimetres and features blue to purple flowers in summer.

Xanthorrhoea; Xanthorrhoeaceae

The 'Grass Tree' of Australia is almost a symbol of the beautiful, vast outback and synonymous with scorching sun and heat. Essentially it is a sub-shrub, but there are also true perennials that are best used in natural Australian native designs but in saying that, this should not be exclusive and they may have a place in prairie and steppe designs, together with other flora from similar habitats. In any case, these plants are an exercise in patience and are slow growing; it will take many years before they show their full potential.

Xanthorrhoea macronema
This tufted, trunkless plant has linear, around a metre long leaves that rise from the ground. A creamy flower spike is held on a sturdy stem of a hundred to a hundred and fifty centimetres in height. It requires well-drained soils in full sun but tolerates a great deal of shade too.

Xanthorrhoea minor
This small, grass-like plant has arching, linear leaves to about eighty centimetres long. The leaves are usually concave in cross-section. This species does not develop an above ground trunk but has a branched subterranean trunk. This trunk can produce a multi-crowned habit with leafy clumps developing at the top of each trunk. Although grass-like in appearance, the leaves are stiffer than those of typical grasses.

Xanthorrhoea preissii
The 'Western Grass Tree' is widespread in south-western Australia and develops over many years an impressive, thick trunk that bears one or more long flower stalks that may stand sometimes two or more metres above the foliage. A superb structural plant for large rockeries, steppes, prairies or grasslands.

Xerochrysum; Asteraceae

The genus of Xerochrysum was split away from what was formerly called Helichrysum and comprises five species. I like using Xerochrysum in the natural landscape design for quick effect among other slower growing perennials, shrubs and trees. Usually I scatter groups (via seed) of them around the young structural plants, where they delight with their long-lasting flower displays and act as living mulch. They are being let go and can self-sow to their hearts' content whilst the long-term structural plans can take their time to fully develop. As they develop, the Xerochrysum reduces naturally and gradually disappears. In cold climates, re-sowing may be required. This way of developing a long-term structure is rewarding, reduces maintenance and gives a great show already in the first season.

Xerochrysum bracteatum syn. Bracteantha bracteata
The 'Yellow Everlasting Daisy' or Straw Flower is a variable species and contains annual and perennial forms. They have been bred extensively and quite a few nice forms are now available in the trade.

275 – Xerochrysum bracteatum
Queanbeyan, Australia

Xerochrysum viscosum syn. Bracteantha viscosa

An up to seventy-centimetre-tall perennial, sometimes annual with sticky leaves and three centimetres wide yellow flowers. Very easy to grow, it is a great filler plant for a large variety of applications like rockeries, prairies, steppes or open woodlands and among shrubs.

Xyris; Xyridaceae

This medium-sized genus contains around two hundred and fifty species of mostly herbaceous perennials. Use in the landscape in moist to wet locations.

Xyris operculata

This nice perennial has terete, rush-like leaves and pure yellow flowers. It is a lovely addition to the wet zone around water features but does also well in the rockery.

Yucca; Agavaceae

The around thirty species of Yucca are mostly sub-shrubs and perennials. They are variable plants and come from central to northern America where they grow in well-drained soils in loamy, often alkaline conditions. Their natural habitats are mostly steppes, prairies, semi-deserts but also forests. They can form a creeping or upright stem that branches. The leaves are usually stiff and some have impressive and fearsome spikes and care needs to be taken around them. Certainly, do not plant these anywhere near areas where children play. They are great as structural plants for large rockeries, semi-desert-like succulent designs, prairie or dry heath and steppe landscapes.

Yucca baccata Torr

In grassy steppes and open woodlands of southern and eastern North America comes this handsome plant with up to a hundred-centimetre-long blue-green leaves. The creamy-white flowers are held in an impressive raceme with the individual flowers up to five centimetres long. They are structural feature plants that may dominate the designed habitat and complemented with Asclepias tuberosa, Anchusa italic, Opuntia, Cistus laurifolius, bearded tall Iris, Artemisia, Eremurus and large bulbs.

Yucca filamentosa L

At home in the eastern United States, where the plant is also called 'Adam's Needle', probably for the thin, hairlike tip of the up to seventy-centimetre-long leaves. White to light creamy-yellow bell-like flowers appear in summer. Easy to grow in moist but not in water-logged soils, this plant may also be informally grouped together in uneven numbers to dominate a design with its unique character.

Yucca glauca Nutt ex Fraser

The plant forms short rhizomes that occasionally rise to a short stem. Grey-green leaves to seventy centimetres characterise this species that bears a gorgeous up to a hundred centimetre long flower stem with a heavy fragrance in summer.

Yucca gloriosa L

The 'Spanish Dagger' or sometimes also called 'Spanish Bayonet' has its name from the very unpleasant sharp spine at the ends of its leaves. When handling the plant, medieval armour is recommended as personal protective equipment. But aside from this the impressive Yucca grows to around two hundred centimetres tall and has pendulous, bell-like flowers in an awesome, sometimes more than a metre tall display.

There are many Yucca hybrids available, best check with local suppliers.

Zantedeschia; Araceae

This rhizotomous perennial has dormant periods during dry times.

Zantedeschia aethiopica Spreng

Large, up to forty-centimetre basal leaves and showy, white flowers with yellow stamens define this water and heat loving perennial. Often cultivated as cut flowers, it is also a tough perennial for moist or wet areas in warmer zones, however in cold climates the plant dies back just like during drought dormancy and reappears from its rhizomes when temperatures rise again.

Zauschneria; Onoagraceae

The 'Kolibri-Trompete' (German for Kolibri's trumpet) is named after the appearance of its bright orange-red flowers that appear in abundance and make for a highly attractive, if a little temperamental, species. The species Zauschneria californica is currently under discussion to be amalgamated with Epilobium.

Zigadenus; Melianthaceae (Liliaceae)

There are seventeen species in North America and one in north Asia and Japan. One of the more ominous common names is 'Death Camass'. They are bulbous perennials with linear, grass-like leaves and multi-flowered terminal inflorescences. They are best used in the landscape in natural, wild planting designs but may also be integrated in perennial borders or steppe plantings. The plant is highly toxic to farm animals and must not be planted where they could have access.

Zigadenus elegans Pursh

In moist forests and meadows from Alaska to Arizona grows this species in altitudes between sixteen hundred and four thousand. A small bulb bears thirty-centimetre-long blue-green leaves and up to a hundred-centimetre-tall flower spikes with greenish to yellow-green flowers in summer. Plant from full sun to semi-shade in any average garden soil.

References and literature

A Guide to Iris; Cambridge	British Iris Society
A History of Kitchen Gardening; Frances Lincoln	Campbell
A year in the life of Beth Chatto's gardens	Beth Chatto
Bauen mit Grün; Parey Buch Verlag Berlin	Niesel
Baukonstruktionslehre für Landschaftsarchitekten; Ulmer	Schegk/Brandl
Beth Chatto's Gravel Garden	Beth Chatto
Design on the Land – the Development of Landscape Architecture; Belknap-Harvard	Newton
Detailing for Landscape Architects; Wiley/Blackwell	Ryan/Allan/Rand
Die Freiland Schmuckstauden Bände 1 & 2; Ulmer Verlag	Jelitto/Schacht/Fessler
Die Stauden und ihre Lebensbereiche; Ulmer Verlag	Hansen/Stahl
Enzyklopädie der Gartengehölze; Ulmer Verlag	Bärtels
Foundations of Landscape Architecture; Wiley/Blackwell	Booth
Gartendenkmalpflege; Ulmer Verlag	Hennebo
Gartendenkmalpflege zwischen Konservieren und Rekonstruieren; Meidenbauer	Hajos/Wolschke-Bulmahn
Geländemodellierung für Landschaftsarchitekten; Birkhäuser	Petschek
Kulturpraxis der Freiland Schmuckstauden; Ulmer Verlag	Köhlein/Bindlach
Landscapes in Historic Building Conservation; Wiley	Harney
Landscape Architecture; McGraw Hill	Harris/Dines
Landscape Architecture Graphic Standards; Wiley/Blackwell	Hopper
Landscape and Memory; Harper/Collins	Schama
Landscape Design and Construction; Gower	Blake
Landscape Site Grading Principles; Wiley/Blackwell	Sharky
Landschaftsarchitektur; DVA	Waterman
Materials and their application in design; Wiley/Blackwell	Sovinski
Pflege historischer Gärten/Theorie & Praxis; Leipzig	Rohde
Plant Propagation; Pearson	Hartmann/Kester
Professional Planting Design; Wiley/Blackwell	Scarfone
Rekonstruktion in der Gartendenkmalpflege; Leibniz	Hajos/Wolschke-Bulmahn
Romantic Gardens, Nature, Art & Landscape Design; Morgan & Godine	Barlow-Rogers/Eustis/Bidwell
Site Analysis; Wiley/Blackwell	Lagro
Site Engineering for Landscape Architects; Wiley/Blackwell	Strom/Nathan/Woland
Soil Analysis; CSIRO	Peverill/Sparrow/Reuter
Some English Gardens; London, New York & Bombay	Jekyll
The Art of Landscape Detail; Wiley/Blackwell	Kirkwood
The Damp Garden	Beth Chatto
The Dry Garden	Beth Chatto
The English Vicarage Garden; Penguin	Read
The Formal Garden; Thames & Hudson	Laird/Palmer
The Gardens at Kew; Lincoln	Patterson
The History of Garden Design; Thames & Hudson	Mosser/Teyssot
The Iris Family; Timbler Press	Goldblatt/Manning

The Landscape of Man; Thames & Hudson	Jellicoe
Trees for Architecture and Landscape; Wiley/Blackwell	Zion
Wood and Garden; Longmanns, Green & Co	Jekyll